W

MW01297042

For Kathryn:

Daughter of the famous
Hugh Lloyd.

Hope you enjoy reading
about my long career
in journalism.

Best
Regards

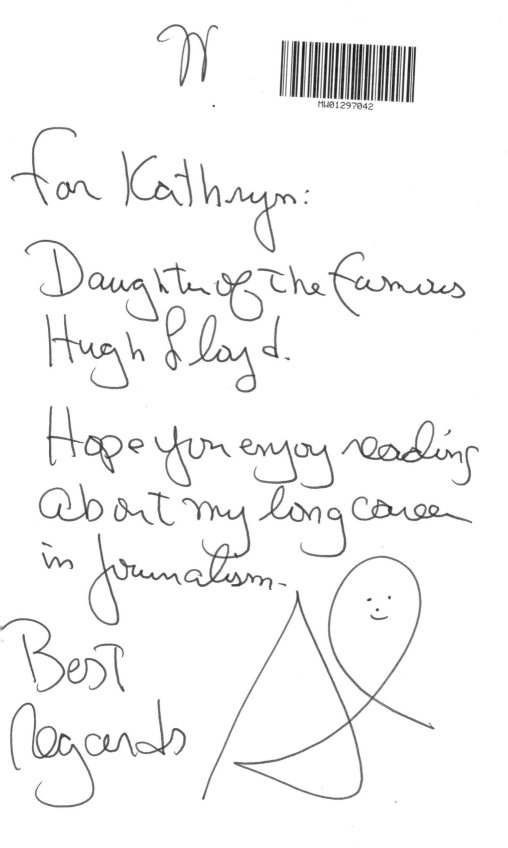

REPORTER

Covering Civil Rights... And Wrongs in Dixie

By

Alvin Benn

authorHOUSE™

1663 LIBERTY DRIVE, SUITE 200
BLOOMINGTON, INDIANA 47403
(800) 839-8640
WWW.AUTHORHOUSE.COM

First published by AuthorHouse 01/23/06

ISBN: 1-4208-6187-5 (e)
ISBN: 1-4208-6186-7 (sc)
ISBN: 1-4208-6185-9 (dj)

Library of Congress Control Number: 2005905854

Printed in the United States of America
Bloomington, Indiana

This book is printed on acid-free paper.

DEDICATION

For Sharon Ann

PREFACE

We all have memories and often bring them up when we talk to friends and relatives. In most cases, they are lost to future generations. Some put their memories into book form and they tend to last a bit longer. Since I'm a journalist who has written about others for the past four decades, I thought I'd make my memories more permanent for my children, grandchildren and those to come. Hopefully, unrelated readers will want to share my experiences as well.

I'd often ask my grandfathers what it was like in "The Old Country" before they came to America. Now and then, they'd mention the eastern European towns where they were born. What they preferred to talk about, however, was the moment, not the memories. They've been gone a long time and, at my age, I don't have many years left. As I get older, my regrets deepen for not having pushed to learn more about my grandfathers and their formative years—about how they left countries where they were second class citizens, about how they came to this wonderful land and raised large families during tough economic times.

Louis Solsky and Albert Benn rarely left their homes once they arrived in Pennsylvania. I did and I've have had the opportunity to experience and report on some of the most important moments in our country's history. Those events happened far from my boyhood home and were quite unexpected for an average student who didn't know what he wanted to do with his life after graduating from high school.

Thanks to the U.S. Marine Corps, I got a chance to see part of the world I would have missed had I remained in Pennsylvania. I also picked up a profession along the way. Thanks to *United Press International*, I got a chance to witness and report history in the making during the civil rights era. Thanks to newspapers in Decatur, Alexander City, Selma and Montgomery in Alabama, Natchez in Mississippi and LaFayette in Georgia, I got a chance to do the same things I did at *UPI*, but on a more limited scale.

If variety is, indeed, the spice of life, I've had a condiment-filled career. During my brief tenure with *UPI*, I felt like Zelig, that Woody Allen movie character who injected himself into 20th century history. Ditto for Forrest Gump, played by Tom Hanks, in the Academy Award-winning movie. Unlike the fictional Zelig and Gump characters, I experienced the real thing for much of my 2 ½ years with *UPI*. After that, I had a chance to roam through three states, sampling events big and small and reporting them to our readers.

During the 1960s, my high school classmates who finished college and were beginning their professional careers read about Martin Luther King Jr., and historic events in Birmingham, Montgomery, Selma and other Alabama cities. I interviewed Dr. King and covered important civil rights activities in those three cities. My friends also read about America's race to the moon. I interviewed Wernher von Braun—the man who helped create the Saturn 5 rocket as well as astronauts who would test it for the eventual lunar trip in 1969. It was an exciting time for a rookie who helped to spread the word around the world about major events in the United States.

Whoever said it's better to be lucky than good at times was pretty accurate. That's been—in boxing lingo—the tale of my journalistic tape. Articles that carried my name and appeared in major newspapers around the world were made more coherent by *UPI* editors in Atlanta and New York. Those of us in the field didn't always have time to sit down and shape our stories. We were too busy racing from one hot spot to another to do that. Telephones were our links to the outside world. We'd often dictate what we saw and heard before moving on to make the next deadline. Experienced editors such as Tony Heffernan,

Jack Warner, Marty Murphy, Al Kuettner and others made us all look good.

When I moved on to newspaper work in 1967, I got an opportunity to experience important events in five small towns in three southern states. For the people who lived in those communities, their daily and weekly newspapers were every bit as important as the *New York Times* or the *Washington Post*. I quickly learned that mundane events often spawned big news in Small Town USA.

Some of my articles are in time capsules buried under courthouse lawns. Grammarians who dig them up in a century no doubt will say they should have stayed in those holes. We all make mistakes in our professions and I've made my share of them. But, I think my journalistic batting average has been pretty good, considering the deadline pressures I've been under through the years.

There is poignancy in some of the stories contained herein. There also are stories about murderers and those who put them on Death Row. There are accounts of heroes and villains, community leaders who kept their reputations intact and those who didn't. I've covered six presidents, lots of governors, including Alabama's George Wallace, along with other political leaders and public figures—from mayors to dog catchers. Most of the stories in this book, however, are about average people who keep our country ticking. Reporting about them can be fun, terrifying, exasperating and unforgettable. In our line of work, we quickly learn to expect the unexpected.

During my long career, the methods of producing newspapers have changed dramatically. I've seen them move from heavy, noisy linotype machines to a quiet system using scissors and paste. The computer age eventually changed everything. Today, a button on a machine can instantly transmit earth-shaking events in a nanosecond. What modern technology cannot do, however, is guarantee that what's being sent is fair, accurate and unbiased. That comes from the heart and mind of the reporter who writes the story being transmitted. Journalistic integrity cannot be duplicated. That's all reporters really have. We never make much money. What we can leave behind is a good name in our chosen profession. I hope I've been able to do just that. There are those who will disagree, but I've tried to be as fair as I could be.

None of it would have been possible without my grandfathers and their decisions to leave their homes in Europe more than a century ago. I appreciate those decisions more than my children, who lack the sense of history I have. The life expectancy of a Jewish baby born on April 25, 1940 in Poland, Hungary, Russia, Lithuania, Latvia or Estonia could be measured in months or a few years at best. I realize, more than most Americans, what a blessing life is—how we should cherish and appreciate each day.

Hopefully, my descendants will keep a copy on their book shelves, in a computer disk or whatever awaits the printed word down the road. For those who read it and wonder why they bought it, well, there is always the trash can. This was primarily written for our children, Dani and Eric and our grandchildren, Ben, Scott, MariCruz and Ilan. It's for them that I've left some of my memories and adventures.

I hope they like them. I hope you do, too.

ALVIN BENN, 2005

ACKNOWLEDGEMENTS

What began as an attempt to relate one man's life for his children, grandchildren and relatives evolved into an effort to expand the potential reading audience. Without the help of friends and colleagues it would not have been possible.

It started a few years ago over lunch with Montgomery book publisher Randall Williams. I mentioned to Randall some of the stories I had covered through the years, beginning with my days as a wire service reporter with *United Press International* in Birmingham, Alabama. Randall suggested that I put my experiences into a book. While we weren't able to get together on the project, I'd like to thank him for encouraging me to do something I had thought about for a long time.

Special thanks are in order for John and Teresa Kelly of Selma. John is one of the city's finest lawyers and was a great help in handling some of the initial legal matters that arose. Teresa, a former English teacher in Selma, read the first draft of my book and made suggestions that helped improve it significantly.

Since computer expertise is somewhat alien to me, I relied on two Selma friends who have an abundance of it. Don King and Dusty Brown helped solve problems as they arose. Don and Dusty were especially helpful when I ran into technical trouble, which was quite often. Dusty spent several days helping to transfer photographs from one format to another to illustrate this book. His patience with me was truly awe-inspiring. Roy Paul of the *Montgomery Advertiser* Information Systems department also was invaluable. He not only keeps our newsroom humming with his technical knowledge, he was always available to answer questions whenever I called him from my office at home.

Montgomery Advertiser editorial page associate editor Jim Earnhardt agreed to write the foreword for "Reporter" and had me beaming when he said he considered it an honor. I feel the same way about him. We've known each other since 1976. He's one of the finest journalists I've ever known.

Of all the assistance I've received on this project, however, the most important was provided by Jim Purks, a friendly rival with the *Associated Press* when I began working for *United Press International* in Birmingham in 1964. Jim's reluctance, at first, to edit my revised manuscript eventually subsided when I convinced him that fate had stepped in to renew our friendship. We had not seen each other in 40 years. He spent many hours reading, editing and making suggestions on how best to improve this book. His sensitivity was greatly appreciated since, at times, I've been sorely lacking in that part of my writing. His keen insight and eyesight were important factors in completion of this project.

FOREWORD

For a few months back in the 1970s, Alvin Benn was my boss. More importantly, at least to me, he has been my friend for nearly 30 years. I was honored—and that's not too strong a word—to be asked to write this foreword.

Al Benn's journalism career spans some of the most significant years of this nation's history. You'll read about some important figures and events in this memoir. You'll also read about people you never knew, people with interesting lives and interesting stories that this ever-inquisitive reporter put into print.

Al would never consider himself a teacher, but he was a mentor to me when I worked for him as a young reporter years ago. If today's young reporters want to learn something about daily journalism, they've got a good model in Al.

He understood that a lot of copy is generated simply by being around, by knowing people, not just the "official" types, but the people in the coffee shops and the garages, the folks who drive the school buses or scramble the eggs. He knows his territory; he always has, whether it was in the Birmingham of the turbulent 1960s, or Decatur or Natchez or Alexander City or, for the last 25 years, in Selma.

In this book, you'll meet all sorts of people—the famous and the obscure, the amusing and the scary. Most of all, you'll experience those moments of history through the eyes of a guy who was there.

It's been a heck of a ride through four decades of journalism. I've been lucky enough to be along for parts of it. Now you can get a look for yourself.

Jim Earnhardt
Montgomery Advertiser associate editor, editorial writer and member of the Editorial Board

TABLE OF CONTENTS

CHAPTER ONE:

UPI

We were being set up. At least, it looked that way.

It happened late at night, in the rain, at a little Alabama park where Ku Klux Klansmen and Klan sympathizers surrounded us.

The date was June 5, 1965 and we had driven 100 miles from Birmingham to watch three accused killers being hailed as heroes.

They were in the Klan and the "star" attractions at a rally held to raise money for their defense, recruit new members and "initiate" some who had been accepted into the racist organization.

We were three vulnerable journalists in the middle of nowhere at a time when civil rights workers, reporters and photographers tended to disappear or wind up in hospitals.

I was a reporter for *United Press International*. With me were Joe Chapman, a *UPI* free-lance photographer who worked at the *Birmingham Post-Herald*, and Vernon Merritt, a *Life* magazine photographer.

Our purpose at the park was to check on Collie Leroy Wilkins, Eugene Thomas and W.O. Eaton. They had been arrested after Viola Liuzzo, a Detroit housewife and civil rights activist, was shot to death following the historic Selma-to-Montgomery march on March 25, 1965.

Klansmen Eaton, left, Thomas, center, and Wilkins after arrests
(Photo by Tommy Giles)

Wilkins, Thomas and Eaton were picked up after a fourth person in their car—Gary Thomas Rowe—called his FBI contact in Birmingham not long after Liuzzo had been killed. Rowe, a paid federal informant, said Wilkins had shot Liuzzo as she was trying to get away from them— driving her car as fast as she could. It was a high-speed race and Liuzzo lost. Rowe claimed he had a good vantage point. He said he was in the back seat, to the left of Wilkins, and saw it all.

We were at the rally by invitation. Klan Grand Dragon Bob Creel and Klan lawyer Matt Murphy extended it to us. Creel probably anticipated a big turnout at the rally and felt that might help improve public support for Wilkins, whose public demeanor wasn't winning him many friends. He was a surly young man with a beer gut and a glare for anybody holding a notebook or a camera.

The three were arrested on federal conspiracy charges, but the state of Alabama stepped in with murder indictments since there was no federal murder statute at the time. Wilkins was the first to be tried for murder in state court, but an all-white, all-male jury couldn't reach a verdict and a mistrial was declared only a few weeks after Liuzzo's death.

Murphy needed money to prepare for the second trial so he took his three clients on the road—appearing at rallies in rural Alabama where many Klan members and sympathizers lived. That's what brought Joe, Vernon and me to Chickasaw State Park in Linden, Alabama on a muggy night in early June of 1965. We wanted to see what kind of support they had in Alabama. We quickly discovered it was still solid.

A platform had been set up in one corner of the little park and speaker after speaker mounted it as they took turns denouncing "Zionist Jews, communists and niggers." They said "outside agitators" were trying to change Alabama's "way of life" and they just wouldn't stand for it. It was dark by the time the speeches began, but I was able to take enough notes for a story to be called to our Birmingham bureau. Other than Goodloe Sutton, who later would become publisher of his family-owned paper in the town where the rally was held, we were the only newsmen covering the event.

Creel, who wore a white robe with red trim and a tall white tipped cap, announced that the Klan was strong in south Alabama "and we are going to stay here and fight for your rights." He didn't elaborate on just how hard he and his fellow Klansmen would "fight" for those "rights," but I couldn't help but think of Liuzzo—slumped across the front seat of her car with a bullet in her brain.

Klansmen end racist rally by burning a cross.
(Photo by Joseph M. Chapman ©)

As rain began to fall, we headed for Joe's Volkswagen. No cross was burned that night, but there was enough light to see that all four tires had been slashed. It had been less than a year since three civil rights workers—Andrew Goodman, Mickey Schwerner and James Chaney—had been murdered in neighboring Mississippi. It was possible somebody who noticed the "UPI" sticker on one of Joe's car windows just wanted to scare us or strand us at the park. Whoever did it accomplished both goals. I had only been with *UPI* for 10 months and the thought of a short career did enter my mind when I looked at those tires.

Luckily for us, Creel saw us standing next to our car. He came over and saw what had happened. No reminders were needed about the Mississippi murders. Creel could understand our concern. That's when he passed around his pointy white hat and took up a collection to buy some new tires.

When we drove away from the park, the rain had stopped and a full moon emerged from behind the clouds. Joe and Vernon began joking about how "funny" it would be if the Klansmen charged with killing Liuzzo tailed us. That's what happened a few minutes later as we drove toward Demopolis, about 15 miles from Linden. Thomas' red and white

Chevy Impala pulled up alongside Joe's VW. With him were Wilkins and Eaton. I was shaking. One rolled down a window and invited us to join them for drinks. The Klan rally story suddenly had become even more interesting. We followed them to a bar near Birmingham. It was after midnight. The six of us slid into a semi-circular booth against a wall where we began to drink, smoke and talk. Wilkins did most of the talking as he downed one drink after another. He had been a nonentity all his life—a Birmingham mechanic who enjoyed beer, cigarettes and Klan rallies. Then, he discovered a worldwide audience. He had become a media darling and didn't shy away from the spotlight. He reveled in it. We sat there for a couple of hours and didn't leave the bar until early Sunday morning.

My bride of six months was frantic when Joe and I walked in about 3 a.m. Sharon was staying with Joe's wife, Sherry, and the two of them had been waiting up all night. So had Lonnie and Audrey Falk. Lonnie was a young reporter with the *Birmingham Post-Herald* and we had become friendly. I hadn't indicated to Sharon when we left that I'd be out drinking all night with Klansmen. I should have found a phone and called her. I learned later that *UPI* put out a bulletin that the three of us were missing after attending a Klan rally. I imagine my editors in Atlanta were happy to hear the three of us got through the night unharmed—unlike the three men in Mississippi who were murdered.

It took most of Sunday to recover from the rally and bar rendezvous with the three Klansmen. By the time I arrived at my office at the *Birmingham News* Building Monday morning, my thoughts were on assignments of the day—not that wild night in the boondocks and at the bar. The phone rang about mid-morning. On the other end of the line was a prosecutor from the Attorney General's Office. He got right to the point.

"We understand you were with Wilkins, Thomas and Eaton Saturday night," said the prosecutor. "We're going to subpoena you and the two who were with you. We want you to testify at the second trial. We want to know what you guys talked about."

I caught my breath. How in the world did he know about the conversation at the bar? I didn't tell anybody about it other than Sharon and she had no reason to call the Attorney General's Office. There were six of us in that booth and a lot of people sat around us. Could somebody have heard us? Could the FBI have been following us all night? Was a federal agent listening nearby? All those possibilities ran through my mind. It seemed like an hour before I responded.

"You can't subpoena me," I said. "Why not?" he asked. "For one thing," I told him, "we were all three 'sheets' in the wind when and if anything incriminating was said. Secondly, I probably wouldn't live long enough to testify anyway. You know they had to keep Rowe in protective custody after he reported Liuzzo's murder." The FBI knew that if anything happened to Rowe, there would be no case against the other three, so they kept him out of sight and away from the Klansmen charged with murder.

The subpoenas never were issued and I was relieved. Being added to a possible Ku Klux Klan "hit list" wasn't what I had in mind in early 1964 after I got back home from a tour on Okinawa with the Marine Corps. I didn't know what I wanted to do when my enlistment expired in August of that year. I did know that I wasn't cut out for a career in the Corps. I never was militarily inclined and, after six years, I realized I wouldn't enjoy spending 14 more in the Marines before collecting a pension and retiring to civilian life. I wanted to walk with the rest of America—those millions of people our drill instructors told us were always "out of step." I was one of them.

My first attempt at a wire service career fizzled. I was staying at my brother's house outside Washington, D.C. when I called the local office of the *Associated Press*—one of the world's most venerated wire services. I didn't get past the receptionist. She told me I would have to go to New York where I would be interviewed, tested and put on a waiting list. My next call was to the Washington, D.C. office of *United Press International*—the Avis of wire services. *UPI* was second in money, manpower and clientele muscle to *AP*, but, as I soon learned, it didn't take a backseat to any wire service competitor. A few seconds after I called, I was put through to the office of Grant Dillman, a *UPI* vice president who ran the Washington office. The telephone transfer impressed me, but not as much as what happened next.

"Sure, come on down," Dillman told me.

I couldn't believe it. Here was one of the busiest journalists in the country and he took the time to invite someone without experience to his office for a chat. I didn't waste any time. We set up an appointment for the next day and I hurried downtown to meet him. Dillman greeted me with a handshake, a big smile and a cup of coffee in his office. We talked for several minutes about wire services and how they differed from newspapers. He did the talking. I did the listening. I wanted a job and was willing to do just about anything to get one. He told me my three years of military journalism wouldn't count toward my start in wire service work. That meant I'd begin at the bottom rung as a rookie. I learned that you had to have worked for an English language daily newspaper to pick up seniority credit with *UPI*. What the heck, I thought to myself. I started as a raw recruit at Parris Island and worked my way up to sergeant in a few years. I was even offered a chance to go to Warrant Officer School, but declined. Dillman said my starting wage would be just under $90 a week—gross. Even by 1964 standards, that was pretty gross. I made more in the Marine Corps where the benefits included a roof over my head and three squares a day—all paid by Uncle Sam. But, careers don't usually start at the top. It's a matter of paying your dues as you learn the ropes and gain experience. As I would soon learn, I'd be starting at the top of my profession—writing bylined stories that appeared in newspapers around the world.

"Where would you like to go?" Dillman asked me.

"Where the action is," I said, without thinking. It's something I've done a lot of in my life. On occasion, I've regretted it.

"OK, you'll be going to the South," he responded. "We'll let you know later what city."

All I knew about the South at that point was the location of Parris Island, known fondly in the Marine Corps as the armpit of South Carolina. The rest came from newspapers, radio and television. The South in the mid-1960s was in turmoil. The civil rights movement was in full swing. It was violent, bloody and deadly. I had no idea what role I'd play, but I knew it promised to be interesting and exciting. A few weeks before my discharge on Aug. 4, 1964, I was told that I'd be working out of the *UPI* office in Birmingham—Alabama's largest city. It often was referred to during those days as BOMBingham because of frequent manmade explosions unrelated to mining. It even had a neighborhood called "Dynamite Hill."

Excitement mounted as my departure from military life neared. I wrote Sharon that I was looking forward to the next phase of my life and that, hopefully, we'd be able to get married soon. We became engaged earlier in the year after a courtship that included only a few dates. Parris Island, my final duty station, is far from Silver Spring, Maryland, a Washington suburb. That was a long way to court. I was the only passenger on the bus that left Parris Island that day, so I had plenty of room to roam and think. Mostly, I wondered if I had made the right decision. I had no idea what would happen next. I knew about the civil rights movement that had blanketed the South from Louisiana to Florida. Alabama is known as the "Heart of Dixie" and square in the center of the region where most of the racial mayhem was happening. Mississippi had its share of problems, too. It had been only a few weeks since Goodman, Schwerner and Chaney had vanished while investigating a fire that destroyed a black church just across the Alabama state line. I knew the *UPI* bureau in Jackson must have been working overtime on that story.

When my bus pulled into Atlanta, I began to have second thoughts about my decision. I knew I hadn't wanted a military career, but I didn't want to sell insurance back home, either. "What the hell," I muttered to myself. "Let's do it. All they can do is fire me. I'm sure I can find something else if that happens." I had been to the *UPI* office in Atlanta a few weeks before my discharge. There, I met *UPI*'s Southern Division administrator Chiles Coleman. He said the company would give me a chance, but it was up to me whether I succeeded. "I think you can do it, Al," he told me. "You don't have any civilian newspaper experience, but that doesn't always say much about ability and desire. You'll be going over to Birmingham and will have a fine boss in Tony Heffernan. He's experienced and willing to teach you what you need to know."

That sounded reasonable. I thanked Coleman, left the building and went back to the bus station for my return trip to Parris Island. It would be only a few more weeks before my discharge and my mind was on anything but firing ranges, physical fitness tests and gung-ho lieutenants. My second trip to Atlanta was to have included an orientation period before I headed for Birmingham. I was to be shown some of the technical wonders of wire service work. As it turned out, my orientation was very brief. The moment I walked into the news department, I could tell something big had happened. The place was in an uproar. Reporters were on telephones, checking their wire machines, reading files and running back and forth. I soon learned what was going on because Coleman spotted me the moment I walked in the door.

"They've found the bodies in Mississippi," he said, referring to the remains of Schwerner, Chaney and Goodman. "Get back on the bus and get on over to Birmingham. Tony will need you there." Coleman's face showed the deadline strain he must have been under. Atlanta was *UPI's* Southeast regional headquarters and was responsible for sending important news up the pipeline to New York where it was transmitted around the world. I had only been out of the Marine Corps a few hours, but already I was being given marching orders. It almost felt good, if not for the fact I was already on edge about starting my new career. I could see the pressure associated with wire service work. I could also see the professionalism. I would find out quickly that the two were one and the same.

When I arrived in Birmingham, I asked a man at the bus station where the *Birmingham News* was located. "Up the hill, on the corner at 4th Avenue and 22nd Street," he said. "You can't miss it. It's a pretty big building." I could have taken a taxi, but I didn't have that much money to spare, so I lugged my heavy duffle bag to what would be my office for the next 2 1/2 years. It was several blocks away and it was August. I was sweating when I left the bus station and, by the time I got to the *News* building, I was drenched. But, the few dollars I had in my wallet had stayed there. I knew I'd need every penny I could save because I wasn't going to make much for awhile—if I lasted with *UPI*. As I walked through the newsroom of the *Birmingham Post-Herald* which shared the building with the bigger, richer *News*, I glanced toward the opposite end where the door to a small office was open. Inside, sitting in front of a large, black machine with large "*UPI*" letters on the front was a white-haired guy pounding on rows of small metal keys. He didn't hear me come in and I didn't want to say anything to interrupt his concentration. A few minutes later he swung around in his chair, smiled and extended his hand.

"Hi, I'm Bill Tome," he said. "Welcome to *UPI*."

Bill's primary job was to sell our news product to newspapers which, at that time, were our major customers. Radio and television stations also bought our service, but newspapers were our main target, especially the bigger ones that also had *AP*. In those days, many of the large papers had both wire services and would tend to rip off the first report of a breaking story and use it. Editors knew one would always beat the other, if only by a few minutes, and they wouldn't have to wait very long when something important happened.

My first big challenge, in addition to finding a place to live and a car, was to master the teletype machine. It was the heart and soul of wire service operations in those days before the arrival of computers. The bulky machines linked bureaus around the world with their regional headquarters where copy was edited and then retransmitted to clients from Alabama to Austria. Teletype machines had keys similar to a typewriter. Instead of white paper, though, it fed yellow tape through a narrow metal slot. The tape would be perforated along the way, forming letters and words, much like Morse Code. After awhile I was able to read the letters and make out some of the words as they flashed through the machine. Mastering the teletype was the ticket to continued employment. Those who couldn't learn didn't last long. Something else was needed as well—writing ability. It didn't matter how fast a reporter was. If he or she couldn't produce an acceptable story, job survival was short in a business where speed, accuracy and dependability were requirements.

I found an apartment on the side of Birmingham's Red Mountain, just down from the Vulcan Statue which honors the city's steel heritage. At least, it did back in 1964. Huge clouds of thick black smoke from steel mills poured out of enormous stacks throughout the day, creating smog conditions not unlike that which continue to annoy Los Angeles residents today. On the days when the mills were really cranking out the steel, it was tough to breathe. Many people had to cover their faces with handkerchiefs. Women knew not to hang their clothes on the lines at that time. They'd be darker than before they were put into washing machines. During the past 40 years, Birmingham has switched from steel to medicine and those who live in Birmingham couldn't be happier. Their lungs appreciated the switch, too. The University of Alabama at Birmingham has become a world class medical presence, turning out general practitioners and specialists while also serving as a great research center.

It wasn't actually "my" apartment. I shared it with a bunch of guys, including some who worked for the *Post-Herald*. I didn't have a bed, so I got a ride to Sears and bought a metal folding cot and a thin mattress. I didn't have a bedroom, so I just leaned the cot against a wall and took it out at night when I needed it. The best times were on weekends when I didn't have anything to do and my roommates, most of whom didn't pay any rent because they were "between jobs," were gone. They had gone home to mom, dad and some free meals. Weekends in the fall of 1964 were devoted to pimiento cheese sandwiches, television sitcoms and football. I picked up a cheap TV set and it provided my entertainment.

Most of my week was filled with learning and reporting. Military journalism is much different from its civilian cousin. When I wasn't going through physical testing, qualifying on the rifle range or standing inspection, I had an opportunity to write articles for my base newspapers. They were closely scrutinized by editors who made sure we didn't give away any national secrets. I was accused of that once when I wrote a story about a helicopter pilot who had recently returned from Vietnam. He explained some of his squadron's tactics, but it was written in general terms without specifics that might jeopardize anybody's life. Besides, I didn't think we had any Viet Cong subscribers at Cherry Point, N.C. where we published the *Windsock*, our base newspaper. The story was chopped up so much that I didn't recognize it when it was returned to me by an editor. We never did run it.

Tony Heffernan had a lot more journalistic experience than I did. More important was his patience in dealing with me. He helped me cope with the teletype machine, explained our responsibilities, edited my copy and made me feel at home which was even more vital to my mental health at the time. I was lonely. I missed Sharon. I didn't have much money. Most of all, I didn't know if I could succeed in the pressure cooker world of wire service work. After finding an apartment, my next chore was getting a car. I didn't have any credit, but that wasn't a problem for the used car salesman who saw me coming. It didn't take long for him to hook me. I left the lot in a 1954 gas-guzzling Buick that had been on its last wheels a long time. It didn't cost me much, either. I had about $350 from my last Marine Corps paycheck and used part of it to make a down payment. I needed the rest of it for my first month's rent and other incidentals.

Tony wasn't about to let me sit around and soak up some of his wire service knowledge very long. He had me write some local stories and then gave me my first major assignment—covering the counterfeiting trial of Pat Sutton, a former Tennessee sheriff who once served in Congress. He also was a World War II hero who came home with lots of medals and a great reputation. He was on the legal ropes in 1964, but, he did have something special—John Jay Hooker, Sr., a flamboyant Nashville lawyer known for his courtroom theatrics. It was apparent from the start of jury selection that Hooker was placing most of his hopes on what Sutton used to be, not what he was alleged to have become. Sutton's war record would be a key ingredient in Hooker's defense. Federal prosecutors told the jurors that what his client did in the past should have no bearing on what they claimed he did 20 years later. Prosecutors felt they had enough evidence to convict Sutton several times.

Sensing his case was in trouble, Hooker tried one last defensive maneuver—his closing argument. That's when he demonstrated in the courtroom how he had gotten his reputation as one of the best in the business. Walking slowly in front of the jury, Hooker—a large, imposing figure—held a polished mahogany box in his hands. That got the jury's attention and Hooker knew it. He had me, too. I kept waiting for him to do a Senor Wences routine—the one from the Ed Sullivan show in which he looked at his hand puppet and said: "S'ok, S'all right." Hooker had a different way of playing with the jury's curiosity as he outlined Sutton's military record and public service as a congressman and sheriff. The box was the ace up his sleeve. Hooker's closing statement to the jury was basically: "Would this man, this war hero, this sheriff, this congressman, throw away all that he has earned through a lifetime of hard work and tarnish his reputation for 50 low-down, dirty, rotten, counterfeit dollars?" His voice rose with each word as he slowly opened the box lid while the jurors strained to see what was inside. "Of course not! He would not!" Hooker shouted.

Then, tears streaming down his cheeks, Hooker opened the box all the way, revealing Sutton's medals earned during World War II. They were neatly lined up on what looked like a velvet background. It was an impressive decorative display as well as a magical courtroom moment when all the elements seemed to come together. Hooker's pleas and tears weren't enough to convince the jurors of his client's innocence, however. They couldn't reach a verdict and a mistrial was declared. Sutton put on a brave front when I approached him in the hallway outside the courtroom and asked for a comment. "They didn't convict me and that means I'm still as innocent as I've ever been," he told me, as he prepared to leave the Federal Building. Before the year was over, Sutton would sign a plea bargain agreement to avoid another trial.

This UPI teletype machine in Birmingham, Ala. sent historic reports to newspapers around the world.

As the weeks passed, I began to have more confidence in myself and my abilities as a wire service reporter. I wasn't very fast on the teletype machine, but Tony told me not to worry. He said it would come with practice and pointed out that he typed with two fingers. I had learned to use them all in high school typing class. The machine included a small metal arm which extended from the front across where the narrow, perforated yellow tape was being processed. Once the tape ran out, it would strike the little arm and shut down the transmission. We had two teletype machines and would switch from one to the other in a chair that had rollers on the bottom. One machine was used for newspaper clients while the other was for radio and television subscribers. It was our job to change the writing style from newspapers to radio and TV stations. Among other things, it meant switching quote attributions and writing jazzier phrases for listeners and viewers with short attention spans. It took deep concentration, but, mostly, it took speed since we were required to file "splits" — wire service lingo for getting copy to newsrooms for their broadcasts. News directors around the state knew the exact times of each "split" and would wait for them to come in for their newscasts on the hour. That meant the men and women in *UPI* and *AP* offices had to be on their toes. They also had to be pretty good at pounding out stories on their teletype machines.

My least enjoyable assignment during those early months in Birmingham was punching into tape all the Southeastern Conference football statistics brought in by Scoop Hudgins, the league's public relations director. Scoop was a mathematical whiz who had every conceivable category prepared for avid followers of the most rabid gridiron section of the country. He had categories for individuals and teams—everything from rushing to receiving, from tackles to touchdowns. On and on it went, page after page of hard-to-see figures neatly lined up in long columns. My job was to measure the width of the page on my teletype machine to make sure everything was lined up just the way Scoop had laid it out.

It took more than two hours to type in all the statistics and up to an hour to transmit the whole thing. Before that happened, I had to prepare a story for papers that week that was related to the statistics brought to me. I liked Scoop, but it got to the point where I hated to see him coming. It meant spending about half the day on his statistics, but that was one of the reasons for our existence—to serve our customers. Most of the papers used them, too. It was my luck to have been assigned to the city which was SEC Central—headquarters for the whole conference. On the upside, it provided great training and helped me concentrate even more on mastering the teletype machine.

In between the football statistics and covering federal trials, I also found myself becoming more familiar with America's civil rights movement. When I arrived in August 1964, the bombing of Birmingham's 16th Street Baptist Church was still a recent, painful memory. Four black girls had been killed in the blast that occurred the previous September. I was working for the Armed Forces Radio and Television Service on Okinawa at the time and remember the vivid story sent by the *AP*'s Jim Purks, who was still with our competitor's Birmingham bureau when I got there. Jim was one of the first reporters inside the 16th Street Baptist Church after the Ku Klux Klan blew it apart in September 1963. Bull Connor was gone as Birmingham's police commissioner after the city's form of government was changed to a mayor-council format, but he remained a major force in the community. He later would be elected to the Alabama Public Service Commission, but his name would forever be linked to police dogs set loose on and fire hoses aimed at black demonstrators in 1963.

Connor was known as "Mr. Bull" by blacks, who used the appellation with deference or disdain, depending on what they thought of him. He provided me with plenty of colorful quotes during that time because he wasn't reluctant to discuss whatever the issue might have been that day. When Martin Luther King Jr. was awarded the Nobel Peace Prize, I was asked to contact Connor for a comment. "They must have scraped the bottom of the barrel," he told me in that growling voice of his during a brief telephone interview. Connor had tried to stay in Birmingham politics by running for mayor, but he lost to Albert Boutwell, who was considered a "moderate segregationist."

Boutwell was Connor's opposite—a courtly southern gentleman who also had a habit of crying in public, especially when a violent act happened. He cried a lot during those days. Boutwell also came up with the funniest, unintentional quote of my stay in Birmingham. It occurred during a luncheon for *ABC Sports* prior to the Iron Bowl game between the University of Alabama and Auburn University. It was and still is the most important athletic event of the year in Alabama. The mayor stood to welcome the television crew and thank them for giving his city a chance to show its positive side on national television. "We are very pleased to have *ABC Sports* and the NAAC......err..the NCAA with us today," said Boutwell, whose slip of the tongue brought down the house. I think he cried then, too, but they were tears of laughter.

EXP216601-2/16/65-TUSCALOOSA,ALA: University of Alabama Center Paul Crane (1) is presented his All-America plaque 2/14 by UPI Birmingham bureau manager prior to the Alabama-Kentucky basketball game. UPI TELEPHOTO ab

Benn, right, presents UPI All-America certificate to University of Alabama center Paul Crane.

By the time football season had arrived in 1964, I felt I had a good chance to make the *UPI* squad. Tony was giving me more responsibility and I had much more confidence in my teletype abilities. Wire service bureau work rarely allowed time for specialty reporting. We did everything—from covering college football games to transmitting chicken and egg production reports to our rural newspapers and radio stations. Civil rights had priority status, however, and the fallout from King's demonstrations and Connor's racist tactics was still being felt. Birmingham was on the road to a more progressive future, but the Klan and other hate groups did all they could to make sure it would be a long and winding road.

A diversion, of sorts, occurred in November of 1964 during the general election pitting the incumbent president, Lyndon Johnson, against the Republican nominee, U.S. Sen. Barry Goldwater of Arizona. Alabama had become increasingly conservative by that time, but few gave the Republicans—other than Goldwater—much of a chance to do any damage. Imagine, then, the shock in Alabama's Democratic Party when five GOP congressional candidates were swept into office. They had ridden Goldwater's coattails and straight ticket voting to Washington. One of them remained in office for two decades.

My election night assignment was to go to Republican headquarters in Birmingham to get reaction. I didn't even know where it was. Few in the state did. I think all the Alabama Republicans did that year was list candidates for several national positions and hope for the best. Little wonder, then, when I walked into GOP headquarters that the place was in chaos. John Grenier, the young lawyer relatively new to Alabama by way of Louisiana, had fashioned a "Ride Barry's Coattails" campaign with the skill of a much more experienced politician. People were jabbering away with "can you believe this!" and other startled comments. The bubble began to burst two years later when one of the five lost. Bill Dickinson of Montgomery lasted the longest, but it was a sign that Republicanism had arrived in Alabama and wasn't going to go away. Today, both of Alabama's U.S. Senators are Republicans, as is the governor and five of the state's seven congressmen. Bob Riley is the most recent Republican governor. He was elected in 2002 over Democratic incumbent Gov. Don Siegelman.

As winter approached, I got the good news. I had passed my probationary period and could stay as long as I did the job. My editors also said I could get married. That was awfully nice of them. The call to Sharon was short and not very sweet. "We can get married," I told her, "but we won't have time for a honeymoon." If that didn't tell Sharon something about the type of work in which I was involved, she'd soon learn once she arrived in Birmingham. Since the wedding was to be held on such short notice, we couldn't get a synagogue. They usually were booked up to a year in advance in the Washington, D.C. area. So, we settled on Solomon's, a catering service with room in the back for weddings, bar mitzvah celebrations and, I imagine, circumcision rituals. I made plane reservations and Ron Tate, a friend from the *Post-Herald*, promised to pick us up at the airport when we returned the day after the Dec. 27 wedding. I rented an apartment on Highland Avenue in south Birmingham. It was a three-flight walkup similar to brownstone apartments in New York and just as dingy with narrow hallways and steps leading to our top floor apartment. But, the rent was reasonable, our landlady was Jewish and I wasn't too far from my office in downtown Birmingham.

The wedding weekend was a blur. Relatives arrived from around the area. I picked up a case of liquor and we all chipped in to help pay for everything. Sharon and I met briefly with the rabbi who would be officiating and came to a quick conclusion that he needed improvement in the area of human relations. Cold wasn't close in describing him. But, we weren't going to argue with the rabbinical selection process because we couldn't have a wedding without him. We didn't have much time for a rehearsal and everybody kept their fingers crossed that everything would be fine when the big day arrived.

The wheels nearly came off the day before the wedding when we got word that my father was in intensive care at a hospital in Gettysburg after experiencing shortness of breath as he and his second wife, Sylvia, drove to Washington. My little brother, Stevie, was with them. Today, he's a grandfather. Meryl and Sylvia Benn had been having problems throughout their year-long marriage. I think it probably began right after they exchanged vows and she realized what a big mistake she had made. Sylvia was well-read, had an extensive vocabulary, dressed impeccably and loved to travel. My father was at the opposite end of Sylvia's cerebral spectrum. They had met at Browns in the Catskills—a place where Jewish widows, widowers and lonely single people went to see if, perhaps, they might find a mate for their twilight years.

When my mother-in-law-to-be—Sophie Boumel Waldman— learned of my father's medical problems, she became frantic—worried that the wedding might be called off. I told her that was a possibility as my brother, Barry, my sister, Eileen, and I headed for Gettysburg. As we left Solomon's where we had been rehearsing, I could hear Sophie's loud sigh behind us. She sighed a lot and, on this occasion, it seemed appropriate. When we got to the hospital, Sylvia came rushing toward us—flying down a hallway with eyes and mouth wide open and a ready explanation. "I didn't do it," she cried. She said she and my father had been arguing again and he began to have problems breathing—a bad sign for anyone at the wheel of a car going 60 miles an hour. They managed to get to the hospital where he was placed in intensive care and given tests. He recognized us when we walked into his room, but wasn't able to speak. We knew then that he wouldn't be able to make the wedding, but we weren't going to delay it. Doctors told us he'd be okay after some rest. As it turned out, he lived another 17 years with anger and breathing problems. He and Sylvia were divorced not long after the "attack."

Sharon Benn on her wedding day—Dec. 27, 1964

Our wedding went off without a hitch—other than the fact my father was in a hospital. Everybody seemed to have a nice time. It was held on a cold, rainy Sunday afternoon in Washington. Our "honeymoon" consisted of one night at a hotel not far from Solomon's. By the next morning, we were on our way to National Airport for the flight to Birmingham where we began our married life. It had been difficult, at first, for me to adjust to my new surroundings, but Sharon took it all in stride. She's always been that way—adjusting to life no matter how many twists and turns she might encounter. As long as she had her family with her, that's all that really mattered.

One of our biggest adjustments during those first few weeks was the apartment. I didn't realize how tough it would be to negotiate those steep steps to our third floor "penthouse." Lugging several bags of groceries up those steps was tough. The furniture inside looked like it had been rejected by the Salvation Army. But, considering the fact I wasn't bringing home much more than $70 a week in 1964, I guess I should have been thankful for small favors.

The funniest moment of our first month together came early one morning after I had gotten home from my 3 p.m.-midnight shift. It had been an even longer day than usual and I was exhausted. Sharon stirred when I came into the bedroom. She did more than stir when I sat on the edge of the bed to take off my shoes. The old bed collapsed—creating a thunderous roar right above the bedroom of an elderly couple just below us on the second floor. After the initial shock wore off, Sharon and I began to laugh. There wasn't much more we could do, but all I could think about was what the old couple must have been thinking. They knew we were newlyweds. After the mini-bomb went off just above them, they must have thought we had been engaging in some lusty chandelier swinging and it broke. We dragged the mattress into the living room and plopped down on it, finally falling asleep after we stopped laughing and made up for lost time. We didn't need the chandelier. The next morning, as I went down the steps and passed the second floor apartment, the door opened and the male half of the elderly partnership peeked out. He gave me a big wink of what I guess was approval. I winked back.

As 1965 dawned, the civil rights struggle in Alabama had moved from Birmingham to the small town of Selma about 90 miles south in the heart of what is referred to as the Black Belt. It's a designation referencing the region's rich, black soil, but everybody just associates it with the color of most people who live there. Most of Alabama's black population is located in the Black Belt which stretches from Georgia to Mississippi through the state's midsection. That's where cotton was grown in abundance during the industrial revolution of the 19th century.

That's where the slaves lived. After emancipation, many blacks migrated to northern states, but most did not. They stayed put and they put up with discriminatory practices by powerful white officials until the drive for racial equality began in the 1960s. Before Jan. 2, 1965, Dallas County's black population was virtually shut out at the polling precincts. The county, of which Selma is the heart and soul, was home for about 55,000 people in 1965. Only about 350 blacks were registered to vote in a county that had a black population majority. White politicians in Selma, which had about 27,000 residents at the time, watched the civil rights activities in Birmingham and resisted a repeat with everything they could muster. They knew it was inevitable, but they weren't going to quit without a fight. King called Selma the most segregated city in America. In reality, most small southern towns were like Selma—one white community and one black community. That scenario hasn't changed much in the 40 years since the Selma movement began.

Instead of seeking more basic civil rights such as access to public accommodations, black leaders chose Selma as the battleground for the voting rights movement. In the end, voting rights would be more important because of what it portended for a way of life that was about to change. Black people had been denied voting rights by the white minority who feared that black voters might cast ballots for candidates who looked like them. In the end, that's just what happened.

The Rev. F.D. Reese invited Martin Luther King Jr. to Selma in 1965.

The catalyst for the Selma protests was a slim Baptist preacher and Selma teacher named for a 19th century black civil rights leader. Frederick Douglass Reese experienced the same discriminatory practices as all blacks in Selma prior to and after World War II, but he vowed to do something about it after returning home from nearby Wilcox County where he had taught school. Reese helped to create the Dallas County Voters League—a group that worked to register black voters. Voter registration classes were held between 1962 and the end of 1964. That's when Reese extended a formal invitation to King to come to Selma to pump new life into what had become a waning movement. King, still basking in the glow of his victory in Birmingham and his epic "I Have A Dream" speech in Washington, D.C. in 1963, quickly accepted the Selma invitation. He had been waiting for Reese to send it to him and wouldn't come unless he got it.

King wasted little time organizing the Selma Movement, as it would be called, once he got Reese's invitation. His top aides were put to work to agitate the local white establishment. It wasn't hard to do, not with the likes of Ralph Abernathy, Andrew Young and John Lewis leading the way. Young eventually would become mayor of Atlanta and U.S. Ambassador to the United Nations. Lewis one day would become a Congressman representing the Atlanta area. The Alabama native, who grew up in Pike County just south of Montgomery, was considered by most who covered the civil rights movement as the bravest of the brave. He was jailed dozens of times, beaten and threatened with death. He ignored it all and pressed on. Four decades later, he still has that same burning desire to help the oppressed.

"Bloody Sunday" in Selma in 1965.
(Photo by Alabama Department of Public Safety)

Mass arrests soon became a daily occurrence in Selma. At one point, so many black demonstrators were being arrested that "Camp Selma" was created to detain hundreds charged with misdemeanors such as blocking sidewalks, parading without a permit and angry words tossed at local authorities. As the days and weeks wore on, Selma became known nationally. On March 7, 1965, it became etched in the national psyche when Alabama State Troopers and mounted Dallas County deputies routed 600 black protesters as they attempted to march across the Edmund Pettus Bridge. It became known as "Bloody Sunday." Lewis was in the front row and suffered a concussion when a trooper cracked him across his skull with a billy club.

I was too busy in Birmingham to pay much attention to what was going on in Selma. My job was to cover anything of interest in my part of Alabama—from Birmingham north to the Tennessee Line. Less exciting news was happening in that area during the first three months of 1965, but we were responsible for covering it just the same. And, we also had to keep informing Alabama's farmers about egg prices. Scoop would pop in with SEC basketball statistics during that time, too. The hours continued to be long, but at least I had Sharon to keep me company.

We were just getting to know each other. A handful of dates isn't much prior to a wedding and we had spent more time together during the first two weeks of our marriage than during our abbreviated courtship.

John Lynch, who had been covering the Selma protests for *UPI*, was on the Pettus Bridge when the troopers and deputies waded into the large group of protesters led by Lewis, Hosea Williams, Albert Turner and Bob Mants. Tony would occasionally drive down to Montgomery to cover a federal court hearing on the Selma protests, but I was told to stay in Birmingham where mundane daily reporting kept me busy. That was fine since I was still learning the ropes after only eight months with *UPI*. They didn't need any rookies around Selma and Montgomery. All that changed with "Bloody Sunday" because we needed as many reporters as possible to keep track of what was going on. I was told to be ready for any civil rights assignment that might come my way. On occasion, somebody from *UPI* might drive over from Atlanta, but it was the responsibility of Alabama's bureaus in Birmingham, Montgomery and Mobile to get the job done. Did we ever!

My first major story during that time occurred two days after "Bloody Sunday" and involved a Unitarian minister, James Reeb. When he saw what had happened in Selma on television that Sunday night, he wasted little time heading south. King had appealed to the clergy to help him. Hundreds answered the call. Ministers, priests and rabbis arrived by cars, planes, trains and buses. By the following Tuesday, King was ready to march to Montgomery to protest what had happened on "Bloody Sunday." The proposed march was stopped by federal court order, disappointing those who had expected to begin their long walk to Alabama's capital city. It became known as "Turnaround Tuesday." That night, Reeb and two other white ministers were leaving a black restaurant when several white men saw them. The whites had just left the Silver Moon Cafe—an eatery that sold more booze than food. "Hey, you niggers," one shouted to the white ministers. Within seconds, a club was swung and Reeb collapsed to the ground. He never knew what hit him. He got little medical help in Selma and was finally taken to a Birmingham hospital. The first ambulance had a flat tire and another one was called out. By the time Reeb got to Carraway Methodist Hospital, doctors knew there was little they could do.

My assignment was to wait for Reeb to die. I was to stay at the hospital until he did. We called it the "Reeb death watch." I got to know some of the doctors and nurses during that time, but there was little I could do other than wait. The end came two days after Reeb arrived at Carraway. His skull had been shattered by the force of that swing back in Selma. A massive blood clot didn't help, either. Reeb had become the second civil rights homicide victim in less than a month in central Alabama. Jimmie Lee Jackson had been shot to death in February in nearby Marion, an event that led to the Selma-to-Montgomery march. A state trooper who did the shooting was questioned in connection with Jackson's death, but was not indicted by a grand jury. Reeb's Selma attackers were acquitted when they came to trial. President Johnson, already furious over the "Bloody Sunday" brutality on the bridge, was even more incensed over Reeb's death. He ordered one of the small jets in his White House fleet to fly Reeb's widow to Birmingham to pick up the body. Tony and I both wound up at the Birmingham Airport at the same time to report on her arrival.

Resumption of the Selma-to-Montgomery march was a foregone conclusion. The country demanded it. *UPI* had a strong presence in Selma when the march began on March 21, 1965—another Sunday. I wasn't called on to do anything. That's why Sharon and I decided to have a bagel brunch at our little apartment. We asked Lonnie and Audrey to join us. Lonnie had a keen interest in the civil rights movement. He was born and raised in Birmingham and was as aware as anyone his age that radical changes were taking place in his hometown. A few minutes after they arrived, the phone rang and breakfast was forgotten by two of us. It was a call from a police contact who told me that a locker box full of dynamite had just been found and Army demolition experts were was on their way to defuse it. "Hold the bagels, we'll be back," I shouted to Sharon, as we headed for the front door. It would be the start of the longest day of my *UPI* career.

BX.*232101-3/21/65-BIRMINGHAM,ALA.:Police officers and FBI man examine
explosives found in Birmingham 3/21. The dynamite was rigged to go off
at noon (EST), but Army demolition experts disarmed the crudely-made
bombs. A total of 140 sticks was found in three places. UPI TELEPHOTO-tp.

Green locker boxes were filled with dynamite.
(Photo by Joseph M. Chapman ©)

Lonnie and I took separate cars to the site of the dynamite location. We didn't know if we'd need to separate, and, as it turned out, it was a wise decision. Lonnie and I were the first to arrive at Our Lady Queen of the Universe Church and we soon found ourselves standing near a large green box—the kind I used to have in the Marine Corps. Instead of clothes, this one had 50 sticks of dynamite, a cheap clock and wiring connecting the whole thing. We were kept several feet away, but I swear I heard the damn thing ticking. Two soldiers—Robert Presley and Marvin Bryan—worked feverishly without special protective clothing and disarmed the bomb. We all relaxed, but, then, it hit me. What a stupid thing for us to have done. If it had gone off, most of the block would have disappeared and we'd have been vaporized.

We learned later that the batteries used in the timing devices were too weak to ignite the blasting cap. Of course, we didn't know that as we strained to hear the ticking. Not long after the first bomb was defused, Arthur Shores—Birmingham's leading black lawyer—found one next to his backyard fence. It was identical to the first and the two demolition experts defused it quickly. Shores and bombs weren't strangers. His civil rights activities had made him a prime target for the Klan in those days. I once asked him how he put up with it all and he said, with a grin: "Well, after awhile, you get used to it." The man had a sense of humor. He wasn't going to be intimidated.

I didn't have much time to get shook up over those initial bomb discoveries because, before we could leave the second site, we got word that a third locker box had been found a few blocks away. This all took place around the "Dynamite Hill" area. Off we went, again. I was still trying to find my way around Birmingham, which has to have more dead-end streets than any city in the South. One of the bombs was found by two black kids playing marbles near Western High School. It was about 25 yards from the school and the ticking seemed even louder than the first one. Presley and Bryan worked their magic again. Police Capt. George Wall told me that the two men "saved Birmingham some heartache and trouble" that day.

As night began to fall and word spread through the black community, fear turned to anger. It was around midnight when the fifth bomb was found and defused. By that time, I was exhausted. I hadn't eaten all day and those bagels were looking pretty good in my mind. I wanted to call Sharon and let her know where I was, but I was focused on calling the details in to Atlanta where it was put into story form. I hadn't counted on almost becoming a statistic.

Jim Purks and I had struck up a friendship, even though he worked for *AP* which was "the enemy" for all dedicated *UPI* reporters. I had admired his work since my days in the Marine Corps when I read his story about the 16th Street Baptist Church bombing. We'd chat whenever we ran into each other on assignments. Jim was a lot thinner and faster than I was and it helped him beat me on reporting discovery of the fifth bomb. There weren't many phone booths in that area and the two of us began looking for one. Jim and I spied one a block away and we both took off to get there first. He won and I lost more than that race. There wasn't much grass in those neighborhoods and proud homeowners protected what they had by placing thin strands of wire around each little patch of green. They were hard to see during the day and invisible at night. As I ran toward the phone booth with Purks just ahead of me, I hit one of the wires and crashed to the pavement, ripping up the right knee of my new trousers. Panting, bloodied and in pain, I looked up to see a large black man standing a few feet away—a shotgun cradled in his arms and an angry look on his face. As far as he was concerned, I could have been a Klansman looking for a new spot to hide a green locker box full of dynamite. "I'm a reporter, I'm a reporter," I shouted. "I'm trying to get to a phone booth to call in a story." The anger seemed to vanish from his face, but he didn't invite me inside to use his telephone.

In addition to the bombs, we also wound up on a wild goose chase that long, long day. It was around 2 a.m. the next day and I was ready to collapse from exhaustion. Instead of a locker box, somebody found a suitcase and it was under the front porch of a house occupied by A.D. King, brother of America's most famous black leader. Reporters were kept a safe distance from the house. After carefully removing the suitcase from under the house, demolition experts opened it to find old clothes and other harmless items inside. No one was quite sure how it got under King's house, but we were happy it didn't present a problem. That discovery even gave us a chance to laugh for the only time that day.

I finally got home around 3 a.m. Monday. Sharon's bagels were but distant, delicious memories. The scrambled eggs and the lox were long gone. I was too tired to even think of food and pretty much passed out after falling into bed. When I awoke several hours later, I learned that the locker boxes were part of a scheme to take attention away from the start of the Selma march. It didn't work, of course. But, it did get national attention in newspapers and on television. I got some nice compliments from my bosses in Alabama and in Atlanta. It made me feel pretty good. I was feeling more confident than ever. I was earning my *UPI* spurs.

The march from Selma to Montgomery accomplished what King wanted—national attention to the plight of southern blacks denied the right to vote. It lasted for almost a week and ended on the steps of Alabama's Capitol—not far from a bronze star marking the spot where Jefferson Davis was sworn in as president of the Confederacy a century earlier. It's only a few feet from the main entrance on the marble entrance. There are no historic markers to designate the spot where King spoke. Gov. George Wallace was inside the Capitol at the time, but he didn't step outside. King, who had pastored a church a block away in Montgomery, wasn't one of his favorite people and he became a verbal target for Wallace during his gubernatorial campaigns. He used King in negative speeches to pick up votes.

The night the march ended, I was relaxing in my office. I had gotten to know most of the reporters and editors at the *Post-Herald* and they'd occasionally step into my office to chat. The night of March 25, 1965 was relatively quiet and I remember propping my feet up on my desk and taking deep drags from a cigarette. Then, the teletype machine began to clank. Bells sounded to alert us of something important. The bulletin said the body of a white woman had been found inside her 1963 Oldsmobile just off U.S. 80—the route used by the marchers to get to Montgomery from Selma. Her name was Viola Liuzzo. I would learn a lot about her in the coming months.

It didn't take long to arrest those suspected of killing Liuzzo. They were taken into custody almost immediately. Rowe had given his FBI contact the names of those he said had killed her. By mid-morning of the next day, I was at the Federal Building in downtown Birmingham, jockeying for position with other reporters who also had gotten word that something big was up in the Liuzzo case. Wilkins, Thomas, Eaton and Rowe were arrested and charged with conspiring to intimidate Liuzzo in her effort to exercise her rights under the U.S. Constitution. At that time, there was no federal statute on murder. Murder indictments would be returned later in state court in Lowndes County where the Detroit housewife and civil rights activist was slain.

Johnson succeeded the assassinated John F. Kennedy as president on Nov. 22, 1963, and quickly picked up JFK's torch on civil rights. He wasted little time injecting himself into the Liuzzo case—appearing on television in Washington the same day Wilkins, Thomas, Eaton and Rowe were being taken into custody by the FBI in Birmingham. LBJ called the Ku Klux Klan a "hooded band of bigots" and said he was declaring war on the group to drive it "from American society." "We will not be intimidated by the terrorists of the Ku Klux Klan any more than by the terrorists of the Viet Cong," said Johnson, who soon would discover that the Klan couldn't hold a candle or cross to the Viet Cong.

In early April, about two weeks after Liuzzo was shot to death, Rowe's connection to the arrests leaked our way. Federal indictments were returned against Wilkins, Thomas and Eaton, but all charges against Rowe were dropped. He wasn't with the other three when they were brought in for their arraignments at the Federal Building. That's where I met the bombastic Matt Murphy for the first time. He loved the press, especially when he was being quoted and his picture was being taken. After the arraignments and the revelations about Rowe, my job was to find as much about him as possible. I drove to the area where he was supposed to have lived and talked with some people who said they knew him. Rowe's reputation didn't seem much better than the three men he had fingered for killing Liuzzo.

The following days were consumed by the civil rights murder case. The march was all but forgotten by then. Our Atlanta editors wanted to know as much as they could about Rowe and the three men charged in Liuzzo's death. As the government built its case against the Klansmen, I got to know Murphy in an unexpected way—up close and personal. It happened on a rainy morning as I was rushing toward the front door of Birmingham's Federal Building. That's where we collided. It gave me a chance to formally introduce myself. We had seen each other at some of the press conferences, but hadn't had a chance to really sit down and talk. In the weeks that followed, I got to know him pretty well. At times, he'd invite me to his office. Wilkins usually was there—sitting across from me. He had that same surly look on his face. Cigarette smoke swirled around him, covering his face in a white cloud. I never knew if Murphy and Wilkins were aware I was Jewish. If they did, they didn't say anything. I'm sure they felt they had somebody they could use to plant some information about Liuzzo's "real reason" for being in Alabama. In a way, I was using them, too. That's the way it often is in journalism—using each other to get what's needed. In my case, I was involved in one of the biggest stories of 1965. And, I was a rookie, to boot.

My association with Murphy paid off in a big way in late April when he gave me a copy of a federal lawsuit asking that charges against his clients be dropped because, he claimed, President Johnson had violated their "constitutional rights." Murphy said Johnson had gone "beyond the bounds of realm and reason" and had already found the three

Klansmen "guilty of the crime." On April 30, 1965, the *Post-Herald* placed my bylined story across the top of one of its pages with the headline: "Klansmen Claim LBJ Violated Their Rights." I had scooped their own reporters who covered the federal courthouse. Not bad for a rookie reporter. Our regional office in Atlanta used the story to drum up more business from other newspapers. Leaflets were sent to editors with the article on top and "Only UPI's Al Benn had this story" below it. That was a nice thing for them to do. We never knew if what we did helped increase business for *UPI*, but we knew we weren't relaxing a bit during the civil rights era.

My assignment during Wilkins' trial was to use my Klan connections, especially with Murphy and to sit by the master's side in the courtroom. That was Al Kuettner, a veteran reporter sent over from Atlanta to handle the bulk of the writing. I was allowed to write a bit myself, but my main role was to make sure I knew where Murphy was and to call him at night at the Montgomery motel where he and his assistants stayed. Jury selection began on May 3, 1965 and the place was packed. Hayneville is a quaint little town with a monument to local residents who were killed during the Civil War. It's in the middle of the courthouse square. The courthouse had no air conditioning and was falling apart. The trial was held on the second floor and the only way to get there was up narrow, decaying steps. At the bottom of the steps, a man sat whittling on a small piece of white oak. He'd sit there and whittle, then spit some tobacco juice on the cement floor. Then, he'd resume his whittling as he watched all the "outsiders" hustle up to the second floor.

The trial attracted some of America's most prominent journalists. Among them were national columnists Jimmy Breslin and Murray Kempton of New York. Another was William Bradford Huie, a successful novelist from north Alabama who, one day, would write about King's assassin. I was in awe of those guys and stood a respectful distance away. Autograph seekers crowded around Breslin and others they recognized. I doubt anybody ever heard of Kuettner, but he was— in wire service circles—a superstar with an amazing ability to describe the smallest details in the most vivid fashion.

The living has always been easy in Hayneville—far removed from the hustle and bustle of big city life in nearby Montgomery. Aware of all the reporters expected for the trial, the local telephone company set up a bank of pay phones on the courthouse lawn. They were in demand throughout the trial and there would be long lines as reporters waited impatiently to use one of them. Today, reporters have cell phones that can be used at most assignments. There weren't many grocery stores in Hayneville and the owners cashed in on out-of-towners with big expense accounts and strange accents. I stopped by around noon each day to pick up some hoop cheese, crackers and a bottle of R.C. Cola for lunch. Montgomery was only 30 minutes away, but too much was happening in and around the courthouse to be gone even for a few minutes. There was no such thing as gag orders back in those days and Murphy was having a field day pontificating about everything, especially the superiority of the "white man."

The prosecution's star witness was Rowe—a fat thug with red hair and a quick temper. Without him the state had no case. With him, it had a man who gave new meaning to mercenary conduct. The question was whether the jury would believe Rowe's account of what happened on the night of March 25, 1965. It was evident from the moment Rowe took the stand that Murphy would be trying him while prosecutors went after Wilkins. Murphy's opening statement to the jurors was as expected. He delivered a long, racist harangue against "Communists, Jews and niggers." He said they had tried to change what he called the "accepted" way of life in the South.

The prosecutors—Arthur Gamble, Carlton Perdue and Joe Breck Gantt—used words that shocked and embarrassed many in the courtroom—especially those unfamiliar with the way it really was at that time in Alabama. The three had grown up in a state where segregation was the law and second class citizenship was bestowed on blacks as part of the racial landscape of the times. Gantt told the jury during his opening statement that he didn't want to talk about Communism or integration because he was there to try a murder case. He also said he believed in segregation. That was no big surprise since most of the jurors felt the same way. Gamble, who would become a circuit judge one day and serve with distinction, had the best description of the Liuzzo case. It was, he said, "a cold-blooded middle-of-the-night killing that you cannot overlook."

The judge was T. Werth Thagard, a wisp of a man who watched the proceedings with what appeared to be mild detachment. In reality, he knew all that was unfolding before him, even if it looked like his mind was elsewhere. I would discover that fact during Rowe's testimony later in the trial. It was obvious from the start that Liuzzo was all but forgotten. She represented people and a culture loathed by many in the South. On trial was a way of life—nothing more, nothing less.

Rowe's presence on the stand was what Murphy wanted. His strategy was to portray Rowe as a man who had betrayed his "own kind," a man who could not be believed under any circumstances. Added to that fact was Rowe's "job" as an FBI spy. The trial was made to order for Murphy. The FBI was hated almost as much as the civil rights protesters. A few feet from Murphy sat Robert Shelton, Imperial Wizard of the Ku Klux Klan. Shelton kept slipping pieces of paper to Murphy as Rowe testified about joining the Klan in early 1961 and becoming an "active" member. After Rowe gave his account to prosecutors of what he said had happened to Liuzzo, Murphy got his chance. He had been waiting for a long time and knew exactly what he was going to ask.

"Did you not sign an oath of allegiance to the Klan?" Murphy asked him.

"Such as it was," Rowe countered.

Murphy then read the Klan oath which required members not to betray fellow members, "yield" to bribes or perform any other disloyal act. It did not mention murder or maiming those who might have disagreed with the Klan or had different lifestyles. Rowe had obviously been tutored by FBI agents on how to conduct himself on the witness stand. No doubt he was told to keep his cool and not allow Murphy to egg him on with belittling personal remarks. It seemed to work from the start because Rowe wouldn't get rattled, especially as he began to recount how the four of them first saw Liuzzo in downtown Selma and then followed her car into Lowndes County.

He said he was carrying a .38 caliber Smith & Wesson revolver and was sitting to the left of Wilkins in the back seat of Thomas' car. He said they got to Selma about 7 p.m. and rode around until they saw a white woman behind the wheel of her car at a downtown intersection on the approach to the Edmund Pettus Bridge. Next to Liuzzo was Leroy Moton, a tall, thin black civil rights volunteer who had been helping get marchers back to Selma from Montgomery so they could prepare to return home.

"You were going to kill some niggers," Murphy challenged Rowe.

"No, sir," Rowe responded as he leaned forward from the stand.

"Shoot niggers," Murphy said, pushing his face close to Rowe's.

"Very definitely not," Rowe said.

"How many shots did you fire, Rowe?" Murphy asked.

"Not any," Rowe said.

And, so it went...on and on as Murphy tried his best to shake Rowe from his rehearsed reflection of a night that would change many lives. As I sat and scribbled notes in my composition notebook, I realized we had a chance to score a major beat over the *Associated Press* because the "dean" of the wire services in Alabama had assigned only one writer to cover the trial—himself. Rex Thomas was a legendary reporter, but he was no match for two competitors, even one as green as I was at the time.

"Al," I whispered to Kuettner, who was taking his own notes, "I'm going to go downstairs and call Atlanta. I figure when I'm through you can finish (Rowe's) testimony." Kuettner flashed a smile, but didn't say anything. I think it was an endorsement sign on what I was planning to do. The courtroom was packed and no one had left during Rowe's testimony. With butterflies fluttering in my stomach, I slowly got up and, as quietly as possible, walked toward the back of the big courtroom. I didn't look back. I didn't want the judge to order me back to my seat. Down on the first floor, I walked into the sheriff's office, called Atlanta and began dictating my story about Rowe's testimony. I told the editor on the other end of the line that I hoped Kuettner would be down in a few minutes to finish, but, if not, we'd still have my report of Rowe's dramatic account. Included was Rowe's testimony that Wilkins fired the fatal shots and then shouted: "She's dead and in hell."

I knew we'd beat *AP* by several minutes. In wire service competition of that period, a couple of minutes constituted a beat of major proportions, especially at newspapers that subscribed to both *UPI* and *AP*. With several editions confronting editors, many just grabbed the first report to come over the wire and put it into a pre-arranged spot on a page. In most cases, updated reports were used from the wire service that was first. Rowe's testimony went according to plan. I've always had pretty good luck during my career and, more often than not, have stumbled into places where the news was happening. When Kuettner came downstairs, he didn't miss a beat—picking up where I had just left off. By the time Thomas came down, we had finished our story. I could see the mortified look on his face. In the end, we had pounded *AP* on the Rowe testimony with a substantial scoop, which meant several minutes.

Thagard called a recess when Rowe was finished and, from what I was told, he wasn't very happy about what I had done. After the recess, as Kuettner and I had taken our seats for the next witness, Thagard let it be known just how displeased he was.

"No one, let me repeat myself, no one, will leave this courtroom while testimony is going on," the judge said, as he looked in my direction. "Anybody who tries to leave will not be getting back in." I could feel everybody begin to look at me. They had seen me leave before the recess. Inwardly, I was crowing. A rookie had just helped score a major victory in one of the day's most important stories. Al nudged me a bit after the judge finished his admonition. I think he was proud of me.

Testimony continued through the week with the prosecution relying heavily on FBI agents who had worked with Rowe or conducted the investigation. Agent Neil Shanahan testified that he had been paying Rowe for information about the Klan since September 1964. He said he paid him $112 a week since the first of April, 1965—a few days after Liuzzo was killed. How he came up with $112 was a mystery. I guess the FBI had a pay scale for snitches.

The defense lawyer couldn't resist having fun with the federal investigator, especially since both of them had surnames from the Emerald Isle.

"You're Irish, aren't you?" Murphy asked Shanahan, who responded "yes" and even managed a smile.

"You're not shanty Irish, are you?" Murphy asked.

"I'm not sure what that means," said Shanahan, who knew exactly what it meant.

Murphy tried without success to break Shanahan's concentration on the stand. The agent wouldn't buckle. He was no stranger to courtrooms and knew most defense tactics. He just waited for Murphy's question and then blasted it out of the park. Murphy realized he wasn't getting anywhere with Shanahan, but he didn't quit. His aim was to show disloyalty to the Klan and the best way to do that was to grill the two men who provided that opportunity—Rowe and Shanahan.

Sharon joined me for a couple of days of testimony and seemed to enjoy it. As she sat in the courtroom, she began to chat with several women who were just behind us, not realizing some were Ku Klux Klan wives. They didn't discuss religion, but, if they did, I think Sharon would have been excluded from the conversations. At one point during a break, I heard one of the Klan wives invite Sharon to join their group—the KKK Ladies Auxiliary. I interjected, saying she wouldn't be able to join because their gatherings might conflict with her Hadassah meetings. The Klan wives didn't know Hadassah was a Jewish women's group, of course, but I got a kick out of it. "They seemed like such nice ladies," Sharon said, as we walked outside the courthouse for a breather.

After the testimony ended, closing arguments began. In Alabama, the prosecution has the burden of proving its case and, thus, has two bites of the apple. Prosecutors open and close with defense attorneys sandwiched in the middle—meaning they had to go all out since the last thing the jury hears is from the prosecution.

In his opening statement, Gantt outlined the state's case and used words that—decades later—would be considered politically incorrect. In 1965, those words were accepted by many in the South. He told the jury he didn't want to talk about "segregation or integration or whites, or niggers or marchers or demonstrators." He described himself as a segregationist, but said he wanted to talk about one thing—a murder in Lowndes County. He didn't want to talk about a white Yankee woman sitting in a car with a black man. By the time the testimony ended, Gantt had hoped it would be sufficient for a conviction. In his closing argument, he called Liuzzo's death a "cold-blooded murder" and said there wasn't "one iota of evidence against it." As he paced back and forth in front of the jury box on that sweltering day in early May 1965, Gantt spoke about the past, the present and the future. "I pray for justice," he told the jury, adding that, while he was a "strong segregationist," the evidence demanded a conviction. "Blood is going to spill in Hayneville," Gantt said, apparently meaning that an acquittal might open the flood gates of continued violence against those attempting to change a way of life. "Is that what our forefathers fought for?" Gantt asked. He followed by invoking the name of Gov. George C. Wallace, the man who used his inaugural address two years before Liuzzo's slaying to promise continued segregation in Alabama. Wallace had used "cowardly" in describing the attack on Liuzzo and Gantt took it one more step. He called the accused killer a "yellow-bellied coward." He also told the jury that it would "take courage" to return a guilty verdict, adding: "We're not going to be intimidated." He ended his summation with: "The decision you make in this case will be a historic one. Law enforcement has done everything it could do."

Murphy knew he had to appeal to the racist instincts of 12 white men who grew up in a county and state where racial separation was legal. That's what he did, attacking anything that wasn't perceived as "the right way" to live—the "white way." It led to the most embarrassingly funny moment of the trial. He criticized Liuzzo for coming south and Rowe for being a "Yankee spy." His client was all but ignored during his closing argument. Murphy described Rowe as a man who had sold out the Klan "for 30 pieces of silver." He told the jurors that they were dealing "with the devil himself...a liar, a perjurer and as treacherous as a rattlesnake." Murphy said Rowe had "sold his soul" and was "worse than a white nigger." As he made a pass of the jury box, Murphy stopped for a moment and glanced out the second floor window that was left open to provide some fresh air inside the muggy courtroom. When he looked down, he saw a CBS camera crew on the grass. The camera was focused on the window and Murphy suddenly found himself in the middle of what he knew would be a national spotlight. At that point, he seemed to forget about the jurors and proceeded to give his closing statement to the world.

"I am proud to stand on my feet and declare white supremacy," he said, as he began to flay his arms in all directions. "You have that bunch of white Zionists who run that bunch of niggers. When white men join up with them, they become white niggers. Then, there was that black nigger who was with (Liuzzo). The Klan didn't bring this thing down here. She turned her soul over to a black nigger. She was hauling niggers and Communists back and forth. The black man hasn't got any decency, honor or courtesy."

Murphy wore a cheap toupee and, on that hot, humid afternoon in Lowndes County, it became unglued—just as he appeared to be during his closing argument. The more animated he became in front of the jury box and in front of the open window, the more the toupee began to flop up and down on his sweaty dome. As he continued his tirade against black people, whites in the courtroom began to squirm. Murphy had, in many minds, gone way too far, especially when he said that black people "never built anything but huts with thatched roofs" and claimed that supporters of the civil rights movement "are using their power in the wrong direction and it will destroy them." Murphy also described the 54-mile walk from Selma to Montgomery as "the most unholy march in the history of Alabama." CBS Evening News, anchored by Walter Cronkite, devoted a segment to Murphy's closing argument. Most television news segments are measured in seconds. I think Murphy's lasted several minutes. I wish I had a copy of it for my personal files.

Despite Murphy's racist histrionics, it appeared from the start of deliberations that the jurors were having problems with the case. There would be no quick acquittal, as Murphy had hoped. An hour after they started, jurors sent a note to Thagard, asking if they could consider lesser included offenses such as second degree murder or manslaughter. The judge said they could do that. Three hours later, the foreman told the judge they were hopelessly deadlocked. Thagard sent them to a motel for the night to rest and resume in the morning. Sleep didn't change any minds and Thagard finally had to declare a mistrial. After it was over, reporters were told the jurors had voted 10-2 for manslaughter which would have carried a 10-year sentence. Supporters of Wilkins had hoped for an acquittal, but they weren't too upset. They felt it had just been an opening act and he'd win the next time. Those who were hoping for a conviction also had reason to be optimistic. After all, to have 10 white men favor conviction of another white man for killing a civil rights worker was almost unbelievable in rural Alabama during that time. Civil rights leaders considered the mistrial a moral victory.

Murphy never got his chance for a second round. Sharon and I were at my sister Eileen's house in Pennsylvania not long after that wild night in the state park in Linden. The phone rang early one morning. It was my father calling. "Your buddy's dead," he said. "What?" I asked, as I tried to clear the cobwebs." "Murphy, Matt Murphy," he said. "He ran his car into a tree." Reports said later that Murphy had fallen asleep behind the wheel of his convertible early in the morning as he was on his way to Klan headquarters in Tuscaloosa where Shelton lived. It was

Aug. 20, 1965 and Matt Murphy's sun had set. He did have one last hurrah, however. The May 21 issue of Life magazine had him on the cover. His right hand, minus three fingers, was held up in a "V" for victory sign and he had that smug look on his face, his right eye framed neatly between his two remaining fingers. I think Murphy tried to buy every copy of the magazine in Birmingham. He was one proud Klan lawyer and autographed them as fast as he could. Mine read: "To my friend, and a true stuff writer who writes the truth and is a real credit to the press. Best Regards. Matt Murphy." Sharon put it in a scrapbook she had begun to fill with clippings of my bylined articles. I never did find out if Murphy knew I was Jewish. It was long before the "Don't ask, don't tell" policy regarding homosexuals in the military. Murphy didn't ask and I didn't tell.

I don't think there was a busier *UPI* bureau in the world than Birmingham during those first few months of 1965. The same could be said of Birmingham's *AP* bureau. Those of us charged with getting the news out to the world seemed to work around the clock at times to meet deadlines. Before the year had ended, Wilkins would be acquitted by another all-white, all-male jury in Lowndes County. Thomas also would be acquitted in another trial. In November 1965, Wilkins, Thomas and Eaton were indicted in federal court of violating Liuzzo's civil rights as in the right to breathe. Wilkins and Thomas were convicted the following year and sentenced to 10 years in federal prison. They served six years. Eaton died of a heart attack before he could be tried. Wilkins and Thomas slipped from sight after they were released, but did make one final splash. The two claimed in a national television interview that Rowe had been the triggerman in the Liuzzo murder. They also testified before a federal grand jury—the same type of investigative body that had indicted them. The grand jury refused to indict Rowe, saying Wilkins and Thomas had waited too long to bring their complaint. Thomas died a few years later. Wilkins died in 1994 of a heart attack at the age of 51. He had had his 15 minutes of fame and they weren't very pretty. Rowe died in 1998.

Wilkins' second trial had a somewhat amusing, if not unexpected, ending. After the jury went out following closing arguments, we sat back to wait on a decision. The first day produced no results and into the second day it went. As the hours ticked by, we wondered what was going on. I asked a Hayneville man who was sitting in the back row of the old courthouse what he thought and he made a prediction I hadn't expected. "They'll be back in with a verdict no later than 6 p.m. Friday," he told me. "Why do you say that?" I asked. "Well," he said, "Hayneville High School's football team has a game Friday night and it's on the road, so to get there in time, we'll have to leave no later than 6 o'clock." "You've got to be kidding," I told him. "A man is on trial for his life and you're saying a football game will be the deciding factor in the jury's decision?" "Right," he said. Shortly before 6 p.m. that Friday, the jury returned and acquitted Wilkins. Most of them then hopped into their cars and pickups for the big road game. Alabama and Auburn also had college games on Saturday, so that meant nothing was going to keep the jury out too long. There's an old saying in Alabama that boys grow up wanting to be one of two things—a football player or a politician. The expression remains popular today.

Before the summer of 1965 ended, two more civil rights era slayings would occur and I'd be involved in both of them. On the night of July 15, Willie Brewster had just gotten off work at a Calhoun County pipe foundry and was headed to his home near Anniston when three white men in a car began to follow the vehicle in which he was a passenger. Brewster, 38, agreed to take over behind the wheel of the 1957 Pontiac when the driver complained his feet hurt. Suddenly, shots rang out and Brewster slumped over the wheel. A bullet had pierced his spine. He was rushed to an area hospital for treatment.

I heard about the shooting the next morning at my office and drove immediately to Anniston, about 60 miles east of Birmingham. I was allowed into Brewster's hospital room. He appeared to be recovering and was able to answer a few of my questions. "This is the worst thing that has ever happened to me," Brewster said, from his bed. He denied having ever taken part in civil rights activities. He said his wife and children came first. He told me he had felt a "stabbing pain" in his shoulder and then noticed the car behind his pulling off the road after passing his vehicle. Doctors indicated that Brewster would recover, but said he would be paralyzed for the rest of his life. Brewster died three days later—the latest victim in what would be the most violent period of the American civil rights era. The victims included Jimmie Lee Jackson in Marion, Viola Liuzzo in Lowndes County, James Reeb in Selma,

Willie Brewster in Anniston and Jonathan Daniels in Hayneville—five activists killed in a seven-month period. Each was killed during protests or in response to a plea for help from Americans denied their basic rights.

During my visit to Anniston, I remained long enough to attend a racist rally on the steps of the Calhoun County Courthouse. A few hours before Brewster was shot, a white supremacist reprobate by the name of Connie Lynch stood on the same steps to denounce integration. He assailed federal court orders, Jews, Communists and anyone or anything else that might change the way things had been for so long. At one point in his tirade, Lynch, who lived in Florida, said: "If it takes killing to get the Negroes out of the white man's streets and to protect our constitutional rights, then I say, yes, kill them." Unfortunately for Brewster, he happened to be at the wrong place at the wrong time. If he hadn't changed places with the driver of that car, he might still be alive today. At the courthouse rally I attended, several Klan-types took turns repeating Lynch's earlier comments. I stood across the street, next to an Anniston police officer, with a notebook in my left hand and a ballpoint pen in my right. As one of the speakers ranted and raved, he paused for a second and looked over in my direction. "There," he shouted, "that's one of them news media people. They're to blame for what we've been going through." A chill ran down my spine when the cop whispered over his left shoulder: "When they rush, get inside the building behind us. I left the door open." All I could do was hope he'd hang around long enough to lend a hand if they did rush us. Luckily, it was just bluster from the speaker and all I got were more choice words from him and some of the others in the crowd.

I went to Brewster's funeral and it was a personally painful experience for me. Even though I had only been with him in his hospital room for a few minutes, I felt as if I had known him for a long time. It was held in a small stiflingly hot church in a rural area many miles from Anniston. I stood in back as mourners passed by the open casket, pausing long enough to look down and bid farewell to a man who believed in supporting his family and loved raising tomatoes. When his wife, Lestine, walked up, she couldn't hold it in any longer. She broke down and cried uncontrollably, repeating his name over and over. "Brewster, don't leave me, Brewster," she cried. Pregnant with their third child, she suffered a miscarriage shortly after the funeral.

A month after the shooting, three white men were indicted on murder charges in Brewster's death. A witness testified that he overheard one of them say after the shooting: "We got us a nigger." It took the jurors 13 hours, but they finally returned a verdict and it had people sitting up and taking notice. The jury convicted Brewster's killer and sentenced him to 10 years in prison. It was the first time a white man had been convicted of killing a black person in Alabama during the civil rights era. The killer died in a brawl at a bar before he could begin serving his term. Anniston had been a hotbed of racist activities in Alabama for more than a decade. Several area men were arrested for assaulting famed singer Nat King Cole as Cole performed before an integrated audience in Birmingham years before Brewster's murder. Cole would never return to his home state to perform after that. One of my personal heroes during that time was H. Brandt Ayers of the Anniston Star. Ayers' paper was referred to by those who believed in segregation as the "Red Star" because of its liberal editorial leanings. Brandy never gave in to the threats that came his way. Fear wasn't in his makeup.

Soon after I finished my coverage of the Brewster murder and funeral, I wound up reporting on another civil rights-related trial in 1965. A month after Brewster was shot in the back, a young Episcopal seminary student from New Hampshire was gunned down in front of a little convenience store in Hayneville—the same small town where the two Wilkins murder trials were held. It would feature some of the same characters and the similarities were easily recognized—a white civil rights worker shot to death in Alabama during the height of the movement.

Jonathan Daniels, who had been attending an Episcopal seminary in New England, answered King's call for help after "Bloody Sunday" in Selma. He arrived in time to lend his support for subsequent developments that included the long march to Montgomery. Unlike the others, however, Daniels remained behind to see what else he could do to help the poor. He spent much of the summer assisting black people in Selma and Hayneville. One of his initial goals was to integrate Selma's Episcopal church. That was a tall order, perhaps even more difficult than integrating the schools. When he saw the brick wall he was facing, Daniels changed his strategy. He took a leadership role in voter registration efforts in Lowndes County where blacks were in the majority as far as population, but not one was registered to vote.

On Aug. 20, 1965, Daniels and a group of civil rights activists were released from the Lowndes County jail after having spent a week in custody for marching without a permit. Daniels and a Catholic priest—Richard Morrisroe—led the group to the Cash Store not far from the Lowndes County Courthouse. Inside was a special deputy sheriff—Tom Coleman—who cradled a shotgun in his arms and didn't waste words. He would later claim he saw what looked like a knife in Daniels' right hand. He said he saw a reflection from the sun and "assumed" it was the blade. Those with Daniels would say later it was a dime to buy a soft drink. As Coleman aimed the shotgun, Daniels pushed a black teen-ager who had been jailed with him. He knocked her out of the way, but took the full blast from Coleman's shotgun. Morrisroe was hit in the back from a second blast. Daniels died instantly. Morrisroe recovered, but the pain remains today. Coleman, charged with manslaughter instead of murder, was acquitted by an all-white male jury in a couple of hours. No one was surprised, including me. It was the third trial of its kind that year at the little courthouse.

By the time Coleman went on trial, I had gotten to know most of the players pretty well—including the old guy who continued to whittle and spit at the steps leading to the second floor. Just before Coleman faced the music, I just had to ask the whittler one question. It was one of the dumbest questions in a long line of stupid queries through the years. "Why," I asked him, "do you seem to be spending your day whittling away here in the courthouse?" He gazed up for a second, spit some tobacco juice on the concrete floor near my right foot and said: "Why do you seem to be spending so much time asking questions in the courthouse?" It was my last question to him.

Liuzzo and Daniels have been honored in the years since their violent deaths and I attended many of them as a reporter for the *Montgomery Advertiser*. A granite monument honoring Liuzzo was erected near where she was killed. It's on top of a hill overlooking U.S. 80 just west of Lowndesboro—about a quarter of a mile from the exact spot of her slaying. Those who put it up wanted a safer location because of the heavy traffic. Highway 80 was a two-lane road when she died. Today, it's a four-lane super highway. Civil rights activists and history buffs from around the world stop by to see the monument on their way to and from Selma and Montgomery. The monument has been defaced twice. Somebody painted a Confederate flag across the front one time. It was wiped off and a large security light and fence have been built at the site. Lowndes County sheriff Willie Vaughner makes sure the monument is protected and the grass is mowed around it. Vaughner, who is black, was a high school student who noticed authorities at the site where Liuzzo was shot to death. He saw them from the window of his school bus. In early 2004, I received quite an honor—selection by the U.S. Department of the Interior to be a member of the Historic Trail Advisory Council. I guess it's because I was the last of the "old breed" still covering civil rights activities. I'm often asked to speak to groups about those days.

It takes more of an effort to get to Daniels' monument which was erected between the store where he was shot to death and the courthouse where Coleman was acquitted. Several groups pitched in to pay for the monument. Ruby Sales attended the unveiling ceremony. She was the young black girl pushed out of the way by Daniels, who gave up his life for hers. Coleman lived more than 30 years after he killed Daniels. In an ironic twist, he became a good friend of Lowndes County's first black sheriff. John Hulett served for 20 years as the county's top lawman and often said he considered Coleman a valuable asset to his office as an advisor and assistant. I went to Coleman's funeral where a black resident served as one of his pallbearers. Coleman's son had a few angry words when he saw me, but cooler heads prevailed. I got an escort from the cemetery. Each time I drive into Hayneville, my thoughts are on those trials I covered and two white Yankees who came south to help poor blacks and lost their lives in the process.

My tenure with *UPI* was filled with many other civil rights assignments and I got a chance to interview some of the most famous and infamous figures of that era. They ranged from Martin Luther King Jr. to George Lincoln Rockwell, who was the leader of the American Nazi Party. Add Hosea Williams, one of King's top lieutenants, Klan leader Bobby Shelton and many others who played a variety of roles during that time and it's easy to see how eventful those 2 1/2 years were. I enjoyed covering King if, for no other reason than to hear him speak. He had the most magnificent voice I had ever heard. James Earl Jones might match him today but, back then, King was in a league of his own. What resonance! What power! What timing! King could have been a great standup comic. He knew a punch line when he saw it and he had the ability to pace himself, especially during long speeches that had several special messages in them. On some occasions, reporters were put on the pulpit behind King because there weren't any seats left in the sanctuary where he spoke. That gave us unusual vantage points. We were able to look out into the audience and see eyes popping, mouths agape, hands clasped together. People hung on every word.

I was surprised by the minimal amount of security for King, especially at a time when he was so despised in the South. When I'd go to the airport to wait for him to board a plane and leave Birmingham, he usually only had one or two bodyguards with him. He obliged everybody who would walk up to him—wanting to shake his hand or have him autograph one of his books for them. How easy it would be, I thought to myself as I watched him pose for pictures, for somebody to whip a gun or knife out of their purse or pocket. He knew he was a marked man, as Memphis would prove three years later, but he refused to allow it to control his life.

King was, in many ways, the commanding general of a huge civil rights army and Williams was his chief of staff. Hosea would lead the shock troops into a town that had been targeted for protests and then stay while King moved on to some other city. He wasn't the kind of leader who stayed in a hotel as others went out to meet the dogs and fire hoses, either. He was on the front lines in Birmingham and Selma where he and Lewis tried to cross the Edmund Pettus Bridge on March 7, 1965, only to be routed by Alabama's State Troopers. As they got to the top of the bridge high above the Alabama River, Williams turned to Lewis and said: "John, I hope you know how to swim."

I got to know Williams pretty well during those days, especially at night when he seemed to enjoy marching through Birmingham to protest one alleged racial inequity or another. In addition to his obvious leadership abilities, he also had a wicked sense of humor and enjoyed picking on reporters as we gathered around him for quotes. After one brutal rebuff by Birmingham police, Williams called another march for the following night. Before it was to begin, we formed a circle around him and began asking questions. He surprised us by asking the first one.

WILLIAMS: "Who wrote the story this morning that there was a riot at last night's march?"

BENN: "I did, Hosea."

WILLIAMS: "Man, that was no riot. Tonight's the riot."

We all laughed. Williams was right because that's the way he planned it. The previous night's violence paled in comparison to the one we were about to witness. It was like that in Birmingham during those days. Local white leaders took offense when we used "riot" in our stories. Perhaps the definition has changed with time. But, back then, I considered it a riot when heads were being bloodied, bricks were being thrown, people were being hauled off to jail and I was in the middle of it.

Rockwell was a world class racist. When he came home from World War II, he brought with him his own vision of what the world should be like. He would have preferred no Jews, blacks, Communists, socialists, homosexuals and others whose lifestyles and religions differed from his. I got to know him briefly during one of his trips to Birmingham. I had just covered one of his press conferences and he invited me to a downtown hotel where he said he had something to show me. As we walked toward the hotel, it began to sprinkle and we picked up our pace, pushing into a slow jog. "Just a minute," Rockwell said. "I've got to buy something." With that, he stepped inside a corner drugstore and came out a couple of minutes later with a small bottle in a paper bag. He swallowed half of it and stuck the bottle back into his right front pocket. "I really need this stuff," he said. It was paregoric, an opium-laced drug used to ease a baby's pain during teething. Some use it to ease other discomforts. I wasn't sure what Rockwell's was, but, for many in America during that time, he was one of the country's biggest pains in the rump.

The drug break seemed to perk him up and, by the time we reached the hotel, Rockwell was in renewed spirits. We took an elevator to the fourth floor and walked into a room where several of his cronies sat around smoking and drinking. "Here, listen to this," he said, as he picked up a record and placed it into a small player. The "song" was titled: "Ship Those Niggers Back" and the group singing it was called The Three Bigots. At least, they had a sense of humor in coming up with their name. That was all Rockwell wanted. I told him I wasn't into the record producing business and really had to get back to my office to report on his press conference. He seemed to like that idea and didn't put another "record" on for me. It was the first and only time I saw Rockwell in person and it was one too many. He would be shot to death by one of his former followers not long after he left Birmingham.

Working for a wire service meant being flexible and, at times, a bit devious in order to get the story filed first. When I was assigned to cover a demonstration in downtown Bessemer—about 20 miles from Birmingham—I wasn't sure how I'd be able to get word back to Atlanta. We didn't have laptop computers or cell phones back in those days. The telephone booth was our primary method of communication. I had a feeling that something bad was going to happen in Bessemer, so I left my car at the office and took a bus there. It was a good decision. Several hundred protesters had occupied the downtown area and weren't going to move unless police did it for them. That's just what happened after about an hour of stalled negotiations over one point or another. The police chief finally had enough. He pounded his nightstick into his left hand and shouted: "That's it. Let's go." Within seconds, demonstrators were scattering to all corners of the community. I had brought a half-frame Pentax camera which meant my 36 exposure roll had become 72 shots. I couldn't miss. Blood flowed, hair was pulled and arrests were made all around me. I kept advancing each frame and snapping the shutter. One of them was good enough to be picked up by *UPI's* wirephoto division and sent around the world.

My next responsibility was filing the story. There were only a few pay phones in the area and each was occupied. I knew that seconds wasted would hurt my filing deadline. Finally, out of desperation, I began pounding on one of the glass-enclosed booths and a woman inside saw my anguished look. She didn't know what to expect, but opened the door a crack. "Maaaaaam," I said in my best southern drawl, "I got to get my story called in. These Yankees down heah are causing all kinds of trouble. We got to tell people." I don't know why she cradled the phone and let me use it, but I was mighty grateful. She might have just felt sorry for me and my lousy southern accent. Whatever, the story was filed and I got on a bus headed back to Birmingham. Then, I began to shake. It finally hit me how dangerous that assignment had been. It took me the 20 miles into town to regain my composure.

Covering the Klan and other hate groups made reporters easy targets for threats, beatings and occasional surprises. During one Klan rally at a Birmingham park, I was approached from behind by a man who tapped me on the shoulder and said "You don't celebrate Christmas, do you?" I didn't know how to respond at first, but finally came up with a solid "no." I had never seen the man before, but his question made me realize the Klan had its own intelligence network, even if "intelligence" may not be the right word. Chanukah was just around the corner and Sharon and I were getting ready to celebrate by lighting the first of eight candles the day the question was asked.

Since I wasn't making much money, I always looked for ways to pick up a few extra bucks. One was to phone in stories to *UPI's* audio division—the branch that fed news to radio stations much in the same way we used the teletype machines to get our stories to newspapers. Whenever I had a chance, I'd slip into a phone booth, call the radio folks in New York and use my best Edward R. Murrow voice. Unfortunately, my high-pitched tones made me sound more like Mickey Mouse. But, I didn't fret. As long as the checks came in, it was fine with me. I was getting up to $50 for each voice report and that was big money for me. I wasn't auditioning for anything. Once, my cousin Linda, who lived in my hometown of Lancaster, Pa., heard me on a local radio station—giving a report from one riot zone or another. She said it was quite a thrill for her. I made several hundred dollars during that time and it was great. The funniest moment came when a large group of black demonstrators prepared to march from a Bessemer church to city hall to protest an arrest. I hopped into a phone booth along the parade route. Moments before the group walked by, the voice from New York told me to place the phone outside the booth to pick up their freedom songs. "OK," I said. "They're just about here." Guess what? Not a sound came from anybody in the group. After a few seconds, I hauled the phone back inside and told New York "this is the first silent march I've ever covered." Then, I hung up the phone and joined the parade.

After my first six months with *UPI*, I knew I had what it took to do the job. It certainly helped during the following two years because I never knew what would happen next. On most occasions, I was on my own. Tony had trained me well and I knew I had the tools by the time he left for another bureau management position. During my 2 1/2 year *UPI* career, I never got back to Atlanta to see any of my editors. I'd get phone calls and teletype messages from time to time but, by and large, it was up to me to cover what needed to be covered—everything from football statistics to farm commodity reports. Of course, civil rights stories took up a lot of my time. On top of that, I also covered developments in the space race and the war in Vietnam. Other than the first half of the 1940s, I can't think of another decade in the 20th century as volatile and as transformational as the 1960s.

Benn, right, covers Wernher von Braun at Miles College in Birmingham. (Photo by Joseph M. Chapman. ©)

Huntsville, about 100 miles north of Birmingham, was in my coverage area and, from time to time, I'd drive up to do stories on the Saturn V moon rocket. Wernher von Braun, the genius who built Hitler's V-2 rockets, led a colony of German scientists, including some former Nazis, at the Marshall Space Flight Center. Their job was to develop a rocket powerful enough to lift a manned capsule into orbit and then head for the moon to fulfill President Kennedy's challenge to get there by the end of the decade. Test burns only lasted a few seconds, but they were something to behold and be felt. The rocket generated 7.5 million pounds of thrust and had a 160 million horsepower wallop.

I took Sharon with me to report on the first test of the five-rocket cluster burn. It was a tooth-rattling experience for her. Reporters and other observers watched from concrete bunkers several hundred yards from where the Saturn V propulsion stage was hooked to steel restraints to keep it from leaving the test pad and heading for downtown Huntsville. The bunker had narrow slits that descended from one end to the other. Short people stood at the end where they could see. Unfortunately, when we entered, we were told a live electrical wire had been creating problems and we'd have to stand at the other end. At 4-11 ¾ inches, Sharon can barely see above the steering wheel of her car. Moving to the opposite end of the bunker meant she'd hear what was going on, but never see it. When the candle was lit on the 138-foot long flight stage, the ground began to rumble, then shake, then appear ready to split under our feet. A look of horror came across Sharon's face as the test continued. Finally, it ended and we were allowed to leave the observation site. I got to know von Braun, some of his engineers and a few of the Apollo astronauts during that time. I knew it would be only a matter of time before we'd reach the moon. I was in Decatur at the time, working for the local paper there. Sharon and I sat on the floor of our little living room, watching at 9:56 p.m. on July 20, 1969 as Neil Armstrong stepped off the ladder onto the lunar surface. Somehow, I felt as though I was a tiny part of the team that got him there.

Although I had left the Marine Corps in 1964 to reenter civilian life, I soon found myself linked to the military again as the Vietnam War heated up. My discharge date, in addition to being the day the bodies of the three civil rights workers were found in Mississippi, coincided with the Tonkin Gulf incident which escalated our presence in Vietnam. By the middle of 1965, large numbers of Marines had arrived in Vietnam and it wasn't long before I began reporting on Alabama casualties. During those early months of the American buildup, the impact of dead Americans being brought home for military funerals was devastating. One of my early stories was about the death of a second lieutenant from Bessemer. His name was Felix King Jr. and he had been assigned to the

First Cavalry Division. I went to the house and interviewed his grieving parents. The young officer had been on a search and destroy mission when his life ended on Nov. 6, 1965. His unit was caught between two Viet Cong units and he was shot twice.

UPI's Joe Galloway, who witnessed some of the most vicious fighting of the war, spent the night in a foxhole with an artillery company supporting the pinned down troops. Galloway, who would co-author "We Were Soldiers Once...And Young" about the first decisive battle between U.S. and North Vietnamese regulars, described King's death. It was included in my story about the lieutenant. Joe wrote about being in a foxhole with another Army officer and learning about King. He was told that King had been popular with the troops and his death had been a major blow to his unit.

"I want you to put in the paper that one of the finest young second lieutenants in the American Army died last night," Galloway was told. "He was the finest All-American lieutenant I've ever met. He was shot twice and killed."

King's parents showed me the last letter they had received from their son. It had been written to a younger son, David, and described Vietnam as seen by a man whose life had ended just as it was really getting started. The letter was written by candlelight a few days before King's death.

"The country is beautiful, Dave," King told his 9-year-old brother. "It has tall mountains with heavy forests all over them. Some of the mountains stick almost up to the clouds. We flew over them all at about 6,000 feet. The country isn't as pretty at six feet though." King said he had been on a secret mission and couldn't say much. He said the mission was so secret that only the officers in his unit were aware of it. King told his brother that he'd explain it all when he got back home. He also said that, from what he could see, the Viet Cong "are afraid of us" and "the big problem we have here is people shooting friendly people."

It had been an emotional interview and I could feel the anguish in the house. He had been a fine student and athlete at Florence State University near the Tennessee line. The Army considered King an up-and-comer—a man with a bright future in the military. All that ended during a secret mission that had claimed many lives. It wouldn't be the last one in a senseless war where 58,000 American men died, many of them younger than King. He was 23 at the time and left behind a widow and two young sons. Who knows what King would have become had he lived. He might have been a general, an educator or a business leader. He'd be in his 60s today. Most likely he'd be a grandfather. What a waste. What a tragedy. I was lucky. I got out in time. I think that's what made me so emotional during the interview with King's parents. I had lost a good friend from the Marine Corps in Vietnam. Jerry Pendell was on a helicopter that crashed in 1962—long before the big buildup. Whenever I'm in Washington, I try to go by the Vietnam Veterans Memorial wall and look for Jerry's name.

By the summer of 1965, I had become a full-fledged *UPI* correspondent. I'd won my job by covering news events of major proportions. My efforts had not gone unnoticed and, even though I still wasn't making much money, the praise directed at me helped make up for it—almost. On July 19, 1965, Jack Griffin—one of our top editors in Atlanta—wrote: "We were logged 32 minutes ahead Sunday on the death of Willie Brewster, the Anniston, Ala. Negro shot last week by nightriders. I understand this beat was due to protection arrangements that you made. Ataway to go, boy. Keep it up."

Another of my stories that seemed to impress the brass in Atlanta and New York involved an unusual interview I had with Klan leader Bobby Shelton who announced he was going to fly to England to save that country from the "creeping black plague." I interviewed Shelton as he drove his new Cadillac from his Klan headquarters in Tuscaloosa to Montgomery. He had taken a liking to me by then and it still amazed me. He had to have known I was Jewish. He didn't give his car phone number out to many people so I guess I should have been honored. Why he spoke so candidly to me remains a mystery. I guess he knew I was the kind of guy who didn't fabricate. I just reported what was told to me. Shelton said Britain's "problems" stemmed from a human relations bill that was similar to America's new Civil Rights Law—a federal mandate springing from the demonstrations in Birmingham. Shelton later was subpoenaed to testify before a federal committee in Washington. It was investigating subversive activities in the U.S. and the Klan topped the FBI list of targeted groups. Bobby stopped by my office and gave me a copy of the speech he had prepared to read to the committee. I told him it was way too long for me to use, but he said: "Just use what you can,

Al. I know you'll treat me right." He obviously wasn't able to convince committee members that the Klan was a benevolent group and when he refused to answer specific questions, he was packed off to prison for contempt of Congress. Bobby died in 2003, no doubt still convinced his way had been the right way.

Griffin wrote me a complimentary letter on my "Klansman Goes To England" story, saying my automobile interview with Shelton was a "fine and hustling response" to a request from *UPI* headquarters in New York. Adding his kudos was Bill Bryant, *UPI* state bureau manager in Alabama. Bill's comments meant a lot. "You've come a long way, Al, since you arrived in Birmingham," he wrote. "No matter what the situation, you always come through like a champ. Never fear that what you do escapes notice. It doesn't." The letter that meant the most that year came from Roger Tatarian, who was *UPI's* top editor in New York. It was dated March 30, 1965 and arrived a few days after all those green locker boxes full of dynamite had been discovered in Birmingham. "Our performance on recent events in Alabama was a joy to behold and a particular vote of thanks to you for superior action on events in Birmingham while a lot of people were looking elsewhere," Tartarian wrote. It took a few days for me to come back to earth after getting that letter.

Two of my biggest stories in 1966 involved an American military disaster and four mop-topped singers from England. One came as a result of my favorite morning radio show while the other came from a tipster.

Mention the Bay of Pigs fiasco and most people will talk about Cuban exiles, dictator Fidel Castro and a botched invasion plan. Few will say anything about Alabama. In reality, the Bay of Pigs "battle plan" was prepared, in part, in Alabama. The invasion that took place on April 17, 1961 had been conceived by officers of the Alabama National Guard and carried out by four brave aviators—Riley Shamburger, Jr., Thomas W. Ray, Wade Gray and Leo Baker. The invasion failed because anticipated American support for the landing force never materialized. Cubans who wanted to overthrow Castro were left to die or be captured on the beaches. That was known by most everybody. The Alabama connection had been kept pretty quiet.

A telephone tipster said the widows of the four Alabama airmen began receiving money from an anonymous benefactor. It was being done to help fill the financial void created by their deaths. As I called the widows, it became clear that I had quite a story in the works. The fifth anniversary of the Bay of Pigs was fast approaching in April of 1966 and I knew I didn't have much time. I began calling the widows and was surprised to find them so receptive. They were proud of what their husbands had done and, five years later, continued to carry the torch to keep their memories alive. They told me their husbands were not soldiers-of-fortune and did what they did out of patriotism and not for monetary gain. I learned that four of the five widows had received about $30,000 each during the five years since the failed invasion. One had remarried, so the financial assistance stopped at that point. That was the main stipulation from the benefactor whose name never was revealed. Since the Central Intelligence Agency played a major role in the invasion, it was assumed it had something to do with the assistance plan for the widows. My story got huge play around the United States and I got newspaper clippings from many of the biggest papers in the country.

In August of 1966, I was driving to work and listening to Doug Layton and Tommy Charles—Birmingham's top disc jockey team at that time. Their unique brand of humor had a wide following in those days. In fact, they became so popular that they bolted the station they had worked for and created WAQY-FM. Their morning chit-chat mirrored the station's call letters—wacky. Doug and Tommy usually tackled local issues, made fun of Birmingham politicians and sold advertising in between. On this day, they took on the most popular singing group in the world—the Beatles.

"Remember to send in all your Beatles records for our bonfire," Layton said. "We need as many as we can get. This will be our way of showing them how we feel."

Doug referred to a magazine interview with John Lennon, the brainy Beatle who teamed with Paul McCartney to write most of their hit songs. The magazine had reported months before that Lennon considered the Beatles "more popular than Jesus." The interview had finally reached U.S. shores and was creating a mini-furor. Layton and Charles had no way of knowing that their bonfire idea would catch on nationally and make them celebrities. I guess I was part of the reason. I know I was the first to report it.

"What's going on?" I asked, soon after I got to my office and called Charles, who enjoyed racing stock cars, running for mayor of Birmingham and doing televised commercial pitches. "We're upset with Lennon and are going to show him just what we think of his comments," Tommy told me. The more he talked, the more I knew it would be something our Atlanta and New York desks would love to get. There wasn't a hotter musical group in the world in 1966 and they were about to begin another American tour. Their closest stop to Birmingham would be Memphis. My story got good play the following day. AP didn't think much of it for a couple of days, but, as word spread from coast to coast, they finally woke up and put something out. By that time, the Beatles, Lennon and Jesus had become the talk of the music industry.

Angry reaction became so intense that the group's manager, Brian Epstein, made a special trip to the U.S. in an effort to deflect criticism on the eve of the lucrative tour that was only days away from starting. As Epstein tried to explain Lennon's "meaning," radio stations around the country held their own bonfires. A station in Kentucky played 10 seconds of dead air each hour to allow "prayer" from angry listeners. The Fab Four held a press conference shortly after arriving in Memphis with Lennon apologizing for what he had to say in the magazine. He tried to put it in "proper context," but nothing he could have said in America's Southland could have ameliorated the situation. New York kept asking me for updates on what was happening and I was happy to oblige. I couldn't resist the following lead paragraph in a story written in early August, 1966: "It's been a hard day's night for John, Paul, George and Ringo since the brainy Beatle suggested the British rock 'n rollers were more popular than Jesus."

Layton and Charles finally held their bonfire and it was a big one. By that time, the two had become national celebrities. Whenever the Beatles are discussed at length in television documentaries, the two disc jockeys are usually shown in their cramped little studio. I got more compliments over that story and somebody even sent me a clipping from the *Okinawa Morning Star* which had picked it up. The headline said: "DJs Start Beatle Ban" and an editor's note explained the Alabama genesis of a bonfire that began with a magazine article months before.

It was a treat to get the paper from Okinawa since I had been stationed there for more than a year.

The only major downside to 1966 was lack of sleep. It happened because I found myself working double shifts for a month at a time. Each time somebody would be sent to Birmingham as an assistant, they'd last about a month. It could have been the pressure. It could have been the teletype machine. It could have been me. Whatever the reason, they'd leave after a month and it would be up to me to keep the place going from 9 a.m. to midnight. The first week wasn't bad, but I'd begin to feel it the second week. By the start of the third week I was dragging into work. The fourth week was a blur. I was a zombie. It really hit me late one night in the cafeteria at the *Birmingham News* Building. I slumped in a booth and began to pour catsup on a liver and onion sandwich. When I looked at what I had ordered I went home. The good thing that year was the money. I made about $2,500 in overtime. In 1966, it was an enormous amount of money for me, considering what my base salary was—$125 a week. It helped us buy our first furniture—nothing spectacular, but it was ours and it was paid for. By that time, I had been named bureau manager. I think I was the lowest paid bureau executive in the *UPI* operation, but it didn't matter to me. I considered it to be quite an honor for a guy who had only passed his probationary period a few months before the promotion.

In addition to the *UPI* regulars working for us in Alabama at that time, we also hired energetic college students who pulled weekend shifts to help pay their way through school. Tim Robinson was the best. He worked for the *Birmingham Post-Herald* at night and attended college during the day. I don't know when he found time to sleep. Tim later got his degree and eventually worked for the *Washington Post* where he helped cover the Watergate scandal. He was a brilliant student, an outstanding journalist and a good friend. Tim later became an attorney, edited a national law journal and wound up as a pioneer in the internet industry. Sadly, he died of complications following colon cancer surgery in the fall of 2003. He was only 58. Mike Atchison was in law school at the time and also did a fine job for us on weekends. Today, he is one of Birmingham's most respected attorneys, specializing in civil law. He also became chairman of the board of trustees of Birmingham Southern, one of the South's elite colleges.

As 1966 began to fade, our attention turned to impending parenthood. Sharon was expecting in late December and my major concern was getting out of that third-floor walkup on Highland Avenue in south Birmingham. Our first home was memorable, to say the least. It played host to friends and even celebrities on occasion. One was Tom Jarrell of *ABC* News. I met Tom at the first Liuzzo murder trial and when he'd come to Birmingham, he'd try to stop by our apartment to say hi.

Mark Dinning, a former singing idol whose *"Teen Angel"* recording had become a smash hit, also paid us a visit. Unfortunately for him, *"Teen Angel"* was his only hit. By the time he arrived in Birmingham to play at the Blue Note—a saloon near my office—he had pretty much hit rock bottom. I pitched a story to my editors about what happens to a teen idol when the cheering stops. They bought it. I interviewed him at his tiny motel room. Parked outside was an old Dodge that Dinning drove from tank town to tank town to make a few bucks singing his famous song. I asked him what had happened to all his money and he said "my ex-wives got it all." Sharon and I went to see Mark one night at the Blue Note and noticed he had second billing to a 6-foot stripper. We had him out to the apartment one night during the engagement. Sharon cooked him a big steak and even sewed a button back onto his flashy red sequined jacket that had seen its share of performances. Mark never did get back to the big time and died of a heart attack several years later. Another of our many guests was Howell Raines, a bright young Birmingham reporter who, one day, would become executive editor of the *New York Times.*

Sharon's doctor suggested that we find another place to live because of the steep climb and the strain it was putting on her. When I explained our plight to our landlady, she was less than sympathetic to our situation. The more I begged, the more adamant she became. She also said she'd haul us into court if we didn't pay up. "Now, how would it look," I told her, "for one Jewish woman to stand in front of a judge while a very pregnant Jewish woman stands next to her crying?" It didn't do any good, of course. My net check at that time had risen from a whopping $70 a week to about $100, but it still didn't leave much room to maneuver financially. We bit the bullet and found another apartment about a mile away. It was newer and much nicer. For six months, we had to come up with two apartment checks. I still don't know how we did it.

Visiting Decatur, Alabama in late 1966

I had decided by the fall of 1966 that wire service work wasn't in my future. What I really wanted to do was work for a newspaper. I got my chance when I was offered a position as assistant city editor of the *Decatur Daily* in north Alabama. Sharon and I drove to Decatur a few days later and fell in love with it. It didn't take much prodding for me to accept the offer. The pay wasn't much better, but the job was what I had been looking for. I informed my bosses that I'd be moving on, but would wait until the end of the year to take advantage of my medical coverage. Sharon had a caesarean section delivery on Dec. 21, 1966 and our beautiful daughter—Danielle Michelle Benn—made her debut. Naturally, I missed it. An assignment had me elsewhere at that magic moment. But, I rushed over as soon as I could and brought along a little orange tree for Sharon. I don't know why I did that. It just seemed like the thing to do. By that time, she understood what a crazy job her husband had. I think she was looking forward as much as I was to the move. Dani was a beautiful baby and has grown into a beautiful young woman with a great husband and two wonderful sons. What more could we ask for?

Two friends helped us pack all we had into a little U-Haul trailer about a week after Dani was born. One was Joe Chapman, the *Post-Herald* photographer who was with me on the wildest night of my career.

The other was Jim Bennett, a political reporter for the *Post-Herald*. One day, Jim would become a state senator and, then, Alabama secretary of state. Joe would become an executive first with the *UPI* Guild and then with Voice of America. I was and still am very proud of them.

Benn, left and Birmingham News editor Jim Jacobson, center, interview future president Richard Nixon in Birmingham in 1966.

As we pulled out of the parking lot that cold late December morning, Sharon and I knew we had just been through something pretty special. I had a chance to cover some of the century's most important people as well as the events they influenced. One was Richard Nixon, who answered a few questions for me at the Parliament House Hotel in Birmingham. It was 1966 and he already was running hard for what would be a successful presidential bid in two years. Instead of living the sometimes dreary life of a Washington, D.C. housewife, Sharon got a chance to rub elbows with the rich and famous herself. One was actor Chill Wills, who got an Academy Award nomination for "*The Alamo*." He took a liking to Sharon at a Republican fund-raising banquet and whirled her around the dance floor. She's never forgotten that. It wasn't the way most marriages begin. We'd have our share of ups and downs along the way, but have managed to stay together as other relationships fell apart around us. I don't know how or why Sharon has stayed with me. I've had a lot of lucky breaks along the way. Having her as my partner and soul mate has been the luckiest of all.

CHAPTER TWO:

NEWSPAPER NOMADS

From the time I was a kid delivering the *Lancaster New Era* in Pennsylvania, I dreamed of becoming a newspaper reporter. I loved to read the *New Era* and I think some of the ink that came off the papers and darkened the white T-shirts I wore must have seeped into my veins. I haven't been able to get it out after four decades—not that I ever wanted to.

My chance came in the fall of 1966 when George Biggers, a friend who worked at the *Birmingham News*, accepted a position at the *Decatur Daily*, about 100 miles north of Birmingham. Sharon and I had visited George and his wife, Carol, and loved the place. It was a long way from the steel mills and smog of Birmingham and not just in distance. The Tennessee Valley, where Decatur and Huntsville are located, is Alabama's most progressive region. It's the area where engineers and scientists helped develop the Saturn V moon rocket.

"Come on up, Al," George told me, one day over the phone. "You'll like it here."

I took him up on the offer and it wasn't long before we embarked on the next chapter of our lives together. It would last 7 ½ years. The three of us got to Decatur on the first day of 1967. It was bitterly cold, but Dani didn't cry very much. I guess breast-feeding had made her a contented baby. Working for a newspaper turned out to be something of a vacation after 2 ½ years with *UPI*. At the *Daily*, my job was to assist George, who was city editor, and fill in for him when he was working on other projects. We worked together to report the news and direct a staff of young reporters and photographers. Our state, national and world news came from an *Associated Press* wire machine near my desk. It seemed strange, relying on *AP* after having been such a part of and so loyal to *UPI*. But, I knew most of the *AP* reporters in the state, so it didn't take long to get over it. They were just as professional as we were.

The news in Decatur was a lot different than Birmingham. Race wasn't much of an issue in north Alabama, which was and still is predominantly white. We handled local stories without having to worry about the big picture that *UPI* focused on most of the time. City Council meetings, sporting events and social activities consumed our days. We had a circulation of less than 20,000 during that time and didn't have much competition. The *Huntsville Times* was the biggest daily paper in the Tennessee Valley and had a Decatur bureau staffed by Chris Bell, an energetic reporter who turned his station wagon into a traveling newsroom. Years later, I'd wind up doing the same thing in a variety of vehicles. On occasion, Chris would beat us on a story, but we usually handled breaking developments first. Mike Freeman was our managing editor. Mike was a low-key editor whose piercing blue eyes could cut through reporters if they screwed up. Our two families became close and I considered Mike one of my best friends. Little did I know how that friendship would help us 13 years later when my bid to become a newspaper publisher flopped.

The 'Old Man'

The publisher of the *Decatur Daily* was Barrett Shelton Sr. We all called him "The Old Man"— an affectionate term that he loved. He called his son, Barrett Shelton Jr., "Boy"—a term that the future publisher loved. The *Daily* weathered the depression when Decatur's major industry—the railroad—closed. Times were tough, but Barrett Sr. helped keep the town ticking. He went to extremes at times to save as many jobs as he could. He was a loyal Democrat, but seemed downright

Republican at times. He disliked government intrusion into local issues, saying it was hurting the country. One day, as he drove me around town not long after I arrived, he pointed out some of his favorite sights, including a factory where a cloud of thick black smoke belched out of a tall stack. It was something that would have federal environmentalists fuming today. The "Old Man" just smiled and said in that gravelly voice of his: "See that, boy? That ain't pollution. That's progress." I didn't need to decipher his meaning. The smoke meant people were working inside. "The Old Man" also had a theory about leadership and it made a lot of sense, too. "Boy," he once told me, "five percent of the people in this country lead, five percent follow and 90 percent don't know what the hell is going on." He had made another point. That's why he did all he could to decrease that 90 percent figure.

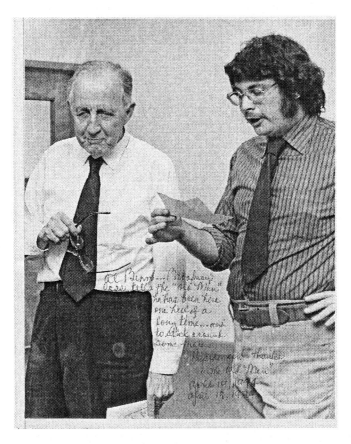

Benn helps honor Decatur Daily Publisher Barrett Shelton.

Shelton was a firm believer in personal responsibility and often set the example. A relative once got into trouble over some missing money from the company where he worked. At some newspapers, crime reports involving relatives of owners are buried inside the paper or not published at all. In this case, "The Old Man" let it be known the story would go "above the fold" which meant in a prominent position on Page 1. That's where it went. The relative went to jail and the company later announced plans to move from Decatur. It would have been a devastating blow to the local economy, so "The Old Man" went to work to save it. He ingratiated himself to the new owner—a man who bought and sold businesses for a quick profit before moving on to other ventures. The two soon developed a fast friendship. The executive gave Shelton an expensive watch made out of a $20 gold piece. "The Old Man" wore that watch with great pride and loved to show it off.

Although he was the publisher, Barrett Sr. preferred to let his son run the show, especially as he got older. It gave him a chance to continue his role of community leader with even more gusto. He supported the Browns Ferry Nuclear Power Plant in nearby Limestone County even though some had reservations about its safety. It was the Tennessee Valley Authority's first nuclear power plant and the largest in the world at the time. During a tour of the facility before it opened, I asked an engineer if he had any concerns about safety at nuclear power plants, especially the one near Decatur. "Well," he told me, "I don't want to be around when they push the button to get it started." Not long after Browns Ferry went on line, a fire swept through a section of the power plant. It wasn't a Three Mile Island scare, but there were some anxious moments in the area during that time. George wrote a long article about Browns Ferry just as it was about to open. He asked: "Is there a tiger in that tank?" It was a great opening sentence to a well-researched story.

During my stay with the *Daily*, I had the pleasure of working with some of the finest writers, editors and photographers in the business. It remained the best staff I had ever been associated with during my long journalism career. We weren't very big, but we were very good. Winford Turner was probably the best newspaper reporter I had ever seen. I don't know how Winford would have done in wire service work because he preferred to develop his sources and take his time. He wasn't the best writer I had ever seen, but, when it came to working a beat, he was outstanding. He could pick up a phone and have all he needed in minutes because he had so many sources. When Gov. George Wallace was shot in Maryland while campaigning for president in 1972, Winford was flown there to report on it for several days. Ben Windham, Bob Lowry, Angie Kirk, Tommy Stevenson, Billy Mitchell, Ray Martin, Mary Wimberly and Libby Jarvinen also were super journalists. Photographers Billy Smith, Bobby Herbert and Ed Bruchac were outstanding, too. We won lots of awards during annual newspaper competitions. Libby and I worked side-by-side after I had moved from city editor to news editor. She and her husband, Bill, met at the University of Florida and lived in Huntsville. Bill was one of thousands of engineers who played important roles in the space program. Libby was more down-to-earth. She loved words and so did I. We made a good team.

On occasion, I'd produce a big story myself, even though I didn't have as much time covering events because of my editing responsibilities. One of my biggest stories involved the University of Georgia football team and its trip to Memphis to play in the Liberty Bowl. The team plane experienced mechanical problems and had to land at the airport in Huntsville. I got wind of it over the police scanner late in the afternoon and headed for the airport with a photographer. When we got there, we saw the players milling around in the waiting room. Within a few minutes, I had my story. The coach, athletic director and players were happy to answer questions. They were only on the ground a few minutes. When the plane left the runway, it dawned on me that Huntsville's two papers didn't have anybody at the airport. So, there we were, scooping the hometown newspapers from 30 miles away. We ran the story across the top of the front page the next day. From what I heard later, editors at the *Huntsville Times* and the *Huntsville News* weren't very pleased.

Libby and I used to go to lunch at C.F. Penn's Hamburgers—a cramped little restaurant featuring a huge black grill in the back where piles of hours-old, cold burgers were stacked against a wall. They must have started making them at daybreak. We'd usually get there about noon. The moment customers walked through the door, somebody at the grill would turn around and shout: "All the way?" Most folks would shout back "yes!" That meant knocking a burger off the top of the big pile and into the grease below to get it hot again. Everything but the kitchen sink would be put on top of hamburgers that seemed to be about 90 percent bread filling. I don't know how they did it, but those hamburgers were the best I ever tasted. They didn't cost much, either, and that was the best part. I think we could get two of them and a soft drink for $1. The buns were enormous and, by the time we got there, the burgers had shrunk to half their original size. They got lost inside the bun, but the cooks put so much other stuff on top of them, it didn't matter how big the burgers were.

Eric Arrives

Our son was born less than a year after his sister. I remember the morning Sharon told me she was expecting again and I responded with a brilliant one-word reaction "WHAT!" I think I may also have asked something stupid like "how did that happen?" Eric Samuel Benn's arrival was met with as much joy as Dani's. He had what may have been Decatur's first *"bris"*—a Jewish circumcision ritual dating back to Abraham. The Jewish population in Decatur was and still is extremely small—only a handful of people. Few Jewish boys are born there. We had our *"bris"* at Decatur General Hospital. You could feel the excitement. I think we could have sold tickets. We hired a *"mohel"* from Birmingham to perform the ceremony. A *"mohel"* is trained to officiate at circumcision ceremonies. The man we hired was the only expert in his field in Alabama. Nurses at Decatur General asked us if they could see him do his thing. When the time finally came, the room was packed. My father had flown down to be on hand. The nurses marveled at the skill exhibited before them. They said none of the doctors could match the snipping they had just seen.

Dani and Eric Benn play outside their house in Decatur, Ala. in 1968.

Not long after Eric's birth, we bought our first house. It was just what we needed—a three bedroom, bath and a half brick structure with a large fenced-in backyard and a central heating system. The best part was the price, only $15,000. Our cars have cost more than that in recent years. We had hoped to buy another one on the same block. It had a den, but we decided we couldn't afford it because it would have cost an additional $5 a month.

The news in Decatur was much different than in Birmingham. Instead of race, the region focused on space. Many Decatur residents worked for NASA. They liked living away from Huntsville and it didn't take them long to drive there. During that time, I was able to interview astronauts involved in the Apollo program as well as the scientists who built the rocket that carried them to the moon. Wernher von Braun not only ran NASA in those days, he seemed to run Huntsville, too. Von Braun never was accepted by some in Decatur, especially those who had fought in World War II when his buzz bombs blitzed parts of England. He was more or less tolerated. Many considered him to be one of our "good Germans." During the 1950s, von Braun spoke to a Decatur civic group. It was before the Soviet Union and its Sputnik launched the space race. I was told that he once predicted America would eventually land on the moon. A member of the club is said to have turned to a friend and exclaimed: "That crazy Kraut doesn't know what he's talking about. He needs to go back to Huntsville."

A Grisly Murder

Mary Faye Hunter loved to play the piano at her church. George and I heard about her disappearance on a Saturday afternoon in late October and joined police in searching for her. We went into the loft at the church. It was hard to see and the sounds from our steps had us stopping every few seconds to see if somebody was behind us. It was around Halloween and that creaky old building was frightening. Not a trace of the piano player could be found. Local police were mystified. Mary Faye's frantic relatives wrote a letter to self-proclaimed seer Jeanne Dixon, who had built a career, in part, by predicting the deaths of famous people including President John F. Kennedy and his brother, Robert. We received a copy of her report on Mary Faye and had it all set to run across the top of Page 1 on a Sunday morning in the spring. According to Dixon, Mary Faye—who was single—was alive and well, but a little "mixed up." Dixon, who also missed the mark many times in her predictions, was partially correct. Parts of Mary Faye were mixed with shoreline debris on the backwaters of the Tennessee River.

The story about Dixon's prediction was scrapped and, in its place, we ran one about finding Mary Faye's remains. I went down to the discovery site Sunday afternoon and couldn't believe what I saw. Police hadn't cordoned off the area. People walked all over the evidence. It was as though they were out on a family stroll in the spring. One man turned to his wife as he peeked under a tree stump and said: "That's where they found part of her." At that moment, the coroner, who also was a scuba diver, emerged from the water a few yards away and held up what appeared to be a long bone. A coroner's inquest determined that the remains had, indeed, belonged to Mary Faye and that she had been raped. How that conclusion could have been drawn when there were only a few bones to work with eludes me to this day. DNA testing was still considered science fiction back then. No arrests were ever made and the case remains open. Faith in Dixon's predictions tumbled a bit in Decatur after people learned what had happened to Mary Faye Hunter.

George Biggers was a man of many ideas. Some were great. Some were weird. He was never at a loss to come up with something new. The funniest involved his "*Dan Daily*" promotion to increase our newspaper's classified advertising revenue. George developed a cartoon-like character that would serve as the paper's classified department mascot. He even came up with a costume—a bright red and blue creation intended to make him look like a super hero. Instead, he came across like something out of *Mad* magazine. At that time, George weighed about 130 pounds soaking wet. He was over 6-feet tall and his legs were like soft drink straws. He unveiled "Dan" on a hot summer afternoon. It was a Saturday and more people than usual were in downtown Decatur where the newspaper office is located. George didn't burst onto the scene from behind a curtain after getting a glowing introduction. He just walked up and down the streets, handing out candy, balloons and whatever else he had in his pockets to bewildered people. Some were too startled to say anything. They just gawked or laughed at the gangly bean pole in the red tights and blue cape. Some must have wondered what asylum he came from. At one point, George ran out of goodies to give away and went to a local five-and-dime to buy more. There he was—looking like a comic book reject—standing in line behind several customers, waiting to pay for balloons and candy. *"Dan Daily"* didn't last long, thank goodness, but George and I still laugh about it when we see each other. He eventually moved to Orlando, Florida. and involved himself in other media-related business. He once bought an alternative music magazine which seemed to make as much sense as his *"Dan Daily"* experiment. But, he learned about it and almost understood what that kind of music was all about before he sold the magazine. I count him as one of my best friends.

We once had a photographer who liked to come up with unusual pictures for the paper. He arrived one day with a bigger smile than usual on his face. He said he had been to a town in Tennessee at night and couldn't resist snapping a shot of a damaged service station sign. It was a Sinclair station with the "C" knocked out. That left "Sin Lair." The service station was next to a motel. The arrow on the sign pointed downward, directly at the motel. No one accused the photographer of taking a rock to knock out the "C," but the thought did cross a mind or two that perhaps he or a local resident had aimed a BB gun at the sign. Another Daily photographer had problems with "motivation" when he was sent out on assignment. One day, we asked him to come up with something nice to go with a high school graduation ceremony. He came back beaming. "Look what I've got," he exclaimed, as he showed us a photo of a chubby girl running through the woods in her cap and gown. The gown was unzipped. She was wearing a bikini. Her right hand held her cap on her head and she was smiling. We didn't. It wasn't published.

One of our photographers itched to be a reporter and got a chance to go on a train trip with a candidate for the U.S. Senate. He apparently didn't realize that first person accounts are fine, if they are written correctly. In his case, he must have thought he was giving a televised account of the trip. At one point in the trip, he wrote: "We are now traveling up the biggest mountain I've ever seen." He followed that by blowing a verbal kiss to his "little heart-breaker" of a daughter. George was hunched over his typewriter, taking dictation from the guy on the train. I leaned over and began to read and laugh. When the last word was typed, George spun around in his chair, a perplexed look on his face. "How in the world could you keep from laughing during dictation?" I asked him. "It wasn't easy," he said, as he finally began to laugh. Then, there was the commercial photographer who tried unsuccessfully to adjust to the hectic world of daily journalism. He was great at taking wedding and baby pictures, but he really couldn't handle the pressure of deadlines. One morning, as he sat in the bathroom contemplating the day ahead, I heard the police scanner alert officers to a burglary taking place a block away from the *Daily*. "We need you now," I yelled into the bathroom. "Be right out," he said. A few minutes later, I inquired again. "Be right out," he said. I finally went up the street with my own camera and covered it. He eventually returned to commercial work and did a great job. His portrait of Dani and Eric hangs on a wall in our house today.

Benn examines outhouse for series on poverty in Decatur, Ala.

One of the things I liked about working at the *Daily* was the freedom extended to us by the Shelton family to dig deep into a story or try something that might be unconventional. We once sent reporter Ray Martin into a department store with orders to see just how light-fingered he could be. We told him to put up a big fuss when "caught." We wanted to check the reaction of clerks and customers. It was akin to *"Candid Camera."* As expected, his outburst caught everybody by surprise. If nothing else, it was a reminder to store clerks to be vigilant because some "customers" aren't there to write a newspaper article. On another occasion, Ben Windham masqueraded as a bum—an unshaven down-and-outer who sat on the pavement with a tin cup and a forlorn look on his face. The idea was, once again, to check public reaction. He got plenty of it—donations from those who sympathized with him and glares from those who wanted him to get up and find a job. His article was so good he won a state award from the *Associated Press*. It was one of the best in Alabama that year. I also got a chance to try my hand at in-depth stories. I once examined the plight of Decatur's small, poor black community. One photograph showed me standing at the door of an outhouse in the backyard of a black family. I also did a series of articles about the need for public buses in Decatur. I rode one of the few remaining buses in town early one morning and quickly came to a conclusion most residents had reached years before—the buses were used by black maids heading to the homes of rich white folks. The series won a state award, but the federal government didn't come up with any money to buy more buses. The Shelton family is among a dwindling number of daily newspaper owners in the United States. Chain operations are gobbling up family-owned papers at a rapid rate. That's one of the reasons I have so much respect for them. The day may come when a newspaper chain makes them a financial offer they can't refuse, but, until that time, the Sheltons are in charge. Clinton Shelton, who was a kid when we lived in Decatur, is expected to succeed his dad as publisher one day.

During my tenure at the *Daily*, a weekly newspaper was launched and Winford Turner was part of its news operation. Winford would leave the *Daily* at least twice before returning and his first departure wasn't greeted warmly, especially by Barrett Jr., who called us into the composing room one afternoon to inform us of the competition and how we would react to it. "We shall be agile, hostile and mobile," he said, as he read a prepared statement to us. Barrett was our Gen. George Patton—ready for action and not willing to give an inch to the competition. As it turned out, the weekly wasn't much competition. Winford would come up with an exclusive now and then, but advertising is what makes a newspaper succeed or fail and the *Daily* had most of the businesses wrapped up in Decatur. When I wasn't handling assistant city editor chores, I also was news editor and had to be at work early in the morning to check the wire service machines. We had moved into our new building across the street from the old one and had installed a burglar alarm system. It didn't always work properly and false alarms often wound up at the police station. One morning, as I was checking paper that came clanking across one of the wire machines, my attention was diverted to movement at my left. "Freeze," shouted the police officer, who had his gun drawn and pointed at me. I not only froze, I nearly soiled my britches. After I had regained my composure I got angry. "What would anybody be stealing in this little room?" I told him. "Use some common sense."

A Spirited Response

The war in Vietnam was raging in 1967 when George and I decided something needed to be done to counter the growing number of anti-war demonstrations across the country. He didn't serve in the military, as I had, but he was just as patriotic. Over coffee one day at the same five-and-dime where he had paraded around in his *"Dan Daily"* costume, George and I discussed some ways to show our national pride. We came up with *"The Spirit of America Festival,"* an event that would be held on July 4 each year. We only had a few weeks to launch the first one, so we needed something to attract regional interest. That's when we came up with a greased pig chase. We convinced a local farmer to lend us a pig and then we found some volunteers to grease it up. Libby was one of them. Watching the greasing was almost as funny as watching the people who tried to catch it. We worried that animal rights groups might try to shut the whole thing down or call the cops, but nobody did. The idea worked and we had a huge crowd that year at a downtown park. Thousands turned out. We had plenty of musical entertainment, lots of hot dogs and hamburgers to eat and, of course, patriotic speeches. We even had our local theatrical group put on a rendition of "*Yankee Doodle Dandy.*"

The inaugural "*Spirit of America Festival*" was a huge success. We eventually ditched the greased pig chases and concentrated on other activities to make the event more successful with the passing years. A planning committee was formed and that helped take some of the pressure off of us. We came up with a beauty pageant but some criticized it as being nothing more than a "meat parade." One year, a majorette from neighboring Athens won the beauty pageant, setting off a firestorm at her church where her father was pastor. Some parishioners thought it scandalous that she appeared in a bathing suit in front of so many people at the Decatur competition. They didn't seem to object to her skimpy majorette outfit which showed a lot more skin in front of thousands at football games. The flap extended to a national magazine after a storm produced a lightning bolt that split the church steeple at the height of the controversy. The headline which appeared over a series of photos read something like: "This is the church, this is the steeple and this is the girl who split all the people." The congregation eventually split and two churches were formed. Despite the criticism, the beauty pageant continued. As a way to attract large crowds, we decided to invite personalities to emcee that part of the program. We had actor James Darren one year. Singer Johnny Tillotson came another time. Darren was a teen idol during the early 1960s and apparently didn't know much about how brutal summer is in the South. He showed up in a wool suit. I thought he'd pass out. Tillotson did a splendid job. He was a popular singer of that era before he and others like him—Frankie Avalon, Fabian and Bobby Rydell—were relegated to lounge acts by the Beatles and other English groups of the mid-1960s.

The personality who created the biggest fuss prior to a festival was actor Troy Donahue—the handsome heartthrob who had set many female hearts aflutter with his role in "*A Summer Place*" with Sandra Dee. It was a huge hit and kept Donahue's Hollywood star shining for several years. When we invited him to emcee our beauty pageant, we had no idea that the Troy Donahue of "*A Summer Place*" was not the Troy Donahue of the Vietnam era. Handsome Troy had let his hair grow down to his shoulders, wore a beard and mustache and, all in all, looked like Dennis Hopper from *"Easy Rider."* When we passed around his glossy promotional photograph to members of the *"Spirit of America"* committee, I thought some of the female members would faint. "We can't invite somebody like that to our festival," one woman said. "Just look at that picture! That's not the Troy Donahue people remember." "Well," I told her, "He's already signed the contract. He's coming." Others suggested we pay him off or let him know we didn't want him. "Wait a minute," I said. "This is supposed to be a festival saluting America, the Bill of Rights, the Declaration of Independence, the Constitution and all the freedoms they guarantee. How can we tell a guy not to come because of the way he looks?" I wrote Troy a letter, telling him about concerns by some members of our committee. He told me he was coming. Not only that, but he read part of my letter on the Johnny Carson show one night. I didn't see it, but was told by several who did. Donahue didn't identify me, but said he was most appreciative of the support he had received from at least one Decatur resident. He came and did a great job as emcee. He hadn't trimmed his long locks that much or cut off his beard, but the female fans who remembered him from *"A Summer Place"* still lined up for his autograph and to have photographs with him. When he died, I wrote a column for the *Montgomery Advertiser* about the day I defended Troy Donahue.

One lasting legacy resulting from the patriotic festival was something none of us wanted. World War II hero and movie actor Audie Murphy had been named to receive an award during the 1971 event. Murphy's movie fortunes had waned during the 1960s after a decade in which he had made his two best films, the classic autobiographical movie *"To Hell and Back"* and the Civil War epic *"The Red Badge of Courage."* He had made some bad investments, too. On his way to a business engagement, Murphy's plane crashed, killing all aboard. It stunned the nation as well as us in Decatur. We wanted to express our appreciation for Murphy's wartime exploits and his continued support of our troops in Vietnam. That's how the *Audie Murphy Patriotism Award* was created. His family received the first one in his memory and it's been awarded each year since that time.

Losing a Friend

Ray Lovett worked in the "Back Shop" as we called it in those days—the place where the paper was prepared for publication. During that period, newspapers had shifted from "hot type" to the offset process which involved pasting and cutting copy onto large pieces of paper that would be photographed and then transferred to an aluminum plate that would be affixed to rollers on the press. It was much cleaner and faster and you could see what you were doing. In the "old days," newspapers were produced by gruff old codgers who sat at linotype machines that clanked out each letter and line. The metal words would then wind up in a device that showed them upside down and backwards. They could read it in a flash and were skilled craftsmen. Ray was a dedicated, punctual employee and when he didn't show up for work on a Monday morning, we all began to worry. I remember saying "goodnight, see you on Monday" to him when we left late Saturday after completing details for Sunday's paper. It would be the last time I saw Ray. A few weeks before he vanished, he had witnessed an accident and was asked to attend a court hearing in the case. Authorities said two people involved in the case went to Ray's house after he got home from work that night and abducted him. Ray's burned remains were found in a shallow grave in south Alabama. A couple believed involved in the abduction were captured and convicted. In 1972, on the day Gov. George Wallace was shot while campaigning for president in Maryland, one of the two walked out of prison. No one's quite sure how he did it, but they say he just walked out the front door. He was recaptured and returned to prison to continue his term. The other person convicted in the case was paroled in 1986.

Wettest Dry Town

Decatur and Morgan County were "dry," meaning alcoholic beverages could not be sold at any convenience stores, grocery stores or gas stations. State liquor stores were out of the question. None of this meant people didn't drink. It was said during our time there that Decatur was the "wettest dry city" its size in the United States. Selling and consumption were two different things. Prohibition in Morgan

County meant big business in neighboring Madison County where alcoholic beverages were allowed. In the tiny town of Madison, some enterprising souls had built several cinder block buildings. Inside, every available inch of space was filled with cases of beer. They were stacked to the ceiling—waiting for thirsty Decatur residents to arrive. Limestone County, located between Decatur and Huntsville, was "dry" and authorities knew where the customers were coming from. They'd park their patrol cars a few yards away and wait for vehicles with the number "52" on their license plates. That meant they were from Morgan County. Then, the deputies would stop them as they drove away. The motorists would be charged with buying alcoholic beverages for use in a "dry" county.

Many efforts were made to end prohibition in Morgan County, but nothing seemed to work. The county's Baptist ministers made sure that they had their best fire and brimstone speeches prepared each Sunday before the scheduled "wet-dry" elections on Tuesdays. Bootleggers and moonshiners also chipped in financially to help the pro-dry forces keep it that way. They didn't want any competition from legitimate beer and whiskey distributors. Campaigns didn't last long and those who wanted the county to go "wet" never seemed to have enough money to get their point across to the public before the elections. I covered one particularly noisy public forum on the subject. It was supposed to allow both sides a chance to speak, but the "dry" forces showed up in much greater numbers. Even in the enlightened decade of the 1970s, most people who supported the public sale of booze in Morgan County kept their heads down and out of the line of fire. That's because many of them drank up a storm at the Decatur Country Club and there was no way the police chief or sheriff were going to raid that place. At the public forum, a spokesman for the "wet" side tried to state his position, but was shouted down. He was followed by a minister who was the leader of the "dry" side. He went into a tirade about the evils of demon rum and ended it with a memorable quote. "Anybody who drinks," the preacher said, "is worse than an egg-sucking dog." His comment was prominently printed the following day, giving rise to the only sparks of that campaign from the "wet" forces. They had about $65 left in their campaign treasury and spent every penny with the *Daily* on one small ad the day before the election. It showed a dog sitting in front of a cracked egg shell with "ALL

YOU" just above the dog and egg and "VOTE WET TUESDAY" just below. It didn't put a dent in the results. The "dry guys" once again won handily. It took another decade or so for the people of Morgan County to catch up with the rest of the state and world and approve the sale of alcoholic beverages.

A Movie and Bob Dylan

Lee Sentell, one of our best reporters, loves movies. So do I. When we were given the opportunity to preview a locally produced film one afternoon at the Princess Theater, we just couldn't resist. Little did we know that *"Blood in the Valley"*—billed as a sci-fi horror movie— would turn out to be an unintentional comedy. We didn't know what to expect, but it didn't take long to realize *"Blood,"* as I would call it, lacked one vital ingredient for movie success—quality. It had to be one of the worst movies ever made. The hero was Ernie Ashworth, a country music star from Nashville. It was only a couple of hours up Interstate 65 from Decatur, meaning he could commute to "work." The villain was called "The Pig Man" and his specialty was ripping off the heads of his victims. A jeweler from nearby Athens played "Pig." The "musical score" was provided by a local disc jockey who strummed away on his guitar as an unsuspecting couple, parked in lovers lane, fell victim to "Pig." The props were awful. They used department store mannequins for the victims. We could see the little prongs that once held heads to bodies sticking up from above their necks after "Pig" killed them. Lee and I tried hard not to laugh. The "producer" sat next to us and was waiting anxiously for a good review. We tried to be as diplomatic as possible, saying something like it showed promise and was interesting. I think I bit through my lower lip. *"Blood"* never saw the light of day and that was a good thing. Lee later went to work in Huntsville with the Space and Rocket Museum. Today, he is director of the Alabama Department of Travel and Tourism. The state is lucky to have him in such an important position.

I had never been to Nashville and jumped at the opportunity to go when Winford asked me if I'd like to join him to watch his hero— Johnny Cash—tape a show for his highly-rated television show. What clinched it was being told that Bob Dylan—that folk-singing icon from the 60s—would be Cash's special guest. "Let's go," I told him. The show was taped at Ryman Auditorium, Nashville's legendary music hall where the Grand Ole Opry was born and was still being used for Saturday night shows. We went up during the middle of the week even though we knew it would be a problem since we had to be back at work early the next morning. As it turned out, my first trip to Nashville could have been to San Francisco. It looked more like Height Asbury than Music City USA. Hippies abounded. Dylan had attracted them. They were his groupies—men and women who traveled around the country wherever he appeared. It was a few years since the Summer of Love in 1967, but beads and headbands were everywhere and a pungent aroma often associated with an illegal substance filled the air. Television productions take time. We watched as crews set up equipment and furniture for various scenes and then shoot take after take. We were disappointed when we couldn't hear Cash or Dylan perform. They were singing into tiny mikes hooked up to a control room. Unless you were five feet away from them, you couldn't hear a thing. There wasn't any amplification and the people who were sitting in the audience were not very happy, especially when they were asked to applaud so it would look good for the finished product in millions of American homes a few weeks later.

A Campaign to Remember

I've covered many political campaigns, but none could compare with the 1970 gubernatorial race between Gov. Albert Brewer, a Decatur boy who made good, and George Corley Wallace, Alabama's former governor. Wallace had run his wife, Lurleen, in 1966 when state law at the time kept governors and other constitutional officers from seeking second consecutive terms. Lurleen Wallace died of cancer midway through her term. Brewer, who was lieutenant governor, took the oath of office a few hours after her death. He served two years and did a good job. His problem was his progressive outlook on life. Wallace had fashioned a successful political career out of race baiting which helped him win his first term in 1962. In reality, he did many good things for all Alabamians, including construction of junior colleges throughout the state. Wallace had already run for president twice and did well. But, without the governorship to use as a political platform for higher office, he knew he'd have a harder time keeping up his national leadership image. At the press conference to announce his candidacy for a second term in 1970, he ignored Brewer. When he was asked about him during the campaign, he'd usually respond with something like "He's a nice young man."

As the Democratic campaign got under way, Wallace quickly realized Brewer would be no political pushover. When the incumbent led the field of gubernatorial candidates in the primary election, panic set in at the Wallace campaign headquarters. Wallace knew his presidential aspirations for 1972 could vanish if he didn't do something in a hurry. Making it into the runoff gave him a second chance. He made the best of it—at Brewer's expense. It was one of those down-and-dirty runoff elections that Alabama has been famous for through the years. Wallace operatives spread as many salacious rumors as they could to derail the Brewer Express. On the eve of the runoff election, the "Old Man" had us represent the paper at a Brewer rally. Libby and I joined several other editors and reporters at the event. We were handed large cardboard signs with Albert's name in big, brightly colored letters. We were there more as supporters than reporters and waved the placards a bit sheepishly before we hid them under our seats. The race was too close to call at that point, but most of us felt Wallace would be able to pull it out, especially in predominantly white areas of Alabama. He was conservative to the core and his campaign used every opportunity it could to brand Brewer a tax-raising liberal. Wallace won and got his chance to run for president again in two years. It was a campaign cut short by an assassin's unsuccessful attempt to kill him at a Maryland rally.

As 1974 dawned, I was growing restless. Working for the *Daily* had been great, but not very rewarding financially. I had won a bunch of awards for writing and editing, but I knew that, with two growing kids, future security was more important than ego. I was paid $125 a week when I joined the *Daily* in 1967 and, seven years later, I was at the $200 level. That's the way it was for journalists back in those days. That's why I spent one of my two off days working as sports information director at Calhoun Community College where I had become friendly with Bob Shuttleworth, the head basketball coach and athletic director. It paid about $100 a month and helped supplement my salary. During the spring and early summer, I also worked to promote the *"Spirit of America Festival."* Thanks to George, it brought in a few more dollars and helped us drive back "home" to spend a week with relatives in Pennsylvania and Washington, D.C. I could have stayed with the *Daily* for my entire newspaper career, but I didn't particularly like the idea of having to plead for a raise every year. When they came, they weren't much more than $5 or $10 a week. That's why I gave serious consideration to a job offer from a fledgling newspaper organization created by the son of a Pulitzer Prize winner from Tuscaloosa.

NATCHEZ

In the spring of 1974, I got a call from a friend who said the *Natchez Democrat* was looking for a managing editor. I hadn't heard much about the Boone Newspaper Group, but, as the days passed, the *Democrat* sounded like a chance to move up the corporate ladder. Jim Boone grew up in a newspaper family, but his vision extended far beyond one publication. He had worked for a newspaper chain for several years and quickly learned how to put together a successful operation of his own. Jim's father, Buford Boone, had won the Pulitzer Prize at the *Tuscaloosa News* for a series of editorials attacking the Ku Klux Klan. Most people thought the Boone family owned the *News*. Not so. It was owned by a non-profit organization based in Washington, D.C. Jim Boone believed in making money the old-fashioned way—through hard work and long hours. He started his newspaper empire in Natchez where he hired the best people he could find and then branched out—buying dozens of other papers around the country. He likes to hire men and women looking for a way to move up from assistant editor positions at other newspapers. That was the offer made to me. I was told that I'd start as managing editor and, if that worked out, would be in line one day for a publisher's job at another Boone paper.

Sharon and I decided to see what Natchez was like. We drove down one weekend and liked what we saw. Natchez could have been the setting for *"Gone With The Wind"* had it not been made on a Hollywood lot. Unlike Hollywood, Natchez is the real thing. It has magnificent antebellum homes, neighborhoods shaded by enormous magnolia trees and, of course, the mighty Mississippi River which flows by on its way to

New Orleans. Located high on a bluff overlooking the river, Natchez, at one time, is said to have had more millionaires than any city in the country. That money was made, in large part, off the backs of slaves who picked cotton. Natchez has always had an antebellum aura about it, but one with an extended Deep South gentility that makes it pretty special. Not that Natchez didn't have its share of excitement. Tourists are told that, on a sand bar not far from shore, Jim Bowie got a chance to use his famous knife to dispatch someone who had offended him. *"Natchez Under The Hill"* also was known to host plenty of late night celebrating at saloons that hugged the river only a few feet away. We settled into an apartment not far from downtown Natchez and I went to work for a newspaper led by a short-tempered, but tender-hearted publisher.

Warren Koon spent his newspaper career in South Carolina and had carved out a solid reputation as a sportswriter, but was ready to try his hand at publishing when Boone came calling. He knew he was in an enviable position since the *Natchez Democrat* was to be the flagship of Boone's envisioned newspaper empire. Warren served in the Marine Corps during World War II and was wounded during the battle of Okinawa. That made me a fan from my first day. I had served with some Okinawa veterans nearing the end of their Corps careers and I had heard the stories about it—about how lucky they were to have survived. Warren was a marvelous writer who was able to take any subject and turn it into a column. I once gave him "aardvark" and it took him all of 10 minutes to complete the column. He oversaw every aspect of an experiment that clicked from the start. Together, he and Boone became wealthy men. Warren's chief assistant was Dolph Tillotson, a bright young Alabamian who knew without anyone having to tell him that journalism is a business as well as a profession. That's something I'd never really grasp, although I was well aware that, without a successful business end, there'd be no profession at the other end. Dolph excelled at every phase. He was as familiar with a profit and loss statement as a city council agenda. He knew all there was to know about circulation, classified advertising and production.

My job was to direct the news department. It wasn't very big, but some of the reporters had promise. We covered city and county government, wrote feature articles about interesting people and made sure that 19th century Natchez would not be forgotten. It would be hard to do, anyway, since the town is built around some of the most famous mansions in the world. Each spring, when the flowers begin to bloom, the town comes alive with tourists arriving aboard hundreds of buses. Tourism is big business in Natchez and everybody seems to have a hand in some money-making endeavor. Black women aren't a bit embarrassed to don bandanas and stand in the sun as they sell homemade pralines at inflated prices. They beam as tourists line up to have their pictures taken with them. It's easy to see who has the biggest smile.

The Natchez Pilgrimage is the town's most popular tourist attraction and two events—the "Natchez Pageant" and "Southern Exposure" were among the highlights when we lived there. Political correctness wasn't a term in use back then and the big event used to be known as the Confederate Pageant. Black woman looking like Aunt Jemima and white women in their hoop skirts looking like Scarlett O'Hara were part of the Natchez scenery. "Southern Exposure" was a locally written and produced play about the tourists who visit during the spring pilgrimage of homes. Sharon and I once played a couple of obnoxious Yankee tourists asking stupid questions. It wasn't much of a stretch for two transplanted Yankees. We had a ball. They also had a golf tournament that wasn't much more than a pretense to get as many oil well entrepreneurs as possible into town. A huge spread was served under tents at the Natchez Country Club. The local airport was clogged with corporate jets and twin engine beauties owned and flown by men who spent their lives gambling that each hole they dug would hit oil. A lot of them never panned out and the wildcatters, as the oilmen are known, went belly up until they could raise enough money to drill some more.

In addition to my job as managing editor, Warren and Dolph gave me permission to write if the urge hit me. It usually did. I've always considered myself a reporter, at heart. When I edited somebody else's copy, I'd be thinking of how I'd have handled it. I also learned some valuable lessons during my stay in Natchez. Unfortunately, advance planning was never one of my strong suits. I was more of a "wing it" than "plan it" editor. When the bell rings, my ears perk up and I'm off to the races, or try to. I've been involved in many long-range, award-winning special projects through the years, but have always enjoyed hustling to the scene of something big. Being around reporters who don't hustle is frustrating and I've often lost my patience with them. I guess it was that great *UPI* training I had received. We were always facing a deadline. We had a police monitor at the *Democrat* when I first arrived, but it didn't provide much more than background noise. The piercing sound of police, fire and ambulance sirens would scream through the room, but nobody reacted until I came out of my office to ask if anybody planned to do anything about it. On one occasion, I called our five reporters into my office and let them have it. "This is a give and take session," I told them. "I'm giving and you're taking." They stared at me. I guess it was the first time anyone had greeted them quite that way. They shaped up, for awhile, at least, until I had to remind them again about the need to hustle.

I learned from Warren that, when writing and editing at a local newspaper, you've got to think "small." I always thought "big" at UPI because so many of the stories I covered in Birmingham and surrounding cities wound up being printed in newspapers around the world. Decatur wasn't much bigger than Natchez, but our location put the *Daily* in a unique position. During the 1960s, our country was racing the Russians to see who could get to the moon first. Decatur is only about 30 miles from Huntsville and that's where the Saturn 5 rocket was being built. It was more than enough reason for us to think global. Not so in Natchez which prides itself in being firmly planted in the 19th century. I got a "local lesson" from Warren one day after a tornado ripped through McComb—a small town about an hour from Natchez. A photographer and I drove over and we covered extensive damage there. Remnants of the storm hit parts of Adams County where Natchez is located and knocked over a couple of chicken coops. When I walked into Warren's office the next morning, I had a big smile on my face—happy about our response and the Page 1 coverage of the McComb damage. Instead of congratulations, I got a glare and a "Why did we go over there?" welcome. "That's where the damage was, Warren," I told him. "We weren't that far away and I thought our readers would like to know what happened to their friends and neighbors in McComb." "I don't give a damn about what happened there," he shot back. "Our readers care more about chicken coops being knocked over in Natchez." He had a point and I didn't make that mistake again, although he hadn't convinced me that what I had done was wrong.

Murphy Givens was one of our best reporters. He looked a lot like Jim Croce, a popular singer during that time. Murph had a bushy mustache, curly hair and an inquisitiveness that made me like him at once. He also liked to argue with me about stories, how they should be written and how they should appear in the paper. He reminded me of me. He often won with persuasive arguments. The story that I liked the most followed a research project at the county courthouse where he examined telephone records. Murph discovered that one of the county's most important officials had been making a lot of what appeared to be personal calls. He tallied the total, wrote the story and it was given prominent play on the *Democrat's* front page. The next day, the embarrassed official hurried into our office with a check he said he was about to present to the county treasurer to cover the cost of all those personal calls. Newspapers are, as it's been described many times, watchdogs for the public and that's just what Murph was.

Eric Benn with mom in Natchez, Miss. in 1974.

Eric honored by Attorney General Janet Reno in Washington.

As we tried to adjust to our new home, we ran into a major medical problem. Eric had kidney problems. He discovered blood in his urine one morning and was understandably upset. Eric was only 6 at the time and was just beginning to enjoy his place on a Natchez youth swim team. He won his first race and was a budding star on the squad. When we took him to a urologist, we got a jolt. We were told that Eric was born with only one functioning kidney and it had stopped functioning. At another time, another place, it would have been fatal. His doctor's last name was "Graves," which, somehow, just didn't seem to go with the medical profession. He also had huge hands and Sharon and I could just see them inside our son's little body as he cleared the blockage. Eric sailed through surgery without a hitch. We tried to calm his fears, but we knew he was having a hard time. Everything worked out well and we couldn't have been happier. We were told not to let him become involved in contact sports and that wasn't easy—not for an outgoing kid who loved to mix it up with his friends. It's been three decades since his surgery and we still remind him to be careful about his kidney.

Warren nominated our little staff for a Pulitzer Prize after we put out a special section on the impending resignation of President Nixon in August of 1974. There were several local angles to the national story and Warren backed us to the hilt. Vice President Gerald Ford had been in Jackson a few weeks before the lid blew off the continuing controversy and we covered his appearance, taking lots of notes and photos. Thad Cochran, who was our congressman at the time and later would be elected to the U.S. Senate, was doing a lot of soul searching over possible impeachment of the president. When I approached Warren with an idea of a special section on the eve of Nixon's anticipated resignation, he pounded on his calculator to get an idea on the cost of the ad-free section and said: "Do it." We worked through the night—just a handful of us—to put out a splendid special section. When I told Warren I thought it was worthy of a Pulitzer nomination, he didn't hesitate. He wrote a nomination letter and gave me a copy. We knew we didn't have a chance to win, but it was a nice gesture from him to our young staff. I had the nomination framed and Eric has it on a wall of his house in El Paso, Texas where he is a federal agent.

ALEXANDER CITY

Two years after arriving in Natchez, we were on our way to Alexander City, a small town an hour northeast of Montgomery. I had gotten the chance to be editor of the *Alexander City Outlook* in a town virtually owned by one family and one business—Russell Corp. I knew that there would be frequent moves as part of the Boone Group and we looked forward to relocating, especially being able to move back to Alabama which had been our home since 1964. As Sharon set up house and got the kids ready to go to a new school, I tried to adjust to a new paper and new employees. Tony Manuel was publisher of the *Outlook*. He had spent his newspaper career on the "business side" which meant retail advertising, circulation and other revenue-producing departments. The editorial end doesn't produce any revenue, but, without it, there wouldn't be a newspaper. That's why I love it. It's a total team effort—from the people who cover city hall to the people who run the presses. Each department depends on another one. If one drops the ball, all the others suffer.

It didn't take long for me to discover that as the size of a newspaper shrinks, so does the staff—meaning more work for those on board. Natchez wasn't very big, but we had an 8-member staff in the editorial department. That number was cut in half at Alexander City. Our "newsroom" consisted of John Paul Wilcox, and Mary Loyd White. John Paul covered area news and sports while Mary handled community news. My job was to oversee the editorial operation as well as pitch in to fill the news gaps when required. That usually was a daily requirement. I learned that my first day on the job at the twice-weekly paper that soon would become thrice-weekly.

"Who covers the council meeting this afternoon?" I asked John Paul. "You do," he said. "Who covers the basketball game tonight?" I asked John Paul. "You do," he said. And, so, it went. When it was decided that we'd publish three times a week, our small staff found itself faced with an even more arduous task. We didn't have a wire service, meaning everything had to be locally generated. With only three people and me to help provide enough copy, it was a race against time to try and be everywhere at once. I wouldn't want to say we threw it together, but there were weeks when it was all we could do to find enough local news to fill up the three issues.

"Al, I want to print the police blotter each week," Tony said, as he stopped by my desk one morning. "Do you know what that'll mean?" I responded. "I have an idea, but I want it done anyway," he said. As we both knew, the smaller the town, the bigger the news, especially when it involves crime. Police blotters generally contain misdemeanor offenses—everything from running red lights to shoplifting. Nobody likes to get caught, of course, and they really hate having their name in the local paper in a negative way, especially when they are accused of thievery. Those not accused of crimes love to read about neighbors who are. I guess it's just human nature—not to mention a great circulation boost for small papers. It didn't take long for us to find out just how much some hated seeing the police report in the *Outlook*. Our phones began ringing off the hook. One day, a huge man walked into the office and I thought to myself that this could be the moment I had mentioned to Tony. I was about to direct the big guy to our publisher's office, when he let me know how "devoted" a father he was. He told me his name and said his son was a "junior," but everybody just called him "Bubba." Seems his boy had gotten into trouble and his name was about to appear in the police report. "Make sure," he told me with a glare, "that when you put his name in the paper that you use "Bubba" or "Junior" or something so people won't think it's me." I was happy to oblige. The guy was enormous and the last thing I needed was for somebody to rearrange our office. We eventually dropped the police blotter, much to my great pleasure.

We wound up living in three houses during our short stay in Alexander City. That brought the total to eight houses or apartments in our first 12 years of marriage. Our only major complaint was a "house" on Elkahatchee Road. It was a rental and had seen better days. We didn't know how little insulation it had until winter arrived. It was our first experience with propane gas and when the first cold spell hit, we turned on the space heaters to keep us warm. Two weeks later, we had to refill the propane tank outside. It cost $100. We decided we'd spend the rest of the winter in our bedroom. It got so cold in that little house that ice formed on the inside of our windows. We slept, ate and lived in our bedroom—using the only space heater and extra blankets to keep us warm. It wasn't all bad. We were able to introduce Dani and Eric to the joys of Charlie Chan movies. Sunday mornings were devoted to bundling up in bed and watching Charlie solve crimes, not to mention uttering all those classic sayings.

As the months went by, I got to appreciate the hard work of those who helped create each *Outlook*. They remain good friends today, especially John Paul and Jim Earnhardt who share the same birthday. John became an educator after picking up a degree at Auburn University. Jim moved on to the *Montgomery Advertiser* where I'd eventually join him. Jim enrolled at Auburn, but never got a degree. I never thought he needed one, anyway, not with his mind. A superb editorial writer and columnist, he is quick to admit that the *Outlook* gave him ample opportunity to write. Before he joined our news staff, Jim worked at a local radio station on Sunday mornings where he supervised live religious programs. I did a story on his efforts. Beginning at about 6 a.m., ministers, congregants and supporters would arrive outside the little radio station where their shows would last from 15 to 30 minutes. It was easy money for the owners and Jim didn't seem to mind the early start to his Sunday mornings. We still laugh about one woman who'd show up at the precise hour, introduce her church program and make sure her listeners also knew she also was a notary public who was ready and willing to record documents—for a fee, of course.

During those days, the Russell family was viewed by some in Alexander City as benevolent, others as dictatorial. There is little doubt it is one of Alabama's most important families—having founded the textile company at the turn of the 20th century and turning it into one of the world's most important makers of athletic wear. The Russell name on a sweatshirt means quality. It is the largest employer in that part of east Alabama. Thousands depend on Russell for daily survival. At one time, not long after the company began, a "village" was created for Russell employees. They may not have made much money, but they had a place to live. If it was a "company store," Russell Corp. had a lot of appreciative customers. Through the years, Russell built or supported construction of a hospital, a high school, a library and an animal shelter. Many of the buildings and services bear the family name. I often wondered why they just didn't change the name of the town to Russell, Alabama. It's unlikely there are any better community angels in Alabama than the Russell family which also started Alexander City's first newspaper—the one putting bread on our table. Unionism is a bad word in Alexander City and Tallapoosa County. It doesn't exist at Russell which also provides the framework for the city's political structure. Russell employees have served as mayors, council members and county commissioners. In short, Russell WAS and IS Alexander City. The company fell on hard times in the late 1990s and thousands had to be laid off as offshore operations by competitors ate into its bottom line. A new president was hired, drastic changes were made and Russell slowly began to regain its standing in the industry.

A maverick politician named Jack Bush upset the applecart not long after I arrived in Alex City. Jack's outspoken assessment of the way things were being run endeared him to many local folks while naturally upsetting more than a few Russell executives and supporters. He campaigned for mayor in an expensive new car and wouldn't take the advice of friends who warned him that the "common folks" might not like it. He said that was the way he was and he wasn't going to change. His election may have been considered an upset by some, but Jack expected to win. It didn't take him long to upset those who had controlled city hall for so many years. Before Jack became mayor, covering the political beat in Alex City was pretty boring. With Bush in charge, we never knew what he'd do or say next. Angered by unsanitary conditions resulting from the inadequate disposal of chicken parts at a local plant, he vowed to crack the whip on those responsible for getting rid of the remains. That happened after he saw chicken innards popping up through manhole covers. "I'm going to do something about that cotton pickin' chicken pluckin' plant," Bush told me one day. He let the plant managers know it wouldn't continue. It didn't.

Jack made national news one day when he and the leader of a nearby town were in Washington, D.C. for an annual meeting of mayors. The two country mayors walked by the Soviet Embassy during a lunch break and decided to go inside to see what was going on. The Soviets were stunned, to say the least, by the two men from tiny towns in far off Alabama—a state they probably never heard of. Bush and his buddy proposed a "trade" agreement in which Alabama opossums—commonly called possums by country folks—would be swapped for something that Americans loved to see at zoos—panda bears. The two apparently were unaware that pandas lived in China, not the Soviet Union, but that didn't dissuade them. As the embassy officials—no doubt KGB agents—scurried to find something out about them, the two Americans finally decided to leave. Their "Possums for Pandas" idea never got off the ground, but they got a good laugh out of it and I wrote a story that was picked up by the wire services and distributed nationally.

I helped cover athletic events as often as I could during those days. In preparation for the upcoming high school football season, I went to a small crossroads community outside Alex City to interview the new coach. He was just out of college and at his first high school. He was so nervous his stomach was flip-flopping during practice sessions as he got ready for his first game. Needing to get back to the office as fast as I could, I fired off several quick questions to him. The last one produced the funniest response I've ever received. "What kinda ball you gonna play this fall, coach?" I asked him. "Without blinking, he said VOIT," giving me the brand name of the ball his team used. I laughed throughout my short trip back to my office.

Occasionally, I'd be able to take Sharon and the kids on trips around the area. It was a way to ease the strain and pressure of constant deadlines at a small newspaper where everybody had several jobs. I couldn't resist the chance to take the family to Tuscaloosa one weekend to watch Elton John, who was riding high as an entertainer in the mid-1970s.

Tickets were hard to get and ours were in the peanut gallery—high up in the packed coliseum. Before the show started, we could detect the unmistakable fragrance of an illegal substance. "Daddy," what's that I smell?" Dani asked me. "Oh," I told her, "that's something older boys and girls smoke from time to time." "You mean, pot, huh, dad," she responded. It was then and there that I realized my baby daughter—who was 10 at the time—was growing up.

Tony Manuel was a cigar-chomping, golf-loving publisher. I always thought his personality was better suited to retail sales and circulation promotions than administration. He always brought along a big smile and a joke when he met people. He would have made a great used car salesman. Tony was succeeded as publisher by Paul Anderson, whose personality was the exact opposite of his predecessor's. Paul liked to mediate disputes between employees and generally was successful. He also had no intention of leaving his home in rural Tallapoosa County. Tony, on the other hand, always was ready for the next challenge in another town. He loved to tell me that "one day, you'll get yours." By that, I assumed he meant a publishing job. In the back of my mind was another meaning, of course. I also wondered if I really wanted to spend part of my day hunched over profit and loss statements and worrying about advertising rates and subscriptions. But, I had committed myself and my family to an opportunity offered by Jim Boone and was ready to ride the horse as far as it would take me.

LAFAYETTE, GA.

I got "the call" on a chilly winter day in 1978—informing me that I'd be going up to LaFayette, Ga. to take over as publisher of the *Walker County Messenger*. I had no idea where LaFayette was or what kind of paper it was, but I'd soon learn. Boone had bought the *Messenger* from the Hall family and hired the second-in-command to be publisher. He had been with the paper for years and was considered the heir apparent, even though he wasn't related to the owners. A big splash was made in that week's edition, complete with a photo of the new boss and a profile of him. All seemed set in place. Then, it fell apart. By nightfall, the new publisher had decided he didn't want to be a member of the Boone newspaper family. That left an embarrassing void and I was selected to fill it. I knew my day would come, but not quite that fast. I was interviewing the mayor of Alexander City at the time and my boss, Paul Anderson, ordered that I be found. After I was contacted, I went home and told Sharon. When her shock wore off, Dani and Eric arrived home from school. "My God," Eric said. After having lived in Decatur and Natchez, he knew moving would be a big part of our family's future.

LaFayette is in the extreme northwest corner of Georgia, just south of Chattanooga, Tenn. and in the same county as Chickamauga where one of the bloodiest battles of the Civil War took place. When I arrived, it was even colder than Alexander City and there was snow on the ground. Soon, it would be falling again. I didn't know what to expect, but I knew LaFayette was now my "bus" and I'd be the driver for as long as I did a decent job at the wheel. Charlie Land, one of Jim's top assistants, was to be my supervisor. I had met Charlie a few times and knew he had a good reputation as a journalist. He was a fine writer, especially when it involved sports. When he became publisher of the *Tuscaloosa News*, he showed he could handle the business end, too. He let me know he'd help me become a publisher. That meant a lot because much was happening in a very short time. In addition to being named publisher of the *Messenger*, I also got part ownership of a little weekly paper in nearby Trenton, Ga. It was the opportunity I had waited for since leaving Decatur five years earlier. Little did I know that my tenure as "publisher" of the *Walker County Messenger* would last all of 18 months.

The *Messenger* was a typical small town weekly newspaper that hadn't changed its style in years. Basically, its editorial motto was: "Don't rock the boat." For someone who had spent much of his journalism career as a boat rocker—reporting about crime, corruption and the sleazy side of life—it was quite a departure. At Decatur, Natchez and Alexander City, we basically told it like it was. At LaFayette, I soon learned that reporting "good news" was generally the preferred way of doing things. The editor at the time of our arrival didn't hustle and seemed to enjoy spending long periods behind his typewriter instead of getting out and tracking down the news. I dubbed him "the professor." He didn't relish the change of ownership and dropped a few subtle hints about it. At one point, he told me he'd give me "two weeks" to see if he wanted to stay. I wasn't overly confident of my publishing potential at the time and that didn't help matters, because "the professor" and I were basically all we had to report the news in and around a huge county. If I'd have had more confidence in myself, I'd have told him I'd give him two weeks to see if I wanted to keep him. As it turned out, he was gone in about a month or so. He did provide one moment of levity during my association with him. We were getting the paper ready one day and talking about our favorite songs. He said one of his was "Send in the Clowns." I knew he wasn't referring to the song. The Boone Group has lots of employees looking for a chance to publish a newspaper, so replacing "the professor" wasn't that difficult. He wound up at another weekly in Georgia. I didn't consider it much of a loss for us.

We quickly changed the appearance of the *Messenger* which was mostly gray with small photographs and lots of type. People began to notice and even Boone was impressed. At one point, he told me I had helped produce one of the fastest turnarounds of any paper in his chain. That made me feel pretty good. Of course, appearance can't compete with profitability and that's the name of the game as far as any business is concerned. I imagine Jim and his people had decided even before buying the *Messenger* that a second weekly edition was in order. You don't pay off a big debt by just sitting around and admiring your new look. You've got to go out and look for ways to increase revenue in a variety of ways. That's why all Boone papers have an annual edition at the start of each year. It salutes local retail businesses and industry with lots of stories that few people read other than those who manage the plants that advertise in them. A new Boone paper usually has a year to get settled before it begins publishing the special edition. They have a variety of names. LaFayette's was "Horizons." They generally are big hits at first because, in addition to spotlighting various industries, they also are ego boosters—giving plant managers and elected officials a chance to have their pictures in the local paper. After a few years, some papers begin to have problems selling advertising as the bloom falls off the rose. They are revenue enhancers at the beginning of the year when ad sales generally slump after the busy Christmas season. But, they certainly help to keep the bottom line in the black and, most of all, make the payroll during the post-holiday advertising dog days. My only gripe was the work entailed to put it all together. Those who sold the ads got commissions. Those who wrote copy for the section got free pizza for late night work.

When we announced that the *Messenger* soon would have a second edition—on Saturdays—the silence was deafening. When we tried to sell the advertising for it, the silence increased. That didn't bring smiles back at corporate headquarters in Tuscaloosa. Mike Pippin, our retail advertising manager and future Boone Group publisher, worked hard to sell the second edition, but nothing seemed to work. We all went out on that first Saturday and delivered thousands of free copies. The sampling was as successful as our initial announcement. When people are accustomed to a weekly newspaper that's all they want. They had two daily newspapers in Chattanooga at the time and didn't care about more Walker County news. By the time we had unveiled our second edition, we had built an addition to our facility in downtown LaFayette and added a press—changing the color of our bottom line from black to red in a few months. The idea apparently was to make our town a regional printing hub for future Boone papers. It didn't work. The publisher of a newspaper is akin to the captain of a ship and usually goes down with it—riding the presses all the way to the bottom. What began with so much promise had deteriorated almost overnight, or so it seemed.

In the spring of 1979, Charlie called to say "we've decided to make a change." I worked hard during the 18 months I spent in LaFayette, but was told I wasn't what they wanted in a publisher there. During one of our "conversations," Charlie indicated that he thought I had "eased up" after being named publisher and wasn't working as hard as I should have. He also questioned my management abilities. He was dead wrong on my work ethic, but he might have had a point about management expertise. Throughout my career, I've always tried hard to manage myself. I lead by example and have helped many young reporters simply by doing my thing. Working for a Boone paper is a challenge. Being publisher of one is even more difficult. Boone publishers don't always last long. They either burn out and quit, are fired or are transferred. Charlie was nice enough to find me a job as managing editor of a Boone paper back in Alabama, so it wasn't all bad. The toughest part was leaving on Mother's Day. Sharon deserved more than that. It was a lonely ride that Sunday and a lot went through my mind as I drove south, including the thought that I should have stayed in Decatur. As things turned out, Boone eventually sold the *Messenger* to another newspaper chain in Georgia, signaling an end to an 11-year failed effort in Walker County. It had been pretty much of a dud and I was the dunderhead in charge.

SELMA

Little did I realize that my stay in Selma would be the longest of my newspaper career. After 7 1/2 years in Decatur, we had moved through parts of three states and four cities in six years and lived in six different apartments or houses. It wasn't easy for Sharon and the kids, but they adjusted well to each move. I was proud of them as they made new friends and attended new schools. Bruce Morrison was publisher of the *Selma Times-Journal* when I arrived and Paul Davis was editor. Within a year and a half, Bruce and I would be gone and Davis wouldn't be far behind. Paul was nice enough to allow our family to spend a few weeks at his house while we looked for one of our own. I am forever grateful for his kindness and generosity. Bruce also made us feel welcome. He was an idea man who had been at several newspapers. I admired him. A year after my arrival in Selma, Bruce left for greener pastures, heading for Tennessee and another newspaper group. He was replaced by Shelton Prince, a Georgia native who began in the press room and made his way up the ranks from that department.

Selma is a lot like Natchez—two small river towns where no one really is accepted unless they can trace their ancestry back at least a century or more. I was a stranger. Before leaving LaFayette, I promised Sharon that, this time, I'd see to it that we'd finally move into a nice house. The others either were apartments or rental houses. As it turned out, we couldn't give away our house in LaFayette. It was an old, wood structure that didn't have any insulation. I sank my only *Messenger* bonus—$1,000—into filling all the holes. We offered it for $19,000 and got no takers—winding up with double house payments for about a year. Boone was kind enough to help us pay for the house in LaFayette before we told the mortgage company to take it back. All in all, our LaFayette experience was a personal and professional disaster. It was the only town we were happy to leave.

I soon learned that Mayor Joe Smitherman ruled Selma. The *Times-Journal* decided to take on "Joe T.," as he's known and failed miserably. It involved Smitherman's decision to come out of "retirement" in 1980 and run against Carl Morgan, the council president who had succeeded him as mayor. The two had been good friends for years, but the campaign was anything but friendly. The STJ backed Morgan and came up with some coverage that turned me off. It's one thing to use the editorial page to endorse a candidate—it's something else to use the front page or a full-page "house ad." Smitherman, one of the most brilliant politicians I ever covered, used the paper's assaults on him to his own advantage and trounced Morgan. He sailed back into office with ease.

Working at the *Times-Journal* provided me with some unforgettable moments, including Howard Tinsley's attempted coverage of a high school football game. Howard and his son, Ray, volunteered to cover games for us and we appreciated it. Ray would take the photographs and Howard would write the story. It was a great way for the father-son team to spend Friday nights together. We all pitched in to cover games and then hurried back to the office to take more results over the phone before we had our pizza. At one time, Howard even became our circulation director. It didn't last long and he returned to a saner profession—directing the local Red Cross office. Our high school football coverage wasn't anything to shout about, but we managed to get the results in and that seemed to please people.

Howard came into our newsroom one Friday night with a frown on his face. He rarely frowned and I knew something was up as he slumped behind a typewriter. Howard had been assigned to cover a game in rural Dallas County—about 20 miles from Selma. I had finished covering my game, which was played in Selma, and was in the process of writing it when I saw him come in. I knew that his game couldn't have been over yet because of the time. Add the distance he'd have to drive to get back and I knew something was wrong.

"What happened, Howard?" I asked. "Darn equipment," he said, using a four-letter word that helped him ease whatever pressure he was under at the time. "The flash didn't work, so I came back." We could have reported the story without the photograph, but we couldn't report on a game that was still in progress and I informed Howard of that fact. "Well," I asked him, "how do you propose that we write the story since you left at halftime?" "I don't care," he said, smoke appearing to come out of both ears. "I'll do the first half and you can get the rest over the phone." That's what we had to do. It was the only time in my career that I had somebody come back with only half a football game to report. Howard did not cover any games after that half effort. But, we remain friends today. I just don't mention it to him—much.

"We've decided to make a change," Prince told me, moments after I had taken my seat in front of his big desk. It sounded like LaFayette all over again, except it was in person and not over the telephone. Davis sat in a nearby seat, not saying a word other than he would give me the "highest recommendation" for a job as a reporter. I had just returned to Selma from a small town where I interviewed a high school coach for our upcoming fall football special section. I handled many of the same jobs in Selma as in LaFayette, Alexander City and Natchez—editor, reporter, photographer, etc. It's tough to delegate when you don't have enough reporters to assign. I probably saved the *Times-Journal* thousands of dollars that year by doing work someone else would have had to be hired to do. But, that didn't seem to fit into the Boone Group's way of doing things. I wasn't deemed to be management material—in any capacity. I had flopped as a publisher and now they didn't want me as an editor. It was a tough night at home after breaking the news to Sharon and the kids.

My 6 1/2 years with the Boone Group had its ups and downs, but I consider myself fortunate to have worked for it. No regrets. Part ownership of a newspaper proved much more profitable than remaining at the *Decatur Daily* where I'd have made a lot less during that same period. Sharon and I were able to save enough money to help Dani and Eric with their college educations. We couldn't be prouder of two children or our own efforts as we assisted them financially in obtaining bachelor's and master's degrees. They both left college without owing a dime in student loans. I can't thank Jim Boone enough for giving me an opportunity to become a publisher. Unfortunately, I wound up a bit like one of Wernher von Braun's V2 rockets during World War II. His autobiography was about "aiming for the stars." He hit London, instead. In my case, I bombed out after a 6 ½ year experiment in trying to become a newspaper executive. All I could think of was Tony Manuel's "You'll get yours one day" comment to me in Alexander City. It was the only time I laughed that day.

MONTGOMERY

My friendship with Mike Freeman paid off handsomely after I left the *Selma Times-Journal* in late August of 1980. At that point, I couldn't have felt any lower in my professional career—bounced out of two newspaper executive jobs in as many years. But, I knew that was a possibility when I went to work for the Boone Group. During my years with that organization, I saw publishers and editors come and go as though passing through a revolving door. I knew that my time might come, as it did to so many others. I called Mike the morning after I was sacked. Sharon had done her best to soften the blow. She could feel the deep depression I was in. She was there to provide support, as she's always done. After I told Mike what had happened, I pitched a possibility to him. "What do you think about opening a news bureau in Selma?" There was a slight pause and he said "Hey, hoss, let me think about it. I'll get back to you."

By the time I had completed the Boone phase of my journalism career, Mike had moved from the *Decatur Daily* to Montgomery where he became executive editor of the *Montgomery Advertiser* and its sister paper, the *Alabama Journal*. Mike was an important cog in a big corporate wheel known as Multimedia. He knew I could still cover city hall and chase fire trucks, so he must have figured I'd be a good investment. The *Advertiser* was and still is the most popular daily newspaper in central Alabama with loyal subscribers relying on it from many miles away. It gets their day started. News from rural counties was handled by correspondents or staff reporters if the story was important enough to send someone. The *Advertiser* had, as I would learn later, a news bureau in Selma at the turn of the 20th century, but nothing since then. Mike knew my idea had possibilities. It didn't take long for him to call me back. "We're ready to start, Al," he said. I had made job inquiries at some other places, but none had newspaper connections and my heart really wasn't in any of them. By 1980, I had been a reporter, editor and publisher for 16 years and it was all I really enjoyed doing. I immediately drove to Montgomery, got a quick orientation and went to work the next day.

Since it was our first bureau outside Montgomery in 80 years, we improvised as we went along. My original coverage area was Selma and surrounding counties. I worked out of my house the first six months before I was able to rent office space in downtown Selma. It was just above the Alabama River and down the street from the Edmund Pettus Bridge which is the town's most famous civil rights landmark. Some of the folks up the street at the *Selma Times-Journal* weren't very pleased. A few thought it was a hoot, though, and would give me a friendly wave when they saw me as they passed by our huge front window. Shelton may have thought he got rid of me, but he soon learned I not only was staying, I began taking away subscribers with more aggressive news coverage. We became so busy with new subscribers that we had to hire a secretary to handle all the phone calls. Instead of coming up with a fancy sign to keep track of customers, I got a bottle of white shoe polish and began updating the total on the front window. We averaged 100 or more new subscribers a month during our first year in operation as a news bureau. We even had a grand opening with local officials, including Mayor Smitherman and Dallas County Probate Judge Johnny Jones, helping us to celebrate. Balloons and bunting adorned the building which had "*The Advertiser*" in big black letters across the front. Our publisher at the time wanted to make us more of a statewide paper, so he did away with "Montgomery" as often as possible. It eventually failed because our readers wouldn't accept anything but the *MONTGOMERY Advertiser*" as their daily newspaper.

Since the *Advertiser* is a morning paper, it had a big jump on the afternoon *Times-Journal* during our first few years in competition. The *STJ* was an afternoon paper for a century. The only disadvantage for us in being a morning newspaper was providing the *STJ* with news tips. The editors and reporters up the street were young and inexperienced and didn't have a clue. So, they began relying on me for "assignments." When I'd have an exclusive story in the morning, they'd come back with the same story in the afternoon edition. They wanted to make it look as though they knew about it all along, but just came out later in the day. All they had to do was read what I had written and then basically rewrite it. That all changed a few years later when the *Times-Journal* joined the national trend of shifting publication times from afternoons to mornings. Television had done that. People stopped reading their afternoon papers when they got home from work. Instead, they kicked off their shoes and plopped down in front of their television sets to watch the news.

By switching from afternoons to mornings, the *Times-Journal* wound up going head-to-head with me and I loved every minute. It was much like my 2 ½ years with *UPI* when we pitted our talents against the *AP*—each trying to beat the other to the story. When the *STJ* went into the morning cycle it meant that if I had something first, they couldn't touch it for at least a day. They couldn't come back that same afternoon to make it appear as though they had the same story all along, but had to wait to publish it. Talk about a boost for our circulation! Head-to-head competition kicked our subscription numbers even higher. Shelton should have had me sign a "non-compete" contract when I left his employ. They gave me a small severance package and let me keep a company car for awhile to look for another job. As it turned out, I just moved a few feet away—setting up shop a couple of doors down the street. Within a few months, whatever money the *STJ* had saved by not having me around was lost along with a lot of subscribers who had deserted them and subscribed to the *Advertiser*. In my mind, it had been a bottom line decision that backfired on the Boone organization. They eventually recovered and got back many of their subscribers, but I think we had made our mark.

When the *STJ* decided to switch to a morning newspaper, Mike had become editor. He had left the *Advertiser* and joined Boone Newspapers Inc. by that time. We remained good friends, but he knew friendship wouldn't stand in the way of an exclusive news story. I did have fun with Mike once, though, when he came up with a slogan for the "new" *Selma Times-Journal*. It was "A New Dawn." I once told him it was still "The Same Old Yawn." He got a laugh out of it. Eventually, Mike moved on and settled in Arkansas with his new wife, bought a weekly paper, sold it and went to work for Wal-Mart for awhile. I asked him if he had become a "greeter." He said he was placed in another position with "less responsibility." He always had a good sense of humor. He and Barbara later moved to Mississippi.

Our bureau experiment in Selma had become such a great success that our publisher decided to add more. Within a couple of years, the *Advertiser* had news bureaus in Birmingham, Mobile, Tuscaloosa, Auburn, Dothan, Troy and, of course, Selma. Phyllis Wesley became our state editor and eventually needed an assistant editor to help with the crush of copy coming in from all over the state. We occasionally had state bureau meetings in Montgomery and the room was filled with reporters, photographers and editors. One time, our publisher—Doyle Harvill—stood in front of a large map of Alabama—looking like Gen. George Patton as he addressed his troops. Harvill didn't have a stick to point at the map, but he let everyone in the room know that, one day, we'd have a bureau "HERE." He pointed his finger at Florence which is far from Montgomery in the extreme northwestern corner of Alabama near the Tennessee line. Doyle didn't know much about Alabama history or geography and I had to suppress a laugh when he said that. It never happened, of course, but, for awhile, we were really humming. Bureau reporters challenged each other for limited space on our state page. After a few years, financial reasons caused us to cut back on our bureaus. By the end of the 1990s, only the Selma bureau remained.

A Quake, A Rig and Gov. Guy

Since I was the senior bureau writer, I was given wide latitude in covering stories. In December of 1990, I wound up in Memphis, covering "The Big Earthquake That Didn't Happen." Several weeks before the "event," stories began to appear in newspapers about the New Madrid Fault which covers a large area of America's mid-section. A seismologist predicted that a major quake would rock the area. I suggested the story idea to one of my editors who told me to go for it because a section of Alabama might be impacted if the prediction came true. I drove my high mileage Grand Marquis to Memphis and crossed over into Arkansas where I arrived in Marked Tree, a little town that some felt would be at the epicenter of the "quake." I almost wrecked my car at one point. It was due to bald tires, not rumblings from below. Nothing happened and I drove back to Memphis where I met with some college professors who had always had their doubts about the prediction. They did make some money by selling sweatshirts and T-shirts. I still have my sweatshirt. It reads: "The Marked Tree Fault Festival" with "Quake, Rattle & Roll" under it. I bought another sweatshirt for Selma lawyer Vaughan Russell, who asked me to bring back a souvenir for his daughter. She wore it for years.

Two unforgettable assignments occurred near Mobile. The first followed Hurricane Frederic, a Category 3 storm with 145-mile-an-hour winds that flattened most of Gulf Shores in September of 1979. I was sent down a few months later to do a week-long series on rebuilding efforts. Part of the series focused on Alabama's lucrative off-shore oil drilling operations. I accompanied a couple of oil company officials to one of the huge rigs in the Gulf of Mexico. The water wasn't very deep, but the rig was pretty high. I asked one of the company's public relation wonks how we were going to get to the top of the rig. He looked at me and then upward. "On that," he said. I looked up and saw what appeared to be a giant black inner tube similar to the kind kids love to splash around in at pools and beaches. The tube was connected to several large strands of rope which formed a cone shape tied to a metal piece above them. "Okay, hop on," the executive said. I stood next to him on a little boat, wearing a camera around my neck, a notebook in a back pocket of my pants, a tape recorder in a front pocket and several pens in the other. "Well," I muttered to myself, "Nothing ventured..." I hopped up onto the tube, linked my arms around two strands of rope and held on for dear life as a crane on the rig began to lift several of us upward. There were no elevators or stairs, but it appeared that helicopters could land on it. They probably were only used for corporate executives and shift replacements. As I looked down, I noticed a steel barge moving directly under us. "What's that for?" I asked the oil company guy next to me. "Oh, that's just in case you fall. We'll be able to see if you bounce off and hit the water." I didn't appreciate his attempt at humor. I spent a couple of hours at the rig, interviewing the men who make a good, but lonely, living drilling for oil in the Gulf of Mexico. All that time, I couldn't help but think of how I was going to get down. I knew it would be the same way I got up.

In late September of 1993, I was getting ready for work one morning when news flashed over the television set in our bedroom that the Sunset Limited, an Amtrak passenger train on its way from Los Angeles to Miami, had hit a bridge about 3 a.m. It plunged into the Connor Creek Bayou near Saraland, not far from Mobile. First reports indicated no one had been hurt. Then, the phone next to our bed rang with Nancy Dennis, one of the *Advertiser's* best editors, on the other end of the line. "Get on down to Mobile right now," she said. "Nancy," I told her, "I'm hearing that everybody's okay. That's what they're saying on TV right now." "Well," she said. "We're getting reports that a lot of people are dead. Get down there." "I'm on my way," I told her. It's a long way from Selma to Mobile, but I drove as fast as I could, watching out for state troopers and road signs. I hadn't been down that way in a long time. It would be a long, difficult day for those of us who covered that tragedy. The most indelible memory for me was driving to the area where the bodies of 40 passengers were neatly lined up in plastic bags on a barge. We could see them from a distance. An aerial photo provided a more dramatic view of the victims. I spent most of the day driving back and forth from the area where recovery operations were under way to a building in Mobile where the survivors were brought in. Most were still in shock later that day—wrapped in blankets and clutching each other for support. It had been the worst disaster in Amtrak history. Most of those who died were inside one of the Amtrak sleepers. They never knew what hit them. That might have been a good thing. Water poured in through the windows and they drowned.

One of the funniest stories I wrote involved the theft of hundreds of cases of Budweiser beer from a railroad boxcar. It was parked on a rail spur at the beer company's distribution center just off U.S. 80 a few miles east of Selma. Next door was a housing project. During the night, somebody broke the lock off the boxcar, setting in motion a mad dash by thirsty folks looking for free beer. By daybreak, there wasn't a beer can left inside the boxcar. Outside, however, it was a different story. It didn't take investigators long to trace discarded Bud cans to front doors throughout the housing project. Several of the culprits were still sleeping blissfully after a party to be remembered. In my lead paragraph, I called it the "biggest beer bust in Selma history."

It wasn't unusual for me to step on a few toes now and then. Ten of them belonged to Dallas County Commissioner Perry Varner, who took exception to an article I wrote about his deplorable driving record. He had been frequently stopped for speeding and his driver's license had been suspended seven times for infractions. He once was clocked at 90 miles an hour in a 55 mile-an-hour zone outside of Selma. The headline which appeared above the article on July 30, 1993 was: "Dallas official just can't drive 55." I didn't write the headline, but I was blamed for it. A few days later, Varner wrote Managing Editor Jim Tharpe a letter threatening a lawsuit for "invasion of privacy" in connection with the article. In his letter, Varner accused me of "racial discrimination," saying my article was done "with malicious intent." Although the article was supported by official state records and he was a public official, Varner still demanded a retraction. What he got was a brief response from Bill Brown, our executive editor, who wrote: "If, as you say, you have not had your driver's license suspended seven times, you may want to check with the Alabama Department of Public Safety and see if someone has appropriated your name and address. Records in that department not only show that a license with your name on it has been suspended seven times, but that the person with that license has a string of traffic offenses over the years that would make a teenage hot-rodder blush." We didn't hear from Varner again on that matter. Bill's support was much appreciated, as it was throughout my association with him. I would have written the same kind of story if it had involved a white politician. I have. Many times.

A story that would be talked about for a long time involved Guy Hunt, a former probate judge from Cullman County who became Alabama's first Republican governor since Reconstruction. It was a fluke victory because two Democrats seeking the party's gubernatorial nomination upset voters so much that Hunt was elected virtually by default. With his folksy twang and habit of fracturing the King's English, Hunt was called "Goober" by many in Alabama. Not long after he took office in 1987, Hunt went to Clanton in the middle of the state to take part in the annual Peach Festival. It's been customary for governors to buy the first basket of peaches and Hunt did just that. When he stepped to the microphone in the middle of a baseball field that Saturday morning in late June, he talked about driving down from Cullman to buy his peaches from local farmers. "I never tried to Jew with them, either," Hunt said. He didn't say "Jew him down," but the crowd roared in support just the same. When Hunt took his seat under a nearby tent with half a dozen of his bodyguards, I walked over and asked him if he thought Alabama's Jewish citizens might take offense at what many perceive to be an anti-Semitic slur. "I kid all my Jewish friends about it," he said. On the way down the interstate to Montgomery, I asked Sharon if I should write about what he said. It was obvious nobody else was going to and the television station reporters never gave it a second thought. Being brought up the way I was, I don't overlook such slurs. The headline across the top of the "Southland" page Sunday morning was: "Hunt's peach festival speech contains ethnic remark." A Montgomery television station picked up on it and used his comments Sunday night. Later in the year, at a funeral for an Alabama trooper who had been murdered by her boyfriend, I saw Hunt again as we walked up a hill to our cars. He looked over and gave me a double-take. He apparently had remembered me from Clanton. Hunt was bounced out of office midway in his second term for violating Alabama's Ethics Law.

Reporters rarely find out who has been offended by one of their articles. At times, however, they will be notified about whatever displeasure they might have caused. Sometimes the names are even real. Most of the time, they're fictitious. Case in point was a letter I received from a man identifying himself as "James Kirklewski." No such person existed. Here's the missive sent to me during the winter holiday season of 1995:

Alvin: wishing you Christmas cheer, hoping bad things happen to you all year. A horrible person like you, bad things should always happen to. So, in this season of fun, maybe someone will shoot you with a gun. The way you dye your hair, looks like paint from an old chair. The lipstick and makeup from a jar shows you for the faggot or queer that you are."

He'd occasionally call me and identify himself as "James Kirklewski" and then make more threats. I had a feeling that he was an erstwhile politician in west Alabama—a man I apparently upset by reporting his legal problems during a campaign. He didn't win his race, thank goodness. He once accused me of having a sexual relationship or infatuation with a popular female official in west Alabama. For someone who was supposed to be a "faggot or queer," I was flattered by that claim. She was gorgeous and I couldn't see her giving me the time of day, let alone anything else. Besides, Sharon wouldn't have approved. She'd have used a frying pan to drive home her point if she felt I had strayed. "Kirklewski" eventually quit calling and writing.

Those of us in the news gathering business often find ourselves targets of "gutless wonders" as I call them. On Sept. 18, 1998, I received a copy of a letter from "Mrs. James Garrett" of "Detroit" who claimed I had molested her son. She said her "son" told her: "He squeezed me funny mommy." It allegedly happened at my Selma office just down the street from the National Voting Rights Museum.

"You have a real problem person on your staff who needs immediate counseling or needs to be fired," the woman claimed in a letter to "Dear Editor," before adding: "At this point I don't know whether to sue for molestation or be satisfied that you have taken sufficient steps to discipline him severely. You will hear from me by the end of October."

We never heard from "Mrs. James Garrett," of course, because she did not exist. Neither did "James Kirklewski" or others who called or wrote my editors during a 20 year period in an effort to get me fired. We published an ad in the *Selma Times*-Journal seeking information about anyone who might have been linked to the letter, copies of which were sent to everybody but me, it seemed. Mayor Joe Smitherman gave me his copy. We offered a $500 reward for anyone with information about me having committed a "felony." There were no responses and it didn't surprise us. Montgomery lawyer Dennis Bailey helped us on that matter, as he has done many times through the years. I've often called Dennis to help me out of one jam or another. He's never failed us or me.

On another occasion, a couple unhappy with articles that I had written arranged a meeting with one of my senior editors. When we sat down, the two were smiling, apparently convinced I'd be booted out the door. My editor stood by me and let them both have it for complaints he felt were unwarranted.

At times, my aggressive reporting style produced a laugh or two. I once called a local politician to ask an innocuous question. He waited a few days before returning my call and when I asked him about the delay, he said: "You know, getting a call from you is like getting a call from Mike Wallace." I told him I viewed that as a compliment. Being compared to the fearless "60 Minutes" correspondent was quite an honor.

It's human nature to dislike negative news. Newspaper reporters often find themselves facing angry readers for writing about events that can be embarrassing to people. In the spring of 2005 in Selma, I covered the arrival of a Vietnam Wall replica that had been touring the country for 20 years. A large group of students from Morgan Academy walked to the wall and spent an hour at the site. Vietnam is ancient history for teen-agers of the 21st century and it was apparent that they didn't make much of a connection with it or the 58,000 names of troops who died there. They seemed more interested in enjoying the sunshine and cutting up with each other. That's how I reported it, along with the dismay of veterans who had served during World War II, Korea and Vietnam. A few days later, the mother of a Morgan student approached me at an event and "insisted" on getting details about what happened. I told her what I had seen, but it didn't seem to mollify her. "Did you have to report it?" she asked, referring to the questionable conduct of the students. "Yes, I thought I did," I told her, adding, in so many words, that I didn't tell her how to do her job and she didn't need to tell me how to do mine. The real blame, in my opinion, lay with Morgan administrators and teachers for not having informed the kids about what they were about to see. It might have helped them show the respect that "The Wall" deserved.

In late 1995, the *Advertiser* and its sister publications in the *Multimedia Group* were bought by the *Gannett Co.*, a corporate giant that owns *USA TODAY* and about 100 other newspapers from coast to coast. It also owns broadcasting and computer-related enterprises. Within a year, we had undergone some major changes. The biggest involved journalistic philosophy. At a time when newspaper readership continued to slump in direct proportion to the steady rise in television viewership and internet usage, *Gannett* executives knew something had to be done to reverse the trend. What they came up with was something called "News 2000," a plan developed to make *Gannett* publications more inclusive. Part of that meant reaching out to minorities to make them feel more comfortable, more inclined to read and subscribe to their local *Gannett* newspaper. It didn't take long for several employees to bail. From top to bottom, editors and reporters who disagreed with the way *Gannett* planned to change the *Advertiser* left. Some described it as "cookie-cutter journalism." Those unhappy with the changes either departed on their own or as a result of management moves that left little doubt their futures would be limited. I didn't know what my future would be, but I wanted to give it a go. After all, I had been able to make it with a very demanding wire service and held several editorial positions at newspapers during the previous three-plus decades.

One of my favorite co-workers was Debra Davis, who covered south Alabama for the *Advertiser*. She did a fine job and could handle any assignment. When the *Advertiser* was bought by *Gannett* and the Troy bureau was closed, Debra was moved to the "home office" in Montgomery. It didn't take her long to begin packing her bags—a few hours. She was assigned to the business desk which had been taken over by a young man who didn't have a clue about business or anything to do with it. After a few hours of listening to him try to explain his business philosophy, Debra gave her notice. Never one to hide her feelings, she let her friends know why she was leaving. Debra quickly moved on to a public relations job with a farmers organization. It paid a lot more, too. Talk about landing on your feet!

Paula Moore joined us as executive editor in 1996 when Bill Brown shifted to the editorial department. Bill decided against continuing in the position he once held, but he quickly adjusted to new surroundings and responsibilities. Publisher Dick Amberg left within a year of the *Gannett* takeover and wound up as a vice president with the *Washington Times*. The departure parade continued in the years that followed. We began to have more black employees, which I thought was appropriate, given the racial percentages in our part of Alabama. We had very few blacks in the news department. Opening it up to all qualified reporters and editors was long overdue. Women also began to pop up more in leadership positions. That was another good move. I've never liked companies that paid men more than women. It's not like that in the military. Personnel of the same rank get the same pay. That's the way it should be in civilian life. By the turn of the 21^{sst} century, the *Advertiser* had begun to reflect the world around it—workers of all races, religions and sexual preferences. It was about time.

After 20 years as an editor with the *El Paso Times*, Paula found herself transported from the Southwest to the Southeast. It must have been quite a culture shock for somebody from New Mexico and Texas to arrive in Alabama where old times are not forgot. Paula proved to be a demanding editor from her first day. She expected professionalism from everybody and had little respect for anybody who didn't give it their best. She informed her subordinates that longer hours would be a given under her leadership. Like me, she led by example. Unlike me, she knew how to manage people. If her editors worked 50 hours a week, she put in 60 or more. Usually it was more. She also did something very nice for me. I started getting overtime pay. During my 17 years with *Multimedia*, I was paid a weekly wage and that was it. I don't think anybody knew what my status was—management or labor. I was the bureau manager in Selma, but, in reality, managed only myself which was a real chore at times. Nobody said anything until Paula arrived. That's when they decided I was part of the labor force and should be paid for extra hours. It was much appreciated.

I wasn't sure what my duties would entail under the rapid changes taking place within our new *Advertiser* operation and continued to report the news in Alabama's sparsely populated Black Belt region. I had been doing that for years and knew just about everybody in west Alabama. I knew we didn't have a lot of subscribers in some of those counties. I also was aware of how small Alabama was and that everybody seemed to be related to or friends with people all over the state. That meant people in the area that I covered were interested in what was going on in Montgomery, Birmingham and Mobile. The same applied for those who lived in big cities. Many came from small towns such as Marion, Linden and Eutaw. But, change is expected after business acquisitions. I figured it would only be a matter of time before those changes would be heading my way. It happened over lunch one day at the restored St. James Hotel a couple of blocks from our *Advertiser* office in Selma. Paula came over with Andrew Oppmann, who was our managing editor at the time. Andrew replaced Jim Tharpe who worked with Bill Brown to direct the Pulitzer Prize winning project for our sister paper, the *Alabama Journal.* The *Journal* merged with the *Advertiser* in 1993 and Tharpe eventually left to join the *Atlanta Journal-Constitution.* I imagine Paula and Andrew met prior to our lunch to discuss how they were going to break the news to me that I wouldn't be continuing my coverage of Marengo, Perry, Hale, Wilcox, Tuscaloosa, Greene and other counties in the Black Belt. In addition to a new coverage area, Andrew also suggested that I begin writing a weekly column, patterned after one by a colleague at one of his former papers in Kentucky. It would be called "Al Benn's Alabama." I've written hundreds of columns since that time.

The changes involving me were gradual. After awhile, they made sense, even though I didn't like it. Why drive 75 miles through the Black Belt to Tuscaloosa when I could be drive 75 miles in another direction to cover events involving more people who took the Advertiser? My miles amounted to the same. Some people at the office wondered why I was getting paid for "commuting." I told them I wasn't commuting—I was just reporting from another area. A Marine general whose division was surrounded by Chinese troops at the Chosin Reservoir in Korea was asked how it felt to be the first general in the Corps to retreat. "Retreat, hell," the general responded. "We're just attacking in another direction." In my case, I was just attacking the news in another direction. I still tried to stay in touch with many of the folks I had gotten to know on the "other" side of Alabama for 17 years. I kept my contacts and they would come in handy from time to time when something big was breaking in their area and my editors wanted something.

My contacts in West Alabama helped on the night of Oct. 23, 2002 when police began to close in on two Washington, D.C. area killers. They were snipers who had fatally shot 10 people. After three weeks of cold leads, police in Montgomery County, Maryland where Sharon used to live, focused on the fatal shooting of a liquor store manager on Zelda Road in Montgomery County, Alabama. Dave Hendrick, one of my colleagues and a good friend who sat next to me in the news department, tipped me off earlier in the day that there was a connection between the D.C. snipers, as they were known, and the Zelda Road murder. I expressed my doubts, but Dave was convinced after getting his information from solid sources at city hall and the police department. Dave did a super job breaking the story locally and won a state award. I was interested in the case, but didn't think much more of it because it wasn't my area of responsibility. Besides, it had been another long day for me and I went to bed about 8:30 p.m. Sharon woke me an hour later to tell me about television reports on a possible connection to the snipers in Perry County which is near our house. Then, the phone rang and one of our editors relayed the same information. I wasn't ordered to go, but I could feel concern in the voice on the other end of the line. Off I went. I got back home about midnight after spending part of the night in the woods where a militia school was located. I was helped by Sgt. Carlton Hogue of the Perry County Sheriff's Department. I had known him for a decade. His comments made the report more relevant, even if the television claims about the Perry County connection were wrong. Two men were arrested the following day in the D.C. area and it was the biggest story of the day for us at the *Advertiser*. Both would be convicted of murder.

Arrests, convictions and sentences all have court connections and it's been one of my favorite beats though the years—from *UPI* to the *Advertiser*. I've seen good and bad judges. One of my favorites was Brevard Hand, a federal judge from Mobile whose demeanor on the bench could send chills through the most cold-hearted criminal. He also had a sharp sense of humor. I once covered a trial involving a guy who claimed he "woke up" on a schooner in the middle of the Caribbean and just happened to be surrounded by a large quantity of illegal drugs. The jury actually bought it and acquitted him. Hand was astounded by the verdict and let the guy have it as he stood before him at Selma's Federal Building. "Young man," the judge told the equally surprised defendant, "I know you did it and you know I know you did it. If I ever see you before me again, you will not be going home." The guy apparently got the message or made sure he didn't get caught again.

Through the years, I've been able to report on lots of lawyers—the good ones and the bad ones. One of the sharpest was Billy Coplin of Demopolis in west Alabama. He may not have had the highest public profile, but he knew how to use at least one reporter—me—to get out of an assignment he didn't want. It happened after Tootsie Prowell, who ran a small post office in the tiny community of Dayton in Marengo County, was stabbed to death at her office. It was a capital murder case and Coplin had a feeling that a state judge was going to assign him to defend the thug who killed her. I called Billy after learning that was going to happen within a day or two. His response was: "They ought to hang him on the courthouse square." Since he hadn't been officially assigned to the case, he knew his comments would be viewed as a bit prejudicial for a defense lawyer to make. The court named somebody else to represent the killer who pleaded guilty and was sentenced to life in prison without the possibility of parole.

Within a few years of my arrival at the *Advertiser*, our seven-bureau operation had been cut back to three—Selma, Auburn and Troy. Then, there was one—mine. Financial concerns caused our editors to reduce our coverage and, of course, our costs. My compensation began at a relatively low amount when I arrived at the paper, but it quickly rose to acceptable levels and continued to increase. I guess they thought I was doing a pretty good job. I know I was saving the company money. By eliminating two bureaus and the expenses that went with them, I became a one-man state bureau. It meant driving up to 300 miles or more a day at times, depending on the area that needed to be visited. Two cars conked out on me while returning from assignments. One blew up at the very moment the Challenger space shuttle exploded. I was driving along U.S. 80 headed to Demopolis—50 miles west of Selma—and listening to the launch on the radio. It was Jan. 28, 1986. I couldn't believe what was happening—to the shuttle and to my little blue car. Smoke began to billow out from under the hood as the announcer, in shock, described how the shuttle was coming apart. I had blown a bolt on my engine crankcase and all the oil drained out—causing the car to smoke and quit running. I had to get a tow into Demopolis. I considered myself pretty fortunate. My troubles were minor when compared with those poor astronauts. On Feb. 1, 2003, I was at home, preparing to head to work when I switched on the television set and saw the Columbia space shuttle disintegrate on reentry. I wrote the main story for our Sunday edition. I was able to contact two Auburn University graduates who became astronauts. I used their comments in the article after chatting with them at their homes in Houston.

I've lost track of the number of cars I've owned since 1980, but figure it's got to be at least a dozen or more. I drive disposable cars. I once had a Mustang that ground to a halt just outside Selma on my way back from Wilcox County and that led to another call to Robert Turner. Robert runs Al's Towing Service in Selma. I told Sharon if I ever bought a German car, I'd name it Schnell. I got a 1999 green New Beetle, bought a personalized license plate with "Schnell" on it and drove "him" 144,000 miles in less than three years. In early June of 2001, the air conditioner died. It would cost me $1,000 for a new compressor and I knew more problems awaited. Johnny Stewart of Victor Nissan in Selma suggested I get a Camry. He also said my VW was worth about $6,000. "Johnny, it's only three years old and it cost $20,000," I told him. "Right," he said, "but you've got 144,000 miles on it." I estimate I've driven just under a million miles since beginning my bureau activities with the *Advertiser*.

As my association with *Gannett* continued, I began to feel more comfortable, even if I didn't think our policy of "inclusiveness" was right. I've always taken great pride in "telling it like it is" when I cover a story. That meant if blacks, Hispanics, Jews, Italians or Soviet defectors were involved, that's what wound up in the story. The policy drilled into us involved seeking out minorities or those not in prominent positions to add to a story. It means contacting "real people" and "mainstreaming" our stories. Basically, that means calling or contacting a minority when writing a story on any subject that might need "inclusiveness." If, for instance, we wrote about the price of tea in China, we might want to call a black cook at the local beanery for his or her opinion on the sudden rise in cost. We even had to prepare a "Minority Source List" which was put into booklet form so we'd know who to call on a particular topic. Those of us the *Advertiser* weren't the only ones who tried hard to fit into the *Gannett* mold. At our former *Multimedia* flagship newspaper in Greenville, S.C., they found just what they needed—somebody who possessed all the "mainstream" ingredients. Somebody in the *Advertiser* newsroom suggested that she must have been a one-eyed, one-armed wheelchair-bound Ethiopian lesbian agnostic New York Yankee fan who did not like sweet tea. It got to the point where reporters in Greenville called her all the time on just about any issue so they would have their "mainstream" source for the day. They had taken it to an extreme, of course, but we all still wondered about a policy of inclusiveness that those of us with experience had followed on a personal basis for years. We also were told not to forget "real people." We wondered if that meant forgetting "unreal people." It meant going after rank-and-file folks instead of elected public officials and other prominent people.

One of my favorite Montgomery stories involved the city's new mayor. Bobby Bright had defeated long-time incumbent Emory Folmar in 1999 and was adjusting from life as a lawyer to mayor of one of Alabama's most important cities. A few weeks after taking office, Bright agreed to take part in a Labor Day charity run. I was assigned to cover what appeared to be a routine event. It started that way, but turned into a major story. Bright didn't show for the run, but did appear about an hour later. He had on his jogging outfit and shook hands with those who had finished the run. I asked him why he didn't participate and he said he had a meeting with three members of the city council. "Oh, is that right?" I asked. "Was the public invited, mayor?" "No," said the former lawyer and rookie municipal leader. "We just met to go over some things." I found out the meeting began about 7 a.m. which would appear to be a bit early for a city council session, especially since it was held on a Saturday morning. The more questions I asked, the more the mayor began to appear uneasy and hedge on what had been discussed. Finally, he looked at me and said: "I know where you're going with this." That was pretty much it for the interview. When I got back to the office, I contacted some council members who didn't know about the early morning meeting. They were as surprised by the 7 a.m. session as the mayor was of my questioning. The story got prominent play the next morning. I think it was the last time Bright did that. At least, I hope it was. Whenever I'd see him after that, I'd ask when his next "secret meeting" would be held. Both of us would get a good laugh out of it. I've always liked Bobby Bright. He's a down-to-earth guy who's trying to do the right thing for his town. His primary focus during his first term was on redeveloping Montgomery's deteriorating downtown area through a bond issue that paid for a $26 million baseball stadium and other improvements. He easily won reelection in 2003.

Taking notes as President Clinton leaves Selma.
(Photo by David Bundy)

Covering racist rally in Montgomery.
(Photo by Karen Doerr)

**Sharon Benn, right, honored by Montgomery Advertiser
Executive Editor Paula Moore. Paula died of cancer in 2004.**

A few years after she joined us, Paula found out she had ovarian cancer. What a trouper she was! She just kept plugging along as she underwent chemotherapy and radiation treatments. She lost her hair, got a wig and never missed a beat. The two of us shared a common trait—hard work. Watching her fight a killer within her made me realize once more that courage comes in many different packages. She was more than a boss to me. She was a friend, someone who was in my corner from the first day I met her. As she fought back the pain and continued to run the news department, Paula found time to approve a new working arrangement for me. I told her in early 2003 that I was ready to retire, but wanted to continue working on a part-time basis—writing columns and chipping in where needed. She jotted down some figures and, within a few days, my retirement date had been set. I became a "correspondent" in early May and then switched to part-time status at the beginning of 2004. It was a good arrangement. When I told her I planned to retire, she told me I'd have three receptions—two in Montgomery and one in Selma. I said one would be fine, but I didn't deserve three. She said I did. I finally agreed after some halfhearted protests. At our newsroom reception, she presented Sharon and me with a Southwest Airlines gift certificate worth $500. Along with flowers came a card that read: "You'll never know how much you are truly loved and appreciated. Love, Paula and the Newsroom." Her condition began to deteriorate at the end of 2003 and the pain finally got to be too much for her. She no longer felt she could do the job and took disability leave. Less than a week later, she died. It was late January 2004. We knew it was only a matter of time, but her death still was a shock to those of us who admired and loved her. We held a memorial service for her at a little chapel overlooking Lake Martin near Alexander City where I once was editor of the weekly paper. I typed up my thoughts the day after she died and gave them to her husband, John. Then, I wrote a tribute column to her. It was tough to walk by her empty office in the days and weeks after she died. I still miss her.

Wanda Lloyd became executive editor of the *Advertiser* after a nationwide search and her management style was evident from the first day. Paula was a hands-on supervisor who wielded a mean editing pen. What we considered words for future generations to savor soon had more marks than a used golf ball. In many cases, she was right. Wanda prefers delegation of authority. She knows what's going on, but prefers to let others under her supervision handle nuts and bolts aspects of putting out a daily newspaper. It didn't take long for her to gain the respect that so many editors never achieve.

One of the most rewarding things about working for newspapers is watching and learning from gifted writers and editors. I've had an opportunity to be around some of the best, especially at the *Advertiser* during my quarter of a century with the paper. Mike Sherman, Mike Cason, Dan Morse, Mary Orndorff, and Carla Crowder were among the best reporters I've ever seen. Their skills helped them move on to larger newspapers with national audiences. Jannell McGrew came to us from the University of Alabama Journalism School as green as the first blade of grass in the spring, but soon developed into a fine reporter. Rick Harmon, editor of our Features Department, can do it all and we're fortunate to have him. Tom Ensey of the *Advertiser's* sports department and Teri Greene of the Features Department are word sculptors and I love to read their stories. Robin Lichtfield and Darryn Simmons consistently turn out quality work. David Bundy, Mickey Welsh, Lloyd Gallman, Julie Bennett and Karen Doerr are super photographers who constantly win awards. Mark Miller was a fine photographer, too. He moved on to *USA TODAY* to take over an important photo editing job in Washington. Many of our editors, including Dan Way who did a fine job, left after only a few years, but Faye Davis and Allison Griffin have anchored their departments for a long time and provide the continuity we miss in other areas of the paper. Likewise for Ken Hare, our editorial page editor whose experience has led to thought-provoking editorials on a myriad of subjects. He was the managing editor when I joined in 1980. In addition to his moral support, he also pushed through several pay raises for me. What a guy!

CHAPTER THREE:

UP FROM THE SLUMS

I was born on April 25, 1940 and spent my formative years in the poorest section of Lancaster, Pa. It was known as the Seventh Ward, but most people just called it the "Bloody Seventh" because of the violence that often occurred there.

My mother, Dorothy Solsky Benn, was a saint, or as close to one as a Jewish woman could get.

My father, Meryl Benn, was somewhat of a sinner—a gambler and a man of few social graces.

Meryl and Dorothy Benn walk down the aisle at their son Barry's wedding in 1956

We were Orthodox Jews who lived in a corner house on, of all places, South Christian Street. My grandfather, Louis Solsky, owned the house and didn't charge us rent during World War II. My father's meager Navy salary didn't go far. He was getting something like $30 a month. I think that's where my mother got her saintly attributes. She found a way for us to survive. So did my Zadie Solsky. "Zadie" is Yiddish for grandfather. He'd come to our house at least once a week— a burlap sack slung over his right shoulder. He was a little man and strained under the weight of the sack filled with canned goods to keep his daughter and three grandchildren alive.

Louis and Sarah Solsky stand outside Congregation Degel Israel which Louis Solsky helped found in Lancaster, Pa. in the late 1800s.

Louis Solsky arrived in this country in the late 1800s. All he had were the clothes on his back and a dream that life had to be better than it was in Eastern Europe where Jews were second-class citizens. In time, he became a wealthy man who built a large house next to our synagogue. Between Congregation Degel Israel and his house was a warehouse where he stored his burlap sacks and weighed them on a huge scale. We'd play in the warehouse and marvel at what a great place our grandfather had built just for us. We soon found out that this modest little man who could barely speak English had realized his American dream. He became known as the "Burlap Bag King" of Southeastern Pennsylvania.

Across the street from his house was a kosher butcher shop. Above it was our Hebrew school. We went there after our secular school ended for the day. Most of us didn't want to go, but we weren't given a choice. Cantor Friedman was our teacher. He was from the "Old Country." We didn't know which one, but we knew that, from his thick accent, he wasn't raised in Lancaster. He tried to drill the Hebrew alphabet into our thick skulls. Most of us resisted. Cantor Friedman used a long ruler for emphasis. He'd slam it across our knuckles to make a point now and then—more now than then. In addition to the strange language and Cantor Friedman's ruler, we also had to cope with the activities below our classroom. That's where the butcher kept his chickens—where a man cut their throats, said a blessing and pronounced them kosher, meaning they were safe for traditional Jews to eat. I wanted to be outside with my friends, playing baseball or engaging in some other useful pursuit. Instead, we looked at strange Hebrew letters on a blackboard, tried not to upset Cantor Friedman and listened to the gurgling sounds of dying chickens. We had some very bright students in our class, excluding me. Twins Alex and Teddy Shear, Bobby Geller and Glenda Siegel were among the best. I always thought Glenda was the smartest in our group, but, in Orthodox Judaism, women generally are ignored. Boys get all the attention. I think Glenda could memorize the Lancaster phone book. She'd run circles around us. We'd have contests to see who could memorize a specific prayer and, more often than not, Glenda would have it down pat and win. I usually wound up in the rear of the pack.

At times, I'd be tossed out of Hebrew School, usually for cutting up in class. I had a habit of doing that. Luckily for me, my zadie was just across the street and I knew he'd have a delicious treat for me when I arrived.

"Alvie, kicked out of cheder (pronounced with a hard 'C' as in Chaaayyy-der) again?" he'd say, using the Yiddish word for Hebrew School.

"Yes, zadie, looks like it," I'd tell him.

"Vel, zit down and have piece pumpernickel," he'd say, as he began to cut a large piece from a loaf of dark brown bread. Then, he'd spread out a large slab of butter. Sometimes, he'd add jelly. I couldn't wait to dig in.

I loved my Zadie Solsky, even if I didn't understand what he was saying most of the time. I knew he loved us because we were his baby daughter's children. My brother, Barry and sister, Eileen, all shared the same opinion of our grandfather. We never got to know our grandmother. "Bubbie Solsky" died in 1947. One of my last memories of her was being in her bedroom during her final moments. I was with an uncle at the time. A small candle burned on a corner table. Bubbie was a typical Jewish mother—making sure the house was clean, the children were properly cared for and the meals were made on time. She was totally devoted to her husband. In those days, it was expected.

The only time I was ashamed of myself around my zadie happened during a fight I had with a neighborhood boy who had called me a "dirty Jew." Our neighborhood was a religious and ethnic rainbow. We'd occasionally exchange more than pleasantries. It didn't take much. I pushed him to the ground, got on top and began popping him with my little right fist. The next thing I knew, an arm was around my right shoulder to pull me off. Instinctively, I reached around and bit the hand attached to the arm—the one that often fed our family. It was my zadie's. I knew I was in big trouble. When I got home, my mother had already been informed of my transgression and gave me a beating that would have made my father proud.

"You ever do something like that to your zadie again and you'll get a lot more than what I just gave you," she said, anger flashing in her eyes. It didn't happen again—biting my zadie or my mother beating me like that.

I enjoyed going around with Zadie Solsky when he walked through the 7th Ward to collect the rent on houses he owned. He was in his

70s at the time, but still managed to negotiate some steep hills. I didn't know anything about rent back in those days, but I soon learned about compassion. Many of the people who rented from zadie didn't have enough money and would tell him. He'd look at them, see the pain and humiliation in their eyes and tell them he'd come back next month "ven you haf it." He just didn't have the heart to demand it or even think of eviction. An old German man would do things for zadie's family when the Sabbath arrived at sundown on Fridays. Orthodox Jews aren't supposed to engage in anything that approaches work on shabbos, as the Sabbath is known in Yiddish, and I was told that flipping a light switch constituted effort beyond opening prayer books. That's why zadie's neighbor was hired to do the menial things normally handled by the Solsky family the other six days of the week. Gentiles who did such things were and still are known as "Shabbos Goys."

Albert and Rose Benn stand outside the grocery store he operated for half a century in Lancaster, Pa.

My other grandfather, Albert Benn, owned a corner grocery store on Laurel Street up on "The Hill," as it was known—far from our poor neighborhood. He, too, was an Orthodox Jew, but not quite as observant as Zadie Solsky. Zadie Benn couldn't read or write very well, either, but his mind was a calculator at a time when no one knew what that was. After taking down the orders, he'd reach into his meat cooler and begin slicing chunks of ham or pick out some choice pork chops for his gentile customers. All of it was *traif* which is Yiddish for forbidden foods. It didn't bother Zadie Benn a bit. Selling that stuff helped provide for his family. He could add and subtract long columns of orders from customers in seconds. He also took mental notes on his inventory and I learned one day just how accurate he was in that department, too.

As a kid, I used to sell soft pretzels. I'd go to a bakery even higher up on "The Hill" with my mother's wicker basket—the one she used when she went grocery shopping. I'd get 200 hot, salty soft pretzels right out of the oven, cover them with a cotton dish cloth and head into town about a mile away to sell what I could. Along the way, I'd sing "Soft pretzeeeelssss, get'em while they're hot...two cents a piece or three for a nickel." Today, you can't get one that size for less than $1. My route would take me through downtown Lancaster. I had it all mapped out. I'd go up to the top floors of department stores where seamstresses altered clothes. They seemed to like me and would buy some pretzels from their chubby little salesboy. Some of my best customers were in saloons. A hot, salty pretzel tasted great with a glass of ice cold beer, or so they told me. "Hey, kid, bring me a couple of them hot pretzels," they'd yell at me. My route would end at the Armstrong Cork plant just down the street from our house on New Holland Avenue where we had moved from the 7th Ward. I knew when the shift ended and made sure I'd be there when they got out because it was during the lunch hour. Whatever was left over didn't do me any good. After a couple of hours, soft pretzels aren't very soft, but they do make great door stops.

One week during the summer, I stayed at my Zadie Benn's house. It was a lot closer to the pretzel factory. Each morning that week, as I headed out the front door, I picked up a small bag of Sunshine cheese crackers. "Zadie won't mind," I'd say to myself. Five days later, he let me in on something about missing merchandise and the importance of taking inventory. "Alvie," he said on the fifth afternoon. "Vy you take cheese crackers?" "Cheese crackers, zadie?" I responded in my most innocent voice. "That's right," he said, in his thick accent. "You took ze crackers, but I'm not going to make you pay. I hope you learn lesson."

The crackers cost a nickel—the price of three pretzels. He had taught me a valuable lesson. He was quite a man, my Zadie Benn. As I grew older, I'd hear stories about the kind of discipline he had imposed on his four sons—Meryl, Dutch, Leonard and Harold. A thick razor strop—the kind barbers use to sharpen their shaving instruments—hung from a nail in the grocery store which was the front portion of the Benn house. I was told of the times my Zadie Benn had used the strap on his sons—providing lessons far removed from nickel bags of cheese crackers. He never used that belt on his grandsons and, for that, I would be forever grateful.

Zadie Benn shared Zadie Solsky's compassion for the poor. He helped keep many of his customers alive during the Depression of the 1930s—delivering food to people he knew couldn't pay. Some eventually paid him back. Some didn't. But, he didn't seem to mind. He and Zadie Solsky believed in helping others if the opportunity presented itself. Zadie Benn became a celebrity one day when a young man walked into his grocery store, pulled out a gun and demanded money. My grandfather, who was in his 70s at the time, calmly reached into the long glass meat display case and pulled out a butcher knife. Holding it up, he told the would-be robber: "Young man, in old country, I vas knife thrower in ze circus. If you don't drop gun, I vil split your skull vit dis." Zadie held the knife over the frightened kid as he called the police. A reporter and photographer from the *Lancaster New Era* rushed to the store to do a story about an old grocer who had turned the tables on a hood with a gun. Zadie Benn waved them off. "He vas just sick young man," he told them. "No story. No story."

Alvin, right, and brother, Barry, in 1943.

I wasn't the only one in my family who sold soft pretzels. My brother, Barry, tried his hand at it once and even came up with an idea to make money without having to walk long distances. During the summer, if we sold all our pretzels every day, we'd make about $10 a week. Barry's idea was to set up a "stand" in front of one of the downtown stores.

"Alvie, if we sell from a stand, we won't have to walk so far and people will buy from us as they go by," he said. "Are you sure?" I asked him. "Right," he said. "It can't miss."

Being his younger brother by four years, I wasn't about to argue. And, it did seem like a pretty good idea at the time. We went to the owner of a store near Watt & Shand, the biggest department store in downtown Lancaster, and he gave us permission to sell from a stand outside. He said he'd allow us to do it on a "trial" basis. Well, we figured, nothing ventured, nothing gained. An hour later, we realized we were going broke as fast as the pretzels were getting hard. Time was running out. After another hour, we hadn't sold many more and came to the conclusion that the "Benn Brothers Pretzel Emporium" had been a miserable failure on its opening day.

"Well, let's go to a movie, Alvie," Barry told me. "We're not doing any good here." We packed up our pretzels, covered them in our wicker baskets and dejectedly headed for the Colonial Theater where "It Happens Every Spring" was playing. It was a baseball movie starring Ray Milland when he was still young and handsome and few knew he was wearing a toupee. It was in the late 1940s and the theater was not air-conditioned, but we didn't seem to mind because we were exhausted. Tickets only cost a dime and, after paying, we walked into the darkened theater, found seats and began to watch the movie about a college professor who had accidentally discovered a liquid that makes baseballs avoid wood—as in bats. That made the pitcher holding the ball almost unbeatable.

Halfway through the movie, Barry turned to me and said, "Alvie, how about a pretzel?" "Sure, Barry," I told him, "they're two cents a piece or three for a nickel." We arrived back home with two wicker baskets filled with door stops shaped like pretzels. It had been a disastrous afternoon, but we learned something—don't extend yourself when you don't have anything from which to extend. When I stopped selling pretzels, I didn't wait around very long and soon began delivering the *Lancaster New Era* after school in the afternoons. As I wrapped each paper at the bundle drop, I'd read the headlines and stories—marveling at how the writers put words together. That's how I fell in love with journalism and the *New Era*. My mother wasn't very happy when I got home during the summer because the sleeves of my white T-shirts usually were lined with ugly black marks from where I had wiped my sweaty, ink-stained face as I delivered the papers.

I got into my share of fights as I grew up or tried to grow up. I won some, I lost some. A black eye here, a few bruises there and an occasional bloody lip. It was all part of my maturation process. I think that I had picked up my father's fighting genes. He didn't care how big the other guy was. He'd go after him if he felt he had been offended. From what I learned, my father felt he had been offended a lot as he grew up. I once was told of an incident in which he belted one of his teachers, knocking him over a desk in his classroom. An older boy at our Hebrew School liked to pick on us. He seemed to enjoy being a bully. One day after class, my friend Roger and I walked outside to find him standing there, waiting for us. He didn't look happy. The next thing I remember, I closed my eyes and came around with a solid left hook before the bully could swing first. He went sprawling. My friend and I looked down on the ground to see him rubbing his chin. He seemed as surprised as I was. We didn't wait around to take any bows. Both of us headed for a quieter location.

At Edward Hand Junior High, fights were held in a wooded area behind the school. In those days, we settled scores with our fists. Today, guns, knives and bombs seem to be the preferred weapons. It didn't take much to precipitate a post-school fight. In fact, it got to the point where a fight card could have been put together. Word spread during the day about who would be fighting whom in the woods. The fights usually only lasted a few minutes and, at the end, the two combatants would shake hands. There'd be a bloody nose or lip, but never anything too serious. I got into one or two myself.

Although we didn't have much money in the 7th Ward, we managed to survive somehow—as did our neighbors. It didn't take much to entertain us. We had a small radio and would gather around it as people do today with their television sets and personal computers at home. Barry and I would lie in front of the radio and listen to the adventures of the Lone Ranger, Archie Andrews, Henry Aldrich and Superman. On Saturdays, we got a special treat—the movies. My mother would give us each 25 cents which got us into the Hamilton Theater and bought us a box of candy, a bag of popcorn and a soft drink. We'd enter the theater at 10 a.m. and leave about 6 p.m. after having seen everything twice.

We'd see a double feature of our favorite cowboy stars, usually Johnny Mack Brown, Roy Rogers, Gene Autry or Lash LaRue. Also on the bill were previews of coming attractions, lots of Bugs Bunny cartoons, the Pathe weekly news, Three Stooges comedy shorts and much more. At times, Filipino yo-yo experts would give live shows on the stage. They'd show us their latest yo-yo moves and then, for a dime, carve our initials or palm trees on the side of the little wooden stringy things. We didn't know it, of course, but those long Saturdays at the Hamilton proved to be a cheap babysitting service for harried mothers. It was the same all over the country in the 1940s.

I knew we were poor, but never realized just how poor, I guess, until the day my mother plopped me into her wash bucket, filled it with water and put me out in our "yard" which was a tiny concrete slab that divided us from our neighbor's house. One day, as I sat there, a black woman walked by and glanced over at me. I think I was about five at the time. She just shook her head and kept walking. It hit me that we must have really been poor for a black person to pity me. The 7th Ward was predominantly black, but just about all of the families were in the same financial boat. We were probably the poorest white family in the area. My best friend was Chuckie Simms, a black kid who lived two blocks away. Joey Jackson lived next door to us. He would join the Marine Corps many years later and lose his life in combat in Vietnam.

We moved "up" and out of the 7th Ward to a house on New Holland Avenue when I was eight. It was across from a cemetery. Our house was in a long row of attached dwellings where you could hear conversations, screaming and noise from television sets on both sides of the walls. We were a lot farther away from our synagogue than when we lived on South Christian Street, but we continued to walk there because, as Orthodox Jews, we were prohibited from doing much of anything on the Sabbath other than attending services. That meant walking more than two miles each way every Saturday morning.

Benn siblings, from left: Alvin, Barry, Eileen and Steve.

I don't remember much about my Bar Mitzvah except rushing through it as fast as I could. Those of us in our Hebrew School class had studied our biblical passage for what seemed like years. We were expected to memorize all of it. The rabbi knew our fathers and grandfathers would be in the sanctuary and would be following every word. They knew Hebrew as well as he did and, during services, it wasn't unusual for somebody in the congregation to "correct" him if he mispronounced a word. Imagine, then, the horror I must have felt as I mounted three carpeted steps to where the rabbi awaited me that Saturday morning in April of 1953. It was as though I was heading up the scaffold to await the placement of a rope around my neck. Somehow, I managed to get through it without embarrassing my family. I even gave a speech.

We eventually moved to Edgemore Court in the Manheim Township district of Lancaster. We had really progressed by that point. The reason was our Zadie Solsky. In his will, he left us the house on New Holland Avenue. My father then sold it to move to the house in Manheim Township. We couldn't have afforded either one and most likely would have continued living on South Christian Street forever.

Our house was semi-detached—meaning only one other house was connected to ours—not 20 or more. Barry and I lived in the attic which had been converted into a bedroom by the previous owner. It served as an insulator for the rest of the house. We kept everybody warm in the winter because we absorbed all the cold air in our "bedroom." It was the same during the summer, only worse. I don't know how hot it got up there, but I do know how unpleasant it was for the two of us in that sweltering little attic.

I made a lot of new friends at Manheim Township High School. It was out in the little farming community of Neffsville and had an all-white enrollment—quite a departure from "The Ward." There aren't many black farmers in Pennsylvania Dutch country. Our school had wood floors, demanding teachers and plenty of scholars who went on to fame, if not fortune, in academia. I, of course, wasn't one of them. Latin was a prerequisite for those going on to college. Advanced mathematics, physics, chemistry and other tough courses also were required. I struggled through and took part in many of the extracurricular activities including football, baseball and theater. In the end, enrolling in typing class would be the best decision I ever made in high school.

If ever there was an All-American boy, it was John Eshleman, who lived a few blocks away from us on Pleasure Road. Butch, as he was known, excelled in everything. He was first in our class both academically and athletically. He was a star in baseball, football, basketball and track. He played the piano, was a soloist in the choir and had the leads in most of our plays. I remember the day he played baseball and competed in a track meet at almost the same time. He finished his track events, rushed to the locker room, changed into his baseball uniform and hustled to the ballpark to take his position at first base within a few minutes. Butch went on to become a doctor and, not surprisingly, served his country with distinction as a flight surgeon who saved lives in the jungles of Vietnam.

Jim Graham, Dick Saylor and Henry Brubaker also were good friends. Jim was the first classmate to greet me when I walked into my homeroom at Manheim Township High School. He was another super student, an outstanding wrestler and a performer who sang "Everything's Up To Date In Kansas City" in our production of "Oklahoma." Butch had the lead, of course, playing Curly. Jim's parents were deaf mutes who were daily reminders of perseverance for him. His mathematical prowess led him to a career as an engineer and he eventually moved to Arizona where he worked for a Fortune 500 company. Dick became a machinist with New Holland, one of the nation's top farm implement companies, and wound up in the Midwest.

Henry's father was an editor at one of Lancaster's two newspapers. I got my first taste of journalistic "power" one night when our basketball team had a road game against Columbia High School. Both teams were excellent and the showdown had been the talk of Lancaster County. The problem was getting tickets. There just weren't any, or so it seemed. "Don't worry," said Henry, who would get his doctorate and carve out a great career with the U.S. Environmental Protection Agency. "My dad will get us in." That's what Mr. Brubaker did. They weren't exactly courtside seats, though. We wound up literally in the rafters of the gymnasium and had to crane our necks to get a look at the action on the basketball court far below. As far as I was concerned, the venue couldn't have been better. They were, to us, ringside seats at Madison Square Garden for a heavyweight championship fight. I couldn't get over Mr. Brubaker's influence. It got me thinking about journalism as a possible career. All I needed to do was learn how to write. My first efforts were horrible attempts at descriptive narratives—covering athletic events and trying to find a ways to add heroic endings for the home team.

It had been a long way from the slums of the 7th Ward to Manheim Township. Our family's financial fortunes had improved but, by my senior year, I had no idea what I wanted to do with my life. Little did I know how many twists and turns waited around the corner. Unlike my parents, who remained in Lancaster and only occasionally ventured away to visit relatives in the Washington, D.C. area, I would soon find myself on a long and winding road. I'd spend time in a strange land halfway around the world and then travel through the South as a journalist— exceeding my wildest dreams of one day becoming a reporter who wrote about famous people. Some would call me by my first name. I even learned to cut back on those corny heroic endings most of the time.

CHAPTER FOUR:

USMC

I wasn't admitted to Millersville State Teachers College in 1958. I've never found out why, but can only surmise it's because the person who graded my entrance examination got a headache after looking at so many wrong answers. I've never been particularly proficient at tests, but did manage to graduate from Manheim Township High School. I even got A's and B's in English, French, algebra and other academic courses.

Money for college would have been a major problem for me since I didn't have any. So, I turned my attention to the military and decided to join the Air Force. In high school, I had wanted to become a navigator on a B-52, but was told to take physics first to see if I could handle the required math. Well, it took me. The only thing I still remember is 32 feet a second. That's the rate of a falling object. That's how fast my grades fell. James Livengood, my science teacher, suggested I consider some other line of work as in lion taming. I quickly changed courses and forgot about a potential career as an officer on a jet bomber. Instead, I took a test to join the Air Force as an enlisted man. Surprise, surprise... I scored in the 99 percentile group. How I could have screwed up on my college admission test and done so well on another still mystifies me. That out of the way, I concentrated on having some fun during that summer. I worked at my uncle Stanley Friedman's aluminum storm window factory to make a few bucks. At night, I played softball.

One miserably hot summer afternoon, I decided to see my Air Force recruiter about details of basic training in Texas. The Post Office wasn't air conditioned, making it even more uncomfortable as I climbed the steps to where the military recruiters had their offices. My recruiter wasn't in, so I walked across the hall to where the Navy recruiter was located to see if he had gone over there. He had and it changed my decision about which branch of the military I wanted to join. There he was, sitting at a card table, playing poker, with his Army and Navy recruiter buddies. They were in their sweaty undershirts. The room was filled with cigarette smoke, compounding an already sticky atmosphere. I couldn't blame them for not wanting to recruit anybody that day, but it just didn't seem very military to me.

I wondered why the Marine recruiter wasn't with them and went across the hall to see if he was in his office. He was and it was a sight to behold. A big, bulky man with close-cropped hair sat behind his desk in the Corps' famous dress blue uniform—his leatherneck collar buttoned to just under his chin. Sweat poured down his cheeks and dripped from the tip of his nose onto the desk in front of him. He was working on some forms when he looked up to see me gawking at him from just outside the door. He raised his right hand and pointed his right index finger at me. Then, with a grunt, he moved it toward him with a "Come here, boy" order. I was hooked. A few minutes later, I had forgotten all about the Air Force and was busy asking questions about the Marine Corps, boot camp and my future, if any.

"What can the Marines promise me?" I asked the recruiter, a gunnery sergeant who looked like he could have gone a few rounds with Rocky Marciano. "Anything special?" In order to meet enlistment quotas, Marine recruiters often offer special incentives. Some offer technical training. Others offer assignments as embassy guards in Paris, Madrid or other exotic locations around the world. When I asked my Marine recruiter what the Corps could offer me, he stared as me as if I had been asking for samples from Fort Knox. "Three months of pure hell at Parris Island, boy," he told me. "That's all we offer. That's all you'll get. If you are good enough to get through boot camp, you can ask for something." Before I realized it, I blurted out: "I'll take it."

Life on the home front wasn't very good at that time and all I knew was I needed to get away from my father. I had heard how tough it was at the Marine Corps' recruit training depot at Parris Island, S.C. and wanted to find out if I could take it. If I could survive my father's brutality most of my life, I figured I could get through Parris Island in three months. I had dislocated my left shoulder playing high school football and fractured my left ankle sliding into second base on the baseball team, but I kept going back for more. I guess I was just a glutton for punishment. I don't know what made me want to go back to those teams, but I did. I was 18 and didn't need parental consent to sign enlistment papers. I think my father would gladly have signed them to get rid of me. My mother wasn't keen on the idea. She had heard about the Marine Corps.

I enlisted with a group of guys in Philadelphia on Aug. 5, 1958. We raised our hands, pledged to support and protect and headed south on a train the next day. When we boarded, we joined a group of recruits from the Buffalo, N.Y. area. Among them was a guy who bragged most of the way south about how he was going to show the Corps a thing or two. He said it would be a piece of cake for him. Midway in our trip, a recruit returning to Parris Island from emergency leave began telling us horror stories about boot camp. The big mouth from Buffalo suddenly became quiet. We didn't hear much from him after that. Our train broke down about 100 miles from Parris Island. It was hot and muggy and we went outside to sit on the tracks while the repair work began. A couple of hours later, we reboarded and continued our journey. We got off at Beaufort, S.C. and boarded buses for the short trip to the island. Most of us had fallen asleep shortly after we slumped into our seats.

"Out, out, out, you maggots," screamed the drill instructors just after our bus stopped. "Be quick about it. No talking."

One of the DIs was rolling a short, thick piece of wood around inside a large metal can. I would learn later it was called a swagger stick and often was used by drill instructors. They swaggered a lot, so I guess that's where the name came from. On this occasion, his intent was to get us fully awake so we could truly appreciate what lay ahead. It was 5 a.m. at the time. During the days that followed, we went through processing which included the shaving of our heads, issuance of recruit clothing and constant screaming at us by men who seemed to enjoy it.

In 1958, the Marine Corps didn't employ the niceties associated with recruit training today. We were the scum of the earth in the eyes of those assigned to train us. It appeared their main goal was to weed out as many weaklings as they could as fast as they could. I don't know how I survived. It could have been something deep inside me that kept me from quitting when things got tough.

The first week of Marine boot camp generally is known as "Hell Week," "Shock Week" and "Why in the World Did I Do This Week?" Our individuality was taken from us. We were part of a team and we didn't open our mouths without first shouting "Sir, yes sir" or "sir, no sir." Our DI's mouth usually was positioned about an inch from ours and he frequently spoke in such a way as to provide a spray—along with an elbow to the gut now and then. Our first day was highlighted by a locker box sprint. Each of us got a large wooden box which would be used to store our stuff. We were several hundred yards from our Quonset hut, but it seemed like several miles as we huffed and puffed our way toward it—carrying the big box in front of us—trying to stay in step with the DI's cadence.

Our first Sunday on Parris Island offered a brief respite from the pressurized grind of that tough initiation week. We lost a couple of guys along the way. One freaked out. He just couldn't stand it. I guess it would have been easy for a bunch of us to do the same thing. One reason for Marine boot camp is to see who might fold under pressure in battle. I came to appreciate my recruiter's words that first week. I didn't enjoy them, but I understood what he meant. The Corps didn't really need anybody who might quit when the going got tough. Our DI lined us up outside our huts which were nothing more than inverted metal frying pans. They attracted the intense heat of South Carolina summers, making it miserable for anybody inside. They had been used to house recruits during World War II and the Corps didn't seem in any great hurry to spend money on new barracks.

We were going to church that Sunday morning. It was a Protestant service and I sat up high with the rest of the platoon, listening to the minister's sermon and wondering what my rabbi would think of it. In my mind, I was the only Jewish recruit at Parris Island and figured that's the way it would be for me during boot camp. The next Sunday, as we lined up once again to go to church services, our DI said quietly "It has come to my attention that we have a member of the Jewish faith in our platoon. Will he please step out?" I guess I was still in shock from the first week and didn't hear him. He repeated his order when he didn't get a response, but it was somewhat more demanding, as in "We have a Jew in our platoon. Step out." I still didn't hear him. Then, he really cut loose. "We've got a %$&%&&$#$(*!@ Jew in the platoon," he shouted. "Get your ass out here." That's when I heard him and stepped out of formation. He came over to me, stuck his face into mine and sprayed "You idiot. Don't you know Jews don't go to Christian services? Get over there with the rest of the freaks." That's when I found out I was one of 18 Jewish recruits at Parris Island. There were thousands of Christian recruits, including many who had found religion after their first week. The way I looked at it, nice Jewish boys didn't join the Marine Corps. They went to college to become scientists, writers and labor leaders. Of course, most nice Jewish boys are intelligent. That's why I was at Parris Island.

We were allowed to go to Jewish services once a week. They were conducted by an old rabbi from Poland who lived nearby and picked up a few dollars on the side ministering to frightened Marine recruits. I was one of three Orthodox Jews and we had to explain to a DI one week that we were required to keep our heads covered during services. In the Marine Corps, covers—the Corps' word for hat—are removed inside, unless someone is wearing a sidearm. It took some explaining and a lot of courage since recruits don't speak to sergeants without bowing and scraping. He seemed to understand after we bowed and scraped. The best time at boot camp came during our High Holy Day period in September. We not only got to go off-base to a nearby synagogue, we also were allowed to drink as much wine as we wanted. When I got back to my Quonset hut after one service, I was a bit tipsy and not ashamed to admit it. One guy in my platoon said he was thinking of converting.

About two weeks after my arrival, I was assigned to "Fat Man's Platoon." It was somewhat of a shock and disappointment because, having played on my high school football team the previous fall and softball during the summer, I was in decent shape and could have cranked out the 25 pushups, 50 sit-ups and completed the other physical requirements. I think they just took a look at my weight and decided I was a candidate for FMP which was one of four platoons in a special battalion for questionable recruits. The others were "Skinny Man's Platoon" for underweight recruits, "Hospital Platoon" for those recovering from injuries and "Motivation Platoon" which was, by far, the worst because those recruits insisted on keeping their individualities. They were getting one last chance to show some willingness to be part of a team. Each platoon had a red flag that included the number of the unit and was carried everywhere on base. Our flag had an elephant on it.

If our first few days at Parris Island were rough, our introduction to "Fat Man's Platoon" was even tougher. We were treated as subspecies. Our DIs were the best conditioned men on the island. They'd berate us at every opportunity, calling us "fat slobs" and "ugly, overweight excuses for men." They vowed to shape us up or ship us out. They succeeded several times. At 198 pounds, I was the lightest member of "Fat Man's Platoon." We had one guy who weighed more than 300 pounds. That poor soul was a lawyer from New York who had signed up for the Marine Corps' Reserve program, but had to undergo six months of active duty, including boot camp. He spent most of it at Parris Island and in Fat Man's Platoon. He was in agony for the 11 days I spent there.

Our daily caloric intake would have delighted an anorexic. We were allowed 1,000 calories...not one calorie more than that. Our staple was warm skim milk, served up in a huge metal bowl. We "ate" in the mess hall with the other recruits and could only stare in despair as they gobbled down thousands of calories at each meal—savoring pasta, ice cream, cake and other delicacies. Our stomachs never seemed to stop growling. In addition to being in Fat Man's Platoon, we were frequently put on display for visiting brass to show them just how serious the Corps was about shaping up its recruits. Early one morning, about 3 a.m., we were awakened by DIs pounding on those big trash cans and told to stand at attention. Then, we were marched to the workout room where we were ordered to lift weights and do sit-ups for retired Army Gen. Mark Clark, a World War II hero who must have wondered why they let us in the Marine Corps in the first place. We wondered why he was there at 3 a.m. to watch a bunch of fat guys lifting weights.

Our DIs seemed to enjoy putting us through hell each day and tried hard to vary their method of physical and mental torture. One day, when the temperature and humidity raced to see which would hit 100 first, a DI told us we would be allowed to go swimming. That seemed odd because somebody in our platoon (not me) had screwed up that morning and the last thing any of us expected was a "reward." The DI did add one caveat. We'd have to duck walk to the pool. Duck walking means squatting and pushing one leg in front of the other while quacking all the way. It is very hard to do over distances of more than five or six feet. Somehow, we all managed to get to the pool which was about a quarter of a mile away, but seemed like a marathoner's distance. "OK, maggots," shouted the DI, "into the pool." We didn't need a second command. Into the pool we went, splashing happily for about 10 seconds. "OK maggots," the DI shouted, "out of the pool." We got out and duck walked back from where we came. The DI smirked all the way, too.

"Fat Man's Platoon" was also my introduction to firearms. I had shot a round or two at carnivals, but had never really fired a rifle with deadly intentions. My brother and I would play cowboys and Indians when we were kids, but there weren't any real weapons—other than our father—around the house. We were given M-1 rifles which, at that time, was the basic weapon of Marine infantrymen. I proudly held my M-1 in front of me as our DI walked by to inspect. I didn't know what a rifle inspection entailed, but would soon learn.

"Maggot," the DI shouted, looking down into my weapon, "what the hell is that clogged in your bolt?" I responded "In my what, sir?" That put him into orbit. "The bolt, you idiot," he screamed. "Look at that little thing and what's in it." That's when I peered down into my rifle and saw a recessed piece of metal that was supposed to be clean. Instead, it was filled with what appeared to be a tiny clump of dirt and part of a dead sand flea. I would soon learn the importance of keeping the bolt and every other part of my rifle as clean as humanly possible. I also learned to field strip my M-1 blindfolded. I could take it apart in seconds and reassemble it just as fast. It was quite an accomplishment for somebody who was becoming proud to be a Marine-in-waiting—also referred to by DIs as a "maggot."

As the first week ended at "Fat Man's Platoon," I didn't feel any thinner, but got the scare of my life. One of my DIs, upset at a minor indiscretion such as breathing near him, ordered me to go to the window in his second story office. He told me to open it and then look down. "What do you see, maggot?" the DI asked. "The ground," I shouted, adding: "and it's a long way down, sir." "Good, jump," he said. "Jump!" I responded, as my pulse began to quicken. "Are you questioning my order, maggot?" the DI said. With that, he and another DI walked over, grabbed me and proceeded to hang me out the window. They held me by my ankles as I stared in horror at the pavement below. "Don't worry, private," one of them said, "we'll just say you were washing the windows and fell out. It happened that way last week." It seemed like hours before they hauled me back inside. They must have gotten quite a kick out of almost stopping my heart before the pavement did.

As the days dragged on, I kept watching one of my fellow recruits melt into total hopelessness. It was the braggart from Buffalo who had boasted that he'd show the Marine Corps a thing or two once he got to Parris Island. He, too, had wound up at Fat Man's Platoon and was having a tough time surviving. "Well, maggot, what did you eat for lunch today?" one of the DIs asked him. "Well, sir, I had some skim milk and a very thin piece of beef," said the recruit. "It was lovely, too." He had been in a state of shock from the day he was assigned to FMP and I never did find out what happened to him. On my 11th day, I was reassigned to a regular platoon to continue my basic training. I had lost 11 pounds—a pound a day.

Our regular platoon had four DIs who alternated between "Good Cop, Bad Cop" throughout our training period. Actually, one of them played "Bad Cop" all the way through. We never did know his first name. All we knew was his initial—"S". I guess the "S" stood for sadist. He loved to play the role, a real bad ass. Once, during calisthenics, a guy behind me didn't like the way I was doing side straddle hops and he popped me. I turned out to pop him back when "S" interrupted our fun and games and called me into his office. "Pvt. Benn," he said, "what am I going to do with you?" Before he got the "you" completely out, he hit me in the stomach with a left hook that knocked the wind out of me. It took a few seconds to regain my composure. Drill instructors can't get away with something like that today. They're not even allowed to spit into a recruit's face. Good grief! What's my Corps coming to?

When we weren't running, jumping and trying to avoid left hooks from angry DIs, we learned all about the nomenclature of the M-I rifle. A Marine's rifle is his best friend, or that's what they told us. That's why we spent so much time with it during boot camp. We rubbed the wood stocks to a high gloss on the outside, rammed a rod through the metal barrel on the inside and provided plenty of tender, loving care throughout our weeks on the island. We were told to memorize our rifle numbers in case we lost our weapon. I still remember it today. I couldn't always remember my Social Security number and it took retirement to help me memorize it. The reason for the rifle adulation was our commanding officer's insistence that every recruit be able to fire his M-I with accuracy. That meant firing at least a 190 on qualification day. A perfect score was 250. Platoon leaders and DIs were judged on how well their recruits did on qualifying day. A Marine who couldn't shoot straight is considered worthless. We each got to fire 50 rounds from five different positions including standing, sitting and kneeling. A bulls-eye was five points—thus a perfect score meant 50 bulls-eyes. Rarely, is that ever done. It's like bowling a 300 game or batting .400 or better.

Practice sessions were called "snapping in" exercises. We didn't have any live ammunition—only DIs screaming at us about how our positions looked. It had been a couple of years since the surgery to repair my dislocated left shoulder, but it still gave me trouble from time to time. When I twisted my body into some of the firing positions, it felt as though the ball was about to pop out of the socket, again. Fortunately for me, it stayed in place and I actually qualified as a Marine marksman on our big day at the rifle range. For someone who had never fired a real weapon before, much less held one, it was quite an accomplishment.

When we weren't learning how to shoot a rifle, we were being taught how to use it to kill in a different way—with a bayonet. We were taught during a drill using what looked like ax handles with thick pads on each end. They were called pugil sticks and we used them to batter ourselves silly. We wore football helmets with face bars, but we could still feel the pain when we got hit. Occasionally, one end would work its way into the helmet and find a nose or teeth. During one drill, I was matched up with a recruit my size and we went at it with gusto. I got in a lucky thrust and popped him good. Somehow, part of the padded end penetrated the face mask and smacked him in the nose—drawing blood.

"Sorry about that," I said as both of us stopped in the middle of what we were doing. "What did you just say, maggot?" our DI screamed at me. "Did you just apologize for killing him? Do you think the enemy will apologize after he kills you? Get your ass over there and give me

20." He had a point. In combat, you don't apologize for killing your enemy. Chances are you'll wind up being killed by his buddy. It was a lesson well worth the 20 pushups he ordered me to do.

Recruits don't have mothers, fathers or wives, our DIs told us. "If the Marine Corps wanted you to have a wife, it would have issued you one," we were told over and over. Getting goodies from home was tantamount to taunting a DI. One day, a recruit got a big box of chocolate chip cookies from his mommy. Our DI assembled us all in front of our hut and told the hungry recruit to step out. "Maggot," he said, "You have just gotten a box of cookies from home and will be allowed to eat them all by yourself." The poor guy was then given a canteen of warm water and told to eat every one of the two dozen cookies in the box. By the time he finished the last one, he was ready to regurgitate everything but the cardboard. From that day on, nobody got anything resembling nice things from home.

I completed boot camp in November. It was a proud day, indeed, as members of Platoon 328 marched by the reviewing stand to the strains of the Marine Corps Hymn. For the first time, our DIs addressed us as "Marines." We had earned it. Our platoon didn't have the same number we started with. The attrition rate at Parris Island can be pretty high at times. After the ceremony, we all hopped onto a bus for a ride to Camp LeJeune in North Carolina for detailed instruction in the art of war and killing people which is what war is all about. It was known as the Infantry Training Regiment and I wound up in what we dubbed Bivouac B—a company that seemed to stay in the woods every day.

One night, we took our seats in bleachers to watch a display of military might. In front of us was a long barbed wire fence. About 500 yards downwind was a large wooded area where "enemy" troops supposedly were preparing to "attack" our position. "Men, we're going to show you just how impossible it will be for the enemy to get through to our lines," said an officer. "We're going to have a progressive firing demonstration for you." What he meant by that was a progressive display of firepower—from the smallest caliber to the big boomers. Tracers gave us an idea of just how many rounds were being fired at the "enemy" five football fields away. Within a minute or two, the sky was lined with bright lights of all calibers as well as loud bangs from rifles, machineguns, mortars, artillery shells and anything else that was available.

After the last round was fired and the smoke had cleared, the pleased officer smiled and asked if there were any questions. A hand shot up in the bleachers and a guy who apparently never got the word that privates are supposed to be seen and not heard, said: "Sir, what happens if we're the ones down there at that fence?" "You're Marines," the officers shot back. "You'll get through." The officer didn't say how many might get through, but, it seemed to me that making it from one end of that long field to the other would be something akin to Pickett's fatal charge. Few of Pickett's men got through that bloody Gettysburg field alive. The private wasn't heard from again that long night.

We had other late night indoctrinations in the wonderful world of ground-pounding. Once, we were put out in a swamp with nothing but compasses and time to get back to base. That was fun—up to our waists in muddy water at times as we tried to figure out where we were. Somehow, we always managed to get back. Our worst experience came on a chilly daytime exercise that turned into a nightmare. We didn't have any jackets or other cold-weather gear and, as the sun began to set, it got colder and colder. We were convinced they'd take us back to base to get some hot chow. Instead, our company commander lined us all up in formation for some last minute instructions. It was getting colder by the minute. We later learned it was the coldest night in North Carolina history at that time. We climbed into our sleeping bags about 10 p.m. Three hours later, I heard a gentle rap-tap-tapping. I unzipped my bag and saw snow flakes accumulating around us. I got out, went over to a tree where I had leaned my M-I and then brought it back inside my sleeping bag to keep it warm. Early the next morning, we were awakened to start a day we were convinced would be spent back at base. I looked over to the tree where my rifle had been the night before and saw four more that hadn't been retrieved by other guys in my platoon. They had turned into icicles.

When we were lined up in formation once again, our company commander informed our platoon leaders to "get rations for three meals." That meant staying in the field for another day in sub-freezing weather without coats, gloves or anything else to keep us warm. Some of the guys began to fall out. Within a few minutes, jeeps were heading into our area to pick them up. They had become ambulances. I wouldn't have minded being in one. A few minutes after formation, we were told to "police" the area, which meant cleaning up any trash we could find. Somebody finally decided to get us back to base. It's a good thing we were told to look around because we found four guys sleeping about 200 yards away from our main unit. If we hadn't found them, they likely would have frozen to death. On our way back to base on buses, we took turns trying to get our circulation back—rubbing our hands, arms, legs and each other to get the blood flowing again. Several weeks later, when I got home on leave, I went to a podiatrist who said I had a slight case of frostbite.

One of our instructors was a Korean War veteran who specialized in reconnaissance missions behind enemy lines. His weapon of choice was a stiletto—a slender dagger-shaped knife with a killer of a blade. He had long, hairy arms and liked to rub the blade up and down them, showing how easily the hair came off. He wanted us to know how sharp the blade was. We only had one "class" with him, but it was unforgettable. "See that tree over there?" he asked us, without waiting for an answer. "Well, I can hit it five out of five with this thing." The tree was several yards away and not very thick, so we waited to see if he could back up his words. He did. He held the knife by the blade and, with a quick twist of his wrist, sent it flying. Each time it dug into the wood. He'd retrieve it, head back to where he was before and do it again—five times in all. When he was finished, he had a smile on his face that didn't need interpretation. We knew that when he went behind enemy lines in Korea, he didn't toss that stiletto at trees.

For some reason, I couldn't handle field food which usually consisted of tuna or pasta packed tightly into small brown cans. I just couldn't keep it down. The result was even more weight loss than at Parris Island. By the time I got back home in mid-December of 1958, my weight had dropped to 165 pounds—33 under what it was when I arrived. I also had a deep tan from being out in the sun all day. It had been several months since early August, but the tan remained. My classmates at Manheim Township marveled at how good I looked. So did I. When I finished boot camp, I was given a military occupational specialty—known as an MOS. Mine was air freight. Each Marine remains a Marine—that means being a grunt if duty calls. Until that time, we have a variety of job assignments ranging from blowing a tuba in a band to loading boxes onto cargo planes.

I arrived at Cherry Point, N.C. in early January 1959 and headed for my squadron at the Second Marine Air Wing. It seemed even colder than that day in the field at Camp LeJeune. The temperature was about 20 degrees and the wind was whipping across the flight line. It was before wind chill factors were used. It had to be well below zero. During my processing, I noticed a few empty desks. One of the clerks looked up and followed my eyes. He asked me if I knew how to type. In addition to academic courses in high school, I also decided to take typing just in case I needed a backup. It would prove to be one of the smartest decisions I ever made. "Yes," I told him. "I know how to type." "Well," the corporal responded. "You now have a choice. You can take a desk or go out to the flight line and start loading freight." "Where's my desk?" I asked.

I often wonder what would have happened if I had reported during the spring or summer. It's likely I would have started my original MOS duties. I'll never know if I would have made a good air freight Marine. My job as a clerk typist involved maintaining personnel files, preparing letters for our officers and handling any other duties that came along. It became boring after a few weeks and that's when I got a chance to resume my first love—writing. In high school, I had written for our newspaper and the yearbook. My writing was horrible and I still keep copies of it to see just how bad it was. I think I've improved somewhat since that time. My Marine Corps writing career began during that first winter when the sports editor of the Cherry Point *Windsock*, the base paper, asked me if I'd be interested in covering some basketball games at night. He was a family man and I wasn't. It was a made-to-order situation for both of us. He got to stay at home with his wife and kids and I got to cover some of the best college basketball players in the country. Most were Marine officers, but they were still college jocks at heart.

One night, I collapsed in my bunk, exhausted from a long day at work and then covering a basketball game. Early in the morning, I awoke in pain. I must have had a bad dream and slammed my left arm on the bunk above me—dislocating my left shoulder. My doctor had told me it was in no danger of popping out of place again. A good friend, Fred Finfrock, took me to sick bay where a young Navy doctor sat behind a desk. He appeared to be interested in getting off duty, not relocating dislocated shoulders of Marine privates. "What's the problem?" he asked. "My left shoulder is out of place," I told him, as I remained in a bent-over position. "The pain's pretty bad." "Lie down over there and I'll be right back," he said, as he pointed to a table covered with a thin mattress. After lying on the table for about 15 minutes, I asked Fred to check on the doctor. The pain was increasing. Fred left, but wasn't gone very long. When he came back, he had an expression that seemed to be a cross between amusement and bewilderment. "You're never going to guess what I saw when I looked in on him," Fred said. "What, what," I said, in agony. "He was reading a book on dislocations," Fred said. "Hell," I responded through the pain, "I can tell him what to do. All he's got to do is ball up his fist, ram it into my left armpit and yank my shoulder down. That'll get it back into place." We were able to convince the "doctor" to put the book down and try the "Benn Method of Repairing Dislocations." He used it and it worked.

During my assignment at Cherry Point, I got to meet a living, breathing, real-life urban legend and experience her special "talents." Lulu was her name. I didn't think she existed. I thought she was a Marine's dream that had spread through the Corps from base to base. I first learned of Lulu on a trip back to base one night. I didn't have a car at the time and it was the practice of many Marines to be driven to the Washington Monument where we'd get picked up by guys heading back to Camp LeJeune and Cherry Point. We'd all chip in $5 or so to help pay for gas. On the way back, one of the guys talked about "Lulu." He said he and a "bunch of Marines" from LeJeune had a "great time" with her one night. On subsequent trips back, other guys would say the same thing. It began to play on my mind. Did Lulu really exist? I didn't think I'd ever be able to "investigate."

I met her one Saturday night in Greenville, N.C. where six of us had gone ostensibly to watch East Carolina College play a football game. For some reason, we decided not to go to the game. Then, one of them said: "Let's go see Lulu." "You've got to be kidding," I told him. "I didn't think she was real." "Oh, she's plenty real," he said. "Once you meet her, you learn that right away." So, off we drove to Lulu's house. She wasn't in, so we parked the car and waited. About half an hour later, a car pulled up in front and a woman got out and went inside the house. We noticed several guys inside the car which soon left. One of the guys in our car got out, went to the front door and knocked. The same woman came out and then got into our vehicle.

Lulu wasn't likely to get a Hollywood screen test—unless it was to play the bride of Frankenstein. During our drive to a secluded spot outside Greenville, she took long swigs from a bottle of Jack Daniels. She also remarked that she once worked in a "circumcision ward" at a military hospital. From the looks of her, it must have been during World War II. She said she had seen more male genitalia than most doctors. We all got a chance to sample Lulu's "wares" that night, providing her with more "inspections." She was most accommodating and when she finished having her way with us, we took her back to her house. She gave each of us a big smile as she got out of the car. I couldn't help but notice that two cars with six guys in each one were waiting outside Lulu's house.

I had just returned to our barracks from covering a basketball game on the night of Oct. 3, 1961 when I saw a chaplain standing in our squad bay. From the look on his face, I knew it wasn't a social call. "I'm sorry to inform you, corporal, that your mother has died," the chaplain said. I was stunned, unable to speak. My mother had never been seriously ill. She gave birth to our brother, Stevie, when she was 40—a relatively advanced age for pregnancies at that time—but she never complained. She always was out helping somebody. She was a volunteer at the local hospital, assisting patients when she wasn't at our synagogue lending a hand. Dorothy Benn died the day her first grandchild was born. She was so excited. She called her friends and made plans to go to Washington, D.C. She wanted to help her daughter-in-law, Donna, take care of the baby. My father found her on the couch in our living room. He had come home from work and couldn't wake her. She must have decided to lie down for a few minutes. Doctors said she had high blood pressure. We didn't know. She never complained, except when we got on her nerves. She was only 50. For someone who was 21 at the time, 50 seemed pretty old. Today, I realize just how young she was when she died. And, it was on Simchas Torah, one of the happiest holidays for Jews. It celebrates receipt of the Torah by the Israelites thousands of years ago. There was deep sadness in Lancaster's Jewish community that day and in the seven days of mourning that followed.

Getting home was a real challenge. Orthodox Jewish funerals are supposed to be held the day after a death. Since I was a long way from Lancaster and couldn't make immediate connections, some allowances were made. I had to take several modes of transportation, but finally arrived by train more than a day later. Some relatives met me at the Lancaster train station and took me home. The last time I had seen my mother, she was sitting on the couch in our living room—crying her eyes out. My father and I had another argument and I had finally decided to leave for good. There had been just too big a wall built up between us through the years. The final straw was discovering that my father had spent hundreds of dollars I sent home to be put into bonds for whatever future awaited me after the Marine Corps. He told me he needed the money and then threw his checkbook at me and told me to go to the bank and see what their balance was. I took him up on it. I went to the bank where I was embarrassed and ashamed. My parents were nearly broke. I wasn't as upset about him using the money as I was in his not asking or telling me he was going to do it. My mother and I communicated by letter after that and I had planned to go up to Washington to see her that fall. Instead, I hurried home to say goodbye one last time.

My father came out of the house to greet me and gave me a big hug. I reciprocated. I knew the pain he must have been in. They say I drank a fifth of bourbon the night I got home. I don't remember. I do recall downing a shot as soon as I got into the house. My uncles seemed surprised that I had put it away without wincing. I wasn't the same "Little Alvie" they once knew. Three years in the Marine Corps had changed me. I remember taking the bottle to a chair, sitting down with it and slowly drinking it as I smoked one cigarette after another and talked with friends who had come by the house. The next thing I knew, I woke up in the morning with a huge hangover. I got a chance to say goodbye to my mother inside a small building at the cemetery. Orthodox Jewish funerals are plain affairs—no fancy coffins or clothes. It's been that way since we became a people....dust to dust. What we leave are memories. Hopefully, they are good ones. My mother's memory is cherished by those who remember her.

Prior to my mother's death, I had begun to do more work for the base newspaper and decided that if I wanted a career in journalism I needed to learn more. That's when I extended my enlistment for three years and went to the Navy School of Journalism in Great Lakes, Ill. Marvin Deaton, one of the senior sergeants who ran the *Windsock*, was my mentor. He encouraged me during that time and suggested that I go to J-School. I can't thank him enough. Capt. Ed Schultze also played a role in my decision to extend my enlistment. I was able to renew my association with them years later—as a friend and not a junior enlisted man. The school was a condensed version of Northwestern University's Medill School of Journalism—a real condensed version. We got the equivalent of four years of study in four months. It was a whirlwind experience, but we still found time to have fun in nearby Chicago. I also found out that Illinois and Wisconsin have the world's best assortment of locally produced beer.

I graduated in the top section of my class and headed back to Cherry Point for what would be a brief stay since I had my transfer papers to Okinawa. My Marine base would be Camp Butler, but I would be assigned to Kadina Air Force Base which houses the Armed Forces Radio and Television Service Network. Marines in the unit—when we weren't going through two weeks of "summer camp" to remind us who we were—comprised the news division at AFRTS. Army, Navy and Air Force personnel usually handled on-air announcing duties, control room switching, camera work or other responsibilities.

I had put on a lot of weight during my month-long leave at home prior to shipping out to Okinawa and when the sergeant in command of our unit took one look at me, he issued an order. "You are going to lose 30 pounds in 30 days, corporal" he told me. "And, how am I going to do that, sarge?" I asked. "With these," he responded, holding out his right hand which contained several little pills. "Take one of these every morning, but make sure you don't take any after 10." "What happens if I do?" I asked. "Don't take any after 10," he said. After a week of taking one of the little pills, running a mile outside our barracks and working until midnight at the station, I was climbing the walls. I later learned I had been introduced to speed—the pharmaceutical kind, not anything produced by my feet. During my second week, I forgot about the time and took one of the pills about 11 a.m. I didn't sleep that night. The sergeant was right, of course. A month after taking that first pill, I had lost the 30 pounds. The good thing was I avoided any addiction to the pills. I don't think the Marine Corps could get away with that today.

Cpl. Benn reads news and interviews a pilot rescued after his plane crashed into the Pacific Ocean near Okinawa in 1963.

During my 18 months in Okinawa, I had developed a very close relationship with a young woman I met one night while making the rounds of nightclubs outside the base. Her name was Yoko and she was pretty. One thing led to another and I soon found myself spending more time at her little house than at my barracks. That led to an incident that nearly landed me in the brig after I had become a burglary victim. Returning to my room one morning, I discovered my 35 mm camera was missing. After looking all over the place, I went to the Air Police and asked for an investigation. The lead investigator looked at me and said. "Boy, you know how many burglaries we get around here? It's all we can do to investigate the big ones, not opening a lost-and-found department."

Undaunted, I decided to launch my own investigation and headed for "The Strip," a long street filled with bars, pawn shops, barber shops and massage parlors located just outside the main gate at Kadina. I didn't think the thief would be stupid enough to pawn my camera that close to the base, but I thought I'd give it a try anyway. I found my camera in the window of the fourth pawn shop I inspected. The dummy even used his real name. I contacted the Air Police and he was arrested, setting up a court martial in which I nearly became the defendant. The thief, I found out, was in the Air Force and had just gotten out of jail for beating up one of his Okinawa girlfriends. During the trial, he sat there as though it was just another day in court for him. He appeared to be familiar with criminal proceedings. Prosecutors laid out the evidence. The guy had been caught red-handed with my camera. His name had been recorded at the pawn shop. Then, it got a bit dicey. I confidently took the stand, thinking the "bad guy" would get his after a minute or two of cross-examination by the thief's defense lawyer. "Why weren't you in your room the night the camera was taken?" the lawyer, an Air Force captain, asked me. "I was...err....sharing accommodations with someone off-base," I told him. "Well, corporal," the lawyer said, "If you had been in your room, this might never have happened." The thief eventually was convicted and returned to another cell. I often wonder what happened to him—whether he had spent the rest of his life stealing. When I got back home, somebody stole my camera. I didn't get it back that time.

A highlight of my 18 months on Okinawa was qualifying as a crack shot. It was my last time on the rifle range and I had always dreamed of reaching the highest level of marksmanship. I fired "Sharpshooter" one year, but never came close to reaching the Corps' most exalted level—Expert. It means being one of the best. I had done well during my first four required firing positions and when I got ready for the last one—firing from a prone position—I knew I had a real "shot" at the brass ring. We were firing from 500 yards—five football fields stacked end on end. The target was a tiny white dot barely visible from where we lay. I didn't need glasses back then, but could have used a pair. My first shot was in the "Four Ring" just outside that tiny white dot so far away. I adjusted my rifle one "click" to the right to compensate for slight gusts of wind blowing across the range. Then, I couldn't miss. The second, third, fourth, fifth, sixth, seventh, and eighth shots all hit the middle of the target. Each time a round slammed into the center ring, somebody in the pits would raise a large, white circular piece of metal to signify a bulls-eye. As I prepared to fire my last shot, I tried to calm myself. It was like a bowler preparing to roll his last ball enroute to a perfect 300 game. I wasn't that close, but knew another bulls-eye would pass the 220 mark out of a perfect 250 score and qualify me as an expert rifleman. All I had to do was hit the target somewhere. A miss would cost me that expert medal. I took a deep breath and peered though the rear sight—lining it up with the front sight on the end of the barrel. Then, I slowly let the air out of my lungs and squeezed the trigger. That's the key—no abrupt motion to yank the rifle. The round sped toward the target. A few seconds later, a large, white metal disk was raised. I let out a yell, attracting some angry looks from other shooters and officials during qualification. I had finished with 223 points. It was a red-letter day for a guy who didn't know one end of a rifle from the other when he arrived at Parris Island in 1958.

I left Okinawa the day President Kennedy was assassinated. He was shot at 12:30 p.m. on Nov. 22, 1963 in the United States. On Okinawa, it was 5:30 a.m. on Nov. 23. We were across the International Dateline. For some reason, I awoke early and somebody had his radio on. Instead of rock music, mournful melodies were playing. Then, a voice announced that "President Kennedy has been shot in Dallas, Texas." Across the squad bay, a Marine shouted: "Good, it's about time somebody shot the sumbitch." Kennedy wasn't the most popular president in the South and I learned the Marine was from Mississippi. Half an hour later, the word was out that JFK had died. We all were put on alert. Nobody knew if his assassination had been part of a Communist plot. When we found out that Lee Harvey Oswald, a former Marine, had fired the fatal shots, some guys spent the day marveling at his accuracy.

I boarded the USS General Breckinridge with hundreds of other Marines. We went below the water line and, for the following 17 days, had no idea where we were. We didn't know a thing about Oswald's death at the hands of Jack Ruby, but we did discover just how vast the Pacific Ocean is. Even short wave radios couldn't pick up anything in some spots. We pulled into port at San Diego where I was assigned guard duty the first night. Then, we made it up to Los Angeles for a cross-country flight to Philadelphia and several days of relaxation at home. When we got to the airport, we found out there were no flights until the next day. That meant having to sleep in a waiting room all night in uniforms that had begun to reek. Four of us tried to unwind on a long bench when a TWA agent rushed toward us and said: "You Marines follow me." We hustled down a long corridor and onto a jetliner. He had found us super accommodations. We were placed on both sides of a rectangular Formica table, only a few feet from the liquor cabinet. A stewardess with a big smile plied us with libation as soon as we took off. I sat on the side that gave me a good view of the first class passengers. They were not pleased. Our tickets cost $75 for the one-way flight. Theirs cost $200 and all they got that we didn't were fancy little blue slippers. We even had better access to the booze. It didn't take long or many drinks to push me into a deep sleep. I awoke over Denver with several cards in my hands. We were playing pinochle which was a surprise since I had never played the game before. The three other guys had just put some cards in my hands and I bluffed my way through. We landed in a blizzard in Philadelphia and I had a major league hangover. I hadn't shaved in a couple of days and my uniform was ready for the laundry. I also lost my cigarette lighter. As the passengers began to leave, they looked down to see me on my hands and knees, searching under the table for my lighter. I found it, but I hadn't given them a good impression of the Marine Corps.

It had taken about five hours to fly coast-to-coast, but would take even longer than that to go 60 miles from Philadelphia to Lancaster. The snow had brought land and rail transportation to a virtual standstill.

Eventually, I was able to board a train for the trip home. When I arrived in Lancaster, I hailed a cab for the last leg of what was a 7,000-mile trip. Snow was piled high on the sidewalk outside my family's duplex house. It took awhile for someone to answer the front door and when it opened, I was in for a shock. "Alvie, you're home," the woman screamed. "Come in." It was Sylvia. I had never seen her before. My father had written me about her, but I never got it because I was on my way across the Pacific. Their marriage lasted about a year. That was less of a shock than her greeting that snowy day.

A few days after my arrival back home, a good friend, Lenny Goldberg, introduced me to a cute girl named Sharon Boumel in Washington, D.C. My original plans were to return to Okinawa one day and resume my relationship with Yoko, but, as the days and months passed, she became more of a distant memory. My father was less than pleased when I informed him by letter that I was thinking of a more permanent relationship. He didn't know anything about her, but, when he did, he took it upon himself to "save me." I found out about it a decade after I got back when he asked me if I wondered why I had not been allowed to extend my stay in Okinawa another six months. No reason was given by my commanding officer, only that I would be going home. What my father did was go with a friend to Headquarters Marine Corps in Washington and demand that I be sent home. The Corps quickly obliged. In the end, it all worked out for the best. Otherwise, I'd never have met and married Sharon or had such a wonderful family that I've got.

**Sgt. Al Benn and his bride-to-be, Sharon Boumel,
had a whirlwind courtship.**

After my leave at home, I went back to Parris Island where it had all started six years before. My last duty station entailed working for the base newspaper and handling press releases when necessary. One of my commanding officers had recommended me for Warrant Officers School, but I declined. Six years in the military had been enough for me. I was discharged on Aug. 4, 1964. No brass bands played for me. Nobody said thanks for my service to my country. I hadn't really expected anything, of course, but it would have been nice for somebody to have wished me well in civilian life. The young lieutenant who handed me my discharge papers seemed bored by it all.

As I boarded a bus for a trip to Atlanta where I would begin my next journey in life, I had one last chore in the Corps. "Hey, Marine," the bus driver said. "How 'bout buying me a carton of Camels? Here's the money." I was the only passenger, so nobody would have been put off by my brief departure into the base store. It only took a few minutes. The carton cost about $3. Today, a single pack can cost more than that. I got back onto the bus, handed the cigarettes to the driver and lit up one of my own. I had learned to smoke when I joined. Unfiltered Lucky Strikes and Camels were my favorites. At 35 cents a pack, cigarettes were easy to get and an enjoyable way to pass the nights at the Enlisted Men's Club where I also learned how to drink lots of beer. My high school friends were out of college or in graduate school, but I had taken quite a detour. I got good grades taking East Carolina College extension classes on base, but never took enough to really matter as far as a degree was concerned. I was just too busy having fun learning how to smoke, drink and enjoy the opposite sex. I think I got "A's" in each of those subjects. Little Alvie had grown up.

As the bus drove over the bridge, I didn't look back. I wanted to think about the future, not the past. Little did I know that the 2 1/2 years ahead of me would be the most unforgettable period in my life. As a kid, I had wanted to be a history teacher or reporter. Within a few days, I would help write history during one of America's most turbulent periods. The voting rights era was in high gear and I was about to wind up right in the middle of it. After that, I'd work for newspapers in three Deep South states. It would be a career filled with exciting, frightening, historic and amusing moments.

Following are just a few of those moments.

CHAPTER FIVE:

GEORGE WALLACE

In 1966, Alabama law prohibited governors and other constitutional officers from succeeding themselves in office. Being the shrewd politician that he was, Gov. George Wallace did the next best thing. He ran his wife in his place.

Lurleen Wallace was a kind, thoughtful woman, but she wasn't a politician. She left that to George while she raised their children. Once she took the oath of office in January of 1967, however, she let her husband know she no longer was a First Lady. He'd be the First Gentleman, or so it seemed.

Wallace still had his finger in Alabama's political pie during her administration—one that would be tragically brief, ending in her death from cancer. He worked out of a large office next to hers and held court there as friends and cronies from around the state came to see him. That's where I had a chance to interview him on Aug. 23, 1967. *Decatur Daily* photographer Ed Bruchac accompanied me. Wallace was running hard for president as an independent candidate and was happy to talk, even if the *Daily*, where I was city editor at the time, had not been one of his supporters.

Benn interviews former Gov. George Wallace in 1967. Wallace was preparing to run for president the following year. (Photo by Ed Bruchac)

In a wide-ranging, hour-long interview, Wallace talked about the war in Vietnam, foreign aid, law and order, his 1968 presidential aspirations and many other topics. His answers made it clear he would be remaining in the public spotlight for years to come. Wallace sat behind a big desk. I was on the other side and Ed walked around, looking for a good angle to photograph the former governor. Most of the questions had been asked and answered before and he seemed prepared for them. It was still quite an experience for me as I asked my questions, aware that he was ready to respond.

Here's how it went:

BENN: How serious are you about running for president next year?

WALLACE: If I run, it will be with the thought to win. You must remember that it only takes a plurality when there are more than two candidates. You must also remember that we have a cohesion— that is a sticking together in the Southland and the people of our own region are more solidified today in their support than ever before. Our region of the country can determine who is the next president. This race will not be sectional. It will be national because the problems facing the American people today are national, not sectional.

BENN: Let's talk a bit about Vietnam. Do you generally agree with the foreign policies of the Johnson Administration as to our involvement there?

WALLACE: It's a complicated, complex matter. We should never get involved in any place in the world again except through multilateral action, that is with allied nations joining together and with the support of the people who are there. Our servicemen are there and since they are there, they deserve the total commitment of the American people. They should be allowed to win the war by bombing targets in North Vietnam and supply routes and the harbor at Haiphong. We should be able to use our sea and military power.

If I was president, I would lean heavily on the joint chiefs of staff in the conduct of the war. I recognize there are diplomatic and political considerations, but I believe the overall military considerations are the greatest at this moment. I would also, if president, stop foreign aid to nations that are trading with North Vietnam. I'm tired of helping to rehabilitate and rebuild nations that later turn around and not aid us by stopping trade with the enemy. Some of the aid may be small, but it's the principle that's involved. In fact, the foreign aid program should be cut drastically. Getting back to Vietnam, I'd like to show Hanoi, Peking and Moscow now that we are unified and solidified behind our servicemen.

Even though there might be good people in this country who disagree with our being in Vietnam, we are there. We ought to take these people who are raising money and blood for the Vietnam Communists and put them in jail for what they are and that is traitors. We ought to also drag some of these bearded college professors who support the Communist government in North Vietnam and put them in jail, too. This would show our resolve in this country to support our servicemen. I am not against dissent, but I am against treason. Anybody who doesn't know the difference between dissent and treason needs to sit down and study the law.

BENN: In other words, you'd consider yourself a hawk.

WALLACE: I consider myself a hawk in the sense that I want to support our servicemen in Vietnam, but I think they ought to be supported toward a military conclusion. Again I would rely on the joint chiefs of staff. We have allies who have signed treaties with us who are not helping us with the Vietnam War. Some of them are even trading with the enemy.

BENN: President Johnson has mentioned an honorable solution in Vietnam. If you were president, how would you view an honorable solution?

WALLACE: I'd have to have all the facts at my command, including information from the State Department and the Defense Department. An honorable conclusion could be a military conclusion. I also would consider a conclusion at a conference table to give the people of South Vietnam an opportunity to decide the kind of government they would want and also one that would require North Vietnamese troops to withdraw back to their own country. I'd also require the Viet Cong to lay down their arms and stop talking about insurrection. The purpose is not to subdue North Vietnam. The purpose is to stop the subversion of the South Vietnamese government by the Communists. I think an honorable conclusion would be to revert back to the status quo which was brought about by the 1954 Geneva Accord.

BENN: What is your opinion of those who would like to see people such as Robert Kennedy and Martin Luther King run for president in 1968?

WALLACE: They have a right to run. And, the more that run, the merrier.

BENN: The troop buildup in Vietnam has been significant. As president, would you try to reduce the military commitment that we have made?

WALLACE: I would work toward bringing the war to a conclusion.

BENN: What is your position on foreign aid?

WALLACE: We ought to drastically reduce our foreign aid program because a balance of payment problem becomes involved. In some areas, foreign aid is good, especially when countries such as South Korea are involved. They are a strong anti-Communist nation that has stood firm against Communist aggression. That type of foreign aid could well continue. But there are billions of dollars in foreign aid that have been a complete waste to America. I, for one, would not want to give any foreign aid to countries that spit in our face, tell us to drink sea water and trade with the Communists.

BENN: Do you think the United States took the right position in the recent Mideast War?

WALLACE: I don't think we should have become involved other than letting the United Nations work out, for the first time, a solution. I do hope that it will bring some stability to the Mideast and we won't have a war over there every five or 10 years. It also points out the fact that the Communists are involved everywhere. They provided Egypt with equipment and war materials that they lost, of course. We need to take a realistic approach to that part of the world, too, by working with the great powers to bring stability to the Mideast.

BENN: Returning home, what do you feel is the No. 1 problem facing our cities today?

WALLACE: There are two No. 1 problems. One is the complete takeover of our domestic institutions by the federal government. A prime example is education, which means our children. The other is the breakdown of law and order; the complete inability to walk the streets and parks of the large cities of our nation as well as allowing anarchists, insurrectionists and Communists to have a complete free hand in roaming our streets. That has just ripped our nation.

BENN: What would you do in that regard were you elected president?

WALLACE: The first thing I'd do as president would be to let people know I stand with the police and firemen of our country who are the thin line between complete anarchy and safety on the streets. I would probably take some of this poverty program money which is a complete waste of money and ask that it be given back to the states in block grants with no strings attached to be used to enlarge their police forces or reducing taxes to allow that to be done. I'd also introduce legislation to do away with decisions by the Supreme Court which made it impossible to convict criminals.

If I were president, I'd make it safe to walk on the streets of Washington if I had to call in two divisions of troops and put one every 30 feet with a bayonet. People are sick and tired of the complete breakdown of law and order and having it explained away by a lot of the newspapers, a lot of the professors, a lot of theoreticians and a lot of the judges as being caused by something other than what it's caused by. The riots are being blamed on everybody and everything except the rioters themselves. The reason for riots is you've got a certain element of people who are anarchists, who are insurrectionists, who are criminally inclined and who don't want to work.

The overwhelming majority of Negro and white people in this country are sick and tired of this small element of people being able to disrupt and make life unsafe for all of us. I'd see that the law is enforced. I don't think you'd have to call out troops from the federal government if you just stood with the police and let them enforce the law. We've got to start trying criminals on Monday instead of policemen.

BENN: Do you think the civil rights bills of recent years have had anything to do with the racial unrest we've seen in this country?

WALLACE: President (Lyndon) Johnson and the late President Kennedy and all the liberals said pass laws and we'll get people out of the streets and into the courts. And the more laws you pass, the more riots you have. You can't satisfy guerrillas, insurrectionists and rioters with any law because their purpose is not to be satisfied. Most of those who have been leading the civil rights movement, including Martin Luther King, are not interested in the solution of any problem. They are interested in disrupting this country. This movement is supported by the Communists and it's been documented and the government of the United States knows it.

We've got departments here in the state of Alabama—the Sovereignty Commission and the Committee on Keeping the Peace—that can convince you and any committee in Congress that the Communists have been behind this movement that's erupted in this country and brought about this chaos from the beginning.

BENN: What specific programs have you and your administration initiated that might be used nationally?

WALLACE: Trade schools and junior colleges are a couple of programs. Education is a program to solve poverty. Everybody who finishes high school in this state or college or goes to a trade school can find a job regardless of color. It's people who quit school in the third or fourth grade and wake up 15 years later and want a high-paying job. Well, there's no place for them in our economy.

BENN: If elected president, would you consider a Negro for a cabinet post?

WALLACE: I would consider any citizen of this country for a cabinet position regardless of race of color, but based on ability.

BENN: You have accused certain courts and judges of conspiring to limit the rights of individuals. How would you attempt to correct this if elected president?

WALLACE: I can assure you that if I were the president, it would be corrected. I don't want to control the courts as chief executive officer of the nation if I were president. I want to have an independent judiciary. You can mark it down in the *Decatur Daily* that if I were president, I would appoint federal judges and supreme court judges who knew some law and not purely for political reasons. The type judges I would appoint would never do the things that the present court system's done. If I'm elected, we're going to have judges whose attitude and philosophy are more in keeping with the Constitution of our country.

BENN: Do you feel you have the full support of the Legislature in most of your wife's programs?

WALLACE: Generally speaking, yes. We don't have the full support of everything we do. No governor does. We have differences of opinions. My wife has had a number of programs that got solid support. She had, yesterday, support on the teacher choice bill that would allow parents to vote on who they wanted to teach their children—Negro or white. That is in keeping with what the government calls freedom of choice. There were only three senators that voted against this bill—Sen. Bob Harris of Decatur, Sen. Stewart O'Bannon of Florence and Sen. Bo Torbert—T-O-R-B-E-R-T of Opelika. Of course, these three distinguished senators had the right to vote against my wife's program that caused parents to be allowed to vote on whether they wanted Negro teachers to teach their children or white teachers.

BENN: Do you think this might prompt federal action?

WALLACE: Well, I'm sure anything we do might prompt federal action. Wouldn't it be ludicrous or asinine for a court to say you and other parents in Alabama do not have anything to say about who is teaching their child. I believe every parent in Morgan County is more qualified to say what is in the best interest of their child than some judge in Birmingham or some judge on the supreme court in Washington.

BENN: What image do you think you project to the American public?

WALLACE: I project a good image to some people and a bad image to others. I'm not one of those folks who is always worried about image.

In 1964, I got 34 percent of the vote in Wisconsin. A week later, all the Ivory Tower folks said we wouldn't get 5 percent of the vote in Maryland and I almost won that election. Many things have happened since then. Both national parties are worried about our prospective candidacy which means they are worried about the people of Alabama and the Alabama movement. It looks as if our image must not be too bad.

BENN: There are many, governor, who accuse you of being a racist. How might that affect your presidential candidacy if you announce one?

WALLACE: Well, it's according to what you call a racist. I see where militants today are calling President Johnson a racist and they're calling members of Congress racists. A racist, to me, is someone who doesn't like someone because of color. I don't dislike anybody because of color. I believe God made all mankind and that all men are the handiwork of God. I am not a racist and our administration has tried to help people of all races in this state. In 1966, my wife received as many or more votes than either of the two candidates from the Negro race. In Selma, where the newspaper said we were so oppressive, my wife got 87 ½ percent of the vote in the Negro wards.

BENN: We are the most powerful country in the world. Where do you think we're headed right now?

WALLACE: Gov. (Lester) Maddox (of Georgia) said the other day, not creapin' socialism, but leapin' socialism. We're looking at an oligarchic form of government where decrees of the federal government run every phase of our lives. We're headed down the road toward bankruptcy and if law and order is not restored, we're headed down toward internal weakness that can make us a second rate power. But, I think the overwhelming majority of people in this country are going to take hold and restore sanity. We are going to stop this plunge toward the depths that we are plunging at the moment.

BENN: When might you announce for president and how would you do it?

WALLACE: I'd just say at a press conference that I had decided to run for president. I'd call for the people of Alabama to support me and I'd call on the *Decatur Daily* to support local candidates in Alabama. Let's see if that miracle can happen.

BENN: How many votes do you think you could get if you run for president?

WALLACE: Well, I got 34 percent in one state four years ago, 45 percent in another state, 30 in another. I think I could get enough votes to win. I think I could get a plurality, a higher vote than either of the two national candidates. Yes, sir. I can win. I say 'I.'" We can win. This movement can win.

In 1968, Wallace demonstrated just how popular his "movement" was at that time. He ran as the American Independent Party's presidential candidate and got financial backing from many wealthy conservatives in America, including actor John Wayne. Getting on the ballot was a major challenge, but he easily met it. In California, he needed 66,000 to obtain ballot space. He got 100,000 names. Wallace knew he couldn't become president, but he did hope to throw the issue into the U.S. House of Representatives if he won enough electoral votes. If he could do that, he reasoned, he could gain concessions for the South.

Gov. Lurleen Wallace died in the spring of 1968 and Wallace was paralyzed by grief. He recovered in a few weeks and headed back to the campaign trail. In the November general election of that year, Wallace carried five deep South states, but Republican Richard Nixon had more than enough support to defeat Democrat Hubert Humphrey.

Wallace, who was elected governor again in 1970, did prove one thing with his presidential forays. He showed that a southerner could win the nation's most important position. Lyndon Johnson's election in 1964 was due, in part, to the power of an incumbency brought about by the assassination of his predecessor. Jimmy Carter of Georgia became president in 1976 and served one term. George Bush of Texas served one term while his son, George W. Bush, was elected to two terms. Bill Clinton of Arkansas served two terms in the 1990s.

In 1972, Wallace was shot five times at a Laurel, Md. shopping center during a presidential campaign stop. He continued his campaign that year and ran again in 1976, but his wounds effectively ended his presidential hopes. He was elected governor twice more—in 1974 and 1982. The last time was with help from Alabama's black voters.

He apologized for past segregationist beliefs and it helped him win an unprecedented fourth term.

Wallace was in pain much of the final 26 years of his life. He died in 1998.

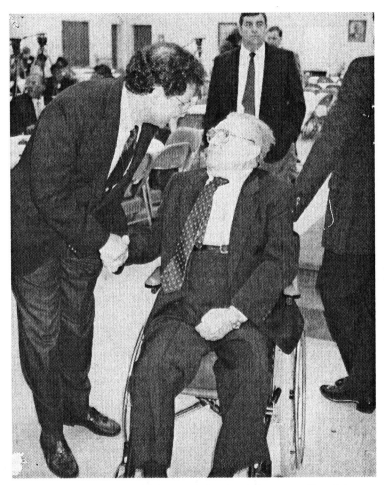

Benn meets Wallace in Selma—20 years after his Decatur interview with him.

CHAPTER SIX:

LITTLE TREE

Could a racist write a book about love, compassion and racial understanding?

Forrest Carter could. Apparently, Asa Carter could, too.

In 1991, I discovered that the two were the same and began writing about it. It was a connection that Carter's publisher tried to keep quiet for as long as possible because a lot of money was involved—millions of dollars over the quarter century since Asa Carter published it under his *nom de plume* of Forrest Carter.

"The Education of Little Tree" was written in 1976 and became something of a minor classic as the years passed and word spread around the country. Asa Carter died three years after its publication. Few knew who he was or had been. No one knew his name in January of 1963, either. But, most of America knew his words—"Segregation today, segregation tomorrow, segregation forever." Carter's words highlighted, or lowlighted, the inauguration speech of Alabama Gov. George C. Wallace. Those who agreed with Wallace cheered. Those who wondered about him could only prepare for a difficult four years. Later that year, a bomb destroyed a black church in Birmingham, killing four girls. That same year, Bull Connor's police dogs and fire hoses scattered demonstrators protesting the city's segregationist practices.

As the years passed, Wallace mellowed, especially after he was paralyzed in an assassination attempt during a presidential campaign stop in Maryland. Asa Carter had become Forrest Carter by then. He started writing books about a variety of subjects, including westerns and an Indian boy who grew up in the mountains of east Tennessee. They were all warmly received. Wallace's inaugural speech seemed so far away for Carter.

State Sen. Hank Sanders of Selma introduced me to "Little Tree." I had just finished an interview with Hank near the Edmund Pettus Bridge. That's where civil rights demonstrators had been routed by Alabama State Troopers in 1965—two years after Wallace had read Carter's "Segregation Forever" speech.

"Al," Hank told me, "You've got to read 'The Education of Little Tree.' It's one of the most powerful books I've ever read. It's a masterpiece."

By 1991, "Little Tree" had made the New York Times' best-seller list. Sales surged and money rolled in for the University of New Mexico Press which had reprinted it in 1986. I contacted Peter Maulson, a spokesman for the university's publication service. He said 500,000 copies had been sold since "Little Tree" was reissued five years earlier. Then, word leaked out that Forrest and Asa Carter were the same men. Maulson said 55,000 copies were sold during the first few days of October 1991—the period when the New York Times ran a story with the headline "Best-Seller a Fake."

The deeper I got into examining the life of Asa Carter the racist and Forrest Carter the loving story-teller, the more fascinating it became. I got a copy of the book and, as Hank had told me, couldn't put it down. It's not that long and I quickly finished it. I have since bought copies for people I'm fond of, especially children. Maulson wouldn't say how much "Little Tree" was generating for the New Mexico Press or Carter's heirs, but he indicated that the paperback version was producing a "substantial six-figure sum" each year.

Asa Carter's racist proclivities had become well-known in Alabama during the post-World War II period, especially on that cold January morning when Wallace screamed "segregation forever" as he became governor.

Nathan Bedford Forrest was a Confederate cavalry commander who later became the first Grand Wizard of the Ku Klux Klan. Many southerners took the general's surname and made it the first name of their sons. In the Oscar-winning movie "Forrest Gump," the main character was named for him. Little wonder, then, why Asa Carter used Forrest Carter as his pen name.

Hank said he had heard rumors about the "true" identity of the book's author and wrote "Little Tree" agent Eleanor Friede in Virginia in an effort to set the record straight. What he got back was a letter denying any connection between Asa and Forrest Carter. She told Hank "there is no truth to that rumor." Obviously, the last thing she wanted to do was kill a literary golden goose. Asked later what he thought about the "name game" that was being played, Sanders said: "All I can say is he was one helluva writer."

The controversy continued to grow and pressure on the publisher and agent eventually got to be too much for them. In late October of 1991, Beth Hadas, director of the University of New Mexico Press, issued a public statement which said: "I don't think there was any deliberate deception on anybody's part." The statement was made a few days after the American Booksellers Association announced that Friede had confirmed the truth about "Little Tree's" author.

"Little Tree" details the formative years of a Cherokee boy growing up in Tennessee during the Depression. It includes black and Jewish characters—two entities that Asa Carter had denounced during his days as an Alabama segregationist. Hadas said she did not subscribe to the belief of many that "Little Tree" had been created by a "right-winger who wrote it to make it look like he wasn't that kind of person." As far as she was concerned, Hadas said, "I think Asa Carter underwent a true transformation before his death. I think he saw the errors of his earlier ways."

In addition to "The Education of Little Tree," Carter also wrote a book which was adapted into one of actor Clint Eastwood's most popular movies—"The Outlaw Josey Wales." Eastwood issued a statement during the controversy, saying: "If Forrest Carter was a racist and a hatemonger who later converted to being a sensitive human being, that would be admirable."

167

There was no way of knowing if Asa/aka/Forrest Carter had a true conversion. If he hadn't and was able to write "The Education of Little Tree" it had to be one of the great literary deceptions of the 20th century. It just doesn't seem possible for anyone filled with that much hate to have written a book containing that much love.

CHAPTER SEVEN

MAMA DAHLING

Her name was Sophie, but I always called her Mama Dahling, often adding "sveethaat" at the end for good measure. She was my mother-in-law and lived most of her seven plus decades in what seemed like a never-ending soap opera script. She weathered one personal crisis after another, but, somehow, managed to maintain her big smile and optimistic outlook on life—even if she'd flash one of "those looks" at her only son-in-law from time to time.

She often reminded me of that character in the Li'l Abner comic strip—the one with the unpronounceable name who walked around with a big black cloud over his head. Sophie Honikman Boumel Waldman Boumel may not have been his female counterpart, but she'd give him a good run for his money. The only breaks she seemed to get in life came from cracked fingernails.

For instance, in 1973, after years of yearning, she and her husband at the time—Morris Waldman—flew to Israel for a visit. They landed as the Yom Kippur War began and spent most of their time hiding under tables and chairs at the airport which had been targeted by Egyptian pilots. I think the Arabs knew Mama Dahling had arrived and were doing their best to get her before she got them—most likely with a large chicken soup ladle. Neither was hurt.

Mama Dahling was a typical Jewish mother, the kind made popular by Molly Goldberg, who had a TV series years ago. Molly's career was based on her ability to mangle the King's English. Mama Dahling was like that, too. Her sigh was as big as the Montana sky and she took everything to heart—from cyclonic disasters in Pakistan to all those years the Dodgers lost the World Series, usually to the Yankees. She spent most of her working days at a Washington, D.C. paper products company, answering the switchboard and trying to run the business in her own inimitable way. She'd answer the phone with "S. Friedman and Sons, how may I help you?" Before she transferred callers to the party they wanted, she had engaged them in a discussion about every hot topic of the day. In the "Old Country" she'd have been a Yenta, which is Yiddish for blabbermouth—usually a lovable blabbermouth.

Behind her big smile and desire to inject herself into other lives in an effort to bring sunshine was a life filled with challenges and personal tragedy. Mama Dahling's mother died soon after she was born in 1919—struck down by the influenza epidemic that killed millions around the world that year. Sophie was born in Chile and came to this country by way of a different route. Most Jews came to America across the Atlantic from Europe. I think that's why she never seemed to understand geography. Sophie grew into a beautiful young, athletic woman. She was an accomplished swimmer and enjoyed dancing. She never knew her mother, but adored her father—a little man who ran a grocery store in Washington, D.C. One day, a thug walked in, pulled out a gun and robbed him. Then, he shot him to death. The killer was arrested, convicted and sentenced to death. Several years later, the sentence was commuted to life and he eventually got out of prison.

Her first husband, Danny Boumel, was the love of her life. They had three children—Sharon, Barry and Jerry—and were just settling in to what they hoped would be a typical middle American existence when Danny died. He had returned home from work and wasn't feeling well. He went upstairs to take a nap and never woke up. Doctors indicated that a blood clot apparently formed after he had bumped his leg at work. No one was quite sure if that's what really happened, but it devastated several families.

Sophie Boumel and her big, happy smile.

Sophie survived. She had three kids to raise. She couldn't do anything else. Relatives tried to help, but there was only so much they could do. She was raised as an Orthodox Jew, but neither of her sons had Bar Mitzvahs—the traditional Jewish male's passage into adulthood. Hebrew instruction wasn't a priority for her. Putting bread on the table was. Eventually, she married Morris, a quiet little man who survived World War II when most of his family members died in the Holocaust. We heard he had spent much of the war hiding from the Nazis. He never talked much about it. Their marriage was a strange one. They didn't communicate. That's understandable—given his thick accent and Mama Dahling's version of English. It appeared to be a marriage of convenience. They divorced a few years later.

Sophie and I got along relatively well after Sharon and I exchanged vows on Dec. 27, 1964. My mother-in-law was too busy working to support her two growing sons to interfere in our lives. Besides, we lived in Alabama and that was the same as telling her we were on the moon.

"So, tell me, dahling, when will you and Sharon be coming down to Washington to see me?" she'd ask. "No, sweethaat," I'd tell her. "We'd be coming UP to Washington, not DOWN." "Up, down, doesn't matter," she'd say. "Just so I can see you."

We made many long trips to Washington after Dani and Eric were born and we lived in Decatur. We stayed at Mama Dahling's little apartment on Georgia Avenue. It didn't have any extra bedrooms and we'd wind up sleeping on the floor, often wedged between a coffee table with little glass animals on top and a big stuffed easy chair. Morris usually avoided her. When he'd come home from work, he'd go into the bedroom and close the door. She rarely saw him.

At times, Sophie would fly down to see us when we lived in Decatur and, later, in Natchez, LaFayette, Ga. and Selma. One of her most memorable entrances was at the airport in Chattanooga, Tenn. which is just north of LaFayette. At the time, I was publisher of a small weekly newspaper. She got off the plane wearing a big cowboy hat and carrying two suitcases. As usual, she also wore a big smile. She loved to smile. As she got older, she got wider and we kept trying to convince her to lose some weight. It didn't seem to work. I think her genes got in the way. So did her jeans. She finally had to stop wearing them. "Mama Dahling," I once told her. "You've got to drop a few pounds. Just imagine yourself carrying around two suitcases with each one weighing 50 pounds." "Well," she said, "At least I'm balanced."

When she reached 70, we began to notice even stranger quirks. She started buying every cheap gadget she could get her hands on. Then, she began digging in the front yard of her house and created a "shrine" of junk. We think she had suffered some minor strokes and was having a tough time dealing with reality. Her son, Barry, didn't help matters, either. After having become friendly with another family, he took their surname as his. That angered and dismayed Mama Dahling. It was, to her, a slap in her face. She felt she had been disinherited by her own son. I don't think she ever forgave him. We tried not to mention his name in her presence.

A major stroke put her in the Hebrew Home in Rockville, Md. and that's where she spent her final years. Doctors gave up on her several times, but she managed to bounce back each time. "Do Not Revive" was on her medical sheet. In late 2000, we went to visit and were shocked by her appearance. Her once robust frame had been reduced to skin and bones. Her face was shrunken. She stayed in bed all day, her eyes staring vacantly at the ceiling. We didn't think she'd be with us much longer. A few weeks later, doctors reported she had "come back" and was eating again. It was unbelievable. Dani got a chance to see her grandmother more often after she and her family moved to northern Virginia. She knew she might not have many more opportunities. She'd take her sons, Ben and Scott, to see her, but it was too frightening for them at times. Mama Dahling had been placed on a special ward for difficult patients. She once slugged an attendant with her remaining good hand.

Sharon, left, Sophie and Dani light Sabbath candles.

We tried to see her whenever we visited Dani and her family. It tended to be depressing because of her surroundings, but it also helped bring back some of the good memories, too. Sophie turned 83 in February 2002 and I think she recognized me. She glared at me as I stood at the end of her bed.

"It's me, Mama Dahling, it's Alvie," I told her. "Do you remember me?" She was paralyzed on one side, couldn't move one hand and was too weak to move the other one, but, those flashing eyes told me she knew who I was. It was her favorite son-in-law. It was her only son-in-law. I even think I detected the crease of a slight smile when she looked at me.

Morris wound up in the Hebrew Home, too, and lived in a room not far from his former wife. He'd visit her occasionally. It appeared as though time had healed the wounds between them. It did for Morris. She appeared to recognize him when he'd walk up to her and say "how are you doing, Sophie?" He'd help feed her whenever he could.

In the spring of 2002, Morris died at the Hebrew Home. We don't think it ever registered on Mama Dahling. She died on Dec. 5, 2002.

Jewish tradition calls for a tombstone unveiling ceremony at the gravesite of a loved one or friend. We missed the first one because it wasn't ready. The day after Thanksgiving, 2004, we gathered at a cemetery about a mile from the Capitol in Washington, D.C. to say our final farewell to Sophie. Unfortunately, we wound up at the grave of Sophie Blum, not Sophie Boumel. The headstone was placed at the wrong spot. It took a few weeks to finally correct the problem and all the credit was due to our wonderful daughter. Dani stayed on top of it and urged me not to take legal action against cemetery management or the person responsible for putting the tombstone in the wrong spot.

I had the honor of conducting the memorial service for Mama Dahling. Rabbi Stephen Listfield of Montgomery gave me some special unveiling prayers to read and I concluded the ceremony by saying *Kaddish* which is a Jewish prayer extolling the sanctity of life.

As we were leaving the cemetery, I mentioned to no one in particular that something as strange as what just happened had Mama Dahling's touch all over it. I could almost hear my mother-in-law's unmistakable laugh over the whole thing, as in…"Over here, dahling, I'm over here."

CHAPTER EIGHT:

PACKY'S PREDICAMENT

It began as a routine patrol for Packy Dempsey, but ended in an incident that nearly cost him his life. I wound up in the middle of the fallout.

Dempsey was a deputy with the Dallas County Sheriff's Department and his specialty was handling dogs. He was one of the best and it wasn't unusual for dog handlers from other counties to come to Selma, Alabama to see him and ask for some tips. On Dec. 7, 1994, he was patrolling Craig Field, a former Air Force base turned into a housing development inhabited mostly by Selma's poor black families. Drug dealing was rampant at Craig at the time and Sheriff Cotton Nichols' deputies patrolled the neighborhoods of little houses where Air Force enlisted personnel once lived.

Packy knew what the area was like and tried not to take any chances. Princess, his German shepherd, was with him. He also had a video camera mounted in front of his sport utility vehicle. It was the only vehicle of that type in the sheriff's department to have one. Dempsey knew the value of video support. As things turned out that Pearl Harbor anniversary day, his faithful companion would help save his life and his electronic buddy would save his job and freedom.

Dempsey had just arrived at Craig when he noticed a young man standing with a group of other black men. He thought a drug deal was in progress and decided to investigate. Within seconds, everybody but Robert Walker Jr. scattered. Walker, 18, had been the central figure in the group. Packy got out of his SUV, walked toward him. Dempsey soon found himself caught in a life-and-death struggle with Walker, who jumped him after the deputy took out his handcuffs. Packy, who weighed about 140 pounds, was caught by surprise. Walker took Dempsey's .40-caliber pistol from his holster during the struggle and threw the deputy to the ground. "He said 'You're gonna die' and I thought I was," Packy told me later. "All I could think about was my wife and my daughter." What he did next helped save his life. He was able to activate a remote bail-out system which opened the rear door of his K9 vehicle to let Princess out.

The dog rushed toward her trainer and then pushed her body against Walker as the two men wrestled on the ground. Walker started hitting the dog with Packy's pistol, but Princess wouldn't be deterred. Then, Walker stood up and pointed the gun at the deputy, who was defenseless on the ground. During the struggle, Walker apparently had jammed the gun with one round lodged in the chamber, preventing it from firing. He kept pointing and squeezing the trigger, but nothing happened. Then, he ran. In an instant, Packy reached to his right leg and took out a smaller backup pistol, whirled around and fired several shots in rapid succession. Walker was hit and dropped to the ground. He was dead within minutes. A quantity of crack cocaine was found on his body.

It wasn't long before dozens of neighborhood residents stepped forward to claim Walker had been murdered by the deputy. It didn't matter that most of them weren't anywhere near the incident. What they knew was a young black man had just been shot and killed by a white cop. Packy was placed on administrative duty, given psychological counseling and the district attorney's office began its investigation. I arrived at Craig not long after the shooting and wrote the first of several stories about the incident. Black leaders immediately branded Packy a killer. What they didn't know was he had a video camera in his vehicle and it picked up almost every second of what turned out to be a fatal struggle. Nichols used the tape as an ace up his sleeve and played it coyly. He didn't want too many to know what he had. Within 24 hours, however, he knew he couldn't keep a lid on it because of the claims from black activists that Walker had been executed.

Nichols invited several black leaders to his office to view the tape. When they left his office, they were somewhat subdued, but not ready to give up their budding protest. It was just too good an opportunity for them. What they wanted to know was what happened before and after the incident taped by Packy's video recorder. The struggle, itself, was picked up square in the middle of the viewfinder, but events leading up to it and just after Dempsey pulled his second pistol were not caught on camera. It would have if he had had a wide-angle camera. He still was counting his blessings that the fight was recorded directly in front of where he had parked his vehicle. The still photographs made from the tape and released by Nichols were grainy and a bit blurred because they were taken several feet away and then enlarged several times. But, it was crystal clear that Walker was trying to kill Dempsey. He kept pointing and trying to squeeze the trigger. The gun was directed at Packy's head. The sheriff told me later that if it hadn't been jammed, Packy would have been dead.

A rally in support of the dead teenager was held at a Selma park a few days after the fatal shooting and Nichols' release of the video tape for the black leaders. I went, as did a couple of television crews from nearby Montgomery. My purpose was to report on the rally, not become part of the protest. But, that's what happened. Activist leader Rose Sanders, who had called the rally, didn't waste any time assailing Dempsey. "Let's call it what it was—murder," she yelled to about 300 black residents who shouted back in agreement. "In the tradition of the Ku Klux Klan (Dempsey) shot (Walker) in the back, cowardly," Rose said. It didn't matter that authorities said Walker had been hit four times in the abdominal area and upper torso. After more speeches, another organizer of the rally—Sam Walker—turned toward me and began shouting that I had not told the "real story" about what had happened. The TV cameras recorded his rants and raves into a bullhorn a few inches from my head. There wasn't much I could do. During the civil rights demonstrations in Birmingham in the 1960s, reporters were important elements and instruments of "the cause" and "anti-cause." Nearly three decades later, it had changed. Those of us who had seen the videotape or got enlarged still photographs showing the kid pointing a pistol at Dempsey's head had become "the enemy" for not taking a different viewpoint. I agreed with Sanders and her troops that the video recorder had not picked up events prior to the shooting, but it was obvious that Dempsey felt his life was in danger and had acted in self-defense.

As the days passed, the momentum hoped for by those who had branded Dempsey a murderer just wasn't there. It wouldn't surface despite demonstrations, marches and whatever else Rose could come up with. The deputy's videotape machine had seen to that. A press release was put out by a Dallas County black group which criticized reporters who had seen the photo enlargements. "The media," it said, "with total disregard of its commitment to fairly investigate and report news, hastily concluded from partial misleading information released by the sheriff that the officer was justified. By such action, the media served as the judge, jury and molder of negative public opinion before a complete investigation was achieved." The group also was critical of Nichols for releasing a "distorted view" of what happened. There was distortion but it was in the grainy photographs. There were no doubts among reporters who saw the photos that Walker was trying to kill Dempsey and the deputy acted to save his own life. That was my personal opinion, but I made sure to report the criticism as well as Nichols' defense of Packy.

Grand juries normally are convened in secret, but the one that met over the Walker case was caught in the glare of statewide publicity. Usually, prosecutors won't say what is being investigated. They couldn't do that in the Craig Field matter and we spent hours outside the grand jury room or in the District Attorney's office—waiting for word. In the "old days" grand juries in Dallas County would have been made up of 18 white men. The Voting Rights Act of 1965—spawned by protest marches that ended at the courthouse where the grand jury met—changed all that. The panel that investigated Walker's death was racially mixed. On March 14, 1995—three months after the incident—the grand jury cleared Dempsey of any criminal act in the fatal shooting of Robert Walker. "We had full facts to show the grand jury," District Attorney Roy Johnson said. "They had the ABI (Alabama Bureau of Investigation) summary, the videotape and eyewitnesses to question." By the time the grand jury had cleared Packy, a new sheriff was in office. Sheriff Harris Huffman announced Dempsey would be returned to duty immediately, but would not be sent back out to Craig Field to patrol.

A month after the incident, an anonymous donor contributed $12,000 to the Dallas County Sheriff's Department to buy five more video cameras for patrol vehicles. The one Packy used had more than paid for itself. It proved beyond a doubt that the deputy had done the right thing in the face of what he felt was imminent death. Nichols had been at a Selma bank shortly after the shooting and a man told him he felt he could raise enough money to buy some more cameras. A few days later, the man brought the $12,000 to the sheriff. Today, it is standard procedure for law enforcement officers to have video cameras in their vehicles.

Thanks to the distraction caused by Princess and the jammed gun, Packy Dempsey is around to tell his story. He eventually left the Dallas County Sheriff's Department and joined a police department in south Alabama. Princess, who went along, died a few years later.

CHAPTER NINE:

RANDY AND ROGER

I first saw Randy Lewellen on July 28, 1979. It was a Saturday morning in east Selma and Randy was pointing a gun at a woman with a jagged-edged knife in her right hand. She was stabbing at a kid who was handcuffed in the back of a patrol car. Lewellen, a young police officer, stopped her. He was a hero that morning. The last time I saw him, he was a disgraced former police chief —hurrying down an alley with his lawyer. He was headed to prison.

The first time I saw Roger Davis, he had a smug look on his face as he sat behind his desk at the Marengo County Courthouse in Linden. He didn't have much to say. He never did. The last time I saw Davis, he was about to be questioned by FBI agents after a bungled attempt at extortion. He would be headed to prison.

Lewellen once had a sparkling reputation, first as a patrol officer, then as chief of detectives and, later, as chief of the whole department. His career ended in handcuffs. He was going to prison for stealing thousands of dollars from the same taxpayers who had provided his salary. Davis once was a respected officer, too—a state trooper for many years before winning two terms as Marengo's top lawman. He went to prison for demanding kickbacks from the owners of a bail bonding company. They got fed up with him and went to authorities who arrested him.

Why the two lawmen did what they did wasn't hard to understand. They wanted more money and got greedy. In the end, it caught up with them. I chronicled Lewellen's rise through the ranks of the Selma Police Department. It was no personal joy for me to photograph him with his hands in cuffs—the bars of the Dallas County Jail as a backdrop. He had his head bowed as they led him away. There was little he could do or say. It wasn't like that the first time I saw him. He had helped save a young man's life, not to mention a lot of money for the city if the woman had carried out her apparent intentions.

I was at the *Selma Times-Journal* on a Saturday morning when an advisory on the police scanner caught my attention. It said police were at a residence on Alabama Avenue to answer a disturbance call. It had been a relatively quiet morning, so I thought I'd drive over to see what was going on. I had no way of knowing it would turn out the way it did. When I got there, I saw a patrol car parked outside a small house. The back door of the car was open and a pair of legs extended from the rear seat. No police officers were in the area. A cop assigned to guard the handcuffed teenager in the back seat had walked away. Then, the woman approached. She was carrying a knife in her right hand. Her face was twisted and she muttered something to the young man in the patrol car. The kid must have said something to anger her. The next thing I knew, she had raised the knife and began plunging it toward the interior of the car. All I remember was raising my Topcon motor-drive camera and shooting. I caught it all—from the moment she approached with the knife in her hand to the thrusts toward the kid and his kicking to stay alive. I also photographed Lewellen raising his service revolver and pointing it at her seconds after he left a house where the incident had started. It lasted seconds, but seemed like hours. I didn't have the right lens on my camera and the shot of Lewellen pointing his pistol at the woman was slightly distorted. The others were sharp though, including the final one of the woman being propped against a police car as she was being cuffed after she was arrested.

My series of photos appeared the next morning in the *Times-Journal*. The *Associated Press* named them the second best set of photographs that year in Alabama. The only thing better was a shot taken by a *Birmingham News* photographer who happened to notice a hand sticking out of the trunk of a car as it zoomed by his vehicle on the interstate. The hand

belonged to a kidnap victim. The photographer not only got himself an award-winning picture, he also helped save a life. I wasn't too upset about coming in second.

As the years went by, Lewellen's star continued to rise within the Selma Police Department. He became a captain and was named chief of detectives. Later, he moved into the administrative end of law enforcement and eventually was named police chief. He was an able leader who made sure those in his department were treated fairly. Somewhere along the way, though, he lot his direction in life. It would cost him his job, his freedom and a reputation that had taken him years to build.

One of his biggest problems was getting hooked up with Mary Ramsey, another "trusted" city employee who had been involved in controversy several years before she and Lewellen conspired to rip off the municipal treasury. Ramsey had been called on the carpet over questionable use of paint that had been paid for by the public and wound up being applied to her house by other city workers. She kept her job that time, but her association with Lewellen led her to a prison cell. It involved a scheme to bill the city for services never rendered on products never ordered.

The conspiracy started two years before Ramsey, Lewellen and two Selma contractors were caught. During that time, investigators said the four stole somewhere between $700,000 and $1 million from the city. The exact amount may never be known because Ramsey was clever enough to hide much of her dirty work. What she did initially was pad billings going to the city clerk's office where she was the city clerk. When she saw how easy that was, she and Lewellen began to create bogus companies and bill the city for work that had not been done. It couldn't have, of course, because the "companies" didn't exist.

As she developed her conspiracy, Ramsey would sit at a big table in front of the huge, curved Selma City Council table occupied by many of her friends, including Council President Carl Morgan. She'd answer questions about city finances and smile a lot. Lewellen would stand outside the council chamber, smoking cigarettes in a long hallway leading back toward offices and stairs above Mayor Joe Smitherman's office. Their scheme began to unravel in the fall of 1997. Council members Yusuf Abdus-Salaam and Nancy Sewell were given documents detailing what Ramsey and Lewellen had done—records that showed the phony companies and padded bills. They took the documents to Smitherman who gave it to authorities. It didn't take long for Ramsey and Lewellen to know the jig was up.

Two weeks before the whole thing blew up in his face, I asked Lewellen about the reports I had received over an investigation that might just implicate him. "Oh, there's nothing to it," he said. By that time, those of us close to city hall knew it was only a matter of time before the other shoe dropped. Lewellen and Ramsey tried to save their jobs by appealing to friends in high places, but it didn't do any good. Both were fired. The probe, led by veteran Alabama investigator Pete Taylor, continued throughout 1998. Ramsey pleaded guilty in February 1999 to three counts of conspiracy and filing a false federal income tax return. She got 30 months in federal prison. Lewellen pleaded guilty a week later to similar charge and got four years in federal prison. The two contractors also entered guilty pleas and were punished.

Several of Lewellen's relatives had been in law enforcement. His father had worked as a deputy with the Dallas County Sheriff's Department before joining Selma's Municipal Court System. His son's thievery was a jolt to him and other members of the family. "I brought shame and disgrace not only on myself, but my family and my department, who trusted me," Lewellen said, as he stood before U.S. District Judge Brevard Hand in Mobile. "I am deeply sorry for what I did." Lewellen used some of the money he stole to buy a four-wheeler and some other "toys."

Disgraced former Police Chief Lewellen leaves jail after booking.

When Lewellen became chief of detectives, we'd sit around his office and talk about the cases he was working on. We had developed a bond, of sorts. It was a mutual trust. He knew I wouldn't do anything to jeopardize any investigation and I had no reason to suspect he was anything but an honest cop. Who knows what drives somebody to steal? We'd usually end our conversations this way: LEWELLEN: "Make me look good, Al." BENN: "You know it's always turned out that way, Randy." As he and his lawyer, Billy Faile, hurried down that long, narrow alley after Lewellen had entered his guilty plea at Selma's Federal Building, Randy had his head focused on the pavement. He never looked up...never asked me to make him look good.

Unlike Lewellen and Ramsey, who tried to finesse their way through their conspiracy, Roger Davis was as subtle as a bull in a China closet. His actions had been under scrutiny long before he finally admitted his guilt to federal extortion charges in 1997. Goodloe and Jean Sutton, owners of Marengo County's weekly newspaper, had been on Davis' case for years—questioning his unique way of keeping the books in the sheriff's department. Their frequent reports hadn't produced anything more than embarrassment for Davis, but, they were enough to lend credence to the belief of many that things were amiss in the sheriff's office.

Crooked Marengo County Sheriff Roger Davis

Davis' law enforcement career ended on Aug. 22, 1997 when FBI agents surrounded him in neighboring Perry County. That's where he had gone to get his latest payoff from owners of a bail bonding company he had told to ante up or lose their business. He promised them he'd keep competitors out of the county. When the sheriff left the Marengo County Courthouse, his movements were monitored on the ground and in the air by the FBI and the Alabama Attorney General's office. At the payoff site, Davis was videotaped and recorded. Agents cornered him, cuffed him and took him to Mobile where he was booked. He didn't offer any resistance when told to "assume the position." He knew the drill. Davis despised the Suttons. In addition to the sheriff, Goodloe and Jean also were exposing others involved in corrupt practices in the sheriff's department. Davis' chief deputy and another deputy were convicted and sent to federal prison after drug trafficking convictions.

When Davis was sentenced to 27 months in federal prison a few months after his arrest, he told the judge he felt "this high"—spreading two of his fingers a fraction of an inch apart. The Suttons were on hand to record the event. Normally, the Davis case would have ended with his guilty plea and sentence, but Davis and the Suttons were involved in a postscript story. In the summer of 1999, Alabama Attorney General Bill Pryor released statements from FBI agents who said a federal inmate claimed Davis had asked him to burn down the Sutton house in Linden when he was released. The inmate said Davis offered to pay him part of $168,000 that the sheriff had buried in his back yard. Davis denied the claim when questioned by the FBI, but, given his habit of lying, few believed him.

Wrangling over ownership of the money dragged on into the 21st century. Pryor felt the soggy cash had been obtained illegally by Davis and, thus, belonged to the state. Davis said he had saved the money over a 30-year period and buried it because he thought the government would think it had been "dirty." It was, of course—literally and figuratively. In the end, Davis was allowed to keep much of the buried money.

The Suttons became celebrities. They were featured in a lengthy Readers Digest article, appeared on nationally syndicated television shows including the Oprah Winfrey program and were invited to speak at international journalism conferences. Davis eventually was released early and returned home to Marengo County. Jean Sutton died in 2003 after cancer surgery.

At one point in the whole mess, Linden Mayor Kathryn Friday came up with one of my top quotes of 1999. I asked her about the buried treasure, Davis' efforts to keep it and reaction in her little town.

"Well, I don't know about all of that, but I can say that people seem to be renting backhoes as fast as they can find one," the mayor said.

CHAPTER TEN:

ROSE

L ooking into a hospital room in 1990 got me into trouble.
People still talk about it today. Friends said I was audaciously aggressive and a credit to my profession. Critics called me a creep for peeking and said I was a disgrace to the Fourth Estate.

What I did was report on a woman who, according to some Selmians, had just made one of the most miraculous medical recoveries in local history or been caught in a big fib. I didn't offer a personal opinion—just a descriptive account of what I had seen. Unless it's an analytical article or a personal column, I've always presented information the way I've just seen it. Readers are smart enough to make their own decisions.

The subject of the article was Rose Sanders, a Selma lawyer and civil rights activist who is loved or loathed—depending on varying perspectives. There never were any shades of gray when Rose was involved. It could be because she often seemed to see things in black and white. "Racism" was not a foreign word for her.

It began innocently enough in early February of 1990 in the waiting room outside Mayor Joe Smitherman's office at Selma City Hall. Rose and her followers had been protesting alleged inequities about Selma's public school system for weeks. They had been at it since December of 1989 when the predominantly white board of education decided not to renew the contract of Norward Roussell, the predominantly black school system's first black superintendent.

When 1990 rolled around, daily demonstrations began against the school board. Pickets appeared outside city hall and the school board office. The black school board members began boycotting meetings, leaving the whites alone to discuss issues about a public school system that was 80 percent black. Within a few weeks, it would be much higher.

I made it a habit to stop by Selma City Hall each morning to see what was happening during the protests. Everything seemed calm when I went into the mayor's outer office on Feb. 5. Rose and several of her supporters were sitting in chairs lining the walls just outside Smitherman's office. The usually demonstrative protesters had been waiting quietly to see him about the school board matter. They sang "freedom songs" and exchanged light banter with Smitherman, who came out of his office at one point to offer them some soft drinks and coffee. It was relatively civil compared with previous protests led by Sanders.

Then, without warning, Rose got up from her chair and headed for the door linking the waiting room and the mayor's office. She muttered something like "I've had it," indicating she didn't want to wait any longer. She knew Smitherman was deliberately keeping her and her friends cooling their heels in the waiting room.

Police Chief Randy Lewellen was sitting in the chair normally occupied by the mayor's secretary. He had been told to keep an eye on things because of possible problems. At about that time, City Attorney Henry Pitts, one of Smitherman's closest advisers, walked into the waiting room. The stage had been set for some municipal fireworks.

Rose hit the door like a fullback and it burst open. She didn't break stride and raced inside. What she didn't count on was running into a 300-pound linebacker of a cop by the name of John Bean. She bounced off John like a ping pong ball. He had been stationed just inside the door to the mayor's office and, in effect, became a door inside a door.

Meanwhile, back in the waiting room, Rose's Raiders, as I called them, began screaming. Somebody hit Henry from behind, knocking him into the air and over the secretary's desk which had been vacated moments before by Lewellen. All I saw were Henry's feet pointing toward the ceiling as he went airborne. Lewellen, meanwhile, grabbed

189

one of Rose's friends who tried to get inside to "rescue" her. The shouting continued and police poured into the mayor's office. I took photographs and notes at the same time, trying to remember the chaos surrounding me.

I managed to get inside the mayor's office as Rose and two men—Perry Varner and Carlos Williams—were being handcuffed. Varner, a member of the Dallas County Commission, was on his knees on the floor as police cuffed him. He looked up and saw me, offering an expression of anger and embarrassment. Williams, a lawyer, was standing as handcuffs were placed on him. Rose sat on a chair that had been damaged during the scuffle. She had a subdued look on her face. Smitherman's anger bubbled over as he stared at her.

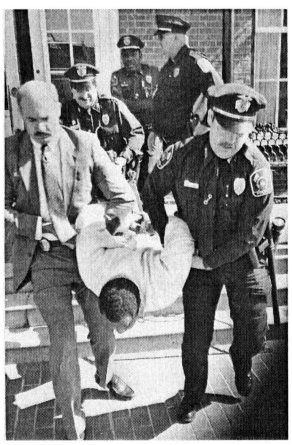

Dallas County Commissioner Perry Varner is forcibly removed by police from Selma City Hall in February 1990.

"You're going to be charged with obstructing governmental operations and anything else we can come up with that's appropriate," he told her. Rose just kept glaring at him. Broken furniture surrounded them. It looked like a bomb had gone off in the mayor's office. Varner and Williams refused to walk out of city hall and police didn't wait for them to change their minds. They carried them outside. Varner, who had helped integrate the county government two years before, went out head-first, facing the pavement.

Rose Sanders makes a point following her arrest at Selma City Hall in 1990.

Rose was saved for last and she put on quite a show. She wore a two-piece, sweatsuit-type outfit. When police carried her outside, she began kicking, squirming, screaming and shouting obscenities. It took several cops to carry her outside and she fought them every step of the way. The police—white and black—looked like hunters returning from a successful safari. Their "prey" was very much alive and kicking, however.

"You motherfuckers, let me go, let me go," she shouted. "I'll sue you. I'll sue you."

At one point, her sweatpants were pulled down to about her knees because of her squirming—producing an unintentional, cheeky mooning of the Smitherman Administration. I got some shots of her being carried out, but my new camera didn't cooperate on the most revealing moment. Rose was placed into a patrol car and driven to the police station about three blocks away. Calm finally was restored at city hall and Rose's followers quickly dispersed. It seemed they were as stunned by what happened as those inside the huge brick building.

According to Rose, she was brutalized by a big cop later identified as Ronnie "Cowboy" Rushing. We didn't hear much more about her or her condition after that, but, the next day, we were told that she would hold a news conference at Vaughan Regional Hospital on Wednesday. By that time, reporters had arrived from around the state and a big crowd awaited her entrance that afternoon.

I went over with Adam Nossiter, a fine writer who covered Alabama for the *Atlanta Journal-Constitution*. Several of us discussed Rose's anticipated appearance. Nobody placed any bets, but there were predictions on how she might appear. One said he wouldn't be surprised if she was wheeled in on a gurney. She made her appearance in a wheelchair pushed by her husband Hank, a lawyer and member of the Alabama State Senate. Accompanying the couple was Dr. Samuel Lett, a Selma gynecologist who, for some reason, was treating her for her alleged injuries at the hands of Rushing.

Rose wore a rose-colored gown and a neck brace. Her left arm was in a blue sling. An IV was hooked up to her left arm. She wore an aggrieved look and tears could be seen trickling down her left eye. Hank looked down at her with great concern in his eyes. Lett said Rose had suffered neck, chest, arm and hand pains. He said she had experienced 100 percent loss of "grip" in her left hand, but was regaining movement since her hospitalization. "She is still in a great deal of pain," Lett said, adding, that she had not suffered any broken bones as she was "dragged" across the parking lot at the police station.

Rose paused for several seconds, as though trying to compose herself. Then, she began to speak quietly. She said the officer who had arrested her took out his billy club "and touched my private parts" with it. She said he then placed it between her body and the handcuffs to "drag me" into police headquarters.

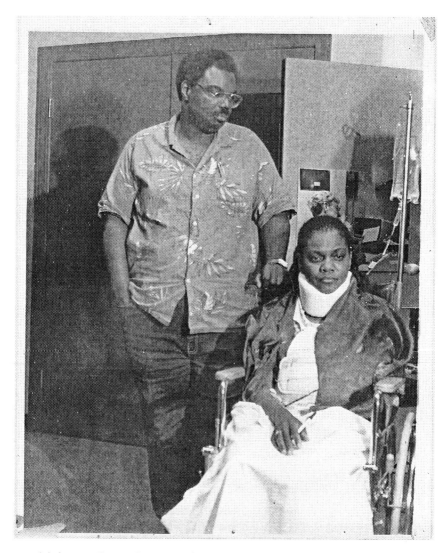

**Alabama State Sen. Hank Sanders with wife, Rose, at Selma
hospital after she claimed policeman injured her.**

Hank said he'd take the matter to city hall, but declined to
disclose what he might say. "It will be between me, the officer and Joe
Smitherman," he said. Rose didn't name the officer who allegedly had
brutalized her, but Smitherman said Rushing had suffered "finger
injuries" as he arrested her.

"(Rushing) said Rose bit him and he had to have medical treatment," Smitherman would say later at his own news conference. "I don't believe it at all when she says she was mistreated. She was given a chance to go peacefully and refused."

Rose referred to her "public humiliation" while being carried out of city hall. "I am a private person," she said, tears streaming down her cheeks. "This society doesn't give a damn about a black woman." She also said that she was handled "the way slaves were treated by their masters 200 years ago."

That's how the hospital news conference ended, but it would be far from the end of the story. As Adam and I turned to walk out of the room, a woman approached me, identified herself as a nurse and whispered: "That's not the way it happened. She's exaggerating her so-called injuries. Check it out. I think you'll find it interesting." Back at my office, Adam and I discussed Rose's remarks as well as the woman's comments. I didn't know who she was, but she insisted she knew what she was talking about. Adam and I both had deadlines to meet, but her claim seemed too good not to investigate before we began working on our stories.

"Come on, Adam," I told him. "Let's go back to the hospital. I don't know what we'll find, but it might be worth the trip." He agreed and we drove back to "The Vaughan," as it's known in Selma. We got there just before 6 p.m.—about four hours after her news conference. We didn't know what floor Rose was on or what room she was in, but we decided to look. We took the elevator to the third floor and, not seeing anything there, went down the interior cement stairwell to the second floor. As we walked down the long hallway, I noticed a closed door. "Maybe, she's in there," I told Adam. "Let's see." I gently pushed the door open. Neither one of us stepped inside, but we did look around the door.

There, lying on her back on the bed, was Rose, sans neck brace and arm brace. The needle was out of her arm and she was talking on a telephone, a big smile on her face—until she got a glimpse of us looking into her room. She was gripping the telephone in her left hand—the one Lett had said was "100 percent gripless" four hours before. We only had a few seconds to take it all in because Rose's mother, Ora Gaines, who was sitting in a chair near the bed, got up and slammed the door shut. But, we had seen enough.

I would be accused later of "sneaking" into Rose's room, but such was not the case. I do know that if we had walked up to the nurse's station, we wouldn't have been allowed down the hallway to her room. I had no idea who was in the room when I opened the door. Of course, that didn't convince those who still believe we used devious methods. I was glad Adam had accompanied me. Without him, there could have been claims I had dreamed it all up. But, even with what I saw, it wouldn't be the focus of the story I wrote when I got back to my office. My lead paragraph said: "Complaining of injuries as a result of her arrest at Selma City Hall this week, black activist-attorney Rose Sanders said Wednesday she was a victim of police brutality."

It wasn't until the sixth paragraph that I mentioned what I had seen in the hospital room after the news conference. If I had wanted to play up the "injury" angle, I could have described what we saw in the room in the lead paragraph, not almost halfway down the story. I felt Rose's claims should have priority status and anything else would be secondary. That's the way I handled it. Unfortunately for me, she saw it differently. The next few weeks would be among the most difficult for me as a journalist since my days of covering the Klan and Birmingham civil rights demonstrators. The day my article appeared in the *Advertiser* I was pushed around outside Selma City Hall. Two of Rose's friends had read it and let me know how they felt. They were among more than 100 demonstrators who were taking part in the daily protests over the Selma Board of Education mess.

I didn't realize how upset I had made some people until three days later when I went to cover a rally at Selma's black First Baptist Church. The featured speaker at the rally was the Rev. Joseph Lowery, president of the Southern Christian Leadership Conference and one of my favorite people. Inside the huge church, I could tell immediately that the school controversy and Rose's involvement had really stirred up the black community. Little did I know that I would become involved. It was standing room only and all but a few in the sanctuary were black. I stood next to a wall at the right side of the church. Next to me was Ron Smothers, who covered the South for the *New York Times*. Ron and I had run into each other from time to time along the civil rights trail and we renewed our acquaintanceship as we waited for the church choir to finish so the speakers could begin.

Not long after the program began, Carol Zippert—one of Rose's friends—walked to the microphone and began to speak. I didn't pay much attention until she began to denounce me and my story about Rose in the hospital room. That's when my ears perked up.

"Al Benn, examine your conscience," Zippert screamed from the pulpit.

"Oh, oh," I muttered to myself, as the television cameras swung around to focus on me against the wall. I turned to Ron and told him to seek a safer place to stand since he could blend in with the crowd a lot better than I could. Instead of ducking for cover, I stood there like a dummy and waved at the cameras. That didn't endear me to some. Two big guys came rushing toward me as the crowd started to shout in unison: "Out, out, out." I could take a hint. It was private, not public property, and I wasn't going to belabor that point. As I got to the door, somebody pushed me from behind and I nearly tumbled head-first down the steps.

As I got to the pavement, Eutaw City Councilman Spiver Gordon came outside and pleaded with me to return to the church. "This is just the thing we're trying to avoid, Al." "No," I told Gordon. "I know when I'm not wanted." In my mind, the scene had embarrassed Lowery, who was in Selma to speak, not listen to a woman screaming from the pulpit about somebody's "conscience." I may not have been wanted inside the church, but I was much in demand by the television crews outside. They rushed up to interview me about what had just happened. They were in the church parking lot when they noticed my hasty departure. I was happy to oblige as I waited for the program to end. I explained what had happened inside and then drove to a street several blocks away to wait for the marchers to reach Selma High School.

As thousands of people marched arm-in-arm up Broad Street, I walked up to Lowery and said: "Sorry I couldn't wait around for your speech, doc, but something came up and I had to leave." He laughed. He and I had known each other for years. I accompanied the marchers up the street—taking photographs and interviewing some in the group. Rose, who had her neck brace on again, quickly demanded equal time. It didn't take her long to line up her own interviews to give her side of the "story" and to berate me for my "intrusion" into her room. She certainly had a right to offer her version, even if it wasn't as accurate as I thought mine was.

Rose quickly returned to the fray and led renewed protests against the school board. At one point, a group of her supporters raced through the hallways of Westside Middle School, scaring the wits out of the children and prompting their parents to come get them and take them home. Some of the same intimidation occurred at Selma High School and the exodus of white students was on. Within a two-week period, about 600 white kids had left Selma's public school system for the town's two private schools or to systems in nearby cities. Selma had the last truly integrated public school system in Alabama's Black Belt up until that time. Not after the demonstrations.

A reporter from a large northern newspaper who had been observing the protests for several days didn't believe me when I told him the departure of all those white students would result in a return to virtual resegregation of Selma's public school system. "Watch what happens," I told him. "It may take a year or two, but that's what's going to happen." That's what did happen. Within two years, Selma's two white private schools, Morgan Academy and Meadowview Christian School were overflowing with students from Selma's public system. Morgan even initiated a $2,000 "transfer fee" for parents who sent their kids over there. Many white parents kept their children in west Selma's predominantly white elementary schools. Then, when it was time for them to send them to the mostly black middle school and high school, they'd enroll them at the all-white private schools. Over the course of five or six years, that meant parents could save $10,000 or more per child in tuition and fund-raising costs.

It was one of the most chaotic periods for public education in Selma's long history. At one point, Gov. Guy Hunt sent in dozens of Alabama National Guard troops as well as State Troopers. They were all armed and formed a ring around Selma High School where a group of black students, including Rose's daughter, Malika, had taken control. Roussell's pleas to give up the "school hostage" protest fell on deaf ears for several days. The students finally ended their demonstration, feeling they had made their point.

A key issue in the school controversy, in addition to the board's refusal to renew Roussell's contract, was Rose's claim of "tracking." It was her contention that, although Selma High School had been integrated by court order by 1970, the white-controlled school board had resegregated it by placing the brightest white students in college-level courses while relegating the black students to lower levels of instruction. Personally, I had not seen it. My two children had every opportunity to take college-level courses. So did their black friends. If they failed French or algebra it was their problem, not the school board's. Rose said some black students were allowed into the "upper levels," on a selective basis, but added most of the black students were kept in what amounted to academic servitude.

As it turned out, the protracted Selma controversy and my involvement in it led to an article in the prestigious *Columbia Journalism Review*. It was written by Emily Bentley, a former reporter for the *Alabama Journal* which won the Pulitzer Prize in 1988 for a series of stories about infant mortality in Alabama. In her opening paragraph, Emily detailed Selma's civil rights background and ended with: "This winter, Selma was the scene of racial strife in the course of which a local journalist became part of the story he was trying to cover."

"In the polarized city, Benn says, his reporting made him "the hero of the white community—the same people who'd wanted to lynch me about a year ago" for articles about the city's black community that whites "perceived to be positive"—and a villain in the eyes of the black protesters," she wrote.

Alabama Journal reporter Jordan Gruener, who also covered the Selma protests, told Emily that he had heard me called an "evil Jew" by one of the demonstrators. Being brought up the way I was, my hearing becomes acute to that kind of language. During one protest march, I heard Rose's mother spit "Jew" at me. I had wanted to shout "Christian" back at her, but, somehow, it just didn't seem to have the same ring. It was the first time in my 11 years in Selma that I had come across such blatant anti-Semitism and I told Emily that. When asked if she had "exaggerated the seriousness of her injuries," Rose told Emily: "It is racist and sexist to imply that."

Years later, Rose sent me a letter after taking exception to an analytical article I wrote about her activism. I wrote that her political stridency had engendered much anger among white voters in Dallas County and they took it out on black candidates she supported. Once again she brought up the hospital incident. In a letter to me on Aug. 28, 2002, she said a hospital employee "was terminated for wrongdoing" in the aftermath of her arrest at city hall. The employee, she wrote, "told me not to wear the neck brace in bed and told you otherwise."

She claimed it was all part of a 'scheme' to make it appear she had been faking her injuries.

The controversy didn't end when the school demonstrations did. Roussell resigned and accepted a $150,000 settlement from the school board to go away. He opened a video store near our house, but later returned to education in another state. In the months that followed, anger continued to spill over in Selma's white and black communities. Several white Selmians wrote letters to the Alabama State Bar, asking that Rose's law license be removed because of her actions.

On and on it went. Rose has never been one to run from a fight. I once described her as a "black Joan of Arc." She has the instincts of a street fighter—a female Roberto Duran. When she received complaints about her conduct during the Selma protests, she struck back with a vengeance, saying it had all been contrived by her enemies. There's no doubt about that. It had been an orchestrated effort to disbar her. Rose eventually emerged victorious. It was no big surprise to me. She usually ends what she starts and, more often than not, wins.

Rose went on the offensive again after the Disciplinary Commission of the Alabama State Bar began looking into the complaints about her. John Yung, who served as prosecutor for the organization that oversees the conduct of Alabama's lawyers, handled those complaints. Rose had accused Yung of leaking information to me and other reporters about "confidential bar proceedings." In a report to the State Bar, Yung acknowledged that he had answered some questions from me about "the Sanders woman" and her "outlandish public misbehavior extending over a period of many weeks." He denied in his letter that he had violated any State Bar rules or regulations as they pertained to public disclosure of private matters, but he let the Bar have it for its "inherently limp-wristed, feckless and fundamentally flawed" disciplinary process.

"I must say that Sanders is a prime example of the ineffectualness of the Bar's disciplinary activity," Yung told the State Bar. "The woman has gone to unsavory, appalling extremes to make herself a rather odd public person. She has diligently made stridency and racism the *sine qua non* of her position on the fringe." Then, Yung got to the point of his displeasure with Rose.

"This woman has been photographed and filmed howling, bellowing and ululating through the streets of Selma at the head of congeries and truant adolescents and flapping about diverse public hallways and chambers like a deranged, featherless egret," he said. "Her unrestrainedly queer public conduct is less appropriate to a member of a "learned profession" than to a member of the steamfitters union. Her pattern of behavior has been infantile and asinine. It has not been merely uncivil, but, rather, uncivilized."

Yung ended his scathing letter with comparisons between Rose and George Wallace, Alabama's four-time governor and a man who attracted, on a much larger scale, the same love and loathing given Sanders. He said the State Bar failed to sanction Wallace "during the period in which he made himself famous by ignoring, defying and ridiculing lawful federal court orders, by publicly and enthusiastically mocking and insulting federal judges and courts and by inciting rabble to violence."

His last sentence called to mind one of Wallace's favorite expressions about not being able to distinguish things—"This (legal) system can never effectively deal with the George Wallaces or the Rose Sanders and there is not a dime's worth of difference between the two."

In the end, all the shouting ended as a whisper in the wind. I got a couple of communications indicating that Rose had received a private reprimand—something her critics told me stopped far short of the legalistic drawing and quartering they had hoped for. They felt it had been nothing more than a slap on the wrist for someone who had turned Selma's public school system upside down.

Rose had the last laugh, as often happened after one of her political or personal crusades. I reported that a settlement had been reached in which the State Bar issued a public apology to her, saying it broke its own rules when it released to me news about the private reprimand she received. If there was one thing I admired about Rose, it was her refusal to turn the other cheek when she felt she had been hit with a cheap shot. Once, when she and her supporters were confronted with accusations over the Selma school protests, she filed a $10 billion lawsuit against her accusers. She emphasized the "B" in billion so nobody would think it was a puny multi-million dollar suit. That led to a settlement which included dismissal of the original claims against her.

The State Bar issued its public apology on the eve of a trial that had been scheduled in federal court. The agreement also included a promise by the State Bar to change its rules and procedures regarding conversations between staff and reporters about reprimands. In other words, the State Bar made its reprimand policies even more secretive. Rose had received her private reprimand in 1990, but she kept fighting. It took her five years to bring the State Bar to its knees, but she ultimately won.

As far as her claims about back injuries at the hands of "Cowboy" Rushing, the Alabama Bureau of Investigation concluded that it could find no indication he caused her anything other than public humiliation.

ABI agents interviewed 32 people, including Van Dailey, who was director of the hospital's Physical Therapy Department. Dailey said he did not observe any lower back injury symptoms that Lett had mentioned at the news conference. He also said he couldn't find anything that might resemble a "loss of grip strength which is a common occurrence in neck injuries."

"Dailey was not allowed to review Sanders' medical file prior to performing physical therapy on her," the ABI report said. "This was done at (Lett's) direction. Dailey said that it was uncommon for him to not be able to view a patient's file and that it endangers the safety of the patient."

In the final paragraph of its report, the ABI concluded that "there was no misconduct by officer Ronnie Rushing."

"Any injuries that may have occurred to Rose Sanders were a result of her resisting arrest by police officers at the Selma City Hall and her resisting (Rushing's) attempts to remove her from his patrol car...," the ABI report said.

If there was to be retribution for those who detested Rose, it would come in 1992 when her husband tried to become the first black congressman from Alabama since Reconstruction. Hank had been inching his way up the power ladder in the State Senate since his first election in the early 1980s. Alabama's congressional district lines had been redrawn to favor the election of a black member by that time. Hank's district included most of the state's Black Belt region which has a decidedly black voter majority. Also running that year was Earl Hilliard, a State Senate colleague and Birmingham lawyer.

As the campaign got under way, many felt Hank would win even if Hilliard was stronger politically in the state's biggest city. Earl's biggest weapon, it turned out, was Rose Sanders. Her critics went out of their way to derail Hank's candidacy. Some distributed leaflets with photos of Hank and Rose on it. It said if Hank won, the people of Alabama's 7th Congressional District would get Rose instead. During that time, I used to have coffee at Ed's Pancake House Restaurant in Selma. I'd meet with Chamber of Commerce President Jamie Wallace, attorney Vaughan Russell and Alston Fitts, a former college professor, historian and fund-raiser for the Fathers of St. Edmund, a Catholic charitable organization which had been helping Selma's poor blacks for decades.

During one of our conversations prior to the 1992 election, I predicted that Hilliard would win a close race because of Hank's biggest anchor—his wife. "I don't believe that," Alston told me. "Well, let's wait for the results," I responded. That's what happened. Hank carried Dallas County, as he should have, but not by a sufficient margin district-wide. Hilliard made history by breaking the 20th century congressional color barrier in Alabama. It had taken nearly 130 years. Hilliard would serve for 10 years and prove to be one of the state's most ineffective members of Congress. I think Hank would have done a much better job.

One of the deciding factors helping Hilliard in 1992 was the vote against Hank in west Selma where many of the city's affluent white residents lived. Most sent their children to the city's two all-white private schools and their disdain for all things Rose extended itself to the ballot box on election day. A decade later, Hilliard's ineptness finally caught up with him—thanks to a lot of money from out-of-state Jewish contributors upset with him over his anti-Israeli actions. Hilliard was defeated in 2002 by Artur Davis, a bright young opponent with a Harvard degree—the same school Hank attended.

After his initial disappointment, Hank went back to work. Within a decade, he had become one of the most powerful politicians in Alabama and Rose was right by his side, generating even more controversy. Complaints were made to the Alabama Ethics Commission that Hank had been funneling hundreds of thousands of dollars in public funds to quasi-public facilities launched by Rose. One was the National Voting Rights Museum a few doors up from the *Advertiser's* Selma office. After an extended investigation, the Ethics Commission ruled that Hank had broken no rules and the appropriations continued to flow toward groups he and Rose either started or supported. Hank's congressional defeat turned out to be one of the best things to happen to him during his political career. Had Selma's white community supported him, he would have been elected to Congress and made history. I am convinced of that.

Instead of being a small fish in a big pond in Washington, however, Hank became one of the most powerful politicians in Alabama—black or white.

I've covered many courageous people in my career, but Rose Sanders is one of the bravest. When she gets behind something, nothing can drag her from it, even if she's arrested. A decade after the Selma school protests, she continued her attacks on alleged academic tracking, even as Selma's public school enrollment and administration changed from white to black. That meant if "tracking" does exist, it's being done by black administrators—something they deny.

Public education is only one of Rose's concerns. She's also taken public stands against black-on-black crime, teen pregnancy and many other issues impacting the black community. An accomplished musician and composer, she has written and directed plays and escorted teens around the country to display their talents. I've also seen her drive groups of talented youngsters to engagements around the South. She would write, produce and direct plays and then make sure the kids got to their designated cities on time to perform them. I remember a cold, rainy night in rural Perry County after one show. Rose was standing outside a van, protecting the kids against traffic whizzing by. She got them into the van and then drove them back to Selma.

There are those who say Rose Sanders lacks a sense of humor. Not so. When the Dallas County Commission had five white males controlling a predominantly black county, Rose came up with a dilly of a protest one day. She and her supporters, upset with a recent decision by the white commissioners, brought five white chickens to the courthouse and set them loose in the hallway outside their meeting room. We all got a laugh out of that. Her law firm spent a decade helping the U.S. Justice Department fight the county's system of electing commissioners. The system was changed and blacks were elected for the first time in 1988. Several years later, a federal judge found fault with the new procedure and whites once again took over majority control. Still, Dallas County's government won't be excluding blacks again.

Rose has also fought a very personal, painful physical enemy the past several years—cancer. She had a double mastectomy and has had treatment on a regular basis. Her energy level isn't what it used to be, but it hasn't stopped her from taking stands on a variety of issues. On Oct. 1, 1994, she was honored by her supporters who organized an "Appreciation, Unity and Recommitment Parade" for her through Selma.

Of all the people I've covered during my career, Rose Sanders has been the most flamboyantly outrageous. Smitherman is a close second. Her career has involved a dichotomy of activism. She ranted and raved against the "white power structure" while building a "black power structure" of her own during that same period. And, it wasn't unusual for her to defend poor white women while verbally assaulting black officials who exercised judicial clout over her clients.

Rose and I have had an ambivalent relationship. She'd get upset at me at times over something I'd write, but usually knew I was available to listen and report on her activities.

"Despite what's happened in the past, I still like you," she once said to me in a letter. "I really don't know why, but I do."

There's no doubt she had a lot of clout. In 2000, she helped lead the effort to get President Clinton to headline the 35th anniversary of the Selma-to-Montgomery voting rights march. During the 36th anniversary of "Bloody Sunday," Rose kept harping about my not "getting the record straight" on a land deed she and Hank transferred to the National Voting Rights Museum—one of their pet projects. Critics accused Hank of using his legislative power to get the state Department of Transportation to improve some of their property adjacent to Selma's famous Edmund Pettus Bridge. The work was done on state right-of-way, but it was almost on top of the couple's land. By transferring the deed to the museum, they were able to put their critics on the defensive— something they proved quite adept at over the years. Those who found fault with them on a regular basis said the transfer was nothing more than taking something out of the right pocket and putting it into the left pocket.

"I was just beginning to like you again," Rose told me at the Bridge Crossing Jubilee. "You owe me an apology, We deeded that land to the museum." I told her I had checked with the Dallas County Tax Assessor and found no records of any deed transfer. As it so happened, the transfer occurred a few days before the Bridge Crossing Jubilee and at a time when the questionable work began on the state right-of-way. I found out the deed was still in a file in the basement of the courthouse and had not made its way to the tax assessor's office. As soon as I got the information, I wrote a story about it. I didn't issue an apology to

Rose, but let my editors know that the story I had written was a way to balance the criticism they had received. I didn't get a "thank you" from her, either.

In June of 2002, Rose decided she finally had it with her "slave name" and changed it. Her new name is "Faya Rose Toure." Even that sparked public reaction which, for Rose, wasn't unusual. One of my many Selma sources sent me an e-mail about her name change and I called Dallas County Probate Judge Johnny Jones, who faxed me a copy of the legal document signed by Rose. The reason she listed was her desire to eliminate her "slave name" while she remained among the living. When I called her, she said "I don't want a slave name on my tombstone." She was smart enough to keep "Rose" as part of her new name so those who wanted to keep calling her that wouldn't be confused over "Faya." Ironically, the man from whom she took her new surname was an African despot who enslaved millions of his own people. Thus, a woman who wanted to rid herself of her "slave name" wound up with the name of a man who engaged in slavery. Rose dismissed it as inconsequential. It didn't really matter anyway. A Rose by any other name would always be Selma's Rose, no matter what her new last name might be. Whenever I see her, I say: "Hiya, Faya." She doesn't get upset.

During my retirement reception in May, 2003, at the Selma-Dallas County Public Library, Rose rushed to the podium with a large green poster in her hands. She didn't want to miss her chance to pop it to me once more—in a nice, gentle way. The poster had two photos of me taken during a Pettus Bridge crossing reenactment and a long, six-paragraph poem. It began: "How does it feel to be on the other side of the camera, on the other side of life? How does it feel to enter someone's space, sometimes without their knowledge or consent, telling your "view" of their story, exposing their pain, their mistakes, their victories, exploiting their glory?"

Rose also "forgave" me in the poem for "reporting lies about my ideas, lies about my health, my actions and my tenuous wealth. But, I am rich in love for God, my people and self. And there were moments through your lens (when) you captured that part of the world that makes me smile. And for this, I say thank you, as you retire."

It was a totally unexpected "salute" and I appreciated it. A woman of many surprises had surprised me once more.

On March 7, 2004, Rose and I walked down Broad Street during the annual Bridge Crossing Jubilee. We exchanged some light-hearted banter, but she let me know she still hadn't forgiven me for "that" article about the hospital incident in 1990.

During the 2005 Bridge Crossing Jubilee, Rose was as feisty as ever and spoke with gusto on the steps of Alabama's Capitol at the conclusion of the 40th anniversary of "Bloody Sunday" and the successful march. Tracking remains one of her concerns, but "miseducation," as she calls it, now has become a priority for her.

Some dislike her because of her tactics. Others can't stand her because, well, she's Rose. Personally, I wish her well—especially physically. As we get older, we realize that time is on the short side and there is just so much more to do.

It's obvious she's not going to give up the fight—whatever that might be for her at the time. No doubt, she'll keep asking me for an apology for looking into her hospital room.

She won't get one.

Rose Sanders delivers poem and photos to Benn at his retirement reception in 2003.

CHAPTER ELEVEN:

THE LETTER

Long after Rose Sanders' activities in the Selma Board of Education controversy had ended, I was in trouble again with her law firm. On Feb. 17, 1992 her senior law partner—J.L. Chestnut—sent me a blistering letter about an article I wrote as a result of the school board flap. His displeasure with me was evident in the first sentence which described one of my articles as "scurrilous, deliberately imbalanced crap." It went downhill from there. The story centered on the Alabama Bar and its disbarment policies. An accompanying article in the same report used the case against Rose as an example of how difficult it is to yank a law license once it is granted.

White Selmians upset with Rose because of her activities through the years didn't waste time complaining to the State Bar, demanding that she be stripped of her law license because of the school situation. Some, no doubt, would like to have seen her in front of a firing squad. Dozens of letters were written. Each demanded disbarment. The Bar investigated and refused to take away her livelihood. The article about Rose and the disbarment effort was written more than a year after the turmoil in Selma ended and was done only after Executive Editor Bill Brown sent me a memo with one of those "whatever happened to" questions. My article should have been written in 1991 when the State

Bar's completed investigation was released, not a year later. All it did was reopen old wounds—not to mention sending Chestnut into orbit.

His letter arrived a day after he called me at my office. He accused me of conspiring to derail the campaign of state Sen. Hank Sanders, his law partner who was making a bid to become the first black congressman from Alabama since Reconstruction. Rose is Hank's wife. In a letter to Bill, I referred to one exchange between Chestnut and me over the phone:

CHESTNUT: "If (Rose Sanders) had been a white woman, you'd never have done that."

BENN: "That's a racist statement if I ever heard one."

His subsequent letter, written on "Chestnut, Sanders, Sanders & Pettaway" stationery and initialed above his typed name, took me to task for writing the article. Among other things, he accused me of being an apologist for Selma Mayor Joe Smitherman and City Attorney Henry Pitts.

Here it is:

"Mr. Benn:

"If you ever write a page of scurrilous, deliberately imbalanced crap about my black wife to satisfy a bunch of low-life, white, racist rednecks in Alabama, I will find 1,000 ways to fix your ass good, election or no election.

"You can't fool me with lame, self-serving explanations. It is insulting as hell to have some white son-of-a-bitch piss in my face and claim it's rain. You white southern journalists and publishers have not written about white female murderers as you wrote about Rose in Sunday's paper. You are clowns and racists of the first order.

"You knew, but didn't write, that five moderate black citizens walked away from and boycotted the Selma school board for nine long months. You knew, but didn't write, that the bottom line was white racism and that transcended (former school superintendent Norward) Roussell's contract. You knew, but didn't write, that so-called tracking had systematically denied most black students even the opportunity to take chemistry, geometry, foreign languages and other standard high school fare.

"You knew, but didn't write, that a committee of Alabama advisors to the Civil Rights Commission documented white racism in the Selma schools and recommended an investigation by the U. S. Department of

Education. Indeed, the committee and not Rose Sanders described this racist cesspool of a town as "two Selmas," one black and one white.

"You knew, but didn't write, that a paid, drug-sniffing police informant knocked Henry Pitts on his ass in Smitherman's office. If you didn't know, you should not call yourself a reporter.

Attorney J.L. Chestnut, left, speaks with Selma Mayor Joe Smitherman outside the Federal Building in Selma.

"You knew, but didn't write, that black parents filed scores of bar complaints against Henry which no one has heard from. You knew, but didn't write that a black woman slapped the shit out of Smitherman after he called her a black bitch. Her husband should have gone immediately to the mayor's office and shot the bastard between his damn eyes.

"You quoted extensively from white parents, but not one word from black parents. You quote at length from this rightwing motherfucker (attorney) John Yung, as if he speaks the gospel. Why didn't you quote from Rose's petition where she described Yung as a racist and political opportunist? You interviewed Commissioner (Perry) Varner, but didn't quote him at all. He is black.

"(The Rev.) Mike Brooks can believe anything he wants to about his family being victims. That hypocrite knows my family and all black families are victims. Some of our persecutors are officers in his all-white church that meets every Sunday ostensibly to worship a Jesus born in Africa. They claim your kind killed their Lord.

"If you knew what else these greedy, WASPish motherfuckers say behind your back, you would get up off your knees and quit kissing all their raw, pink asses.

"Sincerely, J.L. Chestnut, Sr."

I didn't wait long in informing Brown, about Chestnut's letter. I attached a copy, describing it as an "eye-popper of the first order." I reminded Bill of our extensive coverage of the Selma school protests of 1990. More than 100 articles had been written during that time. Every effort was made to provide equal time and balance for both sides in the dispute.

In my letter to Bill, I suggested that we print the letter in the *Advertiser*—with the appropriate editing of Chestnut's interesting choice of words.

"I've always respected and admired J.L. Chestnut," I told Brown in my letter to him. "He always seemed to me to be a man of enormous intellect and good humor, capable of seeing both sides of an issue even if one side displeased him. This letter really makes me wonder about him."

Chestnut's letter was reprinted—in full with editing that didn't leave much to the imagination—on Feb. 26, 1992, under the headline: "Attorney Says Story 'Scurrilous." We used "s..t" and "motherf—ers."

Community reaction was immediate and vociferous. People couldn't believe the language in the letter, but, more than that, they were amazed that a newspaper would print it. We made several attempts to get a comment from Chestnut, but he declined. Bill also added an editor's note at the end of the letter. It read:

"Mr. Chestnut's letter addresses an article concerning the Alabama Bar Association's failure to respond publicly to complaints made last year concerning the conduct of Rose Sanders, a law partner of Mr. Chestnut. The allegations involved her actions during the controversy surrounding the Selma school board's failure to renew the contract of the city's first black school superintendent. The issue was extensively covered at the time."

It didn't take long for the fallout to cover Selma and the rest of central Alabama. Chestnut wouldn't admit he wrote it, but he didn't deny it either. The letter got mixed reaction which wasn't surprising in Selma, which is a racially divided community where blacks cheered him and whites condemned him.

The *Selma Times-Journal*, which had printed weekly opinion columns by Chestnut for more than a decade, applied the brakes and stopped running them. On March 1, 1992, *Times-Journal* Editor John Cameron wrote: "Mr. Chestnut's guest column will not appear in this newspaper in coming weeks and months as the dust settles from this rather profane and disturbing letter."

"To say the least, the contents of the letter were shocking, sad, disgusting and, most of all, disappointing to me and people of both races in this community," Cameron wrote.

Radio talk shows in Selma, Montgomery and Birmingham devoted part or all of their programs to the Chestnut letter, copies of which were placed on the desks of some members of the Legislature which was in session that day. I don't know who did that, but he obviously was taken with Chestnut's letter to me. Central Alabama's most popular talk show host, Don Markwell of Montgomery, told listeners that he tried to reach Chestnut for a comment, but couldn't get through to him because one of the firm's legal secretaries "chewed me out for trying."

Birmingham lawyer Bill Dawson wrote me that "The Alvin and J.L. sideshow is a hot topic in this cosmopolitan area, with even the sports talk shows giving it the once over. At last count, you were seriously ahead."

"I commend your editors for not being intimidated," Dawson continued. "Any reporter capable of finding the Loch Ness Monster in a grease trap in Clanton is bound to step on a few toes. Keep on writing, you budding Pulitzer. We remain confident that a few raw, pink asses or even complete assholes cannot stop the presses."

Bill's comment on the "Loch Ness Monster" referred to a story I wrote about the discovery of a large undetermined mass of something in the McDonald's grease trap at a small town north of Selma. We never did find out what it was, but *AP* picked it up and it went all over the country.

Former Lt. Gov. Jere Beasley of Montgomery decided to have some fun with Chestnut's letter. Beasley, senior partner in one of the city's biggest law firms, wrote his own "letter" to the "editor" of a fictitious legal journal in "defense" of an unnamed attorney buddy of his.

"If you ever write a page of scurrilous, deliberately imbalanced dreck about my Jewish client to satisfy a bunch of lowlife, gentile, rednecks, I will at the request of my proud Semitic brother find a thousand ways to fix your pink tuchus good," wrote Beasley, in an opening paragraph of a hilarious parody of Chestnut's letter. "Dreck" is Yiddish for feces while "tuchus" is the Yiddish word for a person's posterior.

Columnist Charles Mabry of the *Monroe Journal*, a weekly newspaper about 100 miles south of Montgomery, came up with an offering of his own under the title: "Letter reveals Chestnut's bigotry."

"Had there been a contest to determine the most outrageous, needlessly graphic use of barnyard grammar combined with unnecessarily explicit verbiage by a supposedly rational person, Mr. Chestnut easily would have won a gold," Mabry wrote. "The net effect was that of a bantam rooster crowing raucously to disturb as many as possible about matters that are mostly unimportant except as a means of getting attention."

Ches, as I've always called him, is a superb lawyer whose courtroom expertise has garnered him a mostly positive national reputation. He can study a case for five minutes without even meeting his client and then go into court and acquit him. I've seen him do it. He can also be an intimidating barrister in and out of court. What he didn't count on in this case was a letter that backfired.

Instead of being intimidated, Bill Brown showed journalistic chutzpah and illustrated for Chestnut that old newspaper axiom: "Don't argue with somebody who orders his ink by the barrel."

Ches put out word to his staff not to accept any telephone calls from me in the future. Although his column was discontinued in Selma's local paper, he continued to write weekly reflections titled: "The Hard, Cold Truth" for a few weekly newspapers in the state.

In one column, Chestnut said I made my living "gathering information from the black officials he often writes about" and followed it with: "One wonders how much more abuse and unfair treatment these black people will endure before shutting Benn out. How many more black women in public life will suffer before blacks say no to Benn?"

In another column a week later, Chestnut wrote: "Alvin Benn, Jewish reporter for the rightwing *Montgomery Advertiser*, makes a living hustling news stories from black officials, yet, he is systematically unfair to these black officials. Benn, however, bends over backwards to be fair to Joe Smitherman, the arrogant white mayor of Selma."

Seven years after that column, Chestnut was at it again, attacking me in another column in which he described for a group in Los Angeles the "Sol Tepper/Alvin Benn Syndrome." Tepper was a member of Temple Mishkan Israel, which my family attended, and as conservative as anyone in the South. His hero was Confederate Gen. Nathan Bedford Forrest who became the first leader of the Ku Klux Klan.

"These two Selma Jews were determined to out-gentile the gentiles," Chestnut said in his column which appeared in the *Greene County Democrat* on April 14, 1999. "Tepper would have been a robed Ku Kluxer if they had accepted Jews. Benn, on the other hand, is not even a southerner. He is simply an opportunist. He used access to a newspaper in the most biased and racist manner and always at the expense of black people."

I could understand his displeasure over the situation involving his law partner earlier that decade, but I couldn't figure out why he jumped on me once more so many years later. I guess I must have done something to light his fuse again.

"The Letter," as it became known in Selma and Montgomery after it was published in the *Advertiser*, remains conversational fodder to this day. Four years after Chestnut wrote it, Peter Applebome of the *New York Times* included it in "*Dixie Rising*" which examines a changing South.

In it, Applebome describes Chestnut as "amiable and conciliatory at times," but also someone who is "so vituperative that much of what comes out of his mouth can be described as one word—"racist." He then referred to "The Letter" and described me as a "fair, hard-nosed reporter" who has "taken his share of abuse from whites as well (as from blacks)."

Ches and I once had a good relationship and I probably wrote more about his courtroom victories than any reporter in the area. On one occasion, I even accompanied him to interview one of his clients on Alabama's Death Row. As the years passed, things got better and he made my day at my retirement reception at the Selma-Dallas County Public Library in May of 2003. I had not expected him, but he came and brought along a wonderful surprise.

It was another letter, but much nicer.

"Over all the many years we have known each other, my 'enemies' have always been so numerous that the only sensible approach was to ignore them," he wrote. "However, I was never able to ignore you and no one (including my dear wife) could quite get 'under-my-skin' as you often did and always with such ease.

"I can easily think of 10 stories I tried hard to persuade you to publish but failed and 100 stories I wish you hadn't published," he added. "On the eve of your well-earned retirement, I will finally admit that you often covered Selma more effectively by yourself than did all the opposition with teams of reporters.

"Last, our many disagreements notwithstanding, I have always been an unabashed admirer of your impressive skills and professionalism as a journalist," he read to a packed library. You are also a first rate human being; otherwise your wonderful little wife wouldn't have given you the time of day."

Ches' appearance and his letter capped a wonderful event. He was a *mentsh* for coming.

Attorney J.L. Chestnut draws big laugh from Benn at reporter's retirement reception in 2003.

CHAPTER TWELVE:

SELMA, LIES AND VIDEOTAPE

"*Selma, Lord, Selma*" is a fine little book written by a good friend about two girls and their memories of what happened in early 1965 when Martin Luther King Jr. arrived in Selma to lead voting rights demonstrations.

After years of hoping for a movie version of his book, author Frank Sikora got a contract with one of the most respected television production companies in the country—Walt Disney. It couldn't have been a better arrangement. The final product was befitting a Disney fairy tale. They had the name right, but that was about all. Those who put it together defended their work, of course, but their explanation of why they reshaped history didn't go over well with those of us who covered the real thing.

"I'm speechless," said Roy Smith, a former Alabama State Trooper who photographed much of what happened in Selma between January and the end of March of 1965. He was at the Edmund Pettus Bridge when black marchers were routed by tear-gas tossing, billy club swinging troopers. "Maybe I was in a different Selma. That was not the Selma I was in."

Roy was invited, along with four Selma area residents, to preview "*Selma, Lord, Selma*" at the *Montgomery Advertiser* office a few days before it was to be shown at Alabama State University and, later, to a national audience on ABC's "*Wonderful World of Disney.*" We had cookies and Cokes as we watched. As it turned out, the treat was what we ate, not what we saw on the television set in the *Advertiser's* conference room.

Having covered some of the court hearings associated with the Selma movement, I was familiar with factual accounts of what happened that year, especially the dramatic confrontation on the bridge. When I saw the Disney version, it convinced me that Hollywood is, indeed, a dream factory where fact and fantasy often merge for the sake of movie receipts or television ratings.

The movie version included events that happened only in the imagination of the producer, director and scriptwriter. They made a hero out of a young man who wasn't even in Selma at the time of the bridge violence. They had King confronting Selma Mayor Joe Smitherman on the bridge. It didn't happen. They had Smitherman ordering the county sheriff to "take down the barriers" and allow King and his marchers to move on to Montgomery. It didn't happen. They had a cross burned outside a black church. It didn't happen—not with dozens of officers surrounding the church to see that it didn't.

"Dramatic license" is often used to juice up what filmmakers feel is too dull for movie or television audiences. In some cases, it might be justified. In Selma's case, it wasn't needed. There was so much drama during those first three months of 1965 that no embellishment of the truth was needed. It was all there and it was in Frank's fine little book.

Most of the movie was made near Atlanta which was an indicator the Disney people may have been looking more at the bottom line than authenticity. It was cheaper to do it there because many of those who work on film projects live in the area. Thus, costs can be cut on lodging, transportation, food and other expensive incidentals.

The crew did come to Selma for a couple of days of shooting. The reason was the Edmund Pettus Bridge, one of the most uniquely designed and recognizable spans in the country. Its wide, sweeping steel gray arches make it easily identifiable as a place where civil rights history was made. Today, I imagine it could be digitally reproduced, but Disney's decision to come to Selma was one of the few wise things it did in the production.

I spent much of the time on or near the set, watching the crew get ready and occasionally talking to the producer, director and extras. It didn't take long to see that "liberties" were being taken—apparently for the sake of time and finances. What clinched it for me came during one of the most dramatic moments of the movie—at the apex of the bridge where the violence occurred on the afternoon of March 7, 1965.

The march to Montgomery to protest black voter inequities was anti-climactic. It took place two weeks after the "Bloody Sunday" incident. On March 21, King and 4,000 followers walked peacefully and quietly across the bridge as the nation watched. His large group had protection from the Alabama National Guard which had been federalized.

The Disney version had actors portraying Smitherman and Dallas County Sheriff Jim Clark—two men who rarely allowed themselves to be in each other's company—standing side-by-side at the base of the bridge. The actor playing King approaches them and, with a harsh stare, informs them that history awaited. That's when Smitherman orders Clark to "take down the barricades" and allow the marchers through. In reality, there was no need for barricades because the Alabama National Guard had been ordered by the federal government to protect King and his followers. In addition, no mayor has jurisdiction over a county sheriff. But, it certainly made for a dramatic conclusion and that's what Executive Producer Julian Fowles apparently wanted.

As a one-man news bureau, I had my hands full trying to cover the movie. I didn't want to miss the most important moment—when State Troopers routed the demonstrators. I had taken photographs earlier in the day during another scene and needed to get it to Montgomery. So, I drove 53 miles to the *Advertiser*, dropped off the film, got back in my car and arrived in Selma 10 minutes before the big scene was to be shot. I was able to get a pretty good photograph of the "troopers" as they charged into the demonstrators. Then, I hopped back into my car for another 100-mile roundtrip to take that film to my office.

The movie version of the bridge violence had a major historical flaw. Jonathan Daniels, a young seminary student from New England, was depicted as having picked up one of the little girls whose memories led to Frank's book. He is shown hauling her out of the way of the tear gas, billy clubs and Clark's mounted posse. Daniels didn't arrive in Selma until a couple of days AFTER the incident. What the movie showed was a handsome young white man—played by the son of actress Patty Duke—rushing to help a poor, defenseless little black girl. When it actually happened, she had been picked up and taken to safety by one of the black civil rights leaders.

"I know Hollywood has to simplify things, but I was sort of stunned by the way this (movie) was oversimplified, the way everything was forced to fit the need for a young, cute white man to be a leading figure," said Selma historian Alston Fitts, who watched the movie with us.

Joining Alston and Roy at the advance screening were Charlie Jones, a former Selma police officer who had been at the bridge that day, Edie Jones, who helped promote tourism and movies in Selma and Bob Mants of nearby Lowndes County. Bob was in the second row of the march across the bridge and got a good whiff of the tear gas being hurled at his group.

As the closing credits rolled following the screening, everybody sat in silence until Alston came up with a loud "WOW!" He, too, had wondered what he had just seen. Mants, the lone black viewer in the group, shook his head, too. A real life hero during that time, his thoughts were on how future generations might perceive his group's actions.

"My concern is that my kids, my grandkids and other kids will view (the movie) as being historically correct," said Mants, who became one of Lowndes County's first elected black officials as a result of his efforts to force whites to give blacks their voting rights.

What made it even more puzzling was the fact many of those in decision-making positions in the production of "Selma, Lord, Selma" were black. They, more than anyone, should have known that factual history shouldn't be altered, especially when it involves their own heritage. It would be akin to Jewish producers trying to add even more drama to the Holocaust. Spielberg told it like it was in "Schindler's List."

As word of the movie began to spread through Selma, some leaders tried without success to encourage those in charge to at least inform viewers that what they were about to see or had just seen contained scenes that didn't happen.

"We urged Disney to issue a disclaimer at the start or end of the movie to tell people that it was not a true picture of what happened in Selma," said Jamie Wallace, who was president of the Selma-Dallas County Chamber of Commerce. "Our concern is that young people will view this movie as pure historic work when, in actuality, dramatic license was taken in the writing of the script." Jamie is a good friend and a former newspaper reporter who was on the bridge that day and was among those close enough to the action to smell the tear gas.

About an hour before the official screening of the movie at Alabama State University, Fowles joined Sikora, Jurnee Smollett, the young star of the film and Sheyann Webb-Christburg—one of the two girls featured in Sikora's book. At an ASU news conference, they talked about how happy they were to have been involved in the production and expressed the belief that it would be a national hit. Sheyann, an aggressive businesswoman and ASU employee, had a small role in the movie. If she had any reservations about the translation of her book to the big screen, she wasn't sharing them with anybody.

Sheyann told reporters that as the group of demonstrators got to the top of the bridge and started down toward the troopers, she could see "a lot of police dogs" with them. Wrong, wrong, wrong. Police dogs were used against black demonstrators in Birmingham in 1963. There were no police dogs on the bridge that day in Selma. People often confuse Selma and Birmingham because both played pivotal roles in the civil rights movement. Memories tend to become a bit cloudy with age, but Sheyann should have known better. I told her so. Even Frank seemed caught up in the hype. After waiting so long for a movie version, he was just happy to see it finally happen.

"I stand by my book," he said. "I was never asked to help during the filming and I realize they have the authority to make it the way they feel it should be made. I was sent an early copy of the script, but I've never seen the finished product." Frank said he had read books about Gen. George Custer and saw movie versions that portrayed him as the "last man standing" at the Little Big Horn. He said it didn't matter to him if Custer had been the last man or the first man. It mattered to me. Disney now has in its movie vault a fictional, made-for-television version of one of the most important real-life events in American history. It should have been a piece of cake to make "Selma, Lord, Selma" the book into "Selma, Lord, Selma" the movie without changing key elements. It was all there. Fowles didn't need to juice up or spruce up the ending or any other part of the movie.

A few years after the movie made its debut and continued to be rerun on television, a group of visitors from Gadsden in north Alabama drove to Hayneville, where Daniels was shot to death in August 1965. He had just been released from jail on charges related to demonstrations in which he was involved. They toured the jail where he had been kept prior to his slaying and listened to accounts of what happened from those who were there. I covered the memorial to Daniels each year and liked to talk to some of the visitors who may not have known much about the civil rights movement.

A 14-year-old girl stood outside the jail after looking at the cellblock where Daniels and his friends had been kept. I walked up to her, identified myself and asked if she had been familiar with what happened to the young seminary student.

"Oh, yes," she told me. "I saw the movie on television."

"Do you know many of the scenes in the movie never happened in real life?' I asked her.

"No," she said, as she looked at me in amazement. "You mean it wasn't true?"

"A lot of it wasn't," I told her.

It may have made for good television, but "*Selma, Lord, Selma*" alters history in the worst way. The teen-ager is only one of many who now believe fiction was fact.

Here's hoping the video version stays on store shelves for a long time, gathering dust and inattention.

CHAPTER THIRTEEN:

THE BEAR AND THE SNAKE

I had never heard of Bear Bryant when I arrived in Alabama to cover the civil rights movement. Growing up in Pennsylvania, the football coach we all admired was Rip Engle at Penn State. He was a winner, too, but, as I was to learn later, he couldn't match "The Bear" when it came to football success.

When I joined *United Press International* in Birmingham, I was told that one of my jobs—in addition to civil rights developments—was to cover University of Alabama football. They played on beautiful Saturday afternoons in the fall at Legion Field in Birmingham or at home in Denny Stadium in Tuscaloosa, about 60 miles to the west.

Football seemed like a nice diversion from covering protest marches, riots, arrests and police beatings. I had never seen a major college game before. So, prior to the start of the 1964 football season, I got a grand tour of Tuscaloosa from Bill Lumpkin, who was sports editor of the *Birmingham Post-Herald*.

It was a pleasant late summer morning, with the scorching heat of July and August a distant, sweaty memory. After Bill and I arrived on campus, we stopped for lunch at a local barbecue restaurant and then headed for the Crimson Tide practice field.

Bryant was busy with his assistant coaches, so Bill and I ambled over to where a group of players were warming up. One of them had a shock of dark hair and a big grin on his face. From what I would later hear of Joe Namath, he must have had a pretty good night.

The only thing I knew about Namath was that we had something in common. Both of us were from Pennsylvania. I caught his eye during a break and told him I was from Lancaster, Pa. I asked him what he was doing "down here." The transplanted Yankee from Beaver Falls, Pa. asked me the same question. He said it with a big smile. I didn't know if it was as a result of my stupid question or the fun he must have had the night before.

We all knew 1964 was going to be quite a year for Alabama football. With Namath and Steve Sloan, his backup at quarterback, speedy Ray Perkins at end and a bunch of other talented players, the Tide had a super team. By the end of the season, it was Sloan, not Namath, who made the difference, though.

During my first visit to Tuscaloosa, I got a chance to meet "The Bear." Since I hadn't known who he was, I had no reason to tremble in his presence. I didn't have a clue as to what he meant to the people of Alabama—those who loved the Tide, of course. He had returned after the Tide went 2-7-1 in 1957. The 1955-56 teams had a combined record of 2-17-1. The Tide faithful were miserable. Bryant, who was a star on Alabama teams of the early 1930s and once played on a broken leg, was coaching at Texas A&M when he got the job offer. He said it was as though "mama called." He returned to his alma mater in 1958—the year I graduated from high school.

I knew they called him "Bear," but I didn't know why. What I slowly began to comprehend was the deification bestowed upon him by Alabama football fans. It was well in place six years after he returned as head coach. He had already helped them win a national championship in that short period. As we began walking down a narrow concrete path toward the dressing room after practice, I asked him how he got it. He moved closer to me, wrapped a big, beefy arm around my right shoulder and said: "Well, son, it was like this...," then proceeded to tell me about wrestling a bear and acquiring one of the most famous nicknames in America.

I covered the Tide's game against North Carolina State that year and watched as Namath, who was as fast as any of the team's halfbacks, rolled out to his right on an option play. Unable to find a receiver, he headed downfield. All of a sudden, he collapsed. One of his knees buckled. Nobody touched him. Namath would come back after rehabilitation, but he never was the same. His arsenal of weapons had lost a key element. He could pass, but he couldn't run. It would hurt him throughout his professional career with the New York Jets where his arm and flamboyant behavior earned him his "Broadway Joe" nickname and a Super Bowl ring.

It was after the N.C. State game that I got a chance to really see how much Bryant was held in awe by so many people, even the writers who were supposed to be objective, but obviously fell under his spell as well. I was too green and too much of a "foreigner" to be quite the same sports sycophant. With the Tide a winner once more and everybody pretty happy we were all invited to Bryant's house for a post-game party.

The basement was cavernous and fit for a bear. The walls were lined with photographs of Bryant and his players, Bryant with President Kennedy, Bryant with friends and family. The buffet table could have fed my Parris Island battalion. The drinks were plentiful.

In the middle of the room was a large, stuffed chair. It was more like a throne. That's where "The Bear" sat—smoking his unfiltered Chesterfields and sipping one drink after another. It didn't seem he ever got a buzz on. The man could really drink. Whenever he dropped his right hand with an empty glass, one of his "aides" would rush over, grab it, refill it and replace it faster than a center's snap. He was the king and Tuscaloosa was his domain.

I didn't know it, but the "party" also served as a quieter place for a news conference after the game. Once everybody had their fill of food and drinks, Bryant announced that he would answer a few questions. No one had to come up and kiss his ring, but they knew they would be expected to toe the line and not ask any potentially embarrassing questions.

"Men," said Bryant, "The only thing I won't do is compare this team to any of my other teams or one player with another, today or in the past. That's the way it's going to be."

It didn't take long for a sportswriter to blow it with his first question. It went something like: "Coach, how would you compare..." Everybody seemed to freeze, even the writer, who must have known he just screwed up royally in the presence of gridiron royalty.

"That was a stupid question," said Bryant, in that slow, guttural voice of his. He knew how to control his anger. The glare in his eyes took care of that without uttering a word.

"Well coach," the writer responded. "I've got to get back home."

With that, he stood up and tried to find the exit as fast as he could after digging himself out of his embarrassing hole. He eventually got back into Bryant's good graces. No king wants bad press, even from a commoner reporter.

Even with Namath sidelined much of the season, the Crimson Tide won its second National Championship under Bryant despite an Orange Bowl loss to Texas on a controversial last second play. Namath was able to return in the second half and rallied the Tide to a point where there was a chance to win. On the last play of the game, Namath was stopped just short of the goal by Texas' great linebacker, Tommy Nobis. To this day, Namath insists he scored. Nobis is just as adamant that he stopped him. In any event, the wire services had crowned Alabama national champions based on the team's regular season performance. The post-season bowl loss changed that arrangement. Today, no national title is bestowed until the final bowl game is over.

Covering college football in those days was a lot different from the way it's done today. Instead of laptop computers to file our stories from press boxes around the country, we had to dictate our stories over the telephone after typing it out on paper. It meant trying to paint a word picture to somebody in Atlanta who may or may not have known one end of a football from the other.

Dictation, if done right, is a science. Since the person taking it couldn't see anything, we had to insert our own "quote, end quote, continue sentence, graph..." By the end of a story, the parties on both sides tended to be exhausted, if not winded by all the dictation required. We also had to make sure that the person on the other end of the line wasn't confused over particular words, so we'd spell them. I once told a rewriter to make sure it was "bucked" across the line and not a word that sounded like it, but started with another letter.

After Namath graduated, the Tide didn't miss a beat—winning still another national title. As Sloan was finishing his college career, a tall, rangy left-handed quarterback they called "Snake" arrived on campus. Ken Stabler, who grew up in the little south Alabama town of Foley, didn't sprint down the field. He slithered his way toward the goal in a unique running style that gave him his nickname. He was as tough to tackle as his passes were to intercept. I covered Stabler's performance in the Alabama High School All-Star football game at Bryant-Denny Stadium in Tuscaloosa and could tell immediately that he was something special. His passing accuracy, field generalship and self-confidence were obvious from the press box and he was named Most Valuable Player in the game.

When Stabler took over as the starting quarterback at Alabama, he continued a long line of super signal callers who played when Bryant returned. Pat Trammell was the first. Few college football teams had as superb a collection of quarterbacks as Alabama during the 1960s and 1970s. I didn't have the opportunity to watch Trammell play, but, while working for UPI, I did interview him just after he completed medical school. Sadly, he died of cancer before he could show that he was as good a doctor as a quarterback.

It was fun writing about Stabler because he made it look so easy. The only sore spot for him occurred in 1965 and few remind him of that moment. It was against Tennessee. The score was 7-7 and only seconds remained with Alabama deep in Vol territory. Tide fans crammed into Legion Field knew a chip shot field goal would win it. The ball was on the Tennessee 4. Stabler, who had entered the game two plays earlier to replace an injured Sloan, apparently became confused over the down, thinking it was third, not fourth. The Tide coaches on the sidelines apparently had the same problem. The windup? Stabler wound up and tossed the ball about 20 rows up into the stands, hoping to stop the clock and prepare for an easy field goal. Instead, the ball went over to Tennessee and the game ended in a 7-7 tie. I felt for Stabler. Baseball umpires at times forget the count. It was one of the most bizarre games of the long Alabama-Tennessee series. It took longer than usual to explain to the rewrite desk in Atlanta just what had happened.

Bryant took the blame, as he should have.

"When we came off the field, the dressing room door was locked," Bryant would say later in "Bear," his autobiography. "I was so mad I gave it a slam with my shoulder and it came off the hinges. I got them inside and told them I was more disappointed with my performance than I was with theirs." The confusing ending was but a small blip on a screen filled with successes for Stabler who soon moved into the professional ranks. Among his many accomplishments was helping the Oakland Raiders win a Super Bowl.

The next time I saw Stabler up close and personal, he was ready to toss me into Henry Pitts' swimming pool. It happened in 1980 when I went to Pitts' house to ask Kenny if he wanted to comment on a column written by *Birmingham Post-Herald* columnist Paul Finebaum. It centered on a wild night in west Alabama with Stabler, Pitts and friends enjoying themselves at the area's "finer" nightclubs. The colorful column by Finebaum, who would become a $350,000-a-year radio talk show host, helped build his newspaper reputation. It became a statewide story and was used in a *Selma Times-Journal* political advertisement against incumbent Mayor Joe Smitherman. I was managing editor of the *Times-Journal* at the time and our paper supported Smitherman's opponent. Pitts was Selma City Attorney and one of Smitherman's closest allies. The ad questioned the wisdom of electing a man with such an assistant. It didn't work, of course. I think all it did was gain even more votes for Smitherman.

Eric Benn with Ken Stabler at Stabler's football camp in Marion, Ala. in 1980.

I went to Henry's house on a Sunday afternoon to see if Stabler might like to respond to the column and the way it was being used. It appeared when I walked around to the backyard that Stabler had consumed some adult beverages. When I introduced myself, he didn't seem overly happy to see me, especially after I had asked him for a comment. He apparently had read Paul's column.

"I'm just here to see if you'd like to comment on it," I told him.

"You're just here to stir up some shit," he told me, as he moved toward me. "I ought to deck your ass."

At that point, I was mentally figuring out how much I might get in an out-of-court settlement after being slugged by a 6-3, 240 pound very angry professional quarterback. Recognizing that would be the last thing his client needed, Henry —who was Stabler's attorney, agent and friend—stepped in and pleaded with him to calm down.

"Come on, Kenny," Henry told him. "We don't need this. He's just here to ask you a question or two."

I left Henry's house without any bumps, bruises or autographs. Stabler continued playing superbly and I didn't see him again.

The last time I saw Bryant, he was at the Carl Morgan Convention Center in Selma at a 1981 reunion of the Crimson Tide team that beat Stanford, 29-13 in the 1935 Rose Bowl. It was arranged by Pat Morrow, whose husband, Bob Ed Morrow, was a lineman on that great Alabama team. Morrow played on the same side of the line as Bryant and they remained friends long after their playing days ended.

Bryant looked tired, but seemed to enjoy the night which included a showing of a grainy film of the Rose Bowl game against Stanford. He didn't say much, but his mere presence was enough to bring out a big crowd. I asked him to sign an autograph of a picture I took of him several years before. It says: "Eric, see you at Bama. Bear Bryant." Our son went to Troy State University instead, but he has Bryant's autographed picture framed and remains a big Bama fan.

I may have been one of the first people in the country to learn of Bryant's death. I was at my office in Selma which is home for the Zeigler meat-packing plant. Bryant was on Zeigler's board of directors and enjoyed coming to town.

As soon as the phone rang, I picked it up and heard a female voice say she was from Zeigler's. She told me "Coach Bryant has just died."

I knew he had been in ill health for awhile, but I guess we all felt he was indestructible. I called our sports department and told one of the editors. He didn't believe me, so I told him to check it out. It didn't take the wire services very long to spread the word.

The funeral was one of the largest in the state's history. Thousands lined the highway from Tuscaloosa to Birmingham where Bryant was buried. It was a fitting funeral and the end of an era at the University of Alabama.

CHAPTER FOURTEEN:

THE O'SHIELDS CASE

It was a story of tragedies, deception and death.

The cast of characters included an elderly man who spent his final years in a coma after being shot, one son who was shot to death, another son who strangled his ex-wife and a daughter who died after a fall down a flight of stairs.

Welcome to the O'Shields clan—a family ripped apart by violence, greed, sex and a series of strange circumstances.

The central figure was Michael O'Shields, who first was charged with murdering his ex-wife, Ruby, then was arrested on a charge of conspiring to kill his brother, Robert, to collect on part of a $100,000 insurance policy. Seems Michael was also having an affair with Robert's former wife at the time he pulled a Cain.

The strange case first came to light in April of 1994 when Michael O'Shields was arrested, along with his late brother Robert's ex-wife, Shirley O' Shields Watkins. The two were charged with capital murder. Police say they conspired to kill Robert so they could split the insurance money. Shirley, a mother of three, was arrested as she walked out of her doctor's office. Michael was picked up at a campground in west Alabama.

Their arrests prompted police to reopen investigations into the death of Michael O'Shields' sister, Debbie Voegler, who fell down a flight of steps in 1982 and the shooting of Robert O'Shields Sr., who was comatose following a shooting incident. It was a story with numerous twists and turns. Our police reporter at the time, Carla Crowder, did a good job explaining a complicated case filled with extended family connections and violence. Montgomery police originally ruled Robert O'Shields Jr.'s death a suicide and closed the case. Robert was found dead on a couch at his house on June 14, 1989. He had a gunshot wound in his right temple. A .25-caliber pistol had been used. Robert and Shirley O'Shields had just gone through a divorce.

Police Chief John Wilson told Carla that "everything looked on the up and up. (O'Shields) had been depressed and talked of suicide." Prior to the divorce, authorities said Michael O'Shields had begun an affair with his former sister-in-law. Wilson said his investigators learned that Michael then approached Shirley with a plan to hire a man from Tuscaloosa to kill Robert for half of the insurance. Although she was divorced, Shirley was still entitled to the $100,000 from her ex-husband's insurance policy, police said.

The case became a tale of two cities with police in Montgomery and Selma working together to unravel what had happened. In 1996, Michael O'Shields confessed to a charge of conspiring with Shirley to kill her ex-husband. By that time, Michael already had been convicted by a Dallas County jury of murdering his former wife, Ruby. He originally was charged with capital murder—a crime that carries the death penalty—but was convicted of a lesser criminal statute and got life in prison. I had picked up the story at that point after Carla's initial report that had a Montgomery connection. The O'Shields family was from Selma. Other than Robert O'Shields Jr.'s death in Montgomery, most of the events occurred in Selma.

The murder of Ruby O'Shields was a lot easier to prove and it took the jury only 24 minutes to convict her former husband. The main witness against Michael O'Shields turned out to be Michael O'Shields, who had given an emotional, videotaped confession to a boyhood friend, Selma detective sergeant Art Freine. The two had grown up together, went to the same schools and trusted each other. O'Shields felt comfortable around Freine. It wasn't as much a police interrogation as a discussion involving two friends. O'Shields provided explicit details about how he strangled Ruby after the two of them had just had sex and she began to question his manhood.

O'Shields said Ruby told him she was having an affair with one of his former high school friends, a black man she had become "close" to at the time. He said his former wife told him "that she was in love with him and she didn't care anything for me...she had never cared for me and I sexually did nothing for her in any way." O'Shields, who had carved out a good career with the Selma Fire Department, began to cry during his interview with Freine. Part of his statement was read during the trial.

"I just went out of my mind, I totally lost it," O'Shields told Freine. "I cried. She laughed and said that she was going to marry this man, that she was going to have her a life...that I had never meant anything to her...that she didn't care for me. At this time, I knocked Ruby down. I got on top of Ruby and with these two hands, forgive me, God, with these two hands, I choked her to death. I did it on my own. Nobody else was involved in this."

O'Shields told Freine that he paid a friend $600 to help him take the nude body of his former wife—wrapped in a blanket—to the Jones Bluff Lock and Dam between Selma and Montgomery. They waded into the rain-swollen Alabama River and let go. Ruby's body never was found.

"This is what happened with Ruby," O'Shields told Art. "Yes, I had lied in the past to try to cover the trail as to what happened with Ruby, but I'm through lying. This, as God as my witness, is the truth on what happened to her. That is why she has never been found because that's where she is at."

It didn't end there. Not only did Michael O'Shields kill his former wife and cook up a plot to kill his brother, he also went to the district attorney's office in Selma and tried to implicate his mother, Jewel O'Shields, in the shooting of her husband—his father. District Attorney Ed Greene told me that nothing ever came of that because "nobody was buying O'Shields' claims about his mother."

I got to know Jewel O'Shields during that time. She lived just down the street from our house. I first met her in April of 1994 when the bizarre story broke. The anguish was clear in her eyes.

"My family's been destroyed and I don't know what to do," she told me, as we sat in her living room, leafing through a scrapbook filled with photographs taken during happier days. "We are God-fearing people and I think the devil is trying to get us."

Two years after her eldest son was found shot to death in what initially was termed a suicide before her other son was arrested and charged with killing him, police began looking into the shooting of Robert O'Shields, Sr.

"My husband was on nine different kinds of medication when he shot himself," said Jewel, who had been named conservator of her husband's estate as he lay in what doctors described as a "vegetative state" at the Veterans Hospital in Tuscaloosa. The estate was valued at $55,000 plus $1,700 a month from Social Security and a small pension from the Selma Fire Department where he had worked for many years.

Robert O'Shields, Sr. eventually died. He never came out of the coma. Michael and Shirley pleaded guilty to conspiracy to commit murder and both went to prison. Jewel tried to get her life straightened out as best she could. About all she had left was that scrapbook and memories of what once had been.

For those of us who covered the strange story, it was confusing from the start because of all the familial connections to the case. At one point, the *Montgomery Advertiser* ran a list of names, how they were related and the charges lodged against them.

It was much like a baseball scorecard, with one major exception. What happened to the O'Shields family was no game.

CHAPTER FIFTEEN:

THE HISSSSSSMAN

Reginald Wayne Pope was probably the least likely man in America to win "Son of the Year" honors in 1988.

I guess it's because he tried to kill his mother with a rattlesnake.

Reggie met a man in Florida, asked if a rattler could kill someone and was told it could if it struck in the right place. The more Pope talked, the crazier it sounded to the man, but he didn't ignore what he had heard. He knew it could be for real.

Investigators say Pope's plan was to place a rattler in his mother's bed and let it do its business. He then would drag her outside and make it look like she had been fatally bitten while pruning the roses, or trimming the hedges. She lived in the small Marengo County town of Sweet Water where timber rattlers aren't that uncommon.

Reggie's acquaintance contacted authorities in Pensacola, Fla. and a sting operation was put into place. On Oct. 20, 1988, Pope and a snake handler went to Sweet Water to do what Reggie thought would be the deed. What he didn't know was that authorities were hiding nearby. His mother was informed about what was about to happen. She stayed in bed to make it look convincing. Pope had suggested that she take a nap that afternoon. Pope parked his truck around back of the house and made sure his dog was out of harm's way. He didn't want his pet bitten by the rattler. Putting the bite on mom would be just fine, but not his dog.

The trap was sprung long before the snake was ever taken out of the burlap sack it was kept in during the drive from Florida. Pope was cuffed and that was the last time he ever entered his house.

Kathleen Etheridge and her first husband adopted Reggie when he was 7 years old. Reggie , who kept his original surname while enjoying the love and affection of the woman who raised him, was polite to those who watched him grow up. He always wanted to make a lot of money, but never seemed to have any. His marriage failed and he left his ex-wife and two children to return home to "mom."

Kathleen never could understand Reggie. Could be she never knew about the demons that seemed to have possessed him. When she went into his bedroom to tidy up one day, she beamed over copies of "Plain Truth" and other religious periodicals. They were neatly stacked on shelves above his bed. When she tried to sweep under the bed, she found magazines that amounted to a different kind of truth—the "Naked Truth." They were filled with photographs of women without clothes. Investigators later found marijuana in the room—an indication that Reg's life truly had gone to pot.

A year after her son's arrest, Kathleen said she remained "scared to death" of her son, even though he had been in custody all that time. When he finally appeared in court, she was in the front row. Judge Claud Neilson sentenced Pope to 30 years in prison, but even that didn't ease the pain and fright in his mother's eyes.

"I'm very upset," she told me after the sentence was imposed. "I want him to leave today and never return during my lifetime."

District Attorney Nathan Watkins, who prosecuted Pope, thanked the Florida officials who were able to convince Reg that they would kill his mother with a rattlesnake. "The snake has been returned to the state Conservation Department and (Pope) has been committed to jail," Watkins said, before the judge had a thing or two to add.

Reginald Pope, center, with lawyer Billy Coplin, right, at Pope's sentencing in Linden, Alabama

"The method doesn't make any difference, but you did plan for someone to take the life of another person," the judge told Pope, who had been convicted a month before on a charge of criminal solicitation.

Reggie spent $300 as a "down payment" on what he thought would be a contract killing. Florida authorities said they understood Pope borrowed the entire amount from his mother. If so, it meant Kathleen Etheridge had unwittingly agreed to pay for her own demise. Pope denied that claim. He told the judge he had only borrowed $125 from mom to kill her.

After several years in prison, Reggie was transferred to the State Cattle Ranch in Greensboro, not far from where he grew up. He agreed to meet with me, but declined to go into specifics about the case. He maintained his innocence, however. I haven't interviewed any convicted criminals who admit they did anything bad.

"I can't be contrite or apologize for something I didn't do," he said, as we sat around a cement picnic table on a cold, windy day at the cattle ranch in late September of 2003. "Mom said she has forgiven me and I am grateful for that, but I'm not guilty."

Reggie did say he met a man in Florida and said they talked about things, but not about hiding a rattler in his mother's bed. After two parole rejections, Pope will try again, but with his mother's blessings the next time. She said she thinks he's a different man today at the age of 52.

"I really believe he has changed," she told me in an interview after I had met her son. "He seemed so humble and sorry for everything the last time I saw him. I think he was on drugs when all this happened. Deep down, I still love him."

With Alabama's money problems in recent years, Pope could be sprung from prison sooner than he originally anticipated. Thousands of inmates are expected to be released as a way to save state revenue. Since Pope didn't murder anybody, he could be on that long list. Watkins has retired as a prosecutor, but his opinion of Reggie hasn't changed.

"He was a sneaky son of a bitch," said Watkins. "He intended to kill her with the snake and he doesn't deserve parole."

I've seen convicted killers get a lot less than the 30 years Pope received. He hasn't had any disciplinary problems since he began serving his time and is well liked at the cattle ranch.

"The only time I've seen him upset is when he can't get the homemade vanilla ice cream he likes so much from the vending machine," said warden George Free, who approved my interview with Pope.

The motive for Pope's plan to murder mom? Authorities said Reggie was in debt and thought he might be able to collect on his mother's $15,000 life insurance policy. She had named him as beneficiary in the event of an accidental death.

CHAPTER SIXTEEN:

A SORRY IMITATOR

W hen Jack Dempsey was starting out in the fight game, he'd walk into every saloon he could find in Colorado and Montana and offer to take on the house for the price of a drink and a few bucks. He is said to have used different names to make sure his trail would be hard to follow, especially if he had to make a quick departure from the scene of his latest victory.

Willie Smith was no Jack Dempsey. Willy Loman would be more like it. Smith was a real life salesman, much like the fictional Loman in "Death of a Salesman." His product was himself—something he tried to sell under a variety of names to get fights he was bound to lose.

I met Willie while working as managing editor of the *Natchez Democrat* in Mississippi. His name at the time was Muhammad Al. Muhammad Ali was still somewhat in his prime at the time, so Willie thought he'd try to capitalize on the great fighter's fame—at least by using a version of his name. Willie's boxing techniques were better suited for mopping floors because that's what his opponents did with him after a few minutes in the ring.

Muhammad Al became a national celebrity, of sorts when Mike Royko, the Pulitzer Prize winning syndicated columnist for the *Chicago Daily News*, referred to him as the worst athlete on the face of the earth—and that included members of the early New York Mets. In his column, Royko made a pointed reference to Muhammad's 10 knockouts in 10 outings. Muhammad, by the way, was the knockee. I had only been at the *Democrat* a few months when Muhammad began dropping by my office to talk boxing and his next comeback. He said he was a new man and ready to fight again.

"Oh, really?" I said. "Who will you be fighting?"

He said it would be Michall Louis, a former Golden Gloves champ who had comeback ambitions of his own. Originally billed as a professional fight, it had to be changed to a 10-round exhibition a few days before the bout for unexplained reasons. I guess it had something to do with the fact that Muhammad and the words "boxing professional" just didn't go together. It wasn't a fight that attracted a lot of attention. Instead of a big arena on a Saturday night, the bout was held on a Wednesday night at Danny's Lounge in Louisiana just across the Mississippi River from Natchez.

It was about 10:15 p.m. when the two men climbed into the ring at the saloon. It had been erected just above the bar, leaving little room for customers, many of whom had no idea a boxing match had been scheduled. They were there to get a drink. Louis and Muhammad went through some preliminary warmups and then put on their gloves. Louis wore a robe with his name on the back. Muhammad had a robe but no name, most likely because it would have cost too much to keep changing it. When he entered the ring, a buzz could be heard in the crowd. He had been "made" by those who paid a couple of bucks to see what they expected to be a fight.

"That's not Muhammad Al," said one ringside fan. "That's Blackjack Smith. I remember seeing him run down the levee road many times." Before he was Blackjack Smith, he was Muhammad Smith. If names made a fighter great, Muhammad Al would have been a champ instead of a chump.

As it turned out, the warmup lasted longer than the "fight." Muhammad Al may have thought he was like Muhammad Ali in name, but he lacked basic skills needed to succeed in the fight game—like a punch, footwork, speed, stamina and brains. Ali liked to say he floated like a butterfly and stung like a bee in the ring. Al floated like a bee and probably would have been KO'd by a butterfly if it had flown into him.

A sharp right from Louis put him down shortly after the bell rang for round one. Muhammad staggered to his feet and his eyes were glazed. His handlers didn't throw in the towel, but it looked like they were ready to throw him into the Mississippi River, which wasn't far from Danny's Lounge. The "fight" lasted 168 seconds. Muhammad needed only 12 seconds to finish the round, but it appeared to be a good thing he didn't.

The fans weren't ecstatic about the quick ending. But, they should have known something. After all, it was Muhammad Al they had paid to see.

"I didn't get my money's worth," said one boxing enthusiast who had paid all of $3.50 for a ringside seat. Earlene White was even more disappointed by the quick ending. She was the wife of the lounge owner and had hoped for a longer fight to sell more booze. "I turned my head to go see about a customer and when I came back it was all over," she said.

I hurried back to my office to write what promised to be a relatively short story about Muhammad Al's latest comeback disaster. I hadn't been at my desk more than a few minutes when the phone rang. It was Al, wanting to know what I was going to write. "I'm going to say you got your butt whipped, Muhammad," I told him. "It shouldn't take long to write, probably not as long as the 'fight' lasted." "Well, if you do, I'm going to kill you and your whole family," he replied.

The "butt whipping" story ran the next morning, followed by a column a few days later. It ended with a suggestion for Muhammad Al—"Why not take up some other occupation—like steeplejacking. It's much safer." Al wouldn't let it go. He kept calling with threats and stopping by to see me with more nasty comments. We finally told him to cease and desist or the police would be called. That was the last I saw of him. From time to time, I'd hear about him popping up—always on the comeback trail, but never really able to put it all together.

When Royko awarded Muhammad Al his "Worst Athlete In History" designation, it was for good reason. Seems Al once knocked himself out in his own corner. Royko said he tripped over his water bucket and slammed his head into the ring stool.

Too bad the stool didn't knock some sense into him.

CHAPTER SEVENTEEN:

THIS FAT LADY DIDN'T SING

The first time I saw Caroline Corbit, she was waiting to question a former president. The last time I saw her, sweat was pouring down her chubby cheeks and I gave her a couple of bucks for gas so she could get back to Birmingham.

She called herself "The Fat Lady" and she had used it as the title for her 92-page autobiography. After writing about her for several years, it seemed 92 pages could hardly cover the life and times of this strange woman who kept showing up at my office door or calling me.

Caroline first came to my attention—and that of a couple of anxious Secret Service agents—in November of 1987 at the University of Alabama where former President Gerald Ford was to make a speech. Those of us in the legitimate press corps were known to UA officials, but we still had to go through a routine background check to get near Ford. When I entered the room where the former president was scheduled to speak, I noticed a large woman sitting on the front row. "Who's she?" I asked one of the UA press relations people. "I don't know," she told me. "She just came in and sat down."

Moments later, Ford emerged from the wings and made an opening statement. On campus as part of a speaking tour, Ford then graciously asked for questions from the floor. Instead of picking a reporter from

Birmingham, Montgomery, Huntsville or Mobile, Ford—to his subsequent regret—saw Caroline's hand shoot up and he gave her the honor of asking the first question. She mentioned Bert Lance, Jimmy Carter and, it seemed, everybody else in Georgia. Ford listened attentively at first, but began to look uneasy after a couple of minutes. Secret Service agents standing nearby appeared edgy. After all, Ford had been the target of two would-be assassins and they didn't want to worry about any during his Alabama trip. Caroline said she once worked for Lance's bank in Georgia and was doing "research" for her book on "the scandal." She never mentioned what the scandal was all about, but, by that time, Ford had enough and cut her off. She reluctantly sat down and then we were given the opportunity to ask about the Reagan Administration and whatever else was going on in 1987.

When the press conference had ended, embarrassed university officials discovered that they had been snookered. Caroline had obtained a piece of stationery from a Birmingham television station and used it to gain admittance. It apparently was not the first time she had finagled her way into places usually restricted to those with legitimate press credentials. She told me she once ran onto the field at a Super Bowl game in New Orleans and was arrested for her unexpected intrusion. The NFL should have put her in pads instead. She would have made a great defensive tackle.

Caroline told me during an interview at my Selma office that she received $517 a month in disability payments for a mental condition. She denied being of unsound mind, but did tell me that she had been in mental institutions in Louisiana and Alabama.

"I'm not mentally ill," she told me. "I never have been. A Birmingham psychiatrist once told me I was normal."

Unmarried with only a brother in Atlanta to call kin, Caroline, who was 49 at the time, said she had written her life's story to pay off mounting debts. She said she owed individuals, corporations and charities.

"I don't want to take bankruptcy," she said. "I need the money so I can go to a fat farm, lose weight and buy some pretty clothes."

Caroline said she once drove to California to see television producer Norman Lear, the man who gave us Archie Bunker. She said she dropped off a script for a TV series. For some reason, she said, Lear had not gotten back to her. She never seemed to get down on herself whenever

I saw her, but she used "unconstitutional" and "discrimination" a lot in our conversations.

"The rich always get their way and the poor never have much of a chance in life," she told me, adding that she once charged a strand of pearls at Saks Fifth Avenue in New York, knowing full well that she didn't have enough money to cover one bead, let alone the whole necklace. Caroline carried a plastic sandwich bag in her purse. She filled it with business cards and ticket stubs with the names of those who lent her a few dollars for gas. I don't think anybody actually thought she'd repay them. They gave her the money because they knew she didn't have it. I never asked for a receipt from her.

Caroline told me she pawned the small instant camera she used to take snapshots of Ford at that memorable UA press conference. She said she also pawned her diamond ring. She didn't say if the ring had been a family heirloom or had come from a Cracker Jack box.

"I got $7 for the camera and $40 for the ring," she told me. "I didn't have much choice. I needed the money."

As the years moved along, Caroline would occasionally call from her Birmingham apartment or jail where she said she was preparing to bond herself out for one infraction or another. She asked me to return her call, but, I rarely did. Deadline schedules kept me busy and, by that time, I wondered why I had ever interviewed her in the first place.

She'd always make sure I knew she was still looking for a publisher of her memoirs, still looking for a television producer to turn her ideas into sure-fire ratings hits. Caroline, who said she wanted to title her autobiography *"The Fat Lady Sings,"* left a message for me during the summer of 2002. She said she was doing better than ever "and I'm not homeless anymore."

It's a shame Hollywood never took her up on her offers. With all the schlock on television these days, some of Caroline's scripts probably would have been winners. She could teach them a thing or two about reality shows, although it seems much of her world and her concept of reality are strangers at times.

I last talked to Caroline in the spring of 2004. She said she was 65 and had been homeless for two years. She said she finally found an apartment in Birmingham's Southside and was living on about $850 a month in Social Security benefits. "That's about it," she said.

"I'm still going to publish my book," she told me. "I think those people in Hollywood have stolen a lot of my ideas from what I had written before. But, I'm not going to give up."

Knowing Caroline Corbit, I could believe that.

CHAPTER EIGHTEEN:

JAILHOUSE LAWYER

Keenan Kester Cofield's name was enough to send courthouse clerks into orbit. Whenever I called someone to ask about Cofield, the usual response was "who's he suing now?"

Unlike prisoners who spent their time playing basketball, pumping iron, watching soap operas, marking time or looking for ways to escape, Cofield's hobby was suing people and organizations. It didn't matter who they were or how much they were worth. Cofield just seemed to enjoy suing them and spent much of his prison time in the law library, poring over the latest legal journals. He got so good at what he did, that lawyers who came up against him often gave him grudging admiration.

One of Cofield's favorite targets was the Alabama Department of Corrections. Between 1982, when he was sentenced to 15 years in prison for theft, and 1987, when I got to know him pretty well, he had filed 21 suits against the department which oversees the state's penal system. His offense hardly made him a candidate for the FBI's 10 Most Wanted List, but he nevertheless made quite a legal splash for himself all over the state.

In addition to lawsuits against the department of corrections, Cofield also took on newspapers, the state Mental Health Department, lawyers, a sheriff and even a pizza company. His criminal record dated back to 1978. In a pre-sentence report filed by a Madison County court official, Cofield was described as a "very deceptive fellow." On one occasion, officers found in his car a letter indicating he had died—along with requests that speeding tickets and charges against him be dropped because of his "death."

Cofield once sued the *Selma Times-Journal* for $125 million after the newspaper printed his obituary. At the time, Cofield was at the Dallas County Jail, not far from the paper. He sent a telegram to the *Times-Journal* a few days later, saying in his best Mark Twain style, that he was "very much alive." He followed the telegram with a lawsuit that eventually was dismissed—like most of his legal claims.

He once sued me and the *Montgomery Advertiser*—my employer—for $32 million, claiming he had been libeled in an article written about one of his prior lawsuits. A lawyer for a defendant being sued by Cofield had been quoted in my story as saying the inmate's lawsuit was frivolous. Cofield then sued the lawyer for saying his lawsuit was frivolous. It got to the point where the Alabama Supreme Court stepped in to stop him. Noting Cofield's long criminal history, the state's highest court determined that he was "libel proof" and that lawsuit was dismissed.

Cofield once sued a Minneapolis food distribution company for $500, claiming that he had become sick after ordering 10 cases of pizza. When Dallas County Circuit Clerk Bill Kynard asked for a copy of Cofield's prison record for the judge to consider in small claims court, the inmate dropped the lawsuit like a plate of hot pepperoni.

"Please be advised, I wish not to prosecute this matter," said Cofield, in a document that referred to himself in the third person. "Plaintiff Cofield has other legal matters and I'm not able to attend the trial on the date given." It wasn't unusual for Cofield to write some of the companies sued by him with an offer to settle out of court for somewhere under the millions that he originally sought.

Cofield, who once claimed to have been raped by a mental health counselor at the Dallas County Jail, filed a multi-million dollar suit and later received $3,500 in an out-of-court settlement. He didn't always ask for money in his lawsuits. On one occasion, he sued for the right to vote, claiming his incarceration should not stand in the way of casting a ballot for candidates of his choice. He was quickly reminded by the attorney general at the time—Charlie Graddick—that he had forfeited his right to vote when he broke the law. Cofield then announced he planned to launch a prisoner political lobby. He didn't sue Graddick, either.

He once tried to get prison guards an $8-a-day pay differential because, he said, they are "risking their lives every day." That impressed the guards, even though they knew all about Cofield's past.

In most cases, prisoners serving time for theft of property are out shortly after they go in. Some are sent into work-release programs within weeks or months of their incarceration because they are not considered risks to society. Not Cofield. He spent most of his 15 years behind bars. They finally let him out in the late 1990s. He used to call me a lot from jail...always collect, of course. I haven't heard from him in a long time, but wouldn't be surprised if he's still studying law books.

CHAPTER NINETEEN:

A WAKEUP JOLT

The phone next to my side of the bed rang early on a Friday morning. Having covered west Alabama for 15 years, I had gotten to know voices pretty well. I knew right away that the one on the other end of the line was Eddie Hardaway, the first black circuit judge in Sumter County—a rural region that hugged the Mississippi State Line.

"Al, you need to come over right away," said the judge, who had gotten to know me through the years when I'd pop in and cover some of the trials he presided over. "Somebody just shot into my house."

"Say, what?" I asked. "Shot where?"

I didn't waste any time with more questions. It took about 10 minutes to hop out of bed, shower and race to my car. Hardaway lives in Livingston, the seat of government in Sumter County. It's about an hour and a half from Selma. I think I got there in about an hour.

The judge had called me about four hours after two shotgun blasts ripped through bedroom windows in his red brick house near what then was known as Livingston University. Today, it's the University of West Alabama. When I found the judge, it looked like he hadn't completely regained his composure. He told me he and his wife, son and nephew escaped injury, but remained inside the house until they felt it was clear enough to leave. The couple's bed was covered with shards of glass from the shotgun blast that had torn through a window before striking several walls inside their bedroom and one next to it. Shotgun pellets were removed from the walls and doors of both bedrooms.

"This wasn't done to intimidate me," Hardaway told me, as he led me through the house where damage from the shotgun blasts was easy to see. "This was done to murder me."

The shots were fired on Feb. 23, 1996—only a few months after six black churches had been burned and vandalized in Sumter, Greene and other west Alabama counties. As the hours passed that day, black residents of Livingston and Sumter County became upset. It didn't take long for race to be injected into the incident. Within two days of the shooting, Hardaway claimed that "powerful whites" had been behind the shooting. He never mentioned anybody by name. Civil rights leaders spent several days in the Livingston area, holding press conferences and attaching blame before the investigation could really get started.

During one of my interviews with Hardaway in his office, the judge took off his black robe, revealing a pistol on his right hip. He didn't have to explain why he wore it. I took a photo of it and it accompanied my article that appeared in the *Advertiser* the following day.

After the initial shock wore off, it got really messy and personal. Jeff Sessions, who was Alabama's attorney general at the time and later was elected to the U.S. Senate, announced that a personal motive had been behind the shooting. Sessions declined to elaborate, but Hardaway denied any possible involvement.

An Alabama State Trooper who had been a friend of the Hardaway family subsequently was fired from his position for writing letters to the *Sumter County Record-Journal* about the incident. He said he had only been expressing himself as a citizen. His supervisors said he had disobeyed a direct order not to discuss the case publicly.

Instead of a quick resolution, the investigation dragged on through the rest of 1996 and into 1997. In late April of that year, a Sumter

County Grand Jury convened to investigate the Hardaway case was dismissed by Montgomery County Circuit Judge Charles Price.

So, after two shotgun blasts had ripped into a judge's house in the middle of the night, followed by screams of racism, it all ended quietly. No one was ever arrested, the trooper never got his job back and Hardaway continued as a circuit judge.

CHAPTER TWENTY:

BOB ED

When the University of Alabama football team went to Pasadena, Calif. to prepare for the 1935 Rose Bowl game against Stanford, the stars were Don Hutson, who became one of the great wide receivers in the early years of the National Football League and Paul "Bear" Bryant, who would become one of college football's most successful head coaches.

Playing on the right side of the offensive line with Bryant was a man who made up for his lack of size with courage and style. It was Bob Ed Morrow—an important cog in the big Crimson Tide machine that beat Stanford and won the most important bowl game in the land that year.

Bob Ed weighed 170 pounds when he lined up at right guard on New Year's Day of 1935. He had lost a lot of weight after an injury in Alabama's game against Georgia during the regular season. When he squatted into his position for the first offensive play of the game for Alabama, Morrow looked squarely into the eyes of a 245-pound defensive tackle. If he felt any fear at that moment, he didn't let the Stanford player in on it.

**Bob Ed Morrow, left, with University of Alabama classmate
Paul "Bear" Bryant in the 1930s.**

In the years after college, Bob Ed continued to distinguish himself. During World War II, he rose to the rank of colonel and handled difficult logistical assignments as Allied troops drove into Germany after D-Day. Following the war, he became an important member of the Alabama National Guard and a prosperous insurance executive.

Cancer claimed Bob Ed's first wife after 32 years of marriage. They had two children, one of whom, Robert, became Dallas County's district attorney and, later, a state prosecutor. He married again and another son kept Bob Ed young well into his seventh decade. On Oct. 3, 1989, doctors detected a malignant brain tumor. Bob Ed was 78 at the time. He didn't blink when he got the news. Anybody who excelled under pressure as he did on the football field and in war knows attitude is a vital ingredient in surviving through the tough times.

"I have no doubt I will lick it," he told me in a confident voice I had heard many times in the past. I believed him. I had no reason not to. We all succumb to the clock sooner or later, however. In Bob Ed's case, it was a matter of how long he could hang on. He had already gotten his Biblical "Three Score and 10" and was fast approaching a decade after that.

He and his wife, Pat, would take long walks around their beautiful little neighborhood in Selma's Historic District. They had been running a bed-and-breakfast operation for several years. They called it Kelso Cottage and enjoyed entertaining guests. Bob Ed's condition worsened, but he wouldn't give in. He wouldn't give up his most precious gift without a fight. He had grandchildren to spoil. He had memories to talk about along the way.

His faith kept him strong during his biggest battle of all, but he slowly slipped into a zone of no return. His strong heart kept beating as his family, doctors and nurses tended to him. He spent his days at home. That's where he wanted to be at the end.

Bob Ed died in 2000. He had lived 88 years and left behind a large family which adored him. Among them were two great-grandchildren. He also left behind something just as important as a loving family—a splendid history of personal integrity as well as duty, honor and service to his country.

He was quite a guy.

CHAPTER TWENTY-ONE:

WALTER'S 'PUBIC' STATEMENT

Walter Alves didn't think a play with partial nudity and a few naughty words would create such a ruckus. By 1987 standards, his *"Babylon Motel"* was pretty tame stuff, even if one of the female characters was to display purple pubic hair. The catch was location. It was to be performed at the University of Alabama, where Deep South morals and generational aversion to questionable behavior usually takes center stage.

The controversy began innocently enough. Alves, a UA graduate student from Guntersville in north Alabama with dreams of Broadway dancing in his head, penned a play that would have pleased Tennessee Williams. Part of it involved an incestuous relationship between a young boy and his mother. Nobody said much about it until word leaked out to university officials in the spring of that year.

Instead of coming down hard on Alves' questionable scenes and dialogue, the university chose to "ban" the play more on premises than premise. Alves was told he couldn't use Morgan Auditorium which is where he wanted to stage his play. Roger Sayers, who was president of the university at the time, issued a statement saying the issue "in question" was how the school "chooses to manage its facilities." He also said he wanted to "make it clear" to Alves that the university "has not censored your play or asked that you change it."

Right, and Alabama fans love Auburn.

Alves didn't back away. He knew what started out as a play that might not attract more than a handful of curious students, suddenly had begun to garner not only statewide, but national attention. It became a First Amendment issue and he loved every moment. His 15 minutes of fame had extended to months after he was told he couldn't use the auditorium. He also knew that taking on one of the state's most venerable and wealthy institutions was as much a challenge to his pocketbook as his belief in the First Amendment. He called the University of Alabama a "multi-million dollar corporation" and said it could easily "wage a war of attrition against anyone or any idea."

Stan Murphy, one of the university's lawyers, took issue with Alves' attorneys on several points, including a contention that Richard Peck, dean of the UA College of Arts and Sciences, did not have the authority to make "content-based decisions." Murphy responded by saying: "Don't kid yourself. The university administration makes content-based decisions every day."

As the controversy continued to heat up and the case moved from the campus to a federal courtroom, Alves faced a monetary dilemma. He needed money to maintain his fight and that wasn't as easy as writing a play. A Tuscaloosa lawyer, Ed Still, took Alves' case on a contingency basis, meaning there were no guarantees—only hopeful expectations that, if Walter won, he might get some monetary damages. In the meantime, Alves had to find a few bucks to pay his lawyer to keep the case in court. He and his supporters came up with a T-shirt idea and they were sold at campus rallies held in support of the play.

"I haven't even gotten a T-shirt out of this yet," Still laughed, when I interviewed him in mid-December 1987—months after the case first surfaced. "Walter promised to send me one." By that time, U.S. District Judge Sam Pointer had already refused to enjoin the school from prohibiting the play's performance.

In the end, Walter's play never was performed at the University of Alabama. He said he lost a bundle in the process because of legal fees, but never regretted his "free speech" stand.

"I still haven't given up," he told me more than a decade after his failed effort. "I'm working on a way to put the play on up here. I think I'll do it, too."

He moved back home to Guntersville to take care of his ailing mother. After her death, he decided to stay there. In between odd jobs, he works on plays and keeps the script to *"Babylon Motel"* close at all times.

If it ever winds up on stage, he said, there will be one noticeable difference from the original version.

Instead of purple pubic hair, he told me, the female lead will use an "iridescent" dye.

CHAPTER TWENTY-TWO:

HOSPITAL MISADMINISTRATOR

Bruce Rhyne was in tears as he stood before Clarke County Circuit Judge Hardie B. Kimbrough on Nov. 8, 1985.

Once one of the most respected men in neighboring Marengo County, Rhyne was being called on the legal carpet for stealing at least $136,000 from Bryan Whitfield Memorial Hospital in Demopolis, Alabama where he had been the administrator for 12 years. Rhyne apparently didn't feel he was making enough money as director of the only hospital in a 100 mile-area between Selma and Meridian, Miss. So, he concocted a scheme to make more by creating bogus companies, according to prosecutors.

What he did was form a dummy corporation to provide medical examinations for possible asbestos contamination of construction workers. Payments then were sent to Rhyne's phony corporation. District Attorney Nathan Watkins said his investigation showed the address of the bogus company just happened to be the same one used by one of Rhyne's relatives in Mobile.

Some in Marengo County thought Rhyne had swiped a lot more than $136,000 from the hospital, but an audit covering a three-year period was as far as prosecutors could go under Alabama statutes. Several other criminal counts against Rhyne were dropped as part of a plea agreement between Watkins and Rhyne's two lawyers, including future Alabama Supreme Court Justice Bernard Harwood of Tuscaloosa.

Pre-trial publicity in Marengo County caused the trial to be moved to Clarke County. It was obvious that Rhyne's lawyers knew their client would have a hard time finding an impartial jury in a county where he had once been so prominent. They obviously didn't want him facing former friends in a jury box.

They say part of personal retribution is admission of sins. If that's the case, Bruce Rhyne appeared ready to throw himself on the mercy of the court after admitting what a bad boy he had been. As he raised his right hand to take the oath from Kimbrough, who looked down on him from the bench, Rhyne shook noticeably. During questioning by the judge, he began to cry. He lowered his head as Watkins read the indictment against him. Then, he admitted his guilt—confessed in open court that, in effect, he had been greedy and stole the public's money as well as its trust.

The agreement between the state and defense involved a seven year prison sentence and restitution of the money stolen by Rhyne. That was pretty much decided before he appeared in court and the only thing left for Rhyne to do was admit he was "really sorry" for having been such a thief all those years.

"He has imposed on himself an inner punishment exceeding what the court has done," said Harwood. "I don't think even he knows why he did it." Rhyne's sobs grew louder and he continued to shake. Tears streamed down his cheeks. A man who once stood before civic groups and awed members with his knowledge of the hospital industry, had been reduced to a pathetic figure asking for forgiveness—or so it seemed at that moment.

Watkins told the judge that Rhyne had used some of the stolen money to buy a car for a hospital employee as well as a pool table and lawn mower. Some money also went to pay off a personal loan. The prosecutor said Rhyne's bonding company would probably repay $100,000 of the stolen money. He said Rhyne already had paid back $26,000 and would pay the rest within a year. Rhyne had been free on $75,000 bond since earlier in the year when he was arrested.

After the sentencing ended, I hustled outside the courthouse to position myself in front of Rhyne as Harwood escorted him away from the scene of his humiliation. I don't think Rhyne noticed me at first as he walked down the steps, but he did as I raised my camera to get some shots of him in all his apparent contriteness.

Rhyne didn't have a tear in either eye, but he did manage to give me what appeared to be a wink. Perhaps he had just been blinded momentarily by the sun. He also seemed to have a trace of a smile on his face. No one had to tell him that he had just dodged a bullet. He could have gotten 120 years in prison for what he did. He also knew Alabama's lenient laws wouldn't keep him behind bars very long. His seven year stay in state prison sentence lasted only a few weeks before he was placed into a work-release program. He first went to work for a Clanton radio station and then moved on to a bigger city where he worked for a relative's construction company.

I heard he made a nice salary.

CHAPTER TWENTY-THREE:

BUMPING FOR BUCKS

"Attention, ladies," boomed the voice from backstage. "We have just received a severe thunderstorm warning from Montgomery and Selma."

The noisy chatter stopped. Ears perked up. Cigarette smoke swirled to the ceiling of the darkened room. Then, the voice picked up again as everybody strained to hear what would be said next.

"For the next hour and a half, it will be raining men..."

Music exploded, rocking the room with a pulsating beat dominated by a percussion-produced boom-de-de-boom-boom-boom sound that had the walls vibrating. Hundreds of women who had shelled out $6 to see the "rain men" were ecstatic as five tanned guys in tuxedos rushed to the front and began a dance routine. The women whistled and pounded their feet. When the dancers disrobed to bikini briefs, the noise was deafening.

Other than me, the five dancers and an announcer, there wasn't another male in the audience at the Night Owl Club that April night in 1984. I held a notepad and camera and tried to stay out of the way. It was one of my more unusual assignments with the *Montgomery Advertiser*—reporting on the arrival of feminism at still another former bastion of male domination—the strip show. Of course, in this case, the strippers were men, not women.

Why would 300 secretaries, mill workers, clerks and nurses leave husband, hearth and children to drool over handsome young men with "six-pack" abs and bulging "packages?" They were there to have a good time and didn't want any beer-belly, belching, butt-scratching men around to spoil the fun.

I asked one matronly-looking patron why she was at a strip club when she could have been home baby-sitting her grandchildren. She responded with a look that made it clear she was where she wanted to be. "Why shouldn't we?" she asked. "The men have been enjoying it all these years. We're no different than they are."

Anatomical differences aside, it was evident those in the crowd got a kick out of being treated to a show where there was as much tease as strip. Male dance acts back then were popular and the five young men in the dance group "Male Factor" believed that they had the most professional act in the country.

"We make $250,000 a year and our costumes cost us $10,000," Doug Manley, told me. "This is a real business. We're incorporated." I got a chance to interview Manley and the other members of his group a few minutes before they "rained" on the impatient customers on the other side of their dressing room. Some of the women had consumed enough booze by that point to watch any guy take off his clothes. I would have been exempted, of course. My body was and is made for hiding, not feeding female fantasies.

The way Manley saw it that night, he and his friends were providing a much-needed service for the ladies. "Some of these women have never really had a night by themselves," he said. "Their husbands go out and have a good time. We provide an outlet for them."

Each member of the cast had different dance routines with characterizations ranging from Indian chief to Zorro, from cowboy to construction worker. As we talked backstage at the nightclub next to Selma's only movie theater, an announcer standing near Manley and behind the curtain, began using double entendres about the uses of tomahawks, hard hats, whips and pistols. The howls of laughter made it difficult for me to ask questions.

As Manley talked, I began to wonder why I didn't work out six hours a day, shave my chest and prance around in a modified G-string. Manley said one of the dancers recently bought his own airplane. He said each had a nice car, fashionable clothes and an assortment of things associated with the good life.

"We realize this has a limited life span," Manley said. "What we hope to do is use it to propel us into careers like films, modeling and other areas of entertainment. This isn't a piece of cake like some people think, but, if you present yourself in a classy way, the audience will act that way, too. If you act sleazy, they'll be like that."

Seconds after the curtain opened and Manley's group made its grand entrance, it was clear that sleaze had won out over class. "Take it off," screamed the women, throwing sophistication and dollar bills to the wind in the smoke-filled room. They weren't disappointed. There were bumps and grinds, leers, beers, cheers and screams of joy, especially from those women who got close enough to place tips in a spot that would shock a waiter. Manley said he and his buddies didn't go into the audience looking for tips, but they weren't about to ignore them. He said a friend once got a $100 bill stuffed down into the front of his bikini brief. Most of the customers stuck to $1 bills. Some tried to get them as far down the bikinis as possible—perhaps searching for their own tips. That prompted the grinding guys to wave fingers at them in a "classy" way of saying "naughty-naughty."

I took it all in from a spot near where they performed. The owner of the club didn't object to my presence. Neither did the women. Their eyes were on the muscular, sparsely-clad male dancers, not the fat guy with the notebook and camera.

By the time the show ended, most of the husbands and boyfriends left behind that night were waiting outside in the parking lot for their lovely ladies. "Boy, that was fun," one woman said, as she headed for her car and her hubby. "Now I know what we've been missing all these years." She didn't say it loud enough for her husband to hear, but I had a feeling he already knew.

My story ran on April 23, 1984—two days before my 44th birthday—on the front page of the *Advertiser's* Southern Flavor section. The headline screamed: "Strippers Wow Women By Getting Down To Nitty-Gritty." The photograph I took showed five very happy women applauding and holding out their bill-filled hands. There wasn't a frown on any of them. It didn't take long for the reaction to reach me. Some women were livid and took it out on me. I can't imagine why. Those in the photo didn't call to complain, however.

"You are a disgrace to your profession," one woman screamed at me over the phone. "I'm canceling my subscription the *Advertiser*. Don't you have something more important to do than report on male strippers? How dare you write something so distasteful. You ought to be ashamed of yourself."

She was a doctor's wife. I think he wouldn't let her go to the show that night.

These Selma women seemed to be enjoying a male strip show on April 23, 1984.

CHAPTER TWENTY-FOUR:

"ATOMIC MAN"

It was the greatest double-take I had ever seen—one that would have matched Jack Benny or Johnny Carson at their best.

It came from Selma Mayor Joe Smitherman on April 5, 1984 during a press conference in the city council chambers. Smitherman called it because of concerns over the dumping of a suspected "atomic car" into the Alabama River by Jim Rutledge, who, at the time, was the evidence technician at the Selma Police Department.

Rutledge, an electronics genius who dabbled in old cars and new devices that proved interesting to him, had built an electric car to support his belief that vehicles such as that one would eventually replace gas-guzzlers. Jim seemed to be ahead of his time most of the time, but there were some in Selma who thought he had a loose cranial screw or two or three. Rutledge should have been working for Ford, GM or Chrysler because one of his ideas might have caught on nationally. Not in April of 1984, however.

In a statement prepared by him, he explained that his electric car had only cost $400 because it was made out of junked items and ran on batteries. He tried to get federal grants, but was turned down despite a design he said was "radically different in approach to electrical power."

"In the operation of the car, the good and bad features came out and one of them was the source of electrical power," Rutledge said in the statement. "In solving this, I became interested in heavy energy devices to generate power. I then began to develop the heavy energy components, but as predicted, the production of such devices requires equipment and expertise beyond what I had, so my attempts ceased almost a year ago."

Spring in Selma means the annual pilgrimage of stately antebellum homes reminiscent of Tara in "*Gone With The Wind.*" Jim said he and others in his Old Selma neighborhood wanted to clean up their yards for the pilgrimage that always attracts big crowds to Selma. He said he had no place to take his electric car, so he drove it to the river "where I thought I could dispose (of it) with the least fuss and bother." He contended that dumping old cars into rivers serves as a "haven for growing young fish." He also said that the car had no "radioactive chemicals" and, thus, was no danger to fish, fowl, man or beast.

Once it went into the river, however, word leaked out and concern swept through parts of Selma. Some imagined fish glowing in the dark or something similar to "*The Creature From The Black Lagoon*" creeping up the river bank at night. The U.S. Environmental Protection Agency, Alabama environmental groups and, of course, the mayor soon found out what had happened. A search was conducted for the car with several divers, including Dallas County Commissioner Deans Barber, trying to find it in the murky depths of the Alabama River. They didn't find a thing, probably because they couldn't see their hands in front of their diving masks.

In the end, EPA and state officials determined that the vehicle had not been radioactive and that no fish would be glowing at night near the Edmund Pettus Bridge.

I sat in the front row of the council chamber during the news conference and, as I read Rutledge's statement, underlined "heavy energy devices," "heavy energy components," and just plain "heavy energy." Jim and I had had our differences in the past after a couple of run-ins involving stories I was covering, so he wasn't exactly enamored of me. That didn't stop me from asking a "heavy" question.

"Mr. Rutledge, I notice a couple of times in the statement that you mention 'heavy energy,'" I asked him. "Exactly, what did you mean by that? I've heard of the term "heavy water,'" but it usually is mentioned in things like the Manhattan Project."

Rutledge ignored me. He wouldn't answer and appeared to be hoping that a reporter from one of the Montgomery television stations would ask him something else.

"Answer his question, Jim," Smitherman ordered.

"Well, heavy energy or heavy water was a term used by scientists who worked on development of the atomic bomb," Rutledge said, finishing my "Manhattan Project" comment.

"On the what!!!!" Smitherman shot back, turning his head back toward Rutledge in a fraction of a second.

"Nothing like that was involved here, though, mayor," Rutledge said, trying to explain that his had been an innocent experiment that posed no danger to anyone.

In the end, everything worked out for the best. Jim's car never was found and the EPA people went back home. I got to really like him as the years went by and came to appreciate his eccentricities. I've always admired people with overactive gray matter. Jim Rutledge never let age slow him down when it came to special projects. He's still going strong. I don't know what his new project is, but it wouldn't surprise me if it's a "heavy" undertaking.

CHAPTER TWENTY-FIVE:

SAVING MY SOUL

I'm going to hell.

At least that's the impression Ken Scott tried to leave with me each time he stopped by my office on Water Avenue to drop off Christian literature he knew I'd never read. Ken didn't really want me to go to hell, but he was convinced that unless I accepted Jesus as my lord and savior, that's where I'd be going.

Most Jews accustomed to proselytizers have a built-in defense mechanism. I know I do. But, I try to be as courteous as I can before I tell 'em to take a hike. In Ken Scott's case, no amount of hiking suggestions seemed to sink in. He sees himself as a man on a mission to save as many souls as he can.

Scott is a self-appointed preacher who always gives credit to Jesus for saving his soul when it was in disrepair. He was the first to acknowledge that and often did it on Sunday mornings at his church and on his taped radio program. Along the way, he provided plenty of outrage, too. Jews weren't the only ones upset by his sermons and pleas to accept Jesus. He also took on Catholics, Muslims, Hindus and Buddhists. I always considered Catholics to be Christians—the first, by the way—but Ken saw them to be evil on earth. He was an equal opportunity missionary. Call him a fanatic and he'd grin. "They called Jesus a fanatic, too," he once told me. "I've been called that and a lot worse."

Before he got religion or became reacquainted with it, Scott was one of the country's foremost authorities on drag racing vehicles. He designed them, built them and, on occasion, raced them. He also wrote columns for national dragster magazines and his reputation helped build a good life for him and his family. He later sold his business and began living on income from properties he owned and rented. He said he never drew a salary from the church.

They say there's no zealot like a new zealot and Ken Scott fit that description to a Capital Z. His attacks on Catholicism in the early 1980s got him bounced off his Selma television show. The station manager caught too much heat to keep him on. That didn't upset Scott. He just kept moving in high gear with his radio program where the message was the same—hell and damnation without Jesus. As pastor of Joy Baptist Temple, Scott felt he had a calling that could not be set aside for anybody.

In August of 1983, Scott upset Selma's small Catholic community when he claimed that the Pope teaches a "false doctrine" and that Jesuit priests are basically the Mafia of the Vatican. He told listeners that use of Mary as a religious intermediary is as wrong as wrong can be. He doesn't care much for Buddha or Muhammad, either. "If Buddhists and Moslems don't believe in Jesus as the Messiah, they are all lost and will be going to a sinner's hell," he told me once. When I told him there were a lot more non-Christians than Christians in the world, he didn't blink. "They're all going to hell," he responded.

Scott gave me plenty of fodder for columns and news stories during the 1980s. Each time he opened his mouth, something controversial usually came out, often so inflammatory that he upset one religion after another. That's why, during Sunday morning stints at my Selma office, I made sure I tuned to his program, "The Joy Club" on WHBB-AM.

On July 27, 1993, I got a letter from Michael Moorehead, a Montgomery resident and Catholic who was incensed by one of my articles about Scott. "Rev. Scott," Moorehead told me "although probably well intentioned is grossly ignorant of what the Roman Catholic Church actually teaches. The difficulty is that, the way your article is worded, readers could easily gain the impression that Rev. Scott actually knows what he is talking about."

On and on it went through the '80s and into the 1990s with Scott taking on all comers without flinching. He went after *"Playboy"* magazine in 1987 for showing a pictorial "spread" of Jessica Hahn, whose affair with Jim Bakker toppled Bakker's televangelist empire—one that had made him a millionaire. "I thought (Bakker) was a brother in the Lord, but that apparently isn't so," Scott told me, in an interview. "His extravagant living wasn't brought out right away." No one could accuse Scott of an extravagant lifestyle. When his television program was terminated, he had only paid $50 a week for 30 minutes of occasional anti-Catholic vitriol. Scott told me that he had reason to believe that Jessica wasn't exactly "pure" when she and Bakker began their close relationship. "Personally, I don't think she was a virgin when she met Bakker," he said. "Anyone who believes that will believe there is green cheese on the moon."

In 1994, Scott took on W. Deen Mohammad, the spokesman for the American Muslim community. Mohammad had agreed to come to Selma to speak at the annual celebration of Martin Luther King Jr.'s birthday. Mohammad was the son of the late Elijah Mohammad who was the spiritual leader of Malcolm X. Scott called Deen Mohammad a "rascal." That led Yusuf Abdus-Salaam, a member of the Selma City Council at the time and a future member of the Alabama Legislature, to lash out at Scott, describing him as a man who lacked understanding of other religious beliefs. Salaam told me that Islam believes "there is a place in paradise for all of us." He stopped short, though, when I asked him where Ken Scott might wind up. "He will have to be held accountable for his views," he said.

Ken eventually stopped dropping by my office. I guess he figured I was a lost cause and was surely headed for that eternal fire. I told him I had been informed by others about that same predicted destination, but never gave it much thought. It reminded me of the time in Decatur when my wife, Sharon, called to say one of her friends wanted to stop by and ask questions about Judaism. "She's not coming over to ask questions about Judaism, Sharon Ann," I told her. "She's coming over to try and convert you." "No, she'd never do that to me," Sharon responded. "She's my friend." "Well, just wait and see," I said. That afternoon, when I got home, she was sitting on the couch—crying. "You were right," Sharon said. "She tried to convert me."

Her "friend" had turned out to be a female Ken Scott.

CHAPTER TWENTY-SIX:

JOHNNY D

Walter McMillian is a black man who was railroaded in a town once used as a model for a Pulitzer Prize winning book about racial insensitivity.

"Johnny D," as he is known, spent several years on death row for a crime he did not commit. He professed his innocence since the day of his arrest, but it did no good. Freedom finally came because of two lawyers—a black anti-death penalty advocate and a white prosecutor who knew a mistake had been made and corrected it. I got to know both lawyers and saw them work hard for a man who had few resources of his own. A book has been written about the case and a movie ought to be made because all the elements are there for a hit.

The McMillian case began on Nov. 1, 1986 inside Jackson Cleaners in Monroeville, a little south Alabama town that served as the setting for Harper Lee's *"To Kill A Mockingbird"*-a classic book about a black man unfairly convicted of raping a white woman. Ronda Morrison, who had been attending a local junior college, was working alone that Saturday morning. Sometime prior to 10:45 a.m., somebody walked into the store and shot her to death. An autopsy showed she had tried to defend herself. Police believe that, as she ran away from her attacker, she was hit three times in the head at close range.

The town was in shock and remained that way throughout the investigation. Some were reluctant to talk to me during my frequent trips to Monroeville to report on her death as well as any progress that had been made to find her killer. A murder in broad daylight in the middle of a little town where everybody knows each other can be a traumatic experience. That's what happened in Monroeville.

After a lengthy investigation, McMillian and a second man, Ralph Myers, were arrested and charged with capital murder. Myers, who is white, testified for the prosecution and named McMillian as the killer. According to Myers, he saw McMillian standing over the girl's body. McMillian had an alibi. He said he had been at a house far from the laundry at the time the murder was committed. He also said he had about a dozen witnesses who could vouch for him. Some did testify that Johnny D was with them when it happened. The jury didn't buy his alibi and convicted him. The judge then imposed the death sentence. It appeared, at first, to be one of those open-and-shut cases. At least, that's the way it started.

No one tried to paint McMillian as an angel, because he wasn't. At the time of the murder, he had been out of jail under a one-year suspended sentence. He had been convicted of assault in neighboring Conecuh County. McMillian admitted he was no choir boy, but insisted that he had not killed Ronda Morrison. His pleas didn't seem to convince anybody and all he could do was wait and hope that a death sentence date would not be set while his friends looked for evidence to prove his innocence.

Enter Bryan Stevenson, who directs the Equal Justice Initiative in Montgomery. It's a small group of dedicated people who work hard to help those they feel were unfairly convicted of capital crimes. In Alabama, only two verdicts are allowed in capital murder cases—life without parole or death. It used to be in the electric chair. Now, it's by lethal injection. At the time of the McMillian conviction, "Yellow Mama," as the chair was known, awaited him unless Stevenson and his assistants could slow the ticking of the clock. They did the next best thing. Stevenson gathered enough information to clear the dust from the McMillian file and stop the clock altogether for Johnny D.

Walter McMillian, left, leaves with his lawyer, Bryan Stevenson, after being freed from prison.

As the years passed, more people began to express an interest in the McMillian case. One was author Pete Earley, who would write *"Circumstantial Evidence"*—an appropriate title, given the paucity of solid evidence. Another was "60 Minutes" correspondent Ed Bradley. He created a lot of attention when he arrived in Monroeville for a one-day visit. His advance team had set up the interviews and locations. When the segment aired in late 1992, it created national interest in the case. The ball finally began to roll in a positive direction for Johnny D.

On March 2, 1993, McMillian became a free man. Stevenson got most of the praise because of his dogged determination to pursue the case, but District Attorney Tommy Chapman wasn't far behind. As chief prosecutor in Monroe County, he could have refused to reopen the case. He also had the power to slow Stevenson's efforts through a variety of legal options available to him. Instead, he wasted little time correcting an egregious wrong once he became convinced that Myers was lying to save his own skin.

"It's obvious (Myers) was trying to use Johnny D for his own purposes to cut a deal in another murder case in another county," said Chapman, referring to a killing not far from Monroeville at about the same time. Myers got a 30-year prison sentence for robbery in connection with the robbery at the dry cleaners, but escaped the death penalty because he had testified against McMillian.

It was bedlam inside and outside the Baldwin County Courthouse in Bay Minette the morning McMillian was set free. Newspaper reporters and photographers jostled with television crews to get the best vantage point. The actual announcement by Circuit Judge Pamela Baschab lasted only a few minutes. No apologies were offered. It was a perfunctory process. Once the hearing was over, however, the mad rush was on to get close to Johnny D. He held a brief press conference in a cramped room at the courthouse, deferring to Stevenson when legal points were discussed.

When he stepped outside the courthouse—breathing fresh air as a free man for the first time in more than six years, a huge crowd of friends, relatives and reporters surrounded him. I was pushed toward the front of the pack and wound up with what I think was the best picture of the day. It showed Johnny D hugging a friend. It was a closeup shot and the smile on his face told it all.

In the years since his release, McMillian has maintained a low profile. A supporter in the Alabama Legislature filed a bill seeking $9 million in compensation for him because of his years on death row, but nothing ever came of that. Several lawsuits were filed against law enforcement officials who had arrested McMillian. Sources told me that Johnny D, or his lawyers, got "several hundred thousand dollars" from insurance carriers in reduced settlements.

With McMillian freed, the question then was "Who killed Ronda Morrison?" Her death continues to haunt her parents—Charles and Bertha Morrison. She was the sunshine of their lives and her death devastated them.

"We're very disappointed that this case hasn't been solved," Charles Morrison told me in an interview eight months after McMillian's release and conducted during the 7ᵗʰ anniversary of her murder. "That's what hurts the most. Somebody did it, but all we get is speculation."

Whenever I see Chapman, I ask him the same question. He gives me the same answer. He said he believes he knows who killed the teenager, but there is little he can do. The person he suspects was given a lie detector test, but the results were "inconclusive." He said the suspect still lives in the Monroeville area.

"You know, Tommy," I told him when I saw him for the first time in more than a year, "many people believe there is a 'higher judge' and that the guilty eventually are punished one day." Chapman looked at me and nodded, but didn't say anything. He didn't have to. I think we both have the same hope.

Monroe County District Attorney Tommy Chapman.

CHAPTER TWENTY-SEVEN:

TODD ROAD

Two Montgomery detectives investigating a missing persons report were driving through a black neighborhood when they noticed several cars outside one of the houses. Most were expensive late model vehicles with out-of-state tags. They got out of their car just as a man approached the house.

Moments after they began questioning the man, he struck one of the officers and ran into the house. The detectives followed him inside and came face-to-face with more than a dozen very angry people who had driven to Alabama from Ohio and Michigan to pay their respects to a deceased relative.

What happened next remains open to dispute, depending on which side is recalling the incident. One thing is clear, though. Officer Eddie Spivey was beaten and stabbed. Officer Les Brown was beaten and shot. Brown saved his own life by pushing a finger into the hole left by a bullet that hit him in the chest.

Police soon surrounded the house and the two investigators were rescued. Within a few minutes, 11 people were under arrest, charged with everything from attempted murder to kidnapping and robbery. Police Chief Charles Swindall said those in the house were like "wild animals that had their prey on the ground."

Brown and Spivey, who nearly died, still carry the physical and emotional scars of that night. So do the mourners inside the house on Todd Road.

Feb. 27, 1983 was a Sunday night and it didn't take long for the national spotlight to focus on the "Cradle of the Confederacy." It was just too good a story for some newspapers to pass up—two white cops bursting into a house filled with black mourners in a town where civil rights violence was still fresh in many memories. A few years before the Todd Road Incident, as it became known, Montgomery had its own "Watergate" scandal when white cops placed a "throw-down gun" next to the body of a young black man they had shot in the back during a chase. That incident led to the resignation of the mayor and a major shakeup in the police department. Some of those arrested in the house on Todd Road complained that they had been beaten by white cops at the police station. The FBI announced it would look into the matter.

I read about the incident, but didn't think much of it because I had my hands full covering Alabama's Black Belt out of our Selma office. Five different reporters had covered the beatings and arrests. That's why I was surprised to get a call from one of my editors who said I would be flying to Michigan and Ohio to see what I could find out about those who had been arrested. It wasn't hard to figure out why I'd be sent. Our editors didn't want to send one of their police reporters because it might jeopardize their relationship with those at the "cop shop," especially if they discovered the accused were honest, hard-working, church-going people whose only mistake was being in that house on Todd Road.

Selma lawyer J.L. Chestnut, who represented some of those arrested, made some contacts for me. It was invaluable assistance because I had never been to Detroit before and didn't know how long it would take. Ches said those who'd meet me at the airport would be at my disposal and would drive me where I needed to go. "Write whatever you find," he said. "There are no strings attached." I flew first to Warren, Ohio where one group of relatives lived. Then, it was on to Detroit where I was picked up and driven to Pontiac, Mich., about 30 miles away, to interview more relatives and check more police records.

I wrote several stories during that time. My findings did not reflect the picture painted by Montgomery police. No doubt, my articles did not endear me to them. Those who had driven to Alabama were, indeed, hard-working, church-going pillars of their communities. I researched records at the local police and sheriff's departments and couldn't find anything. No felony arrests had been made against any of the 11 who were arrested. I did find one speeding ticket. It was obvious to me what they must have gone through. Black mourners from the North suddenly found themselves confronted by two white cops from the South—two men who burst unannounced into their house. It was a volatile mixture. Those in the house overreacted. That was obvious. Brown and Spivey were lucky to escape with their lives.

When my plane arrived at Dannelly Field in Montgomery after my last story had been filed, I was greeted by my state editor, Phyllis Wesley, my family and the lead article on the front page of the *Advertiser*. The story ran under the headline: "Charges leave family's friends in state of disbelief, anger." A large photograph showing 11 relatives of one of those arrested accompanied the story.

"These are honest, civilized people and they're being described as vicious fanatics. My God, they went down there for a funeral, not to attack any policemen." Pearl Kennedy's comment was printed in large type and set apart from the rest of the story. "Civilized" and "Wild Animals" just didn't seem to go together.

A month after the violent incident, all charges were dropped against 7 of the 11 who had been arrested. Chestnut, who represented some of them, said the judge's decision not to bind them over to a grand jury for lack of evidence showed positive change in Alabama.

"Those who say justice is not possible in Montgomery ought to take a look at what happened here this morning," Ches said. As the weeks and months dragged on and tempers cooled, a clearer picture began to emerge. The two white cops had made a serious miscalculation about what they thought was going on inside the house. They got more than they bargained for from people upset over the intrusion. It's too bad there weren't any cooler heads around that night.

Some of those arrested then took the offensive—filing lawsuits which claimed Montgomery police roughed them up at the station. Similar charges had been filed in the past after white cops apprehended black suspects. It was a sorry situation, but not nearly as bad as the Whitehurst case because of cover-ups that followed the fatal shooting incident. It took a long time to finally resolve that matter, but the stain remains.

Former Montgomery Police Chief John Wilson had a lot to do with improving the image of the department since taking over from Swindall. He was criticized at times for his handling of cases after he became chief, but there weren't any Whitehurst or Todd Road incidents under his administration. Detectives now are required to wear blazers with their badges clearly visible in the breast pocket. Brown and Spivey didn't wear any badges when they entered the house and they didn't have much time to identify themselves because they were jumped as soon as they came through the front door.

In 1983, Montgomery's police department did not have a public relations office or a specific spokesman. During the Todd Road case, it seemed everybody in the department had something to say. Swindall's "wild animal" comment didn't go over very well, as might be expected in the black community. Swindall rectified that by naming Wilson, who was a young lieutenant at the time, as the department's first public information spokesman.

"I was the administrative assistant to the chief and he said we needed a public information spokesman," Wilson recalled. "Then he looked at me and said 'you're it.'"

One of the first things Wilson did was establish a better relationship with Montgomery reporters. He took them out to Todd Road and explained what had happened. Two biracial groups were formed at that time to help ease tensions. They met to talk, break bread and get to know each other better. It was a good start and things kept getting better.

"There's no doubt we got a black eye over the Todd Road case," said Wilson, who retired as chief in 2004. "But, you learn from these things. We did our best to make sure our officers were more sensitive to diversity and cultural differences. I don't doubt for a second that my appointment as public information spokesman played a role in my becoming chief."

I had always liked the way Wilson ran the police department, but he really sparkled during the D.C. sniper case that impacted the city in 2003. Montgomery, Alabama became linked to fatal shootings in Montgomery County, Maryland where two snipers had fatally shot several people. A few weeks earlier, in Alabama's Capital City, a package store employee was fatally shot and a second employee wounded by one of the snipers before he and his friend began their rampage to the north a few weeks later. After their capture, reporters from around the country converged on Montgomery to find out about the Alabama connection to a case that had transfixed the country. Wilson stood tall in the face of mounting pressure from news crews. Unlike some law enforcement officers in other states, Wilson came right to the point and laid it out for all to consider.

"We have the death penalty in Alabama and we use it," he said, staring into a camera he knew was sending his message around the United States.

Wilson's career with the Montgomery Police Department did not end as he had envisioned. He retired after being arrested on a charge of drunken driving—a charge he denied. It eventually was dropped.

CHAPTER TWENTY-EIGHT:

THIN EVIDENCE

"Pretty Woman" was a movie about a hooker who became a lady of virtue—thanks to a suave, sophisticated "customer."

"Skinny Woman" was a tabloid story about a female said to weigh 31 pounds. Since my right leg weighed more than that, I had to read on, of course.

Walking by the tabloid stand at a local supermarket in June of 1993, I saw an impossibly thin woman hoisted atop the arms of her beloved. That attracted my attention, but not nearly as much as the type which said "Joyce-Ann Siskel" lived just outside Jackson, Alabama. At that time, Jackson was in my coverage area for the *Montgomery Advertiser*. The photograph appeared on the cover of *Weekly World News*—my favorite tabloid—and served to spark even more interest. I had sent "*WWN*" some of the more bizarre stories I'd covered in Alabama through the years.

"We've got to go down to Jackson to find the skinniest woman in the world," I told Sharon Ann. "The who?" she asked.

Jackson, about 70 miles south of Selma, is the home of Joe McCorquodale, former speaker of the Alabama House of Representatives. It's not a big town and Joe knew everybody there. I felt he'd know if "Joyce-Ann" lived in his fair town or "outside," as the magazine claimed. Of course, "outside" to the *Weekly World News* could have been Afghanistan.

"No, I never heard of this woman or anybody fitting that description in Jackson or Clarke County," Joe told me after inviting us into his house for a chat. "No doubt we'd all know somebody who looked like that."

According to the tabloid cover story, "Joyce-Ann" had an insatiable appetite and could "gobble candy, peanuts and ice cream—-and never gain an ounce!" The photograph showed her being held aloft in a swimming pool by a man who appeared to be no stranger to a buffet line. The two-page article inside described her as a "string-bean brunette" who was 5-feet-2 inches tall and weighed one pound less than a "Brazilian who had been considered the thinnest woman in the world at 32 pounds."

"I may be skinny, but I'm all woman and I'm proud of the way I look," the magazine quoted "Joyce-Ann" as saying. "I don't have any desire to gain weight." I spent part of the day interviewing several others in Jackson. Each said the same thing McCorquodale told me. George Bradley said "I think it's a hoax." That seemed like a pretty good assumption since the *Weekly World News* and other tabloids have been known to print stories that strain credulity—everything from Hitler being found working at a massage parlor to presidents having affairs in the Oval Office of the White House.

I called *WWN*, which is based in Lantana, Fla. and was connected to a woman who told me the magazine was standing by its story. As if she was going to tell me the whole thing was made up. She also said she couldn't produce the writer of the article for verification. Ditto for his editor. The woman may have been the only one left in the building. I guess everybody else must have been out getting a massage from a little man with a tiny mustache and thick Austrian accent. The article claimed "Joyce-Ann" had visited a doctor in Huntsville who referred her to a friend who specialized in anorexia. I made several other phone calls, but was unable to find anybody who knew "Joyce-Ann" or could give me the real skinny on what was going on.

We all got a good laugh out of it, especially McCorquodale, who had a big smile on his face as he raised the *WWN* front page showing "Joyce-Ann" being held up by her "cotton broker husband" who was identified as "Junior."

CHAPTER TWENTY-NINE:

TAKEN FOR A RIDE

Johnny Stewart could be the poster boy for car salesmen. He has that big grin, an "aw shucks" southern accent and a sales pitch that's irresistible. Our family has bought about a dozen cars from him through the years and we've never regretted it. He's also provided me with plenty of stories along the way.

The one we still talk about is the time he met his match after becoming involved with a con artist who took him for a ride he's never forgotten.

It happened in May of 1991. The dog days of summer were ahead, Alabama and Auburn football fans were in deep mourning because their favorite season was still months away and Johnny's car lot was filled to overflowing with all types of new and used vehicles.

That's when he met "Angelia" Hendley. Actually, "her" name was Mark Hendley, who enjoyed dressing in female attire and traveling the country posing as a movie starlet. Along the way, "she" also ran up thousands of dollars in bills for services rendered and never reimbursed. Selma police discovered that "Angelia" was no angel. "She" was such a good imposter that unsuspecting merchants wined, dined and treated "her" like royalty, or the budding Warner Brothers movie star "she" claimed to be.

Johnny fell for the impersonation lock, stock and bustier. "Angelia" worked "her" charms with a wiggle and a wink. She said "she" needed a nice car and his "personal services" as a driver in central Alabama. Stewart, as good-natured a man as any I've met, grabbed the bait. He even decided to use his own 1976 Lincoln Town Car to drive "Angelia" through Dallas, Wilcox and Montgomery counties that spring. In addition to selling cars, Johnny also ran a chauffeur service. Even though his Lincoln had seen better days, it was still long and shiny enough to fill the bill for those with limited incomes.

Somebody in Selma recommended "Angelia" to him since he was one of the few people in town who operated a chauffeur service. Johnny had just spent a month in the hospital, recovering from appendicitis when he got the call. He didn't need to be asked twice. "She" told him that he'd get $85 an hour plus expenses. That provided a considerable lift to his spirits. "I was in a lot of pain at the time and that made me feel a lot better," Johnny said later. "I normally charge $25 an hour."

"Angelia" said she wanted to use him for two weeks. Johnny did some quick mental calculations and came up with $1,200 for that time period. He couldn't resist, even when he got a gander at "her" at a Selma motel where "she" had just taken a dip in the pool.

"She was one ugly woman, but, for $85 an hour, I figured I could overlook her looks," he said. They spent Saturday on the road. He didn't get home until 5 a.m. Sunday. All the while, his mental calculator was working overtime. During their long trip, "Angelia" regaled him with stories of "her" Hollywood future and how famous she would become. Johnny had only been home an hour or two when "Angelia" called him again and off they went to Montgomery, a 50-mile drive east. He said he bought several $35 bottles of "her" favorite wine and paid for a motel room. "She" complained that the one originally provided proved unsatisfactory.

As it turned out, "Angelia" had left more than a few "unsatisfactory" motel rooms along the way. Lack of funds can prompt hasty departures. Johnny paid $42.87 for another motel room for "her" to spend the next night. By the time "Angelia" had disappeared from the area, "she" owed Johnny $3,500 for his personal services contract." Hendley was caught later in Mobile and charged with defrauding people out of promised payments.

It was a valuable lesson for Stewart, who has never needed reminders that car salesmen don't have the world's best reputations. "We already rank down there with lawyers and preachers so I don't think we can be tarnished any more than we already are," he told me later that year, as he waited for "Angelia" to be tried.

The worst part for Johnny was the ribbing he got from friends, especially one guy who sent him a comical card kidding him about his experience.

He was a used car salesman who had just been used.

Johnny Stewart still loves selling cars in and around Selma.

CHAPTER THIRTY:

THE GENERAL

Nathan Bedford Forrest was one of the Confederacy's best generals, but he wasn't as well known as Robert E. Lee or Stonewall Jackson because he did most of his fighting on the "Western Front" in Tennessee and Alabama.

Known as the "Wizard of the Saddle" for his daring cavalry campaigns and personal bravery in hand-to-hand combat with Yankee troops, Forrest probably would have remained part of revered Rebel history had it not been for a group of Confederate devotees who raised $25,000 for a monument in his honor and placed it in an area that upset the descendants of slaves. The 5-ton monument, topped by a bust of Forrest, was designed, in part, by a Yankee sculptor from Maine. When the marker was unveiled in October 2000, more than 100 Forrest fans were on hand to praise their hero. So were about a dozen black residents of Selma who considered Forrest the devil incarnate.

Nobody said much about the statue until the actual unveiling. The genesis of the flap was relatively low-key. Former Mayor Joe Smitherman gave his blessings to the project in early 2000 after a local Forrest supporter sought his approval. Permission was given to place the monument in the courtyard outside the Smitherman Historical

Building which once was a Confederate hospital and is named for the man who was Selma's longest-serving mayor.

At the dedication ceremony, speakers were constantly interrupted by the jeering black protesters, led by Sam Walker, an official at the National Voting Rights Museum. Sam brought along a dummy outfitted with a Ku Klux Klan robe that adorns it at the museum. In addition to his cavalry heroics, Forrest also was the leader of the Klan following the Civil War. He has been accused by some civil rights activists of ordering a massacre of black troops who fought for the Union at Fort Pillow in Tennessee. Selma was one of the main reasons for the Forrest monument. He tried to defend the town during the final days of the Civil War, but knew he didn't have a chance because only old men and young boys were left to fight. The Confederacy was on its knees during the first week of April in 1865 and the war would be over by the end of the month. Union Gen. James Wilson rode into Selma with more than 10,000 veteran Yankee troops using the latest Spencer repeating rifles. It was a rout. Selma fell in a few hours and Wilson's Raiders, as they were known, torched the town. Forrest managed to escape and lived out his life back home in Tennessee. He died in 1871.

It didn't take long for vandals to defile the Forrest monument after it was unveiled. Somebody once tossed a cinder block at the bust, but it didn't make a dent. It was barely scraped. A few weeks later, a group of black women showed up with a plastic garbage bag and dumped it around the base of the monument. Forrest supporters were standing several feet away in the dark and one of them had a video recorder. It showed about a half dozen women who didn't try to hide their identities. They seemed delighted, in fact, to be "featured" on the tape. No arrests were made. On Martin Luther King Jr.'s birthday celebration in January 2001, hundreds of black marchers veered off their scheduled route and stopped long enough to place a rope around the Forrest bust. It was purely ceremonial because the rope broke after a few tugs. A thin piece of rope was no match for a 5-ton granite monument.

Not long after the dedication and the vandalism, Selma's first black mayor—James Perkins—called a press conference to address what was becoming a thorny issue for his young administration. The last thing he needed was dealing with a Confederate controversy. Perkins announced his concern about the matter, but quickly pointed out to reporters that "thank goodness, no public funds were used" to build the monument. I couldn't pass up a comment of my own, based on what I knew about that matter.

"Mayor," I said, after raising my right hand, "are you aware that several members of the previous administration used part of their contingency funds to help pay for the monument?" Perkins looked stunned and said "I didn't know that." I had been told more than a week before the press conference that some members of the city council donated part of their contingency funds—money assigned to them for neighborhood projects—to help defray costs of the marker. I had been so busy with other assignments that I didn't use that information in a story about the monument. Once Perkins made his claim, I knew I had to use it then and there.

Glaring at me from the council table was Jean Martin, a woman I admired for many years. We had worked together at the *Selma Times-Journal* and I quoted her many times following her election to the city council. If looks could have killed, I would probably have been six feet under Selma City Hall for asking my question. After Perkins said he'd look into the matter of council funding for the Forrest monument, I walked up to Jean as she prepared to leave. She let me have it. "Don't you ever speak to me again," she said, as her voice began to crack. "I thought you were my friend." Jean said she donated a few hundred dollars from her contingency fund, but thought it was to help pay for a reception after the unveiling of the Forrest monument. Two other members of the council, Rita Franklin and Glenn Sexton, also used part of their contingency funds to help pay for the marker.

Jean and Rita went down to the city clerk's office and I accompanied them. I wanted to take a look at the canceled checks to see if they had, indeed, reflected public funding for a private project. Jean was still upset and she tore into me again at the clerk's office. I was beginning to get a bit miffed myself, especially since Jean once worked for a newspaper. "I'm just doing my job," I told her. "That's what I'm doing in this case."

It didn't take long for Jean and Rita to refund the money to the city's general fund, not the "general's" fund. It had been an embarrassing moment for both of them. The money was repaid within a few days, but the controversy was just beginning. Black protesters took their anger from the site of the monument to city council meetings and constantly interrupted proceedings. Some were tossed out by President George Evans. Some were arrested. It got nasty.

As the demonstrations continued, area television crews became regular visitors at council meetings. That didn't do much for Perkins' new administration—one which began with so much promise only a few months before when he made history by becoming Selma's first black mayor. Perkins and Evans would ask for calm at the meetings, but activist Rose Sanders and her followers refused to listen. Members of the Sanders group felt they were answering to a higher calling. Sanders eventually relented after an appeal by Perkins and elected to stay away from council meetings.

The controversy finally was resolved in late February 2001 by Martin, who had forgiven me by that time and resumed answering my questions. Perkins had let his feelings be known that he wanted the monument moved from the Smitherman Building, but left the door open a bit by suggesting several alternate site options. He seemed to be leaning toward a spot in the "Confederate Circle" at Old Live Oak Cemetery where several Rebel officers are buried.

When it came time for a vote on the matter, the council was split and not along racial lines which seemed to surprise many in the packed chamber. Two black council members voted to allow it to remain where it was. Martin, who is white, cast the deciding vote to move it to the cemetery. She also issued a written statement, saying she was becoming "increasingly concerned at the controversy surrounding the Forrest monument." She pointed out that "television, newspapers and news magazines and radio seldom let a week go past without at least a mention of it."

Jean's vote made it 5-4 in favor of moving the monument. As a part of "Old Selma" and a descendant of Selmians who suffered at the hands of Wilson's Raiders, Jean knew what would happen if she voted with those who wanted to move the monument. She was right. Forrest supporters criticized her and ignored her argument that what she had done was "best for Selma." One former friend from Florida sent her an e-mail, asking her what she planned to do with her "30 pieces of silver." I suggested to Jean that she e-mail him back with a one-word response: "Dillards," a popular southern department store. Another angry Forrest fan accused her of selling her "southern birthright." Jean stood her ground and I was proud of her. She knew her vote would no doubt cost her votes if she chose to run for a third term, but she didn't let that influence her judgment.

Perkins wasted little time moving the monument. Once the council voted, he issued an order to transfer it from the Smitherman Building to Old Live Oak Cemetery and the Confederate Circle. As a foundation was poured at the cemetery, a city crew yanked the Forrest monument from its original site. Predictions that it would crumble because of a steel rod inserted from bust to base didn't materialize. It was lifted as easily as Wilson's Raiders raced through Selma in 1865. There was little fuss or fury over its relocation, but I did discover one interesting tidbit when I went to the cemetery to inspect the new tourist attraction—a Confederate flag fluttering near the Forrest monument. It apparently had been there awhile. Nobody had said a word about it. I was told it was placed in the cemetery during a Confederate memorial service months before.

Doug Buster, a Selma commercial photographer and spokesmen for the monument, called a day after it was moved to its new location and said I needed to go back to the cemetery. "It's kinda like what they did for Princess Di," he said, referring to the outpouring of love and floral arrangements for the late, lamented Princess Diana after her death in Paris. In volume, the outpouring for Forrest was considerably below that for the adored princess. A wreath was placed in front of the monument and several small bouquets were behind it. A steady steam of cars kept circling the Confederate Memorial site at the cemetery, apparently wanting to take a look at the Forrest monument and to see if anybody showed up to deface it. A few days later, somebody called me to say the general would be "safe" at Old Live "because you know black people are afraid to go into cemeteries, especially at night."

A federal lawsuit was filed by Forrest supporters to return it to the Smitherman Building, but that wasn't likely. A compromise eventually was reached, but legal fees exceeded $100,000 and the city government was billed for a big part of that. Legal arguments continued into the summer of 2004 over payment of attorney fees. There even was talk of moving the general's monument from its current position to one in which it would face NORTH!

During the 2004 municipal elections, those who despised Martin for her key vote used the incident in an effort to remove her from the council. They placed "Martin's Got To Go" signs in her ward. At the top was "Remember The General."

Jean had the last laugh. She won easily with solid biracial support at the polls.

CHAPTER THIRTY-ONE:

MEET JOHN DOE

I once knew a man who sued a rumor for $10 million.

His name was Frank Harvill and he had a lot of courage to do what he did because his lawsuit opened him to public humiliation, embarrassment and whispers in a small town where news travels swiftly.

Frank's complaint was filed in September 1984—five months after he was admitted to a Selma hospital for treatment of rectal pain which he had been experiencing for several weeks. On May 9, he underwent a surgical procedure known to correct the condition that had caused his discomfort.

Not long after Frank was released from the hospital, rumors began circulating in Selma that he had been hurt while engaging in deviant sex with a woman other than his wife. The rumors claimed that was the reason for Frank's pain and that the object of his distress had been lodged in a place where the sun doesn't shine.

During the weeks that followed, Frank and his wife, Ginger, put up with rumors that caused sleepless nights and anguish during the day.

They felt as though they were sleep walking, that eyes were on them wherever they went.

Frank lost 10 pounds in a few weeks. Ginger suffered, too. She did her best to support her husband, but she was as aware as anyone that rumors aren't easy to dispel, no matter what the accused party does to clear his name.

"It's like fighting a shadow," Frank told me during an interview at his house. "We can't get hold of anything."

Until the rumors began, the Harvills had been living the American dream. Frank was vice president of a Selma bank. Ginger had a good job, too, and their daughter was finishing up her college education. Their son had been elected to his high school student council. The Harvills lived in a beautiful house. The future looked exceedingly bright.

The rumors continued to filter through town during the summer of 1984. Then, a friend walked up to Frank at his bank and said he needed to see him at once.

"He said 'Look, we've got to talk in private,'" Frank told me. "He said he had heard this story about me." The comments also explained some strange phone calls Frank had received in the days before he was approached at the bank by his "friend." Frank said one caller asked him "When did you get out of the hospital?" while the second shouted an obscenity into the phone before disconnecting.

I had heard the rumors, too. It was as though every house in Selma had been privy to Frank and Ginger's nightmare.

I drove over to their house one afternoon and we went to their back porch. The sun had slid behind nearby pine trees and an early autumn chill enveloped us.

"I kept asking myself how this mess could have started and what we could do about it," Frank said, as he took out his falcon head pipe and began to fill it with his favorite tobacco. "I talked to people and asked them how I could fight it." At that point, fighting a rumor of unknown origin seemed as probable for the Harvills as determining the final destination of the smoke from Frank's pipe as it floated away with the late summer breeze.

As a loan officer at his bank, Frank had approved and rejected many requests for money through the years. He wondered if one of those he had rejected might have planted the rumor. Ginger ran a small advertising agency in Selma and she asked herself if, perhaps, she had done something to upset a client.

They were targets of a nameless, faceless enemy. But it didn't stop them from considering possible options. They felt they had three of them—let the rumor run its course, pack up and leave town or stay and fight it in court. They decided on the final option and went to see John Kelly, a Selma lawyer who is one of the best in Alabama. John promptly filed the $10 million lawsuit.

What made the lawsuit so unusual was the name of the defendant. It was John Doe. They didn't know the name of the person or persons who started and then spread the rumors, but they had to list somebody as a defendant in the lawsuit. What they did was select the most common name associated with anonymity in the United States.

They also became amateur detectives, going around town and asking as many people as possible if they had heard anything. Some were reluctant to say anything. Others were too embarrassed to even consider a response. A few admitted they had heard something, but it came from "so-and-so who got it from so-and-so."

"It was one of the most amazing cases I've ever been associated with," Kelly would say later. "People just began hearing this rumor on the streets and it was passed along as fast as it was told. Of course, it wasn't true, but, stopping something like that usually isn't an easy thing to do."

In Harvill's case, it was easy. Once word got out that a $10 million lawsuit had been filed, the rumors seemed to stop as fast as they had begun.

"It was like a blanket had just come down from heaven and covered it up," John told me. "We never did find out who started the rumor. When we started, we felt that all we could do was sue everybody in the world. That's what we did and it seemed to work, but Frank was never the same after that."

Frank knew his back was against the wall when he went to see Kelly. As we sat on his back porch that summer night, we talked about a lot of things. Among them was a negative trait of human behavior. We both agreed there is no substitute for personal honor and respect.

"Banks operate on trust," Frank told me. "What happens when the person you deal with no longer has that trust in you?" It was a rhetorical question. Frank knew the answer before he asked it.

Ginger was feeling the same hurt and pain as her beleaguered husband, but she was just as determined to fight to the bitter end.

"We're not doing this for revenge," she said. "We just want his name cleared. "We could have let it drop, but years from now, somebody could look at him and say: "That's old Mr. Harvill. Did you know..."

By the time Kelly headed for the Dallas County Courthouse to file his lawsuit, the rumors had spread all the way to Birmingham and Mobile.

Newspapers generally don't print rumors. But, when a lawsuit is filed and a rumor is the reason, it's in the public domain. It also makes for quite a story. Add "John Doe" as the defendant and the story is bound to attract reader attention. It also provides more grief for the plaintiffs because the lawsuit serves to add fuel to the fire—especially for those who hadn't heard about it in the first place. I wrote articles about the lawsuit and Frank's dilemma. What he had hoped would remain a private matter found a place in the public for weeks.

Kelly and the Harvills knew their chances of uncovering "Doe's" true identity were slim, but they also knew that if they sat back and did nothing, they'd always be on the defensive. By hauling "Doe" into court, they felt chances were good that the rumors might stop.

The lawsuit accused "Doe" and other unnamed defendants of spreading "malicious and slanderous statements about Harvill on numerous occasions and in public places and in the presence of numerous persons and they have made these statements in reckless disregard for the truth."

It said Frank had been "humiliated, embarrassed and subjected to public ridicule (and) he had lost the respect and affection of friends, associates and acquaintances (and) had suffered severe extreme mental and emotional distress (and) he had been caused to worry and lose sleep (and) he had been made sick."

John ended the lawsuit with a loud, legal emphasis—demanding TEN MILLION DOLLARS in actual and punitive damages.

The decision to file suit against an unknown defendant for spreading a rumor turned out to be the right thing to do. Silent suspicions lingered for a long time, but Frank and Ginger didn't have to put up with quite as many stares and glares after that.

The couple eventually moved out of town. Frank died several years later of a heart attack.

CHAPTER THIRTY-TWO:

RUNNING FOR OFFICE

"**M**y dive into Morgan County's political waters last Saturday caused more than a ripple."

"I sank."

That's how I began an unexpected column that not only got good play on a Monday afternoon in 1970, but also wound up winning a writing award from the Alabama Press Association that year.

It began innocently enough when I decided to run for a place on the Morgan County Democratic Executive Committee. I did it because I discovered that all 44 places had been hand-picked by Chairman Sam McClendon.

I've never felt that people should get a political pass simply because they know the person in charge of the party—be it national, state or local office. I decided that I'd give it a try, if only one time.

I was the news editor of the *Decatur Daily* that year. It was and still is a wonderful little family-owned newspaper in the heart of the Tennessee Valley not far from Huntsville. My job was to select important stories, edit them, write headlines, lay out the front and inside pages, prepare photographs and do a myriad other things that the position entailed. My long day each week was Saturday when I went in at 9 a.m. and usually didn't get home until 1 a.m. Sunday.

The deadline for qualifying to run for a spot on the Democratic Executive Committee was on a Saturday, which meant I'd have to really hustle in order to announce my candidacy and do my job at the same time. McClendon wasn't aware of my hours, but he sure didn't make it very convenient to qualify.

Sharon didn't think my candidacy would be a problem for her or our two children—Dani, 3 and Eric, 2. I told her it wouldn't cost much and she seemed to like that best of all since she wasn't working and I wasn't making much money at the *Daily*. My plan was to buy some campaign cards and go around the neighborhood knocking on doors and soliciting support. I got the idea after a candidate for Morgan County constable knocked on our apartment door and asked for my vote. I figured if he could do something like that, so could I. I voted for him because he took the time to knock on my door.

McClendon told me to be at his "office" by 9 a.m. that Saturday and that's what I did. It meant delaying my arrival at work, but I didn't think it would take more than a few minutes to qualify for an unimportant political position.

Morgan County's Democratic Party headquarters was located in McClendon's real estate office. When I entered, his secretary informed me he was "out," but would return "shortly." When I asked her when that might be, she said she didn't know. I noticed a woman standing in the same office, also waiting to see McClendon about running for a spot on the same executive committee. She apparently had asked the same questions and got the same answers. She said she couldn't wait much longer because she had a beauty parlor appointment.

The qualifying deadline that day was noon and I knew time was rapidly running out. So did the woman who also wanted to run.

"I wouldn't know (McClendon) if I saw him," the woman told McClendon's secretary.

"He's wearing a yellow sweater," the secretary said. "And, it's a real good looking thing, too."

A few minutes before 10 a.m., I decided to look for McClendon, myself, so I walked across the street to a coffee shop where I thought he might be hiding. No luck. On my way back to his office, I spotted a man wearing a bright yellow sweater.

Back inside his office, I asked McClendon about running for a place on the executive committee which had been expanded to 44 members that year.

"I wouldn't if I were you," McClendon told me.

"Why, not?" I asked.

"Because you wouldn't have much chance of winning," he said.

That wasn't exactly the kind of encouragement I needed at that time for my first political foray, especially when he added that committee members could "spread the word' and have me easily beaten at the polls.

"I'd still like to run," I told McClendon.

Trying a different approach, he asked me if I was a Democrat and had I voted for Democrats. Alabama did not then or now have a law requiring registration of political affiliations and I told him that along with the fact that I had voted for Democrats in the past.

"Who have you voted for in the past?" he asked me.

"I'm not going to tell you who I voted for," I shot back. "That's my right...the secret ballot, you know."

After some more verbal sparring, McClendon asked me if I would like to become a member of the executive committee's "advisory council." If so, he said I would receive—suitable for framing—an attractive parchment certificate, saying that I was a member of the council "in good standing."

Somehow I was getting the impression that McClendon didn't want me to run.

After I insisted, he told me there were only three available positions in the district where I lived. That didn't seem very equitable, but I jotted down the names of the three "sure" winners and left to decide which one to run against. All the other positions were filled by rich Decatur businessmen.

Shortly after 11 a.m., I returned to the Democratic "headquarters" to announce my decision about which slot to run for. McClendon was gone again.

"He's out trying to make some copies of the qualifying forms," his secretary said without any reference to his "bright yellow sweater." I waited and waited. No McClendon. It seemed strange that, on the final day of qualifying, there wouldn't be any registration forms.

At 11:30 a.m., two men came in, followed by McClendon a few minutes later. One of the men had wanted to run for a place on the committee, too, but he lived outside Decatur. When it was finally established who he would run against, McClendon informed the man not to qualify.

"He's old and not feeling well, so what I'd do is ask him if he decides to resign from the committee, you'd like to fill his vacancy," McClendon said. Apparently, the would-be candidate took McClendon's advice and left with his friend. That left me alone with Sam.

McClendon told me that he had no more qualifying papers and that he wasn't able to make any copies. He then "suggested" that I drive up to Athens and pick up some papers at the Limestone County Courthouse. It was 11:40 a.m. and it would take more than 30 minutes to get there.

"Who do I see at the courthouse?" I asked McClendon.

"I don't know," he said.

"Who is the chairman of the Limestone County Democratic Committee?" I asked him.

"I don't know," said McClendon, obviously having a hard time keeping from laughing.

A friend in Limestone County picked up a copy of the qualifying papers and brought them to me early that afternoon. I filled them out and hurried back to McClendon's office. He wasn't in, of course.

"Where does he live?" I asked McClendon's secretary.

"On Somerville Road," she said. "But, he's not there. He's playing golf."

No doubt he was wearing his "bright yellow sweater" when he teed off. He had teed me off long before he hit the links.

Undeterred, I called Bob Vance, who was chairman of the Alabama Democratic Party, and told him of my predicament. Vance, who later would become a federal judge and be murdered by a mail bomber, told me he'd let me run anyway—given the circumstances of my first aborted attempt.

I told Vance I didn't want to run, but my experience that Saturday had given me great material for a column. I went to work on it the next day and, when I finished it, took my copy to Mike Freeman, who was our managing editor.

Mike took one look at it and started to laugh. He liked it and said it should run the next day.

It was published on Monday, March 2, 1970 across the top of Page One. The headline was: "Citizen Pitches Hat But Misses Ring." I loved it.

One of my final paragraphs tried to sum up what I had gone through, stressing that it wasn't peculiar to any political party.

"The old saw about the Republican Party being controlled by 'men in smoke-filled rooms' and 'hand-picked candidates' may be true, but, from my experiences last Saturday, the Democrats aren't far behind...if not on a par," I wrote. "Perhaps this account of one man's struggle might prompt others to run in the next election.

I couldn't resist using "par," given McClendon's "bright yellow sweater" and his decision to play golf instead of meeting potential candidates.

Reaction was immediate and, for the most part, positive, throughout Morgan County. Our publisher, Barrett Shelton Sr., thought it was great. He didn't care much for McClendon in the first place. In the coming weeks, he'd pat me on the back and say "we got him."

A few days after the article ran, the county Democratic Committee met to organize for the upcoming election. I assigned a photographer to be there with instructions to take a picture of McClendon's hands. His nickname was "Fate" and it seemed only appropriate to caption it: "The Hands of Fate."

Nothing much came of the election that year. All of McClendon's hand-picked candidates won. How could they lose? They didn't have anybody running against them.

Several months before the election of 1974, a group of young professionals met to plot a bloodless political coup. It was led by Decatur lawyer Bob Milam, who wanted a Democratic Executive Committee free of political hanky-panky.

Bob called me one day and asked if I'd be interested in running. He liked the 1970 article, too, and felt I could be something of a standard-bearer for a more democratic Democrat Party in Morgan County.

"No," I told him. "I've had enough of politics. The first time was my last time."

"Come on, Al," he said. "You're just the kind of person we need to help straighten out this mess in Morgan County."

I then asked Bob if he had ever acted before. That seemed to stop him for a second, but he regained his composure and said he had. That's when I came up with an offer he couldn't refuse.

"Tell you what," I told him. "I'm directing 'Harvey' and I need somebody to play the attendant at the insane asylum where Elwood P. Dowd is being kept. If you agree to play him, I'll run for the executive committee."

"Deal," Bob said. "Let's do it."

The play went off without a hitch and Milam brought down the house with his comedic timing. I ran for the executive committee slot and was overwhelmingly elected. But, then, how could I lose? Nobody ran against me. It was like 1970 all over again, but, with a big exception. Anybody could have qualified. McClendon had been set straight on that count.

Not long after my "nomination," I received a congratulatory letter from U.S. Rep. Bob Jones, who sent similar missives to all Democratic nominees. It's unlikely he knew the circumstances of my "campaign" and what had happened four years previous when I was given the runaround by McClendon.

"Your unopposed nomination is a splendid tribute to your service and your abilities," he wrote, in a June 18, 1974 letter. "This should be a source of pride and encouragement to you."

I was elected in the spring of 1974. At about the same time, I had accepted the position of managing editor at the *Natchez Democrat* in Mississippi. Coincidentally, the organizational meeting was scheduled for the very day we were to leave Decatur for Natchez. I knew in advance that the main order of business was to dump McClendon—at least that's what Milam hoped would happen.

"Al, we've got to have you for the meeting, Saturday," Bob said over the phone. "It could be a close election. Every vote could count."

"I don't know," I told him. "We've got a long drive ahead of us. If we stop for an hour, it could mean getting to Natchez pretty late."

After more haggling, I agreed to meet with the rest of the committee at a restaurant in Hartselle, about 10 miles south of Decatur. I felt it was the least I could do, considering my 1970 political involvement.

On the big day, I parked outside the restaurant. I went inside while Sharon and the kids stayed in the car. I had a feeling it wouldn't take long. It didn't. The meeting opened, a motion was made to elect a chairman and McClendon's name was proposed by one of his cronies.

As it turned out, it was a "FATE"ful day for Sam. We booted him out of office and elected one of Milam's young Turks. Enough of them had been picked for the executive committee to make the difference. My one and only political vote had been cast and it couldn't have been more enjoyable.

Chris Bell, a friend who was a correspondent for the *Huntsville Times*, but lived in Decatur, was well versed in the 1970 incident. He couldn't resist driving down to Hartselle to cover the removal of McClendon as county chairman.

He wrote a column about it and my only political vote.

CHAPTER THIRTY-THREE:

RAP BROWN

I knew it was going to be a long night when I neared the little Lowndes County town of White Hall about 6 p.m. on March 20, 2000.

Lots of blue lights were flashing to my left just off U.S. 80 about 30 miles west of Montgomery. As I looked to my right, I saw six people sitting handcuffed on County Road 23 which intersects with the federal highway. Some of the men walking around the cuffed group had "FBI" in large yellow letters on the back of their blue jackets.

I knew they had either captured or were looking for Jamil Abdullah Al-Amin, known to most Americans with long memories as H. Rap Brown. He was a 60s radical and "Burn, Baby, Burn" adherent who claimed to have gone straight after completing a prison term.

My long night began in the morning at the *Montgomery Advertiser* when I saw an *Associated Press* article about the nationwide search for Al-Amin in connection with the fatal shooting of a deputy sheriff and the wounding of another officer in Atlanta. Scanning the story, I came across reference to a vehicle with an Alabama tag that had "45" on it. I knew immediately that it was from Lowndes County, a predominantly black county between Selma and Montgomery where Brown and Stokely Carmichael, another 60s radical, worked to register black voters. From that effort sprang the Black Panther Party—a violent group that surfaced primarily in California after the southern civil rights movement of the 1960s waned. A black panther was used as the symbol for Lowndes County residents who ran for office and it was picked up by the California group.

I drove over to Hayneville, the county seat, and began asking questions. Probate Judge John Hulett, who had served as the county's first black sheriff for 20 years before being elected judge, heard about the search for Al-Amin. H said he didn't know if he had been hiding in his county. After checking a few more sources, I went back to Montgomery and reported to my editors what I had learned. They seemed interested in a local angle to the national Al-Amin story, so I decided to go back to Lowndes County to flesh it out a bit with more comments and quotes. I had finished my regular assignments for Tuesday, so I knew I had time to work on the Al-Amin story. Most of us just referred to him as "Rap" because "Al-Amin" wasn't a name with which we were that familiar.

Born Hubert Brown in Baton Rouge, La. in 1943, he picked up the nickname "Rap" because of his ability to speak foreign languages and gutter dialects with ease. He went to Southern University in Louisiana from 1960-1964. After that, he joined Carmichael and became an official with the Student Non-Violent Coordinating Committee (SNCC) which spread through the South during the 1960s to push for black voting rights and racial equality in other areas of society. He later spent five years in prison for inciting a riot in Maryland, adopted Islam, a new name and moved to Atlanta where, ostensibly, he shifted gears and became a community activist. In 1995, police arrested Rap in connection with a shooting incident. The charge later was dropped and he resumed his role as a neighborhood leader. Then, the fatal shooting occurred and he was on the run again.

I knew enough about Rap's background to realize this wasn't just any ordinary fugitive-from-justice story. Those aren't unusual in this country. This was H. Rap Brown, the revolutionary.

I slowed down and looked for a spot to park along the highway. Cops were all over the place. I finally found a place between two trucks and my green New Beetle—dubbed Schnell—slipped nicely into the little location. It was almost dark by that time and it was getting cold. It was warm for late March and I had worn a short-sleeve shirt. By 6 p.m., as the sun disappeared behind the towering pine trees facing Selma, I began to shiver as I approached FBI agents standing guard over the six Muslims.

"What's going on?" I asked one of the agents. "We've got a situation here, so stand aside," he responded. "We'll give you more details as soon as we get them." "You lookin' for Rap?" I asked. "Well, you could say something like that, but I can't say anything else," He replied.

A large man wearing Muslim garb was lifted to his feet at that point and positioned against one of the FBI vehicles. They frisked him for weapons and anything that might help lead to Brown. Alabama State Trooper Terry King lent a hand as the agents looked for evidence. By that time, the word was out. It seemed every law enforcement agency but the Secret Service was converging on White Hall—a tiny, predominantly black town where Rap once lived before many of the agents were born.

After the shooting in Atlanta, investigators considered several areas where he might try to hide. One was White Hall. The FBI knew Rap still had friends there and agents were sent to Alabama to set up a surveillance operation through the weekend. They worked around the clock, checking every building in town, including vacant barns, trailers and rusty, discarded vehicles.

"It's been a long two days for us," FBI agent Bill Imfeld told me, after he had walked out of the darkness and we shook hands. "I think most of us have only had about two hours of sleep during that time." Imfeld ran the FBI's Mobile office, but he hadn't seen much of Mobile since the shooting in Atlanta. He told me the six Muslims—two men and four women—had been sitting on the cold ground for an hour, but hadn't said a word. They just sat there and stared into the approaching darkness.

By 7 p.m., the first television crew from Montgomery had arrived at our site and I was freezing. Luckily, I had my newly acquired cell phone and had been able to call my office a couple of times to let them know what was happening. I hadn't gotten one before because I knew I could always stop at a pay phone and dial our toll free number to the newsroom. There aren't many pay phones in Lowndes County and I was far from the nearest one. "How long do you plan to stay there?" asked city editor John Hasselwander. "I'm not sure, but I know our first edition deadline isn't far off, right?" I had dictated enough information to beef up my story of earlier in the day, but, from all indications, they were closing in on Rap and could have him in custody soon. "Let me play this one by ear, John," I said. "We can always go with the AP story if they get him later in the night. Just give me a few more minutes." "OK," he said. "But, we can't wait much longer."

After I disconnected, an FBI agent walked up with a request. "Can I borrow your cell phone?" he asked. "Sure," I said. "Is it a local call." He laughed and said: "I'll be done in a couple of minutes. Mine just died." He finished his call, gave it back to me and walked away after saying softly: "It won't be long now." No way was I going back to Montgomery at that moment.

Rap was trapped near an abandoned church about 8 p.m. Lowndes County Deputy John Williams, known as "Big John," took him into custody. At 6-feet-5 inches and 250 pounds, Williams usually got his way when it came to making an arrest. Rap did try to run away at one point, but Williams tackled him. The site was a few miles from where I stood on the highway and I knew there was no way of telling how long it might be before they brought him out. I thought they'd drive Rap to Montgomery. That's what they did. By 9 p.m., I was back at my office while one of our photographers had staked out the county jail.

I had finished the story of Rap's arrest for the first of our three editions. Then, I asked Hasselwander how much space he could give me for a separate, descriptive story from Lowndes County. We call them sidebars. It would be about what I had seen in the two hours before they caught Rap. "We don't have room for anything else," John said. That set off a spirited debate between the two of us. Having been in the business for more than 35 years, I knew a story when I saw it and this one screamed for at least an accompanying article about waiting in the dark for the law to grab Rap Brown. "John, this is the biggest story in the country right now and we're sitting right on top of it." He knew it as much as I did. "Hassle," as I called him, also was an editor with deadlines to meet and bosses to please. Changing a page's appearance approved six hours before could mean trouble. I guess it must have been the reddish color of my face and the steam coming from my ears that convinced John to give me a few inches to add to what was the lead story on network television that night.

"When H. Rap Brown led voting rights demonstrations in White Hall 35 years ago, he used to pass by "Tent City" where black sharecroppers evicted by angry white landowners had been forced to live." That was the lead paragraph to my sidebar. The second paragraph said: "On Monday night, Brown—now known as Jamil Abdullah Al-Amin—passed by the same area as a passenger in handcuffs." Then, a third: "Instead of tents, the intersection looked more like an armed camp—filled with special weapons team members, men in camouflage uniforms, state troopers, Lowndes County sheriff's deputies, U.S. Marshals and dozens of FBI agents."

It had been well worth the effort that night—the cold, the long wait, the pleas to get my second story approved. Tuesday morning's front page reflected that effort. "Fugitive caught in Lowndes," was the headline. Our photographer had gotten a good shot of Brown being taken to the Montgomery County Jail by two men wearing flak jackets and "FBI" on the front. Rap, bald-headed and wearing sunglasses, stared ahead emotionless. The sidebar inside had a headline that read: "Gut feeling led to arrest of fugitive in Lowndes." It wasn't my gut feeling—it was the FBI's—but I felt that if he was going to be arrested anywhere, it might be in Lowndes County.

The following day was filled with legal maneuvering with Rap's lawyers trying to keep him in Alabama and as far away from Georgia as possible. The charge against him was murder. Execution or life in prison was a possible final chapter in his controversial life.

By Thursday afternoon, I was spending my time updating the Al-Amin story. I also fielded calls from all over the country from reporters wanting details about his capture. Around 4 p.m., the phone rang and I thought it was another call about Rap. Instead, it was a producer for "Geraldo Live," a popular cable television program anchored by Geraldo Rivera. "We'd like you to be on our show tonight," she said. "Tonight!" I said, thinking of a private jet already parked at the Montgomery Regional Airport, fueled and ready to wing me to New York for my 15 minutes of TV fame. "Right," she said, bringing me out of my wishful thinking. "We've got a room just up the street from you. The crew will let you in the building. Hope you can make it."

Deflated a bit, but not about to give up a chance for some national exposure, I agreed to do the interview. After borrowing a sport coat from Bill Brown of our editorial department, I hurried up the street and found Selma lawyer J.L. Chestnut already there. Ches represented

Rap. We sat side by side on the makeshift set and went through our microphone checks. Then, Geraldo came on to say 'hi' and introduce himself, as if he had to. The first half of the show was about a different subject and, by the time the Rap Brown segment started, I knew there wouldn't be much time for us. Geraldo had a couple of New York lawyers on first and they pontificated for about 15 minutes before he had to take a commercial break. With 10 minutes left, he told his audience that he was shifting to Alabama to speak to two people who either knew Rap or had covered his recent arrest. Ches did most of the talking and, by the time it was my big chance, time had about run out.

I joked to Ches that if I ever got a chance to be on Geraldo's show, I'd do what most guests did when he asked them a question. They'd say: "Well, Geraldo…" Naturally, when he asked me the first question, I came right to the point and forget to say "Well, Geraldo…" I answered his questions and put in a plug for the *Advertiser*, telling the world that we had a "scoop" in our Friday morning edition. It concerned a legal twist in the case. I also told him I wasn't surprised about Rap's arrest in White Hall because of his activities there during the 60s and the friends who could possibly have harbored him. Then, it was over and I drove home after still another long, long day at the office.

It hadn't been a total loss. I told Geraldo's producer that I'd be on the show if he sent me an autographed photograph. He did just that, with a nice comment to boot. It had been my first national audience since those exciting UPI days when I sent in audio reports during the civil rights era.

Rap was extradited to Georgia where, after a year or so of delays, he finally came to trial. The evidence against him was overwhelming and the jury didn't waste much time convicting him. He was sentenced to life in prison. He couldn't have claimed racism because the deputies he shot were black, as were most members of the jury. Rap came back to Montgomery for a hearing in late 2002 to face new charges. He was accused of firing at three U.S. Marshals in White Hall as they closed in on him. Ches described the Alabama charge as an "insurance policy" just in case Rap beat the murder rap in Georgia.

That seemed unlikely.

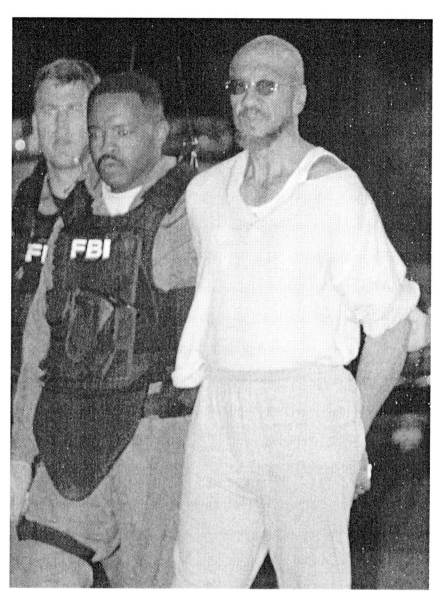

Former 60s radical H. Rap Brown in custody. (Photo by Todd Van Emst)

CHAPTER THIRTY-FOUR:

A PASSIONATE PLAY

It's known as the Passion Play and it's been surrounded by controversy since the curtain first went up in Oberammergau, Germany in 1634. That's when people in the little village created it as a way to thank God for sparing them from the bubonic plague. Or, that's what the Germans would have you believe.

The play—about the final days in Jesus' life—has been called anti-Semitic, too long, too boring and so wonderful that it's something not to be missed during a Christian's lifetime—sorta like Mel Gibson's "Passion of the Christ" movie that attracted millions of people in 2004.

Leave it to Selma, then, to wind up in the middle of a controversy over it.

"Jesus" refused to go up on the cross and "Judas" wound up being crucified.

An American touring company had been holding performances of the play during the early 1980s and, like rock groups looking for an extra payday between contracted engagements, settled on Selma as an easy way to pick up a few bucks as they moved from one city to another.

The catalyst for the production was Ann Kelley Balfour, the widow of the touring company's original producer. Black and white photographs of Balfour, which appeared in the *Selma Times-Journal* to promote the play, obviously had been taken years before her group arrived in town—many years before.

The performers had just completed a successful run at the famous Fox Theater in Atlanta and were headed for Vicksburg, Mississippi for more shows when a member of the advance party stopped in Selma. After crossing the Edmund Pettus Bridge which leads into town, she reportedly told local residents later, that she had a "vision" and was informed by a voice of unknown origin that "The Passion Play must be performed here in Selma."

At least, that's the way Kathryn Tucker Windham, Selma's noted author, heard it from local sources and reported in her delightful book—"A Sampling of Selma Stories." It's the last chapter and, is appropriately titled: "The Passion Play, Selma Version."

I first heard about the play from Allen Edwards, one of Selma's leading lawyers at the time. In addition to his legal activities, he also was president of the Performing Arts Center which had opened a few months before and was in need of a big opening act to wow the locals.

Allen approached me in nearby Marion where I was covering a story about a business he represented. He couldn't wait to break the news about the play because he knew advance publicity in the *Montgomery Advertiser* might draw people from outlying areas since we covered a wide section of central and south Alabama.

"Al, you won't believe what we've been able to come up with," he said. "We've got the Passion Play coming to Selma."

"The Passion, what?" I asked, informing him that Jews usually don't attend plays known to have caused riots and the deaths of their ancestors in Europe. He went on to provide details and to let me know how "lucky" Selma was to have been "picked" for an interim series of performances.

"We need your help, Al," he said. "People spend a lot of money to fly to Germany to see the play. These will be the only performances in Alabama."

Why the Balfour group decided to bypass Montgomery, Mobile, Birmingham and Huntsville for little Selma seemed somewhat strange. Allen also didn't explain what, if anything, Balfour knew about that "vision" on the bridge. Could it have been a vision of an empty bank account? We never did find out.

I eventually wrote a couple of stories because it was a good local angle for Selma's theatrical community and might entice some of our readers to drive over to take in one of the shows. Tickets cost as much as $20 each and that limited the night performances to the city's affluent citizens. Six shows were scheduled—three matinees and three evening performances—all at Selma High School.

Elementary school children had the honor of watching the opening matinee. That wasn't a good omen, especially since the cast and crew arrived late from a previous performance in Atlanta. Some of the costumes didn't fit and dozens of local volunteers who wanted to be in the play didn't have much instruction on theatrical essentials. Selma High School drama teacher Jim Freeman made sure that the chaos was held to a minimum backstage at the school's auditorium where the play was performed.

All went well until the crucifixion scene. That's when the wheels began to come off the Passion Wagon. Accounts of what happened are somewhat sketchy and there are several versions, but all seemed to agree that "Jesus" got into it with the stage manager over the stability of the cross he was supposed to mount in the show's most critical scene.

Two local volunteers portraying the thieves crucified with Jesus took their places on crosses that appeared to be to their liking. Not so with the star of the show. It was akin to one of those campy B movies about early aviation when the young pilot looks at his plywood plane and tells his commanding officer: "You want to send a kid like me up in a crate like that?" Of course, the "kid" goes up and, of course, he dies heroically as he tries to save western civilization.

Jesus had other ideas and told the stage manager where to get off. He wasn't referring to the cross, either. At least, that's what some privy to the exchange between the two would say later. The two men got into a shouting match behind the closed curtain as the antsy youngsters out front wondered what was going on. Shoves apparently led to punches and, according to one version, the stage manager decked Jesus with a right cross to his thorny crown which dug into his forehead, causing blood to run down his cheeks instead of his rib cage.

The next thing anybody knew, Jesus ran from the stage, into the hallway and toward the principal's office to call the police. He was dressed only in a loincloth at the time, so the sight must have left some indelible impressions on those in the hallway.

"Call the police, call the police," Jesus is said to have shouted. "He's trying to kill me." Our executive editor, Bill Brown, told me later: "Isn't that the purpose of the play?"

Principal Roy Wilson, a tobacco-chewing hulk of a man who was more familiar with turning double plays or blocking defensive ends as a young man, found himself in the middle of a theatrical crisis. But, he performed nicely and was able to calm Jesus and keep him from calling out the cops to arrest the stage manager.

Meanwhile, back in the auditorium, the man in charge of special effects must have wondered what was going on. The curtain had remained closed far too long and music heralding the start of the crucifixion scene kept repeating itself. The kids were ready to go home.

When the curtain finally opened, audible gasps could be heard in the audience.

"That's not Jesus on the cross," one youngster was heard to exclaim, while another chimed in with: "They're crucifying the wrong man."

Indeed, they were—figuratively speaking, of course.

After the commotion backstage, those in charge had to find somebody to take Jesus' place on the rickety old cross. Since Jesus had left with the only available loincloth, there needed to be a quick adjustment in personnel, not to mention costumes.

An understudy was pressed into service, but his appearance left something to be desired, according to Kathryn whose research revealed that the young man: "Hung on the cross wearing a pair of dirty green gym shorts with a yellow stripe down each side. His arms were bare, revealing bold tattoos (showing) a bright red rose on one arm and "Mother" encircled by hearts and flowers on the other. And, the fellow had flaming red curly hair."

It didn't take long for word to spread through Selma and surrounding communities. If the Balfour team needed something spectacular to spur ticket sales, it couldn't have come up with anything better than Jesus' refusal to climb up on the cross.

The show that night was a bit rocky, especially since Balfour sent the actor playing Jesus into exile. That meant coming up with another replacement. Poor stage lighting didn't help, either.

Somebody called me at home late that night. He tried not to laugh, but, once he started, I joined in. I knew this was a story of Biblical proportions. The next morning, I drove over to the Holiday Inn where Balfour and her troops were staying. I found her in a booth with three young actors, drinking coffee and looking like they had just been put through a wringer worse than any Broadway critic could conjure up in a post-show review.

"Mrs. Balfour," I said, after introducing myself as being a reporter from the *Montgomery Advertiser*, "I understand you had some problems yesterday during the first show."

"Oh, young man, I hope you won't write anything about it," she said. "It was just a big misunderstanding. We've got it all worked out."

The story ran the next morning across the top of page one—mentioning the backstage tiff and subsequent loincloth dash down the hallway. The remaining shows were sellouts. They had become the hottest tickets in town. Lisa Wallace, who was the wife of Gov. George Wallace at the time, came over from Montgomery as a guest of singer Anita Bryant, who was living in Selma after fleeing Florida following her unappreciated comments about homosexuality.

Aware of the "star power" in the audience, Balfour relented and allowed the original "Jesus" to return. I guess it had something to do with forgiveness being divine, or something like that. Jesus, living up to the character he played, forgave the man with the wicked right hand. The stage manager also shook hands with him. All went well for the remaining performances.

I've had some memorable quotes through the years, but the one offered by Freeman that day topped them all. It still does.

"In this play, Jesus was the star, but he should have known that, in the theater, the stage manager is God," Jim told me.

CHAPTER THIRTY-FIVE:

PHIL LUCY AND A BAG OF BONES

C rawling around under a creepy old house in the middle of winter must have been bad enough for the two men hired to inspect it prior to renovation. Imagine their horror, then, when they hooked a root and came up with a bag of human bones.

The gruesome discovery in January of 1994 set in motion an American Gothic tale in the little Alabama community of Uniontown. The house belonged to Phillip and Margaret Lucy. Four children lived with them. One was an adopted son. His name was Allan and he was only a few weeks shy of his 14th birthday when he vanished in the spring of 1985. Friends and neighbors wondered what had happened to him. Phillip Lucy said he had "gone to Florida" to be with friends. He didn't seem too concerned about the disappearance.

During the nine years that followed, questions about Allan Lucy would pop up from time to time. Most people weren't buying Phil Lucy's claim that Allan had just walked away—not someone as young as he was. He was just a kid and lacked the street smarts to fend for himself.

In late 1993, the couple decided to sell their house. It would be the biggest mistake of Phil Lucy's life.

Kelly Kirby lived in the state of Washington, but he often spent time thousands of miles from home, restoring old houses. He took one look at the big, white Victorian structure in the little town 30 miles west of Selma and knew he just had to have it. Kirby and the Lucys worked out a purchase agreement in October of 1993. Shortly after that, a team was sent in to give the house a thorough check.

Alabama may be in the heart of cotton country, but it's still cold in January and Kirby's men were dressed warmly as they inspected each room in the house. Two of them eventually decided to go under the porch to check out the foundation. They were concerned about possible termite damage and wanted to make sure everything was all right.

The two worked in an area with only a few inches to spare between the ground and the base of the porch. It took a long time for them to crawl around, military-style, to examine the house's underbelly. They held flashlights in front of them. As they reached the front of the porch, Ron Adams felt something in the dark. His rake snagged a large root that had been sticking out of the ground.

Adams heard about the missing teen-ager, but had no reason to believe he had hit anything other than a thick root. Of course, there was always that dream that diggers have—buried gold, diamonds or cash. Deep down inside, however, he had a chilling feeling that it might be something else.

"I had heard stories that a treasure or a body had been buried under the house and I started digging with my rake," he told me, during an interview a couple of days after his discovery. "I kept thinking 'I'm going to be rich.'"

Instead of buried treasure, Adams uncovered a layer of red bricks. Under the bricks he found some plastic bags and in one of them, he felt what appeared to be bones. He had no doubts that he had found Allan Lucy.

Scurrying out as quickly as they could, Adams and his friend told their supervisor. Police were contacted. When the bag was opened, it showed what appeared to be the skeletal remains of a small person. The bones had been wrapped in a cotton blanket with Disney characters on it, including Mickey Mouse.

Phillip Lucy told police he had no idea who the bones belonged to. It wasn't long before newspaper reporters and television crews were camped outside the Lucy house. We knew this was one of those bizarre stories that people loved to read about—something that just doesn't happen every day.

As forensic experts began taking a close look at the remains, the Lucy family lived several miles away in the Marengo County town of Lamison. They had moved into another old house and were renting it as negotiations proceeded on the purchase of their Uniontown house.

Authorities eventually began questioning Lucy. He continued to say he was "shocked" by the discovery of bones under his house. He insisted they did not belong to Allan. As far as he knew, the boy was living somewhere in Florida. I saw a lot of Lucy during that time. He was always open to questions. He seemed to enjoy all the publicity. His wife shied away from the television cameras and reporter notepads. She left it all up to her husband to explain the mysterious discovery under their old house.

The couple's two youngest children—8 and 6 at the time—were cared for by relatives. Their parents were questioned repeatedly. The bones believed to have been those of Allan Lucy were being kept in a cardboard box at the Alabama Forensics Laboratory in Tuscaloosa. One small box contained a skull. The other held the rest of the remains.

Preliminary hearings are conducted before trials begin. They afford defendants a chance to hear what the prosecution has against them and it also gives a judge an opportunity to set bond in the most serious cases. They usually are routine matters, disposed of in a few minutes. But, as in most aspects of the Lucy case, that hearing was anything but routine.

Lucy's biological son, Jason, testified that he saw his father kill Allan in their kitchen—striking him on the head with a crushing blow from his right fist. Phillip Lucy was a bull of a man, solid as a rock and a former professional fighter as a young man. He was court-martialed and then dishonorably discharged from the Army during the Korean War for punching another soldier. Jason Lucy's testimony in June 1994 stunned those in the courtroom. He said his father and Allan began arguing in the kitchen when the fatal blow was struck.

"My father hit Allan...in his left facial area (and) Allan fell to the floor," Jason testified. "He did not seem to be breathing. His mouth and eyes were slightly open."

Jason said his father ordered him to his room and told him to "stay quiet." Several hours later, Jason said he saw his father with dirt on his clothes and a shovel in his hands, coming into the house from the back yard. He said he could see him from a window on the second floor of the weather-beaten old house.

Jason's testimony continued for about an hour. He didn't need much prodding and Lucy's lawyers didn't do much to contradict or ask questions. Phil Lucy, who had been charged with murder, just sat and stared at a son who was calling him a killer. It appeared as though he was ready to attack Jason, who had plenty of courtroom protection.

Circuit Judge Jack Meigs turned the case over to a Perry County grand jury and reduced Phil Lucy's bail from $150,000 to $100,000. Dayle Lucy had been implicated, but not charged with as serious a crime as her husband. Prosecutors felt they had the one they were after. They said Dayle would, at most, have been an accessory. She was allowed to return to Lamison to take care of their two young children who had been taken to Montgomery to live with their older sister.

Phillip Lucy spent most of the following five years in and out of mental hospitals, being examined for a variety of problems real or imagined. At times, he'd be returned to Marion, Alabama for more hearings on his mental competency. That's when I usually got a chance to drive up from my office in Selma to interview him at the county Jail.

Each time I interviewed Lucy, he'd have a different story. He seemed to like my company and didn't have a problem with my little tape recorder taking down every word. He had become a celebrity, of sorts, and he appeared to thrive on it.

On July 31, 1998, we sat in a small room away from his cellblock. Lucy brought with him a thick stack of papers accumulated during his years in confinement. They included legal documents, letters to him and letters written by him, but not delivered. They all proclaimed his innocence.

"They weren't Allan's bones," he told me at one point. "Jason thought he'd scare some of the neighborhood children around Halloween and put the bones together from a cemetery to hang outside the house."

A Selma dentist had already determined through his records that the teeth in the skull—which had been detached from the rest of the remains for closer inspection—belonged to Allan. That pretty much wiped out Phil Lucy's claim of a cemetery prank.

After the interview, Lucy was returned to the Taylor Hardin Secure Medical Facility in Tuscaloosa. A year later, he was back in Marion and I got another chance to interview him. It was June 13, 1999 and Phil Lucy had just observed his 67th birthday. By that time, he didn't celebrate birthdays. He had a lot of reasons not to. A jury had convicted him the previous month of killing Allan and he was sentenced to serve 25 years in prison. It was as close to a life sentence as possible for a man his age.

We met on a Saturday morning and it was evident that the past year had been tough on him. He had suffered a stroke since our last interview. It followed a heart attack not long after he was arrested. The stroke left his speech slurred but he still was able to mumble enough to be heard. His tongue kept flicking in and out of his mouth in reptilian fashion. He had trouble swallowing.

After having interviewed him so many times since his arrest, I was familiar with his story line, but, when he mentioned "Sheck," I knew I had something new and fresh.

Sheck's first name is Barry and he was one of O.J. Simpson's "Dream Team" members who helped convince a Los Angeles jury to return an acquittal verdict. Sheck's specialty is forensic science and DNA evidence. That's what made him popular with Phil Lucy.

"Those bones ain't Allan's and (Sheck) is the one person who can prove it," Lucy told me. "I may not be able to get him to take my case, but I'm going to try."

Lucy said he tried, but never got that appointment with Sheck. He told me he had spent $80,000 on lawyers to defend him and had been wiped out financially. His opinion of them was, as expected, not very high. His fourth lawyer was court appointed.

In the fall of 2000, a new trial was ordered for Lucy. The Alabama Court of Criminal Appeals found fault with the way Lucy's initial jury had been selected. The court said sufficient reasons had not been given as to why a black member of the jury pool had been excluded. As with most of the developments in the Lucy case, this one also had an interesting twist. Most "Batson" appeals, as they are known, involve black defendants who claim too many of their black peers were excluded from possible jury duty without race-neutral reasons. Lucy was white. But, it was a legal avenue to explore and it worked for his Tuscaloosa lawyer, Paula Watkins.

In early February 2001, Lucy was brought back to the Perry County Courthouse for still another hearing. Circuit Judge Tommy Jones had taken over the case by then and discussed the upcoming trial and possible bond for Lucy. At that point in his life, Lucy seemed to be a beaten man with few friends to lend a helping hand. A year or so before, he had been bonded out by a friend in Uniontown. That upset most of the people who lived in the neighborhood.

As he waited for his lawyer to sit down with him for a pre-hearing discussion, I walked over and shook hands with him. He offered a smile, but his heart wasn't in it, not like before.

"Sometimes I wonder if it wouldn't just be better if I died," he said.

In Alabama, parole is a possibility for inmates almost as soon as the steel doors slam behind them. Lucy had been in custody for seven years and would be given credit regardless of what sentence might await him on conviction. By the time his second trial was held, prosecutors were amenable to a deal. They told Lucy's new lawyer that if he'd plead guilty, he'd be in line for a possible parole in 2002. Lucy turned it down.

On Nov. 26, 2001, I drove up to Marion for the start of Lucy's latest trial. I parked across the street from the courthouse and walked to the county jail where Lucy was getting ready to leave. Sheriff James Hood arranged for me to talk with him—as we had done many times after Lucy's arrest in 1994. Lucy carried a plastic bagged filled with notebooks and other items. He flashed a smile—or what passed for one on that stroke-induced face of his—and we began to walk slowly across the street.

I held a tape recorder under my notebook and fired questions in his direction each step along the way. Lucy hadn't changed his tune since the last time I saw him. He was still furious with Jason, who had been found and subpoenaed to testify at the trial. Prosecutors had Jason's testimony from the preliminary hearing seven years before and that no doubt would have been enough to convict his father. With his live testimony, it would be all the jury needed to convict.

"Jason's a damn liar," Lucy said, as he shuffled across the street to the courthouse. "That boy ain't never told the truth in his life. Allan's still alive as far as I know."

As the trial progressed, it was obvious that Phil Lucy's chances of an acquittal were slim. He knew it, too.

"I know now how Custer felt at the Little Big Horn," he told me, with a half smile as he walked into the courtroom after a recess—a deputy sheriff escorting him in.

When Jason began to relive that moment in the kitchen of their house in 1985, the final chapter was being written from the witness stand. At one point, he stood up, pointed a finger across the way and said in a shaky voice: "That's the man, my father, who killed my brother

Allan." Phil Lucy glared at him. If looks could really kill, Jason Lucy would have crumbled on the witness stand.

It didn't take the jury long to convict. Instead of murder, it was manslaughter, but the end result was the same. Jones sentenced Lucy to 25 years in prison. As he was being led out of the courthouse, Lucy insisted that he would appeal once more. He would have been eligible for parole soon because of the credit he received for having been in custody so long.

Lucy vowed to win his freedom one day. He said he had rejected any deal involving a guilty plea from him. He said it would be an admission of guilt and he wouldn't do it. He said he'd rather go down swinging.

That's just what he did—at the end of a bed sheet in a lime green cell at the Perry County Jail.

His body was found at 5 a.m. on Nov. 29, 2001.

Investigators said Lucy had fashioned a noose out of the sheet and tied one end of it to an overhead bar in his cell. Then, he tied the other end around his neck and stepped up onto a horizontal metal bar at the bottom of the cell . He was only inches above the cement floor. It was dark outside, but he apparently wanted to get one last look at the outside world before he left it.

Then, he stepped off the bar, still facing the darkness.

Phillip Lucy led into court for his final appearance.

CHAPTER THIRTY-SIX:

MISSING DOG TAGS

I had just gotten home from a Montgomery assignment on a Saturday night in the spring of 1985. The phone rang as Sharon and I walked in the front door. It was one of my editors, asking me if I knew anything about a Roger Patterson and some dog tags found in the jungles of Nicaragua.

"No," I told him. "Who's Roger Patterson and why should I know anything about him or any missing dog tags?" "Because he's from Selma and he's supposed to be dead," I was told.

I thought it would be a needle-in-a-haystack search, but I told my editor I'd give it my best shot. It was 10 p.m. and I was told they'd hold the final deadline for 30 minutes to give me "time" to find him. It took me 20 minutes, thanks to a friend at the Selma Police Department who happened to know Patterson. He also gave me his telephone number.

"Man, I don't know what you're talking about," Patterson said. "I've never been in Nicaragua."

That's when I told him that the Nicaraguan Defense Ministry had him listed as "killed in action" while fighting Contra rebels. Somebody on our copy desk came across a report from the U.S. Defense Department which said dog tags had been found on the body of a dead American who had been fighting with the rebels. The little metal ID tag had Patterson's name on it and it didn't take long to trace it to him.

What made it even more interesting was the fact that the "dead American" was white. Patterson was black.

When I contacted Roger that Saturday night, he had already gotten word about the dog tags and the "body." He had been watching a television news program when he heard his name mentioned.

"I said to myself 'Wow, how could that happen?'" he told me, "and then I wondered how I could collect on my insurance or how my wife could benefit from it."

Unemployed and facing a bleak future, Patterson began thinking of himself, as in how he might be able to cash in on his unexpected international fame. The next morning, he thought even harder outside his little brick house at Craig Field where he had been living. He found himself surrounded by television crews that had just flown to the former Air Force base five miles east of Selma. Whatever composure he might have had vanished in a few seconds as microphones were thrust in his face. Network correspondents asked him how his dog tags could have wound up in a jungle thousands of miles from home. Among those questioning him was a correspondent from "This Week With David Brinkley." Patterson, who couldn't afford a television set and had to watch somebody else's, discovered he was being watched by millions of Americans.

During his interviews, Patterson displayed a set of Army dog tags he said were his. Then, he added: "Somebody could have printed some dog tags and just happened to use my name." That explanation didn't go very far with reporters looking for an answer that might have more sinister implications.

The little metal tags were found at a time of heightened tension during the Nicaraguan crisis. The Reagan Administration was doing all it could to help the Contras overthrow the socialist Sandinista regime in power at the time. In Reagan's mind, the Contras were much the same as American colonialists trying to form a new government two centuries earlier.

Into this mix came a bewildered Roger Patterson, who also learned that he had been "buried in the jungle." That bit of information came from Angela Saballos, a spokeswoman for the Nicaraguan Foreign Ministry which claimed Roger had died "in combat."

"If the Patterson family had been interested in seeing (the body) we would have made all efforts to look for it in the jungle, since we do not know exactly where he was buried," Saballos told reporters.

Meanwhile, back at Craig Field, Patterson acknowledged that he had served with the Alabama National Guard in Honduras—Nicaragua's northern neighbor, during the last three months of 1983. He said he had spent most of his time helping to build airstrips and working on "classified projects." He also said he began to experience mental problems about that time.

"We were told to stay away from the press and not to discuss anything we were doing," Patterson told me, during my interview with him that Sunday morning. He wouldn't discuss what those "classified projects" entailed.

Discovery of the dog tags placed another spotlight on the Nicaraguan situation. Washington observers speculated that the Nicaraguan socialists might have staged the whole thing to embarrass the United States and possibly slow continued aid to the Contras. The incident occurred at a time when Congress was debating whether to approve $14 million in aid to the rebels.

Patterson said that, while in the Army, he was sent home from Germany where he was stationed. He said his commander told him he was "acting weird and talking funny."

"It seems like I lost touch with reality," he said. "My commander recommended that I go see a doctor and that's what I did. All I know is that I wound up in a hospital and then was sent home. I got shot in the arm with medicine and flown to the United States."

Patterson told me he had been classified as a paranoid schizophrenic and was drawing $450 a month in disability payments. He said he had been a corporal in the Army and was looking forward to a military career. Instead, he wound up living in a housing project without much money or hope.

"I couldn't believe it," he said. "My career just slipped out from beneath my feet. All of a sudden, bam! Everything just fell apart."

Patterson may have had some mental problems, as he claimed, but he was sane enough to know he was—for a few minutes, at least—sitting on a potential gold mine if he could work it right.

"Hey, man," he kept asking me, "you know how I can make some money off of this?" I didn't, but I did offer him a job delivering the *Advertiser* to our customers in the Selma area. He gave it some thought but didn't accept the offer.

People have wondered since that time how Roger Patterson's dog tags could have wound up in that Nicaraguan jungle. I've wondered myself, along with another question in early 2001—how did my dog tags wind up in a field near Georgia Avenue in Washington, D.C.?

My brother, Barry, said someone had called him because there weren't many "Benns" in the D.C. phone book. When the caller read "Alvin" to him, Barry knew immediately those were my Marine Corps dog tags. He made plans to get them to me. My mother-in-law once lived in an apartment on Georgia Avenue and I could have misplaced them there during one of our visits to see her.

Finding my dog tags didn't create an international incident, of course, but it did make me wonder about such things.

I never did get them back. And, I lost track of Roger, too, until I checked the Selma phone book, saw his name and called. His wife, Pam, answered, but said Roger wasn't available. She said he shot himself to death several years before. She said he was never able to chase the demons from his life.

"He had problems before, but I think what he did to himself really began that day with the dog tags," his widow said to me on a chilly, rainy late February Sunday afternoon in 2005. "He just never could cope with things after that."

She sat on a couch next to her 16-year-old daughter, Nikki, who was three when her father ended his life. She never knew him. Roger Patterson, Jr. was being held by his dad in a photograph I took for the article that appeared in the *Montgomery Advertiser*. The little boy is 23 now with children of his own. He also has a void that will never be filled because of his father's death.

CHAPTER THIRTY-SEVEN:

A SAD LIFE

Willie was a wino, but he went out in style.

For most of his life, Willie Millhouse depended on the generosity of others to make it through the day. It was a hand-to-mouth existence. His home was an alley or at the bottom of the Dallas County Courthouse steps where he curled up at night to ward off the chill.

At times, he thought his best friend was a bottle of cheap wine. In the end, however, it was the long arm of the law. It reached out gently to bid him farewell. The men who knew him best laid him to rest.

Millhouse, 57, died at a local hospital. Kidney failure may have been the cause, but those in the 'street corner crowd' were aware of what really took his life.

"He killed hisself," said Big Lee, who sat on a bench near the police station. He and Willie often would sit on the bench, waiting for someone to come by and ask them to do odd jobs for a few bucks. The liquor store is around the corner and Willie was a regular.

"Willie stayed where he could," Big Lee added. "He stayed at the courthouse 'til somebody beat him up. Some boys jumped on him. He talked about what might happen if he got sick. He didn't know what to do. Last time I saw him he didn't feel good. He didn't take care of hisself. He stayed up all night."

Willie was arrested for the first time in 1947 on a charge of stealing a bicycle. The charge later was dropped, but it was only the beginning of his troubles.

From 1949 to 1976, he was jailed 134 times, most as a public drunk. It became a monthly event. Willie would show up at night, flash a smile that would light up Alabama Avenue and ask for a place to stay at the Selma City Jail.

Usually, he was allowed to sleep in a cell or in the city courtroom. During the winter, Willie had no trouble finding a place to stay. By the mid-1970s, he was being referred to as a "sleeper" and wasn't booked.

"If somebody complained about him, all we had to do was pull our patrol car up to him and he'd get in," said Capt. William Zachry. "He never gave us any trouble.

Zachry, Assistant Chief Charlie Jones, Capt. Billy Bobo and others trusted him so much that Willie was hired to do menial chores around their houses. Each year he would help with the police barbecue, spending the day at the Fraternal Order of Police lodge. He cooked the food, cleaned the tables and served his friends.

"'He lived a typical bum's life," said Zachry. "Everything he got was the hard way. He usually wore a trenchcoat and kept food in his pockets. He was heavy when I first met him, but in his last days, he had become very thin."

Jones said the last time he saw Willie was behind the station. It wasn't unusual to see him going through the trash cans, looking for scraps of food.

One of Willie's best friends was known only as "Rat." The two were pals, looking for work or a handout, until "Rat" just disappeared. Some said he was in a hospital. Others said he had died of the same disease— liquor and self-neglect.

Illness finally began to take its toll on Willie and his days appeared to be numbered. On Nov. 14, 1980 he asked two police officers to take him to a hospital. He stayed there for a few weeks and was transferred to another for kidney dialysis treatment. It was Thanksgiving Day.

His heart stopped the following Monday. When word of his death circulated in Selma, the city opened its arms to a man who left five cigarette butts, a penny, a comb, matches and sunglasses.

The funeral procession was led by two patrolmen on motorcycles. Two police cars followed and his casket was removed from the hearse by Zachry, Jones, Bobo and the others. It was made of pine.

There were flowers, too.

Willie would have liked it a lot.

CHAPTER THIRTY-EIGHT:

CHURCH FIRES

The first black church burned to the ground three days before Christmas in 1995. Two more were destroyed within a few days of that, followed by more. By the end of January of 1996, half a dozen were gone. Panic began to spread through west Alabama's black communities.

Churches were destroyed in Greene, Hale and Dallas counties—all within a 75 mile radius. Each had black congregations. The Ku Klux Klan or some other radical group were the initial suspects, but authorities couldn't focus on one person or organization. A white teenager who lived near Selma torched an old black church he thought wasn't occupied. He was a member of a volunteer fire department and said he wanted some "practice" so he set it on fire and then showed up a few minutes later to help his unit put out the blaze. After he confessed, he was ordered to help build a new church for the little congregation.

Mount Zion Baptist Church was destroyed on Dec. 22, 1995. Within the next two weeks, Little Zion Baptist Church and Mount Zoar Baptist Church also went up in flames. Into the spring and summer of 1996 it went—one black church after another in Alabama and around the South. The U.S. Justice Department became involved and reward money was posted. Few, if any, suspects were caught and convicted.

"The devil was responsible for what happened," the Rev. W.D. Lewis, pastor of Little Zion Baptist Church in Greene County, told me on Jan. 16, 1996. "All good comes from God and evil from the devil." Lewis' church and Mount Zoar Baptist Church had been burned within hours of each other late one night—not long after Mount Zion had been destroyed.

The churches were located in isolated areas of Greene County. In some cases, it was hours or days before they were even noticed. Most had only a few congregants and relied on circuit riding preachers to tend to their spiritual needs. There was little money for upkeep, especially fire alarms or sprinkler systems. Arson was the cause of most fires. Those who burned them didn't try very hard to hide their methods. A gasoline can was found outside one church. Jim Cavanaugh, special agent in charge of the Treasury Department's Bureau of Alcohol, Tobacco and Firearms, spent a lot of sleepless nights trying to figure out who might be responsible.

I joined investigators at several of the burned church sites. Walking through the rubble of what once had been the heart and soul of so many religious people in rural Alabama was tough to take at times. Pews were blackened and still smoldering at some of the churches. Pieces of stained glass windows, along with charred Bibles and Sunday School lesson plans were scattered inside the gutted sanctuaries.

Much of my time during those six months involved reporting on the church fires, efforts to find the guilty party or parties and reporting on fund-raising campaigns to rebuild those that had burned. I also was kept busy answering questions from reporters who called me at my office in Montgomery. Some worked for papers in states where other black churches had burned. Arson had been the cause in those states, too. We compared notes and tried to help each other as much as possible.

It didn't take long for claims of racism to surface. Joseph Lowery, then president of the Southern Christian Leadership Conference, arrived in February of 1996 after the three black churches in Greene County had been destroyed. He said he hoped the fires would not signal more "terrorism" against the black community. Lowery's comments followed the sentencing of two white men for vandalizing black churches in neighboring Sumter County. He pointed out that a white church in the same area had not been damaged. I always admired Joe Lowery, but, at times, he seemed ready to cry racism at the drop of a hat. He had seen much of it in his lifetime commitment to equal rights, but, in this case, it appeared to me that he was being a bit too presumptive. There wasn't a bit of evidence, only assumptions based on prior experiences.

Selma lawyer J.L. Chestnut suggested in a column written for a few small Alabama newspapers that anyone charged with destroying black churches might be "honored." Chestnut, whose skepticism of most things Republican was well known in Alabama, opined: "Don't hold your breath until the feds or (then-Attorney General) Jeff Sessions find and prosecute the terrorists who have returned to the bloody and dastardly act of bombing black churches." There never was any evidence of churches being bombed. Ches also said in his column that "if and when they find these bloody cowards who destroy black churches in the dark of night, they will not be placed on chain gangs as a deterrent to others; rather they may be given medals in secret."

Although black churches were being burned all over the South, Alabama found itself being thrust into the spotlight again. That's when I got an unusual assignment—escort duty.

"Al, we'll need you to take Deborah Mathis around to where the fires happened," said Bill Brown, the *Advertiser's* executive editor. "Deborah, who?" I asked. "She works for *Gannett News Service* and is a columnist," he told me. "Bill, I don't want to do this. It'll take me away from my other assignments. I'm swamped right now." Bill then passed along a corporate "suggestion" by saying "this is coming from the top. We need you to do this."

He didn't need to say anything else. The *Advertiser* had just been bought, along with other papers in a large group, by *Gannett*, the country's largest newspaper chain. You don't make points with the brass—especially if it's new brass—by failing to follow orders as fast as they come down the corporate pipeline. I didn't need to be reminded about what a chain of command was, not after having served six years in the Marine Corps.

"When do we start?" I asked Bill. "In a few days," he said. "We'll work out details pretty soon. We want you to get on it right away."

When Deborah arrived, I had already made plans for us to meet with pastors of the burned churches as well as officials in the towns where they had been destroyed. My contacts in the Black Belt had paid off again. I knew right away that Deborah and I had a lot in common. Both of us loved what we did and we didn't watch a clock at work.

Getting to Greene County can be an adventure at times, involving a circuitous route through the heart of Alabama's Black Belt. Highway 14 stretches for more than 100 miles through isolated little communities, cotton fields, pastures and pine trees. There isn't much out there and when a church burns, it's big news. We drove through Selma, Marion, Greensboro, Eutaw and Boligee. Most are tiny towns far removed from the environment Deborah was familiar with in the Washington, D.C. area where she lives and works. At one point, it seemed we were in the middle of one of those Pink Panther movies. We kept going round and round in an area without directional signs or traffic lights. There were cows, crows, snakes and deer, but few people. I was doing the driving which made it even more interesting. I had a habit of flying along rural roads, munching on hoop cheese and crackers and downing it with a can of Coke or R.C.—all the while looking for where I was supposed to be. I often got lost.

Deborah got quite a tour of Alabama's boondocks. We stopped at town halls, cafes, fire houses and courthouses. She got to interview a lot of people. As a columnist with a growing national reputation, it, no doubt, gave her enough material for months. I made sure we didn't leave Greene County without stopping by to see Boligee Mayor Buddy Lavender—a man with a salt-and-pepper beard and an abundance of animated country expressions. He basically ran the little town out of the kitchen of his house when he wasn't out tending to his crops or goats. He and Deborah got along famously. She knew a character when she saw one and he helped highlight her brief visit to Alabama.

By the summer of 1996, Buddy's demeanor had changed dramatically. He still used country expressions in his responses to my questions, but it was evident he was upset by accusations that he had personally benefited from the fires and rebuilding efforts. When I dropped by for an interview on June 18, 1996, he was livid.

"It's like feedin' a rattlesnake," he told me as he settled into his favorite green rocker on the front porch of his house. "You feed it and get it fat and then it'll turn around, bite you and kill you." He referred to critics who had accused him of thievery, but he wasn't about to name any names. Lavender had launched one of three fund-raising efforts to help pay for a church rebuilding project in the town of 268. *USA TODAY*—the *Gannett*-owned newspaper read by millions every day— had an extensive report about the church fires and included Buddy's fund drive. Lavender began getting letters from all over the country. They all praised him for his efforts to rebuild the church and most of them contained cash or checks made out to the fund. Buddy was leery of turning any of the money over to the main rebuilding fund in the county because a spokesman for it was a convicted sex offender.

As the weeks dragged by, more money arrived—along with more accusations against Lavender. It wasn't long before lawsuits were filed and the humanitarian effort of so many became bogged down in the blame game. In the end, the burned churches were rebuilt. The new ones were much nicer than those that had been destroyed. Hundreds of thousands of dollars from around the country helped build new brick houses of worship with air conditioning, central heat, stained glass windows, red carpet and plenty of pews. They were like gifts from heaven. In the end, it all turned out for the best. Nobody had been hurt in the fires.

The man most deeply involved in the church fire investigations was John Robison, Alabama's State Fire Marshal at the time. He had years of experience in determining causes of fires, but nothing he had done in the past could have prepared him for the onslaught of questioning from reporters who called his office from around the country in 1996.

What upset him most, in addition to the fires themselves, was the assumption by some that they were caused by racists. I had known John for years and he got to trust me enough to open up not only about the investigations, but some very interesting statistics. More than half of the churches destroyed by fires in Alabama in the five previous years had white congregations. Robison said arson was the cause in 33 of 38 church fires between 1990 and 1995.

Taking the information he provided me, I began to call pastors at white and black churches. Across the top of the *Montgomery Advertiser* on June 12, 1996 was the headline: "White churches also targets in arsons." The story didn't please conspiracy theorists and black civil rights leaders, but it helped balance things a bit.

A few days after the story ran, I got a letter from Robison. It had my name on the top of the page, his name on the bottom and one word in between.

"Thanks."

CHAPTER THIRTY-NINE:

THE MAXWELL CASE

His name was Will Maxwell and he was a Baptist preacher surrounded by mystery and fear in east Alabama.

Some whispered that he practiced voodoo at his little house near Alexander City where I was editor of the *Outlook*, a weekly newspaper with loyal subscribers who were well versed in past tragedies involving the Maxwell family.

I first heard about Maxwell shortly after arriving from Natchez, Miss. Four of his relatives had died under seemingly mysterious circumstances over the years and the minister's name was listed as the beneficiary on their life insurance policies.

When Maxwell's 16-year-old niece, Shirley Ann Ellington, was found dead on June 11, 1977, his name was the first mentioned as a possible suspect. The main reason was the location of her body—beneath the left front wheel of Maxwell's 1974 Ford. As word spread about Shirley Ann's death, people didn't need the *Outlook* to tell them what they already assumed had happened. We tried our best to print the basics. For many, that wasn't good enough.

Maxwell's first wife was found dead in 1969 and he was charged with first degree murder. He was acquitted. In 1973, his second wife was also found dead. The official cause was asthmatic bronchitis. Maxwell's brother and nephew also died under what police said had been strange circumstances. Investigators believed Maxwell's brother had been forced to drink an extraordinary amount of alcohol. Toxicologists determined his brother's blood alcohol level had been .48 at the time of his death. At that time, the legal limit of intoxication in Alabama was .10—meaning his brother's body contained almost five times the limit.

Maxwell's second wife was found dead in her car, less than a quarter of a mile from their house in the Nixburg community of neighboring Coosa County. Her car had struck a log and proceeded through some shrubbery, but investigators didn't think that was a factor in her death. The minister collected $40,000 in insurance on her death. In February of 1976, Maxwell's nephew was reported missing by relatives. Four days later, his body was found in his car which wound up in a ravine—hidden by bushes. Investigators said his nephew had died of natural causes.

Shirley Ann, who had been raised by Maxwell's third wife, Ophelia, was his fifth relative to die under questionable circumstances. The last time she was seen alive was the day she left in the minister's car. She was found under the rim of the vehicle on a lonely stretch of road in Nixburg. If there is such a thing as a quiet uproar, that's what it was like in the Alexander City area after news of the teen-ager's death made the rounds. Having heard about Maxwell since my arrival, I decided to drive to his house to see if he, as some believed, was, indeed, a master of voodoo who stuck pins in dolls or had been dickering with car rims and heads in recent days.

He greeted me with a big smile and a handshake. His house was a small, modest structure. If he had cashed in on several life insurance policies as a result of relatives' deaths, he sure didn't put much, if any, of the money into housing. We got right down to business. I asked him about the "rumors" and he said he didn't need to be reminded of them.

"I feel they're at me and it's not true," he told me. "I know they're talking about me. Whenever I come up on a wreck and people gather together, I know they're talking about me. If Shirley hadn't been in my car, there would have been no suspicions."

Rumors linked Maxwell to each of the five deaths and there were those who thought he wore a bullet-proof vest wherever he went. I asked him if he expected questioning from authorities in his niece's death.

"Not justly so," he told me, during that Tuesday night interview at his house.

Before I left, I had to ask Maxwell one last question.

"How about showing me your voodoo room," I said, trying to suppress a smile.

"Sure," he said, breaking into a big grin. "It's right down here."

He took me down a hallway and opened a bedroom door. Inside was inexpensive furniture. I didn't see any pots filled with frogs or punctured dolls. He said that's all he could provide.

I saw Maxwell again four days later. It was at the funeral home where Shirley Ann was being memorialized.

He was slumped backward against one of the pews. His head was tilted upward. His eyes were open and staring at the ceiling. A bullet hole—one of three—could be seen high on his right temple. A thin stream of blood had begun to coagulate as it moved down his right cheek. I took his picture, but it wasn't very good because of backlighting from the funeral home windows and problems with my flash attachment. But, it showed the damage that had been done to the minister.

I assigned Jim Earnhardt, one of our new reporters, to cover the funeral. Jim was and is an outstanding writer and editor with a droll sense of humor that has endeared him to those who know him. At Maxwell's funeral, he skillfully described a shocker he had not expected.

"It was about 3 p.m. Saturday," he wrote in his first-person account. "I was standing in the back of the crowded House of Hutchinson chapel as the Rev. E.B. Burpo delivered the eulogy for Shirley Ellington. Burpo's resonant voice sounded an "Amen" and the eulogy was over.

"The story had already been mentally written," he continued. "Now, a few minutes at the typewriter and I'd be done. Several others standing with me began making their way out the back door of the chapel. Shirley's family remained at the front of the building."

Shirley Ann's aunt—the minister's third wife—was overcome with grief and was led to a red-velvet pew where she listened to Burpo's eulogy. Maxwell cradled his wife in his left arm. He had a handkerchief in his left hand, a fan in his right hand. Moments later, one of Shirley Ann's eight sisters shouted from the front of the funeral home: "You killed my sister and now you're going to pay for it."

The dead teen's uncle, Robert Louis Burns, provided "payment." He stepped up onto one of the pews and pumped three slugs from a .25 caliber pistol in Maxwell's head at close range. State Toxicologist Carlos Rabren determined later than any of the three shots would have been fatal.

Already outside and drenched from the blistering heat, Jim was preparing to return to the office to write his story when he saw people running from the funeral home. He could see the fear in their eyes. The warning from Shirley Ann's sister had been enough to send them scurrying for cover.

"It was then I heard the first shot," Jim wrote. "I wheeled and looked toward a window near the front of the building. Then, I heard the second shot and quickly knelt behind a nearby car. There is nothing quite so chilling as a gunshot. Nothing sounds quite so deadly and so final."

There was bedlam inside the funeral home. Hundreds of people had just witnessed a violent death. Some would call it murder. Some would call it a justified homicide. The following day, I drove back to Maxwell's house and interviewed his grieving widow. She sat at her kitchen table, shook her head and stared out a window.

"It's just a dream," she said, tears welling in her eyes. "It's like I'm living in a nightmare. It's just horrible."

Ophelia Maxwell had gone to mourn the loss of a niece and left a widow.

"He went out of his way to help people," she said. "I never saw him do bad things. Sure, he would get upset at things now and then and we didn't agree on everything. But, I don't recall him doing bad things."

She had been married to Maxwell for three years. She said she had "heard it all" during that time, but never let it bother her.

"I believe I would know if he had done anything," she said, without elaborating on what "anything" might have been. "People listen to gossip on the street. People want to hear about gossip. They're not satisfied until they are in the gossip crowd."

She said Maxwell's arrest in the death of his first wife had made him a marked man in the eyes of the Coosa County community.

"Just because he was accused of one thing I don't think it's right to think he's involved in everything," she told me. "It's not right in the sight of God. They didn't allow him a chance. I believe he's at rest."

Friends began to arrive to offer their condolences. She went into a back bedroom and stayed there for several minutes. When she returned, she had regained her composure.

"God has been with Rev. Maxwell down through the years," she said. "I'm glad God is a just God."

On successive Saturdays, she had lost a girl she considered as much a daughter as a niece and her husband. Our interview was being conducted on Father's Day, but there was no reason for joy in the Maxwell household. Ophelia Maxwell was preparing for her second funeral in as many weeks.

Enter Tom Radney, one of east Alabama's most prominent lawyers.

During his lifetime, Maxwell retained Radney to handle the estates of the four relatives who had died prior to Shirley Ann. When Radney built his stately new law office across the street from the town hall, people began calling it the "Maxwell House." Tom got a kick out of that. Now, instead of representing Maxwell over any estate that might have been left in the wake of his niece's death, Tom was defending the man who killed him. Radney knew it probably wouldn't be too difficult to defend Burns. The jury's biggest problem, it seemed to me, was finding a way to slap the killer on the wrist without making it look like that's what they were doing. If they could have given him a medal, that probably would have been fine with them.

It didn't take the jurors long to find Burns not guilty of murder. Radney's insanity defense had worked well. He was sent to a state mental institution, but it was only a matter of weeks before he was back driving his truck. No one raised much of a fuss over that.

District Attorney Tom Young would comment on the case years after the verdict. He'd say he may have been the only prosecutor in the country who failed to convict a killer "who shot a man in front of 300 witnesses."

After having covered the first funeral, it seemed only fitting that Jim go back to cover the second one. It turned into a media circus. The Maxwell story had slipped the bounds of Alabama and spread nationwide. The Rev. Chester Mardis welcomed reporters with open arms, even if the Maxwell family objected. He had presided at many funerals through the years, but this was one he knew would top them all.

"Mardis is my name," he told me outside the Peace and Goodwill Baptist Church in the Cottage Grove community near Alexander City. "Put it in the news."

I was on hand to do an article to accompany Jim's main story. I was joined by newspaper reporters and television crews from throughout the state. They swarmed around anybody who might have known Maxwell or who had any knowledge of his controversial past.

An *Associated Press* reporter approached Maj. Herman Chapman of the Alabama State Troopers and began asking a few questions. Chapman quickly denied a statement attributed to him that the teen-age girl was dead before her body was found under the wheel of Maxwell's car.

"Do you mind if I ask you why there is so much security here today," the reporter asked. "I don't mind you asking, but you're not going to get an answer," Chapman responded.

By that time, the funeral procession arrived at the church. Maxwell, who served in the army during World War II, was laid to rest in a casket covered with an American flag. Services were held under tight security because no one knew if there might be a repeat performance at the funeral for Maxwell.

"He made mistakes, just like you do, just like I do, just like Moses did," said Mardis, whose next comment caught Jim's attention, along with everyone else in the church. "Maxwell is coming back to help judge somebody."

Mardis didn't say who that "somebody" might be, but his words sent chills through many of the mourners. According to Jim, a lot of folks attended the funeral "just to make sure Maxwell was dead."

The Maxwell case could have been turned into a book or even a movie because it had all the ingredients. Jim and Radney helped Pulitzer Prize winner Harper Lee with background information, but she eventually decided not to do anything about it. Jim said she apparently thought it would wind up being more about the insurance industry than conspiratorial intrigue.

I still think it could be made into a television movie. With all the channels we have today, some enterprising soul could easily come up with a script about a pulpwood-cutting preacher gunned down in a funeral home during a services for his niece. And, that would just be the opening.

CHAPTER FORTY:

KILLERS I COVERED

Grady Gibson was an intelligent man with a college degree. He had been a Marine who served in Vietnam and seemed to have an impeccable law enforcement career going for him after he left the Corps and college. He also was a cold-blooded, calculating killer who thought he was too smart to get caught. Joe Duncan was dumb. He thought he could get away with murder by ambushing his sweetheart in the dark of night at an isolated spot behind a church. He considered it to be a fool-proof plan. Turns out he was the fool. It only took a few days to nab him.

The two were at opposite ends of murderous extremes. In the end, both were arrested, convicted and sentenced to long prison terms. The same could be said of Roy Loid Dossey, Earl Jerome McGahee, Douglas Griffin, Randy Turpin Bell, David Leitner and many other killers I've covered through the years. Some of them are still on Death Row. In some cases, they've been awaiting a lethal injection for nearly 20 years. Justice works slowly in Alabama.

Those who murdered used various methods of dispatching their victims, but guns, knives, blunt objects and hands seemed to be the weapons of choice. They also left behind much more than the person they murdered. Relatives continue to grieve today. They are residual victims in tragedies that seem without end.

Following are condensed versions of murder cases that drew my attention and led to extensive reporting—from the crimes to the convictions:

GRADY GIBSON

You'd think a man who had a college degree in psychology would have or should have known better. Not Gibson, a law enforcement officer who considered himself intellectually superior to the snitches, thugs, dopers and investigators with whom he associated.

In the end, his arrogance on the witness stand and lack of background preparation combined to trip him up. Assistant Attorney General Don Valeska and Alabama Bureau of Investigation agent John Perdue had done their homework. It was a circumstantial murder case, but, most are. Unless a killer confesses or there is an eyewitness to the crime, it's up to prosecutors to present enough evidence to bring a conviction. Valeska and Perdue presented plenty of it to the jury.

Dana Hart was the victim. She was 19 and from Wetumpka, a little town just outside Montgomery, Alabama. Dana married Eddie Hart in late November 1984, but she didn't have much of a honeymoon. She was dead four months later. Her badly decomposed body was found off Interstate 65 in rural Butler County about 50 miles south of Montgomery. An autopsy showed she had been stabbed and beaten, most likely on Feb. 28, 1985 or early the next morning.

Gibson was with the Alabama Bureau of Investigation—a cop who made drug arrests during the early 1980s. Eddie Hart was his informant, a snitch who ingratiated himself to drug dealers and then reported back to Gibson who paid him for his "services." They made a good team and Gibson received commendations for his work. When Dana Hart's body was found, investigators focused on her husband, which isn't unusual. That road led to Gibson, who was most responsible for Hart's paychecks.

For someone as smart as Gibson professed to be, his plan was amateurish. Prosecutors said money was the motive, as it is in so many murder plots. In this one, Hart took out a $150,000 double indemnity life insurance policy on his bride. Dana signed the contract three days before she disappeared. Perdue located a couple of witnesses who said they heard Gibson tell Hart they needed to take out some insurance on Dana "if we're going to knock her off." Eddie Hart applied for the full $300,000 a few days after his wife's body was found. The insurance company refused to pay at first and a settlement eventually was reached with Hart receiving $80,000. Valeska said Hart gave part of it to Gibson.

Gibson had an alibi—a fishing weekend in Baldwin County in south Alabama. Other law enforcement officers were invited to go along—as supportive witnesses. By that time, investigators said Dana was dead. They were never able to pinpoint the exact time of her murder, but it apparently was prior to the fishing trip. Gibson would say later that any comment about "knocking her off" would have been made in jest.

Valeska had a scenario about the girl's last, terrifying moments and he laid it out for the jurors. He said Gibson stabbed her seven or eight times as Hart stood nearby and watched. He visualized Dana begging her husband to help her as he looked on without moving. An autopsy was able to determine that the girl had, indeed, been stabbed seven or eight times in the chest, neck and head. There wasn't much left of Dana when her remains were found. Animals had seen to that.

Gibson, who was 37 at the time of his trial, liked to boast about his service record, but it cost him dearly during his testimony. He claimed he got the Bronze Star for action in Vietnam. Valeska and his prosecuting partner, Bill Wasden, didn't waste much time getting Gibson's service record. The Marine Corps not only didn't give Gibson a medal for bravery or splendid service, it also refused to recommend him for re-enlistment. Gibson was court-martialed for going AWOL (absent without leave) after he got home from Vietnam.

Gibson must have tried his best to use whatever psychology lessons he had learned at the University of Alabama. A few months before he was indicted for taking part in Dana's death, Gibson—still an ABI agent—filed a lawsuit against the Alabama Department of Public Safety for allegedly slandering him. Valeska said it was a smart move because it helped turn the spotlight away from Gibson and onto the investigators and prosecutors who were after him. It worked at first, but didn't fool anybody. Gibson's lawsuit wasn't the only problem the state faced. Some of Dana's relatives were upset, feeling Gibson wasn't being actively pursued as a suspect because he was a member of the law enforcement community.

As the jury debated whether Gibson should live or die after convicting him of capital murder, Dana's mother waited anxiously at the courthouse in Greenville. Her daughter hadn't known much happiness during her short life.

"I was 19 when Dana was born," Louise Morton told me. "That's how old she was when she died."

Gibson was sentenced in 1987 to life in prison without the possibility of parole. Hart was convicted of manslaughter and sentenced to 50 years in prison. He was released in 2004 and got a job with a landscaping business in Tuscaloosa, Alabama.

In 2001, a former state narcotics officer whose testimony led to Gibson's conviction claimed he had been "pressured" by his ABI superiors into giving false testimony. Richard Mobley said in an affidavit that he had "manipulated" Gibson's statements "into a confession because of the threats against me." Nothing ever came from that and Valeska said Mobley's claim "doesn't change a thing." "(Gibson) just doesn't like being in jail," the prosecutor said. "We don't pressure anybody to testify."

Gibson's relatives haven't given up hope that he'll be released one day. They have spent thousands of dollars in an effort to overturn the conviction. In early 2005, a cable television network aired a documentary about the Gibson case, raising questions about his involvement or lack thereof in Dana Hart's death.

JOE DUNCAN

Elizabeth Cobb's dream was to become an Alabama State Trooper. She had worked as a clerk for the state Department of Public Safety, but her goal was to wear the blue uniform of a trooper one day. She finally got her wish, but her career lasted only a few months.

She died on the night of Oct. 11, 1987—murdered by the man who told her he loved her. What he loved more was money. Less than two weeks before she was shot to death on a lonely stretch of road just off Alabama Highway 41 south of Selma, Cobb had taken out two life insurance policies—one for $250,000 and the other for $100,000. Joe

Duncan, who had been Cobb's first and only trooper road supervisor, coincidentally, was the primary beneficiary. To make it look good, he had taken out similar life insurance policies on himself at the same time, naming Cobb as his chief beneficiary. After all, they had planned to be married shortly. Or, so, that was his claim.

State Troopers Joe Duncan and Elizabeth Cobb.

I got word that Cobb was missing on the morning of Oct. 12. It became my priority assignment and I walked quickly from my office to the Dallas County Courthouse a block away. Seconds after I walked into Sheriff Cotton Nichols' office, he headed in my direction, on his way out. "They found her," he said.

I followed him outside the courthouse and hopped into the passenger side of his pickup truck. I knew I wouldn't have time to get down to my office and follow him in my own car. I had known Cotton for a long time and he didn't mind. I didn't know where she had been found and whether she was alive or dead. It seemed the latter was the case by the look on Cotton's' face. It's about 10 miles from the courthouse to the abandoned church, but we got there in less than 10 minutes. As the sheriff turned right toward Dallas Lake and the small church, we could see the excitement ahead of us. Several trooper cars and other law enforcement vehicles also were there.

Cotton never had a chance to pick up speed toward the site where all the activity was taking place because a trooper approached him from his left and ordered him to stop. "You can't go in there," he said. "The hell, you say," Nichols responded, in a gruff voice I had come to know through the years. "I'm the sheriff of Dallas County and I'll go where I want to go." The trooper didn't back down and ordered Nichols to stop. That's when it got hairy. As Cotton began to get out of his side of the truck and the trooper moved closer to him, two of Nichols' deputies moved toward the trooper. It was a tense moment, but, thanks to Capt. Roy Smith—who was the official spokesman for the Alabama Department of Public Safety—the confrontation ended peacefully. The trooper who had ordered the sheriff not to proceed was an instructor at Craig Field—the trooper training center a few miles from where Cobb's body was found. He should have known Nichols was the chief law enforcement officer in Dallas County. If he did and he was just trying to exert his authority, it was a stupid thing to do. I considered it stupidity. In my story the next day, I mentioned the run-in without listing the trooper's name. "He was about to get a faceful of door," I quoted Nichols as saying. "I told him who I was and he wasn't going to keep me out of an investigation scene in my own county." Several years later, the apparently clueless trooper and I would meet again at another homicide scene. He let me know he hadn't forgotten me or my reporting of the incident. I didn't recall his face, but I let him know my opinion still hadn't changed. He should have known better.

Cotton was allowed into the scene while I was ordered out of the truck and told to stand along the roadside. Without a vehicle of my own, I knew I'd have to hitch a ride back to Selma later that morning. It appeared I'd be there for a few hours. That's what happened. I wasn't able to get very close and, even with my camera's telephoto lens, I couldn't get much of a shot of what was happening several hundred yards away. That's where they found Liz Cobb's body.

She had been shot at close range, probably less than a foot away. She was wearing a bullet-proof vest, but Duncan shot her three times in the head with a .22 caliber pistol. He knew about the vest since he was in the same line of work—assigned as her road adviser not long after she graduated from the State Trooper Academy. Cobb probably died the instant the first round from Duncan's gun slammed into her skull.

Suspicion quickly focused on Duncan because of his relationship with her. They had planned to marry. What Cobb didn't know was her "lover" also planned to kill her. It had been the best time of her life. Her dream had been realized and she was an Alabama State Trooper. Then, she met a man she thought she'd share the rest of her life with. She thought taking out the life insurance policies was just part of the pre-marital routine. She had not been married before. Duncan had been divorced twice. He also was behind on his child support payments. He was broke and looking for a way out. He thought he found it in rural Dallas County.

Alabama Bureau of Investigation agent John Perdue was assigned to the Cobb murder case. He was familiar with Cobb during her days as a clerk with the state Department of Public Safety. It didn't take him long to put Duncan under a microscope. Cobb's ticket book and the keys to her patrol car were missing, but Perdue was aware of Duncan's "connection" to the dead trooper. He found out about the life insurance policy within a day or two.

It wasn't made public right away, but I learned from a reliable source in the Department of Public Safety that the driver's side window had been rolled down when they found Cobb's body. That meant she wasn't meeting a stranger. She knew who was behind the church. The investigation would show regularly scheduled trysts between the two at the church. The state said that Cobb was the first female trooper in the United States killed in the line of duty. Some within the department took issue with that since her meetings with Duncan weren't exactly linked to public safety endeavors. Duncan made it look good at Cobb's funeral. He accompanied her grieving relatives to the cemetery in Birmingham and even carried the American flag to her gravesite. He was right behind Gov. Guy Hunt, who had joined the family to express his condolences.

With one of its own charged with a heinous crime that involved one of its own—the state Department of Public Safety found itself in a dubious spotlight. That's one reason why the investigation seemed to have been placed on such a fast forward pace. The department was in a no-win bind. If it dragged its feet, the public perception might be that it was trying to protect itself because Duncan was a trooper. If it made an arrest in a couple of days, the public might think it was trying to get the case out of the way too soon. As it turned out, the evidence against Duncan was so overwhelming that it didn't take long to nail him. His alibi was a card game—played with some law enforcement friends not long after he had killed his paramour. Those who played cards with him that night said he was laughing, cutting up and having a good old time. He didn't seem like a man who had just put three slugs into his lover's head.

Perdue and his fellow investigators had come up with enough evidence to wipe away any feeble attempts by Duncan to cover his tracks. Just to make sure, they brought in Glen Foster, one of the country's most skilled interrogators. It didn't take Foster long to break Duncan. At one point, Foster asked Duncan: "What would you do if someone came forward to say you had been seen entering or leaving the area where Elizabeth's body had been found?" That's when Duncan cracked and said he had "found" the body, but "panicked" and left the area. He didn't say he had found the body because he was responsible for the body, but it was close enough. Duncan was arrested and charged with Cobb's murder less than two weeks after her body was found.

Each time local reporters would see Duncan as he was being brought to the Dallas County Courthouse for hearings or pre-trial conferences, he'd stare at us and say "I'm not guilty. I loved Elizabeth." Duncan's relatives, including an ex-wife, showed up at some of his court appearances wearing yellow ribbons. It was their way of showing they felt Duncan was being held "hostage" by the authorities. The trial was held quickly and that surprised a lot of courthouse observers familiar with frequent delays, especially when the death penalty was a possible outcome.

Duncan's Selma defense team—Henry Pitts and J.L. Chestnut—tried to direct the jury's attention to the "real" killer of Elizabeth Cobb. They suggested that Cobb's missing ticket book and her killer were connected. They concocted a theory that Cobb had seen someone in a black TransAm speed along the Selma Bypass and gave chase. Could the TransAm driver have been involved in drug trafficking? That was their scenario. Could the driver have killed Cobb to protect the drug cartel's' tracks? At one point, Pitts suggested that the "drug queen from Evergreen" might have been involved. Henry, who never gave the "queen" a name, even maintained a serious expression as he paced back and forth in front of the jurors during his closing argument. Evergreen is about 90 miles southeast of Selma and if the "killer" had been heading in that direction, he must have taken quite a detour. The little church where Cobb's body was found is about 20 miles from the road that leads toward Interstate 65 which leads to Evergreen.

The jury wasn't buying any of the defense's arguments and convicted Duncan of capital murder on March 21, 1988. They also recommended on a 10-2 vote that his life be spared and that he be sentenced to life without parole. Dick Norton, the presiding judge, had the authority to overrule the jury's recommendation and that's what he did a few weeks later. He also issued a blistering condemnation of Duncan, calling his actions "diabolical" and "outrageously wicked." The judge likened the murder to "the slaughtering of cattle in a stockyard" and to the "killing of a dog." Duncan's lawyers tried to use Norton's comments to their advantage when they filed their appeal which took years to decide. In the end, another trial was ordered by a higher court on a technicality, not for any evidentiary reason.

The second trial, held in June 1995, lacked the courtroom fireworks and theatrics of the first one seven years earlier, but it did include a Saturday morning "movie" that had the jurors watching in rapt attention. It showed Duncan at the murder scene, reenacting how he "found" Cobb's body. It had been videotaped. Jurors could hear crickets chirping and see the flashlights focused on Duncan's face outside a trooper patrol car.

"I went up to scare her," Duncan said, on the tape, as he stuck out an arm and pointed his hand at the driver's side of the car. "Then I went POW! According to Duncan, his "beloved" was already dead behind the wheel. He said her body was still warm and he could smell gunpowder. Duncan said he was "scared" that someone might be around so he left the area as fast as he could. Prosecutors agreed with Duncan on a couple of points. For one thing, Cobb's body had to have been warm because he had just pulled the trigger. For another, he had to have smelled gunpowder because it came from the gun he used to shoot her.

During closing arguments in the second trial, prosecutor Don Valeska referred to Duncan in derisive terms, scornfully calling him "dumbo" and "loverboy." Duncan, a former weightlifter with broad shoulders, sat quietly at the defense table as Valeska mocked him. It appeared as though the fight had gone out of him. His weight had dropped to about 120 pounds. Those who hadn't seen him in years were stunned by his gaunt appearance. Despite the evidence against Duncan, one or more of the jurors didn't think it was enough and a deadlock appeared imminent. Judge Jack Meigs wouldn't allow it, however, and ordered the deliberations to continue. Duncan's lawyers, fearing another conviction, encouraged their client to accept a deal that would involve a 25-year prison sentence with time served—more than 7 years—credited to his criminal account. Duncan agreed and went before Meigs to accept the deal in June 1995.

He agreed to every condition but one that Cobb's parents would have liked to hear—an admission that he had murdered their daughter. He stood before Meigs and said he was pleading guilty to "the charge against me." He would not say what it was. Meigs never asked him and I thought that should have been done. It appeared during the backroom negotiations which I was allowed to attend that Duncan would have walked away from the deal if he had been required to admit that he had, indeed, murdered Liz Cobb. As it turned out, he pleaded to "the charge" and let his relatives believe that it was part of a deal—that he really hadn't done it.

It had been a long murder investigation and was linked in an indirect way to the Grady Gibson case. Before she had become a trooper, Cobb's clerical duties with the state Department of Public Safety included typing up some of the investigative reports on the Dana Hart murder. Valeska told me there was a possibility that Cobb may have discussed the Gibson case with Duncan. Both murders had one major similarity— life insurance policies. Cobb was murdered two weeks after Gibson had been convicted and sentenced to life in prison. The policies in each case amounted to about the same amount of money the killers had hoped to collect. In each case, the victims had signed the policies just before they were murdered and the men later charged and convicted were the primary beneficiaries. Did Duncan get his murderous idea from Gibson? We'll never know unless Duncan admits he did. That's unlikely.

In the spring of 2002, the Alabama Board of Pardons and Paroles once again rejected Duncan's bid for freedom. He'll eventually get out, but he'll be an old man by then. He wasn't at the hearing, but Liz Cobb's mother and other relatives were on hand to ask the board not to let

Duncan go free until he served every day of his sentence. The board agreed and scheduled Duncan's next parole hearing for 2007.

As Duncan's relatives left the hearing room, several of us went after them for a comment. They had little to say and walked quickly to an elevator. I kept after them. Duncan's brother turned abruptly and glared at me, pointing his finger in my direction and shouting: "You should be on the state payroll." He obviously had been following my accounts about his killer brother since the murder. He got into the elevator before I could respond, but it wouldn't have done any good. In his eyes, his brother could do no wrong.

Not long after Duncan's guilty plea, prosecutor Bill Wasden, who had come out of retirement to rejoin Valeska in the second trial, stopped by my office with something in his hand. He had a big grin on his face.

It was a framed photograph of a black TransAm. I hung it in a prominent place on a wall near my desk.

EARL JEROME MCGAHEE

He walked into Selma's Wallace Community College with a gun in his pocket and murder on his mind.

Within a few minutes, Earl Jerome McGahee's former wife, Connie, lay dead on the floor of her nursing classroom. Behind her, Cassandra Lee was slumped over her desk. She would die 10 days later at a Selma hospital. A third woman, Dee Ann Duncan, tried to feign unconsciousness, but it didn't work. She was severally pistol-whipped by McGahee as she lay on the floor.

It was one of the bloodiest, most brutal murders in Selma history. McGahee, a former Coast Guardsman who had served time in a Louisiana prison for child abuse, walked unnoticed into the junior college on Sept. 11, 1985. When he emerged from the school a few hours after he entered, he was in handcuffs and charged with capital murder.

I stood outside the nursing building that morning. We weren't told much except that a violent incident had occurred inside. After McGahee was brought out, we began to piece together what happened earlier in the morning. As the months passed, hearings provided more details.

When McGahee took the stand in his own defense, he gave one of the most chilling accounts of cold-blooded murder I had ever heard.

He was upset with his former wife and called her into the hallway outside her classroom. When she went back inside, the fright on her face was evident. Moments later, McGahee burst into the room and began firing his .357 Magnum. Screaming students scattered. All but three were able to get outside. Connie McGahee had been struck by at least one bullet. Lee was hit by other shots and her head fell against her desk. Duncan tried to play dead nearby.

During the trial, Duncan described what she had seen. She saw McGahee drag his ex-wife to the front of the classroom and then rip off her clothes as she begged for her life. "I could see that she had no clothes on below the waist," Duncan testified. "Then, I heard him say 'get up, bitch, there's nothing wrong.'" McGahee began to sexually abuse her at that point, all the time screaming obscenities at her. Blood was everywhere. He hit her so hard with his pistol that part of the hammer broke off. The jagged edge of the hammer cut into her face as he continued to pound her with the pistol. By that time, it didn't really matter. Police said she was already dead.

McGahee's lawyers quickly announced a defense of mental incompetence. They had him examined by state psychiatrists and then filed motions claiming he did not have full use of his faculties when he entered the college. They also asked that the trial be moved far from Selma where they feared they couldn't find an impartial jury. Prosecutor Jim Sullivan called McGahee's classroom assault a "terrorist act."

During his trial, McGahee displayed the same cold-blooded mentality that had been shown in the classroom. Asked by Sullivan at one point why he had attacked his wife so viciously as she lay dying on the floor, McGahee looked at him and said: "Because she made me mad. She got blood all over my new white sneakers."

Earl Jerome McGahee, second from right, escorted into court.

McGahee at first indicated he wanted to die for what he did. In the years that followed, however, he had a change of heart. Seems he had considered his options and decided to hang around for awhile. Once, as he was being led into the Dallas County Courthouse for a hearing, he looked at me and flashed a big smile. Around his neck was a huge wooden cross that he apparently had made himself. "I've found Jesus," he told me. The jury wasn't buying his "conversion" and quickly found him guilty. Judge Jack Meigs imposed a death sentence on McGahee.

Another trial was held several years later. By that time, McGahee was intent on living. "I ask that my life be spared," he asked Meigs, who had taken over the case from the original judge who had retired. "I know I can't change what happened but in some small way I might be able to help others." He never explained how he planned to do that because, even if Meigs reduced his sentence from death to life without parole, he wasn't going to get out of prison. An appeals court overturned McGahee's original death sentence on a technicality, but not the conviction. The first jury recommended that his life be spared, but the original judge refused and used his discretion to impose the death sentence if he felt it had been a particularly heinous crime. There's no doubt what happened at the college was just that. Meigs endorsed the death sentence and McGahee was taken back to Death Row. That was in 1992. At last report, he remains behind bars.

I hear about Dee Ann Duncan from time to time. She married and settled down several miles from Selma. Dee Ann declines interviews, but agrees to testify about what happened in that classroom so long ago. McGahee keeps appealing and she keeps doing her best to see that he gets what he deserves.

DAVID THOMAS LEITNER

Of all the killers I've covered, David Thomas Leitner had to be the sleaziest. He was married to an old woman who was almost blind and had no idea that her husband was draining her assets. While that was going on, he was also having fun with his young male lover. Then he became jealous of a man he claimed had been having an affair with his "property."

The object of his anger and the man he murdered was a Roman Catholic priest.

In early January, 1989, a charred body was found in a wooded area near Tuscaloosa. It was the Rev. Francis Craven, who had disappeared several days before the gruesome discovery.

Leitner, who once spent time at a state mental hospital, had been a member of Craven's congregation in Guntersville, a little town in Alabama's Tennessee Valley region. After the priest's body was found, Leitner began taking an interest in the investigation and kept asking questions during trips to the Guntersville Police Department. Authorities had already arrested somebody else and charged him with killing Craven, but eventually dropped the case against him.

Detectives began to focus on Leitner because of his incessant desire to inject himself into the case. It was almost as if he had wanted to be arrested. Eventually, that's what happened. Then, it got interesting. Police learned of Leitner's four-year relationship with Gregory Little, a 20-year-old homosexual who had plied his trade on the streets of Atlanta. It wasn't long before Little turned on Leitner and agreed to testify against him at trial.

There had been suggestions of an even more unsavory element to the priest's murder, but it had been kept under wraps until the trial started. Detectives announced that they had found a personal journal in a closet at Craven's apartment. The journal contained sexual fantasies and, although no one ever was able to prove it had been the priest's thoughts or penmanship, the fact it was found at his apartment was enough to convince many that it was his and contained some pretty perverse thoughts.

"His murder resulted from a sexual misadventure, a fantasy gone bad," Leitner's Mobile lawyer, Lee Stamp, told the jurors. "In this case, we're talking about a masochist looking for a sadist and finding one who killed him." It was Stamp's opinion, of course, that the "sadist" wasn't his client.

The murder was hard enough for Craven's relatives to take. Add to it claims that he had been involved in sexually twisted practices and it made for an almost unbearable cross to bear for them. I got to know the family prior to and during Leitner's trial. They were adamant that Craven had done none of the sordid things Leitner alleged. The family was, in effect, speaking out in defense of not only their late, lamented loved one, but the entire priesthood which would be answering claims of sexual abuse in the years to come.

Leitner and Little had a grand time together, according to investigators who delved into the murder case. On one occasion, the two took Leitner's 83-year-old wife to Europe for a vacation and some sexual pleasures. Little lived with the couple in Guntersville and Leitner got it into his head that the young man he had befriended and took to his bed had begun a sexual relationship with their parish priest. That's all Leitner could think of as the days and weeks passed.

The two men met Craven at the Birmingham airport after the priest had returned to Alabama from visiting relatives in Florida on Jan. 7, 1989. Craven had no reason to suspect anything was wrong. After all, the two men were members of his parish. Craven followed Leitner and Little in his van, but, instead of heading due north on Interstate 65 to Guntersville, they veered to the northwest toward Tuscaloosa County. Little told the jury that they wound up in a wooded area and they all got out of their vehicles. Moments after Craven got out, Little said Leitner struck the priest on the head with a metal pipe. Then, Leitner hit him again and again. "I heard something that sounded like a stick break," Little testified. One of the prosecutors told the jurors that Leitner hit the priest so hard "his head exploded like a ripe melon." Then they poured gasoline on the priest's body and set it on fire. It was difficult to tell, but forensic pathologists felt Craven was dead by the time he was burned—or, they hoped he was.

Leitner was convicted twice of murdering the priest. The first one, in 1992, was overturned on appeal due to a technicality in Leitner's favor. The judge had refused to allow into evidence sexually explicit entries contained in Craven's personal journal. The entries were described by Stamp as "homosexual fantasies" with descriptions of someone being dragged by a dog chain through a wooded area. When Craven's charred body was found, a strand of electrical wire and a dog chain were attached to his neck. The new evidence didn't make a bit of difference as far as the new jury was concerned. Leitner was convicted a second time in 1994 and got the same sentence—life.

I drove down to interview Leitner at Easterling Prison about a year after he began his term. He'd write me occasionally, always maintaining his innocence and pointing to someone else as the "real killer." After I bought him some cookies, candy and a soft drink, we sat down for an interview that lasted more than an hour. He didn't say anything that I hadn't heard before, but I took it all in and wrote about it a few days later. "I'm here to die," he told me, as he sipped his soft drink and took a puff from a cigarette. "Why not electrocute me and let me have peace?"

Claims of innocence aren't rare for convicted felons, especially those on Death Row and I had heard many of them. People don't admit they've murdered somebody unless they're proud of what they did. In Leitner's case, Little spilled the beans in return for a break on a criminal case pending against him in Georgia. Three people knew what happened that day in the woods of Tuscaloosa County. One was dead, one saw what happened and one—David Leitner—did it.

In September of 1996, Leitner stopped waiting for his "innocence" to be proven. He attached a sheet to his cell bars at Easterling. Then, he slumped forward. He left a note behind, but prison officials never released it or disclosed what he had written.

Prosecutor Don Valeska, who had ripped into the priest killer during both trials, called Leitner "as evil a person who ever lived. He corrupted our youth with money to feed his longings. He was a demented person."

What really angered Valeska was what happened to the priest's standing in his community.

"Leitner tried to destroy a good, decent man twice—first by murdering him and then ruining his reputation," the prosecutor told me. Stamp didn't desert his client, even in death. He continued to maintain Leitner's innocence, but did acknowledge the convicted killer was "eccentric and different from most people."

RANDY TURPIN BELL

Charles Mims was a truck driver and a man some thought frequented the "dark side" of life. Randy Turpin Bell is a man who waits on Alabama's Death Row to be executed for executing Mims.

The catch is nobody's ever found Mims' body.

When a Chilton County jury convicted Bell of capital murder and he was sentenced to death in 1983, it was believed to be the first time anyone in the United States was scheduled to die for a murder without a body to eliminate all doubts.

Bell is on Death Row because of Michael Joe Hubbard, a convicted felon, who told the jury that the two of them overpowered Mims on the night of Dec. 14, 1981 at the Church of God Campground near Clanton. A couple of Mims' friends said they saw him with $700 in cash just before he disappeared.

Bell's defense lawyer, Paul Harden, described Mims to the jury as a "man of the night" and suggested he had dealt in stolen property. Hubbard testified during the 1983 trial that he and Bell had tried to sell Mims two shotguns and a rifle and were upset when he refused to buy them. After tying Mims up and putting him in the trunk of Bell's Cadillac, Hubbard said they drove to a secluded spot deep in the woods. Hubbard testified that when Mims asked Bell what was going to happen, Bell told him: "Shut up or I'll blow your damn brains out." Then they climbed over a fence where it ended in seconds. He said Bell pushed Mims down to his knees and quickly pumped two slugs from a .25-caliber pistol into the back of his head.

That's that last time anybody saw Mims alive, or so Hubbard claimed. He indicated that Bell returned to the body and might have poured acid over it so that it would decompose faster than if he allowed nature to take its course. Bell's sentencing set in motion a series of appeals in a state where it isn't unusual for killers to sit on Death Row for 20 or more years. The twist in Bell's case, of course, was lack of a body. In most cases, victims are found full of holes or with sharp objects stuck in them. Some are run over by vehicles while others are dropped from high places. Some die from beatings while others are ignited. In nearly all cases, prosecutors are able to produce a body or photographs and DNA evidence.

Mims vanished just before Christmas. I interviewed his frantic wife, Faye, at their little house in Chilton County. She had bought her husband a new shirt and wrapped it carefully in brightly colored paper. As the years went by without any sign of her husband, she lost any hope he might be alive. She remarried eight years later.

Every few years, somebody will step forward and claim they saw Charles Mims alive. In 1987—six years after Mims vanished—defense lawyers filed a motion claiming he had been seen in the Birmingham area. In 1994, former Chilton County Sheriff James Earl Johnson said he had been told by a trucker that he saw someone who looked "just like" Mims. The "witness" claimed he saw Mims with a "Mexican female" at a restaurant in Texas and when he said "Hey, Charles" to him, the man "headed back toward Mexico."

Although Bell has maintained his innocence throughout the two decades since his conviction, one of his lawyers stepped forward in 1987 to say his client was willing to lead them to Mims' body in exchange for commutation of the death sentence. Prosecutors rejected the deal because they felt they had the right man. They also pointed out that if Bell was, indeed, an innocent man, why would he lead them to the body of a man he denied killing?

So, Bell sits on Death Row where he paints and draws and, perhaps, waits for another Mims sighting to argue again that he didn't do anything wrong.

ROY LOID DOSSEY

Friends described Roy Loid Dossey as a devoted family man. Imagine their surprise when they learned Dossey murdered his wife on a bogus hunting trip. Then, he blamed her death on his mother-in-law.

Roy and Mary Dossey were in the woods on Jan. 1, 1984, ostensibly looking for deer. He told her to take up a position near a tree and wait. Then, he claimed later, he walked about 100 yards away and took up a position near a large tree to wait for a four-legged target. He said he heard a shot, walked toward his wife and found her lying on the ground. Dossey said he picked her up, placed her over his shoulder in deer-like fashion and climbed over a barbed-wire fence to take her to a hospital. Investigators didn't find any blood at the scene or along the path where Dossey claimed to have found his wife. Mary Dossey had been hit in the back with 14 shotgun pellets from a 20-gauge.

Prosecutors said money was the reason for Mary Dossey's murder. They said Dossey wanted to collect $300,000 from several life insurance policies on his wife. The largest one, a $100,000 double indemnity policy, was taken out three months before her murder. Dossey got $25,000 on an automobile credit life insurance policy on her, but never received the $300,000 he wanted.

A helicopter pilot stationed at Fort Rucker in south Alabama, Dossey was a block of ice on the stand. As he testified, he stared straight ahead, answering questions in an emotionless manner. Some jurors became upset over one of his comments. Some courtroom spectators gasped when prosecutor Johnny Nichols asked Dossey if he knew of anyone who might have had a grudge against his wife and Dossey said "yes, her mother." The victim's mother bolted upright in her seat and glared at him. Dossey testified that his mother-in-law was upset because she had not been named as a beneficiary on one of her daughter's life insurance policies. "It's absolutely untrue," Mary Dossey's mother told me during a recess.

Dossey was sentenced to 99 years in prison. He then filed an appeal challenging his lawyer's competency as well as claiming his wife may have killed herself through careless handling of her shotgun. Since Mary Dossey was shot in the back, it was unlikely she was able to twist her shotgun at an angle to do that.

The Dossey case didn't stop with his conviction and sentence. Prosecutors also disclosed that he was a suspect in the drowning death of his 9-year-old mentally retarded daughter. Mary Marcelle Dossey died six days after her father took out a $5,000 double-indemnity life insurance policy on her and named himself as chief beneficiary.

He collected on that policy and also got $10,000 from a neighbor's homeowner's policy. His daughter drowned in the neighbor's pool. Dossey's decision to take out a $300,000 life insurance policy on his wife two years later made him "our only suspect," Nichols told me.

Shortly after Mary Dossey's murder, authorities exhumed Mary Marcelle's body, but forensic pathologists were unable to determine if her father had contributed to her death. The death certificate said the little girl had died of "cardiopulmonary arrest due to water emersion and oxygen deprivation." It never was determined whether the water "emersion" was accidental or deliberate.

Authorities researching Dossey's background uncovered another interesting court nugget. In 1971, Dossey was involved in a vehicular homicide in Florida and placed on probation for seven years.

Dossey was released from prison long before his term was up. So much for 99 year sentences.

CHARLES LEE BUFFORD

He was convicted of murder, got a second chance and then blew it again.

Charles Lee Bufford admitted that he fatally beat former Alabama State Sen. Roland Cooper with a garden tiller guidebar on April 30, 1977. It happened on Cooper's farm in Wilcox County. Bufford gave detectives detailed statements—in writing and on tape—about how he had tied Cooper's hands behind his back and repeatedly beat him with the tiller as he lay defenseless on the ground. A year after he killed Cooper, Bufford was brought to trial, convicted of murder, sentenced to death and sent to prison to await execution.

Normally, such a case would be considered cut and dried. Not this one. Cooper was white and, at one time, one of Alabama's most powerful politicians. Bufford was a young black man who had been at the Wilcox County Jail when Cooper picked him up that day to work on his farm. As Bufford waited to die, a portion of Alabama's death penalty law was declared unconstitutional and a second trial was ordered.

I had been at the *Selma Times-Journal* only a few months, but had become interested in the Bufford case as well as Alabama's capital punishment statute. Before the next trial started, I accompanied Selma lawyer J.L. Chestnut to Holman Prison to interview Bufford for a lengthy report on capital punishment.

If anyone could be considered a candidate for prison it was Charles Bufford. A high school dropout, he had served six month for assault before escaping from the Wilcox County Jail in 1974 and joining the Army. He was kicked out in 11 months for being absent without leave. During his short stay in the Army he spent time at a halfway house because of his drinking. In 1976, he was back in Alabama and doing time for stealing a truck.

Security is understandably tight for Death Row prisoners and when Bufford came into the room where Chestnut and I were waiting, his hands were cuffed behind his back. Guards moved the cuffs to the front so he could be free to smoke his Kools. Bufford began to tell us about the day Cooper was killed. Little did we know that he'd drop a bombshell along the way, one which angered some people in Wilcox County.

Bufford said that, while in jail, he was offered $5,000 to kill Cooper, who also had served as probate judge in Wilcox County. Cooper had a practice of picking up prisoners from the county jail to work on his farm. Some of the black inmates claimed it was akin to slave labor, but they weren't going to argue with a man as powerful as Roland Cooper.

Audio and written confessions sealed Bufford's doom. I've always wondered why people would go to extremes to admit their guilt, especially when it could land them on Death Row. They've done it for years and likely will continue doing it. It usually isn't long before they realize what a dumb thing they had done. That's when they start looking for ways out of the mess they created for themselves. In Bufford's case, he took the most popular approach—blame somebody else without being too specific.

He said he had been picked up by Cooper that April day in 1977 and taken to the farm. His Death Row version differed sharply from the one he gave detectives after he was stopped driving Cooper's truck through Selma. According to Bufford, he had just returned to the spot where Cooper had been standing. He said he had picked up some seed to plant. When he got back, he said he saw Cooper's body lying face down in the dirt.

During our conversation, Bufford claimed he had been "set up" and that some "powerful people" in Camden had killed Cooper. I left him alone with his lawyer for a few minutes as they discussed possible strategy. Ches and I later compared notes. Had Bufford been "set up" in Camden? Ches' obligation to his client prevented him from openly discussing his conversation with Bufford. The condemned killer's comments during the interview were printable, however. I've interviewed many killers through the years and most of them blame somebody else. Bufford didn't give me any names during our interview, but I reported his claims. I was criticized by some in Wilcox County as being irresponsible, but I did not view it that way. A jury had convicted Bufford after hearing extensive admissions from him about how he had killed Cooper. They could draw their own conclusions as to why anyone would so readily place himself at death's door when he could have denied everything.

It's not easy obtaining a capital murder conviction on circumstantial evidence. Bufford wasn't arrested next to Cooper's body. He was in his truck, but claimed finding the body and then stealing the vehicle. That's the scenario he gave us during the prison interview. His timing was just bad. He didn't think of an alibi until he was on Death Row. In his initial statement, he said he had killed Cooper and stole his truck.

Bufford's second trial wasn't much different from the first one, but there was one major exception. Bufford's taped confession wasn't allowed into evidence. Prosecutor Bob Morrow still had Bufford's handwritten confession, along with the garden tiller guidebar which he slammed onto the jury rail during his opening statement. It was done to emphasize the force with which Bufford originally said he had killed Cooper. Defense lawyers John Kelly and Billy Faile didn't call Bufford to testify—not with his sorry background. If he had taken the stand, Morrow would have ripped into him over his previous run-ins with the law and his dishonorable discharge from the Army. Kelly and Faile focused on what they claimed was "sloppy police work" during the investigation.

Both juries were either predominantly or completely black. The first one had 10 blacks and 2 whites and the second one had no whites. Defense lawyers couldn't claim racial bias either time, but some white Wilcox County residents had their own opinions. They saw Bufford's second trial as "reverse discrimination" because of the evidence against him in his first trial. Most of it came from his own mouth. Imagine their anger, then, when it took the jurors just over two hours to acquit an admitted killer.

After the verdict was read, I walked up to one of the female jurors as she headed toward the courtroom door. I asked her how she and the other 11 could free a man who gave explicit details of how he had killed Roland Cooper. "Well," she told me, "we felt four years in prison was long enough for what he did." I've been amazed, at times, by juror responses, but that one took the cake. Bufford didn't have much to say, only "I trust in God and felt he would take care of everything for me. I'm very happy." That wasn't enough for me. I drove out to a relative's house where he had gone as a free man for the first time in four years and knocked on the door. I learned later he was hiding in a back room. The last thing he needed to do was screw up and admit his guilt again.

Morrow was outraged by the verdict and he wrote Charles Graddick, who was Alabama's attorney general at the time, to look for help in the federal court system. It had worked in the past in other cases. Two Ku Klux Klansmen accused of killing civil rights worker Viola Liuzzo at the end of the Selma-to-Montgomery march were acquitted on a murder charge by an all-white, all-male jury, but later were convicted by a federal court jury of violating Liuzzo's civil rights.

It didn't take much to convince Graddick to go after Bufford in federal court. When he was a district attorney in Mobile County, Graddick convicted two men of murdering a pawn shop owner as the man's daughters watched in horror a few feet away. A question of which one of the two killers would be the first to die didn't bother Graddick. "You can put one on the other's lap and fry both of them until their eyeballs pop out," he said. In the end, the federal courts didn't intervene as they had in the Liuzzo case which occurred not far away in neighboring Lowndes County.

Bufford left Wilcox County, but he surfaced a couple of years later. In his own peculiar way, he justified Morrow's belief that leopards do not change their spots. He had gotten a job as a handyman for a 65-year-old woman in Stamford, Conn. In October of 1983, he raped her several times in her apartment. Connecticut authorities did not do a thorough background check on Bufford. If they had, they would have found out he once was convicted and sentenced to death for murder in Alabama. Bufford, who pleaded guilty to sexual assault, worked out an agreement which resulted in a 17-year prison sentence.

"He should have been confined to Death Row," Graddick told me, during an interview after I had found out about Bufford's latest brush with the law. "As far as I'm concerned, 17 years is a very short time for what this man has done in his life."

Bufford would be pushing 50 by now. I never did find out what happened to him, but did check once and they said he remained in prison in Connecticut. Once people leave prison they tend to vanish. Knowing the kind of person Bufford is, it wouldn't be surprising to learn one day that he's in trouble again.

ROBERT HALL

A mailman found Raymond Dozier's nude body near the Cecil Jackson Bypass on Oct. 6, 1987. It shocked many Selmians. Dozier was a popular social studies teacher in the Selma public school system. He had many friends.

According to his killer, Dozier also had been involved in a sex ring that involved young boys from Selma, Montgomery, Camden and other Alabama cities. The more detectives probed, the more sordid the story got. I accompanied two of them to a house not far from Selma Middle School and watched as they looked for more evidence. Sexually explicit material was found inside, along with other items that convinced the cops they had enough to at least set the stage for a more thorough investigation.

Robert Hall was charged with murdering Dozier. Before Hall came to trial, an elementary school principal was charged with sodomy and other sexual abuse offenses. Soon, others were charged or implicated in the case. The Selma Police Department issued a statement which said it had uncovered sufficient evidence to arrest a group of men "who were using children for homosexual and drug-related involvement."

In addition to being a murder, the case also proved to be a huge embarrassment for Selma's public school system. Parents entrust their children to teachers to teach, not molest them. Henry Pitts, an aggressive defense lawyer who enjoys high-profile trials, represented Hall, a troubled 24-year-old man who traced much of his problems to Dozier.

In addition to the murder of a respected teacher, Selma residents also learned that there were fears Dozier had AIDS. Actor Rock Hudson had died of the incurable disease two years earlier and it was still viewed in many parts of America as a plague of bubonic proportions. That's all Selma needed. An autopsy quickly determined that Dozier did not have AIDS, so that relieved some of the tension in town.

Mayor Joe Smitherman usually let the police department handle murder investigation announcements, but the Dozier case was so sensitive he felt he needed to do or say something. He was worried parents would remove their children from the public school system. "Hall said Dozier was a homosexual and had been sexually molesting him since he was in the 8th grade," Smitherman told me. "He said it had been on his mind for years and he couldn't take it any longer."

Hall, who had returned to Selma after living in Atlanta for several years, said Dozier attempted to renew their relationship. He said he went to his former teacher's house one night and strangled him. Hall claimed the sexual abuse he suffered at the hands of Dozier and other Selma teachers who "shared" him with each other was too much to bear. When police searched Dozier's house, they found beer cans, rum bottles and traces of cocaine. A large mirror was believed to have been used to prepare cocaine lines for those having their "parties."

Detectives found a Bible that had been opened to the 18th and 20th chapters of the Book of Jeremiah. One chapter included this passage: "For thus saith the Lord, behold, I will make thee a terror to thyself and to all thy friends and they shall fall by the sword of their enemies." Not far away, a coffee cup sat on a ledge, proclaiming in bright red letters: "No. 1 Teacher."

For those who knew Dozier only from a classroom, he was a respected teacher who went out of his way to help his young students. For those who got to know him later as a result of his other "deeds," he was a pervert. Young boys from neighboring counties were driven to Selma for sex and drug parties. No one ever found out just how many were involved, but police believe dozens had been abused.

Although he was charged with murder, few expected Hall to be convicted of that offense, not after details of the case were published. A homicide had been committed and it is rare for anyone to walk away without some form of punishment. In Hall's case, he got 12 years for manslaughter. He was out long before he served the entire sentence.

DOUGLAS GRIFFIN

Patrick Dale was enjoying a beer at a popular club near Evergreen in south Alabama in July, 1983 when he met Douglas Griffrin. After having a few drinks, they got into Dale's car and eventually wound up in neighboring Wilcox County.

That's where Griffin ordered Dale out of the car and into a field. Seconds later, he fired a shotgun at point-blank range, killing Dale instantly. Griffin drove to Tuscaloosa where he partied with a girlfriend. It wasn't long before he was caught and charged with capital murder.

What made the Griffin story so unusual was the involvement of the state of Alabama. A few months before he murdered Dale, Griffin had been treated at Bryce State Hospital where the criminally insane or those who try to cop pleas to that to avoid the death penalty are examined.

On April 22, 1983—less than three months before he blew Dale apart with the shotgun—Griffin sent a letter to his wife. He said: "I love you so much, but I am going to kill myself but first I am going to kill a lot of (people). It (might) not be you. I don't know. I am not going to be here long because I am going to sneak out."

Bryce officials knew of Griffin's letter, but still discharged him on May 4. Dale's dad, Emmett, filed suit against the doctors who treated Griffin, claiming they negligently released a man who had just vowed to kill people. Emmett Dale claimed in his lawsuit that the state mental hospital owed a duty to protect the public from patients such as Doug Griffin who had "dangerous propensities." The state claimed it was "unforeseeable" that Griffin would kill Dale and insisted that it had no duty to protect unidentifiable victims from "criminal acts of their patients."

As prosecutors prepared to try Griffin for murder, the victim's family hired one of Alabama's best lawyers to represent them in their civil lawsuit against the state. Former Lt. Gov. Jere Beasley said the criminal aspect of the case was pretty clear, but let everyone know that others were also involved.

"Douglas Griffin pulled the trigger of the gun that killed Patrick Dale, but it is obvious that he is not the only one who was responsible," Beasley said. "The motive of the (lawsuit) was to make sure it won't happen again. The mental health system has done a terrible wrong and people need to know about it."

The trial contained some grisly evidence and prosecutor Ed Greene didn't try to hide any of it. He knew the more shocking the photographs of the victim, the better his chances of gaining a conviction. In his closing argument, Greene told the jurors: "Griffin gave Patrick Dale half a second in front of a double-ought shotgun. He decided it was time for him to die and he carried it out in the most horrible and gruesome way." Searchers located Dale's remains by following the buzzards that had been circling overhead, occasionally dropping down to what was left of the victim.

Griffin took the stand and said he was sorry. Dale's relatives were unmoved. The jury sentenced Griffin to life in prison without parole. Although he appeared contrite on the witness stand, Griffin was anything but that whenever he saw me. I was the only reporter who followed him through the court system as the case progressed. Not long after the jury convicted him, Griffin was escorted from the courtroom into an elevator on the third floor of the Wilcox County Courthouse. I knew I wouldn't be allowed into the elevator, so I sprinted down the steps to be on the ground floor when the doors opened. I lined up my camera, hoping to get a good shot. I wound up getting more than that.

Conecuh County Deputy Sheriff Jimmy Lambert was next to Griffin as they stepped out of the elevator. When Griffin saw me, he snarled and tried to kick me with his right leg. Unfortunately for Lambert, Griffin's aim wasn't as good as he had displayed with his shotgun. He kicked the deputy instead of me. Lambert uttered a loud "ouch," before taking Griffin to a waiting patrol car. By that time, I was there and got my photo. Griffin didn't apologize for trying to kick me.

Three years after the trial, a Montgomery County civil jury awarded the Dale family $11.4 million in damages from Griffin and the doctors who had claimed he was able to rejoin society. It would be a monetary verdict the victim's family never saw.

"There was a small settlement, but not nearly what the victim's family should have received," Beasley said.

STANLEY KIDD

Some fathers go to extremes to avoid parental obligations. They refuse to make child support payments or delay them as long as possible, often spending the money that would have provided food for the children they helped produce.

In Stanley Kidd's case, he decided to eliminate his obligations by killing his 14-month-old twin daughters—Kierra Letitia and Cierra Tyeshia. He strapped them into their infant seats in the back seat of his car and filled it with carbon monoxide pumped in from the exhaust pipe. Then he closed the garage door. It didn't take long for the babies to die.

Kidd thought he'd benefit in two ways—avoiding child support payments and collecting insurance on the twins at the same time. Not much money was involved. He would have collected only $16,000 in insurance, but, without two children to support, he would have been able to avoid paying a total of $806 each month. Kidd wasn't destitute. He was making about $50,000 annually at a paper mill not far from where he murdered the girls. That's pretty good money now. It was even better in 1993.

Kidd claimed that he had found the lifeless bodies of the girls on a bed in his mother's house after spending 45 minutes working on his car outside. His lawyers maintained that a defective natural gas space heater in the house might have caused the two deaths. They said if that wasn't the reason, the twins might have died from an "accidental infusion" of carbon monoxide fumes in Kidd's vehicle as he drove them to an appointment. Both claims were quickly dismissed by authorities who said it would have been almost impossible for that amount of carbon monoxide to have killed the twins. Their scenario had Kidd directing a lethal amount of toxic gas at the twins as they sat in the back of his car.

The Alabama killings occurred in the wake of the Susan Smith murder trial in South Carolina. Smith had pushed her car into a lake at Union, S.C. after making sure her two young sons were unable to get out. She at first blamed it on a black man. Then, she admitted she had done it to avoid any "complications" for her boyfriend had he decided to marry her one day. The Smith case was not lost on the jurors.

District Attorney Tommy Chapman and one of his prosecutors, Dawn Hare, did a masterful job of putting the Kidd case together. During his closing argument, Chapman told the jurors that when the bodies of the twins were brought to the Monroeville hospital, their mother asked for permission to hold them one last time.

"We want them to hear how this mother held those babies and rocked them in her lap after she learned they were dead," Chapman told me during a break before he addressed the jurors.

Stanley Kidd comforted after jury convicts him of murdering his twin daughters.

Kidd, who was married to one woman when he fathered the twins after a relationship with another, maintained his innocence throughout the trial and after the jury convicted him. As he stood before Judge Sam Welch awaiting sentencing, Kidd turned toward Sandra Dale and told her he was not guilty.

"I hope that one day you'll see it in your heart to forgive me," he said. The grieving mother shook her head. Asked later if she could ever forgive him, she said "no."

Kidd got two life sentences.

A 'BORN' KILLER

Lumbie Ransom was born in 1948 in the Wilcox County Jail. It was Christmas Day and his mother was serving time for murdering another woman. The baby was named for the county's legendary sheriff—Lumbie Jenkins, a lawman known for his unique ways of arresting criminals. He rarely carried a gun, preferring to call people to come in and surrender to him. Most did.

As Lumbie grew up, he displayed a passion for long fingernails and crime. When they arrested him for stabbing his father 42 times with a butcher knife, his nails had grown out to three inches in length. Friends said Lumbie felt he had been a "bad seed" most of his life. Certainly, his actions on Aug. 8, 1979 underscored that assessment. That was the day he kept plunging a butcher knife into the body of James Ransom—the man who helped give him life.

It happened on a dirt road in the Yellow Bluff community between Camden and Pine Hill in south Alabama. Investigators determined that the son had stabbed the father dozens of times in his back and along the right side of his head. Evidence indicated that the stabbing took place over a considerable distance along the road as James Ransom tried to escape. When Lumbie came to trial, he wasn't at all contrite. Apologies can help mitigate savage slayings. What he did was brag about how he did it.

"He seemed proud of how many times he stabbed him," Lumbie's Selma lawyer, Charlie Morris, said. "He wanted to make sure the jury knew the number. I tried to talk him out of that, but he wouldn't listen to me."

As I sat in the courtroom and listened to Lumbie testify, it seemed that this was, indeed, a very troubled man. He said he killed his father because he wouldn't give him enough money to buy a bus ticket to Illinois. "I got tired of it and I did what I had to do and I wanted to do it myself." Lumbie said.

During his closing argument to the jurors, Deputy District Attorney Ed Greene told the jurors that Lumbie had plunged the butcher knife into his father's body with such ferocity and velocity that the handle of the knife broke. Each time Ransom stabbed his dad, the other end of the blade penetrated his own hand.

It didn't take the jurors very long to convict him of murder. The judge sentenced Lumbie, who was 32 at the time, to life in prison. He served less than half when he was released.

"What!" shouted Greene, when I called to tell him what the Alabama Parole Board had just done. "This is a clear example of the need for a truth in sentencing law in this state. People would like to think that when somebody is put away for life, it means for life."

The parole board felt Lumbie had done just fine while he was in prison. He had even accumulated $1,200 during his years on the work-release program to help pay for his own upkeep. There would have even been enough to buy that bus ticket to Illinois.

CHAPTER FORTY-ONE:

JOE T.

Joe Smitherman grew up as a poor kid in a Selma slum. His father died when he was young and his mother did all she could to raise her large family. They were as poor as any of the black families in east Selma. Smitherman's memories of those days never left him—even when he became a man of means and had gained a national reputation as mayor of the town where he was raised.

His was a mostly self-taught street education—one of survival. He was tall and skinny with protruding ears and an ability to get along with just about everybody. He learned the art of compromise long before he'd need it as mayor—first as a young politician and, later, as perhaps the last white leader of a predominantly black town.

In 1960, Smitherman decided to run for a seat on the Selma City Council. He had been an appliance salesman, but wanted more. He quickly demonstrated an ability to campaign and was swept into office that year with other progressives who had taken on the local political establishment. When Smitherman defeated incumbent Mayor Chris Heinz four years later, he wound up redefining "political establishment" in Selma.

No one could have predicted in the summer of 1964 that Selma would become a focal point for the civil rights movement. The new mayor had been in office only a few months when Martin Luther King Jr. and other leaders of the Southern Christian Leadership Conference arrived to begin voting rights demonstrations. It began on Jan. 2, 1965. During the following three months, there would be violence, deaths, thousands of arrests and a negative national spotlight on a little town that had been known mostly for its antebellum houses.

Smitherman didn't endear himself to King and his followers when the protests began. At a news conference, shortly after King's arrival, he blamed the city's problems on "outside agitators." He said they had been led by "Martin Luther Coon...err..King." Blacks were furious, considering it a deliberate slap at their leader. Smitherman maintained then and through the years that it was an accidental slip of the tongue. Selma had a councilman named Coon at that time and the mayor said he got "confused" when he began to pronounce King's last name. Black leaders weren't buying his explanation and it followed Smitherman for decades, especially when national newspapers or television networks arrived for interviews. It usually was one of the first questions asked.

I had heard about Smitherman during my tenure with UPI in the mid-1960s. I hadn't thought much about him after I joined the Decatur Daily and began moving through the South in search of executive positions in the newspaper business. When we arrived in Selma in the spring of 1979, it didn't take me long to get to know Smitherman. Unfortunately, it wasn't a positive introduction and it would take a few years before we developed a relationship of mutual respect.

"Joe T.," as he's called by many in Selma, had been in office for 16 years when we arrived. Political burnout had taken its toll. Add the four years he spent on the council and he had served the city as a leader for two decades. By 1980, he had decided to resign. My bosses at the *Selma Times-Journal* decided to give Smitherman a royal send-off and make a few bucks at the same time. We came up with a special section, called "Joe." It was loaded with tributes to the mayor and, of course, contained lots of paid advertising to make it all worthwhile. It was a huge undertaking for a small staff, but we all chipped in and it was a smashing success—editorially and financially.

Smitherman was succeeded by long-time Selma City Council President Carl Morgan, who had served just as long. Unlike Smitherman, who didn't always follow procedures to get things done, Morgan went by the book. Morgan was a parliamentarian who lacked Smitherman's flair and Deep South Machiavellian abilities. As the weeks and months passed, Smitherman realized he had made a mistake. He was a political thoroughbred and wasn't ready to be put out to pasture, even by himself. He had gone to work for an old friend, Larry Striplin, and even made a trip to the Middle East for the company. When he got back, he was bored. He missed the rush of being mayor of Selma. As he pondered his future, the *Times-Journal* began a series of stories about questionable conduct involving the placement of water lines. Some Smitherman detractors immediately thought he might have been involved. He was furious and when the time came to prepare for the 1980 mayoral elections, announced plans to run for his old job. At the age of 50, he had had enough of political retirement. Joe wanted back into the game.

The *Times-Journal* backed Morgan and all but forgot about Jean Sullivan, a Selma Republican leader who was the third mayoral candidate that year. If the *STJ* endorsement wasn't a political kiss of death, nothing else could have been. The local newspaper and Smitherman were often at odds and the decision to support Morgan was just what the former mayor wanted. In the end, it was a blowout. Joe T. was back in business. His friendship with Morgan ended during that time and he wasn't all that happy with me either, since I had written some of the stories about the water lines. A lawsuit was filed against the *Times-Journal*, but it was just a way to keep the paper off-balance. Nothing really came out of it.

By the fall of 1980, I had gone to work for the *Montgomery Advertiser* and Smitherman hadn't forgotten my involvement with the local paper. He seemed to be waiting for a chance to let me know about it, too. Little did I realize how personal it would become. He had already let me know how much he despised the paper and brought up the special section that the *STJ* printed when he retired. "You built me up in that thing and made money off of me and then you tried to put me in prison later with that water line stuff," he said.

My worst moment with Smitherman occurred over a controversy involving the Selma Fire Department. I went to his office and asked to see some department records, knowing the response I'd probably get. Three women were sitting on a couch across from the mayor's desk and one of his cronies was in a chair to his right. I had an idea that he might not let me see the records and, when he said I'd have to put in a "request"

I knew would never be granted, I let him know in a less than respectful way that it was the answer I had expected. Today, it would be one of those "whatever" responses. Whatever, I infuriated him. By then, I had turned around and was walking through the little room that served as a waiting area adjacent to his office.

Before I could leave the doorway to the outer office, Smitherman came barreling toward me. He grabbed me by my shirt and slammed me against the door, muttering an obscenity. The next few seconds were a blur, but I remember pushing him back, throwing a half-hearted slap in his direction and saying, in a loud voice: "You pushed me, you son-of-a-bitch." He stopped at that point, but neither of us had calmed down. We walked out into the hallway where I told him that I just wanted to, in pre-Rodney King fashion, "get along" with him. He didn't buy it. He kept yapping at me about what I was trying to do to him and his newly installed administration.

I think he may have realized that what he had just done might be construed as assault, but I wasn't thinking of signing a warrant against him. Tempers finally cooled and, when I next saw him, it was as though the blowup hadn't really occurred. In a way, it was a good thing for me since I was trying to establish myself with my new newspaper and the last thing I needed was to have my editors having to decide what to do with a reporter who got into a scuffle with one of Alabama's most important mayors. I guess the anger I inherited from my father must have resurfaced. It's a demon I've tried to suppress without much success through the years.

The issue wasn't over by a long shot, though. One of the women in the mayor's office was Jean Martin, who worked for the *Times-Journal*, my former employer. She told colleagues what she had heard. She didn't see anything, but she heard my "SOB" comment and the noise coming from the secretary's office. That led to a column in the *Times-Journal* by Nikki Maute who suggested that two grown men should act more responsibly. She had a good point.

As I got to know Smitherman better, I began to realize just how remarkable he was. He had little formal training beyond high school, but was able to handle one of the most difficult jobs in the state. He mastered the intricacies of bond issues, put together multi-million dollar municipal budgets and deftly settled internal disputes involving his aides or council members. He knew all about compromise and was able to give just enough to get what he wanted. I often saw him work his magic. At times, he would flash that Smitherman scowl at somebody on the council who disagreed with him. When that happened, he'd mutter something just loud enough for the council critic to hear and then walk into the hallway for a cigarette. Before the night would be over, his critic would be looking for a way to work with the mayor, who was smiling inwardly.

The image I've always had of Smitherman is from the doorway to his office. He'd be sitting behind his desk, often with his feet propped up on it. He'd be smoking a cigarette and a cup of coffee would be nearby. Joe also loved to go out to the waiting room to see who was sitting there and wondering what they wanted. It wasn't unusual to see him fish $5 out of his pocket to give to one of the local panhandlers in need of a meal. He knew the guy would never vote for him, but it didn't matter. I think he might have seen himself in them. He knew if he hadn't hustled for a living he might not have become the success he was. He knew how to reward his pals, too, and always considered himself something a populist, a small town George Wallace. "People say I always give jobs to my friends," Smitherman would say, before echoing Wallace by adding, "Well, who do you expect me to hire, my enemies?" He knew where the political bodies were buried or what closets the skeletons were in and wasn't reluctant to use the information to achieve his goals. I don't think Alabama has ever had a mayor quite like him. His black critics would agree with that assessment. As far as they are concerned, he was nothing short of a demagogue.

Smitherman's antics often made news far beyond Alabama. He took on France and the Soviet Union over wine and vodka and once threatened to arrest Alabama State Troopers because he felt they were operating out of their jurisdiction. One of Smitherman's sons, Steve, proved a major headache at times. He left the police department where he had been a detective after driving his patrol car into a moving train. Steve, who had a drinking problem, recovered, left the police force and became a successful real estate executive. The mayor once told a railroad company to repair its tracks through town or he'd do something drastic. Railroad executives thought he was bluffing, but soon found out he wasn't. Smitherman placed a police car across the tracks and vowed to arrest the crew if it tried to continue its run. The rail officials quickly capitulated and promised to repair the tracks. Joe T. had won again and let the train resume its run.

One of the funniest moments occurred when Smitherman, as a member of the Alabama Alcohol Beverage Control Board, angrily led a campaign to suspend the sale of French wine and champagne at 152 state-owned liquor stores. It was in response to the French government's refusal to let U.S. bombers use its airspace during a strike against Libya in 1986. An outraged Smitherman pushed through an ABC Board resolution which said: "Our country came to the aid of France in World War I and World War II and it is inconceivable to us that France refused to allow our airplanes to fly over their country in our battle against international terrorism." The State Stores, as they are known, sold about 200 cases of French wine a month. That wouldn't make much of a dent in overall sales in the U.S., but Smitherman's resolution reached all the way to Paris just the same. I thought it would be interesting if I took a "survey" of Selma's wine "connoisseurs," so I walked down to a corner near the Alabama River and interviewed three winos. They were delighted to express their displeasure with the French and tout the superiority of their favorite brands—Thunderbird and Ripple. I got a picture of them holding up their bottles. Smitherman did basically the same thing when the Soviet Union rattled its nuclear saber when it still existed. He ordered a ban on Soviet vodka, but it had about as much of an impact as the boycott of French wine. I didn't take a survey that time. Selma's winos couldn't afford vodka any more than French champagne.

Smitherman's driving abilities should have led him to a career on the NASCAR circuit. Going with him on inspection trips around Selma could cause heart palpitations. If he got into tight traffic, he'd just drive up on the sidewalk to get around the vehicles in front. If a destination was 10 minutes away, Joe would get there in five. The Alabama Ethics Commission once cited him for driving his city vehicle to the Gulf Coast. For a politician with such a long career, he maintained a remarkably clean record. He mastered the spoils system, though, and, in a way, established a job placement agency in city hall.

Few favors are ever extended without something sought in return. In Smitherman's case, it was loyalty. In most cases, he got it from the many people he had hired. During his career, he held the power to hire and fire department heads as well as rank-and-file employees. The only major disappointment for him involved thievery on the part of two respected department heads who stole hundreds of thousands of dollars from the city treasury in a contract scam. Police Chief Randy Lewellen and City Clerk Mary Ramsey both were sentenced to federal prison for their roles in the scheme, but the glares they got from Smitherman had to have been even worse to take. The mayor felt both had not only embarrassed him, but bit the hand that had fed them and their families for so many years. He would have nothing more to do with them. They were, in his mind, traitors. As the black voting presence took hold in Selma, Smitherman quickly began appointing blacks to department head positions. That meant he not only had their votes, but the votes of their relatives as well. He was, in many ways, a small town Dick Daley, the late mayor of Chicago. Daley ran Chicago with an iron fist, but knew he'd never be reelected without wide support. It worked for Smitherman for three decades until white flight and a rising black birth rate made it inevitable that his luck was about to end. It happened in the fall of 2000 when James Perkins Jr., a man he had twice defeated in the 1990s, became Selma's first black mayor. Smitherman knew what the outcome would be long before the final votes were counted. He'd often correctly call elections around the state. In his own bid for a 10th mayoral term, he knew he didn't have a chance.

Benn with Selma Mayor Joe Smitherman in 2000 when the mayor lost his bid for reelection. (Photo by Mickey Welsh)

The primary reason for Perkins' victory was activist lawyer Rose Sanders, who waged a long campaign to beat Smitherman—a man she despised as much as he despised her. She formed a "Joe Gotta Go" campaign and it was an immediate success. By election day, it was pretty much over but the shouting. There was plenty of that with Perkins' supporters on street corners screaming "Joe Gotta Go" for hours. Perkins won easily and Smitherman, showing the class and chutzpah that had won him elections for nearly four decades, walked through the screaming throng that had voted against him to personally congratulate the mayor-elect. At one of his final council meetings as mayor, Smitherman stood and extended his hand to Perkins, telling him "you'll make a good mayor."

Before Smitherman left office, there was one thing I wanted from him. In the 20 years after our rocky start, we had gotten to know each other pretty well. I respected him for his political abilities and I think he liked my writing style. He said on more than one occasion that he thought the "curly-haired Jew down the street" was one of the best he had seen. He said if he had to be chewed up by a newspaper reporter "I don't mind if it's by a professional and Al Benn is one of them." That meant a lot to me. I overlooked the "Jew" reference because that was Joe T. I asked him if I could get one of his "Friendship Sticks,' as he called them. They were small wooden batons with rectangular brass plates that said: "Friendship Stick" with "Joe T. Smitherman, Mayor—City of Selma, Al." under it. He gave one to me and I keep it on display at my house.

Smitherman preferred staying out of the spotlight in retirement. He got phone calls from friends and supporters, but the old fire was gone. He had heart problems and his beloved wife, Ouida, died several years before his last campaign. His eldest son, Tommy, also died after a lengthy illness. Smitherman and George Wallace were two men cut from the same political mold. They loved the chase but once they won the race, they often got bored with mundane matters of city or state.

On Dec. 25, 2004, I wrote a column about Smitherman, who was born on Christmas Eve. He was 75. I called him a "diamond in the rough." He told me he didn't want to be interviewed and declined a request to sit down with me, so I did it my way—reminiscing about him and chatting with some of his friends. He told me later that he liked it.

If there was a special point of pride for Smitherman, it was his mayoral longevity. During his final term in office in 2000, he would say that he had served Selma in political capacities more than anyone else in the city's 180-year history. It amounted to about 40 years—four on the council and just under 36 years as mayor.

"I'd say that's pretty good," he said to me one day. "I'd say that, too," I told him.

I was in the upper deck of RFK Stadium in Washington, D. C., watching the Braves play the Nationals, when my editor—Carol Lewis—called to say Joe had died earlier in the day.

Sharon and I left the game and took the Metro back to our daughter's house where I spent the next couple of hours making long distance phone calls to prepare the story.

It was Sept. 11, 2005—the anniversary of a national tragedy and a jolt for Selmians, many of whom thought Smitherman was indestructible.

We got back home in time for me to attend his funeral. I wrote one final column about him and the big turnout to bid him adieu.

Joe Smitherman was one of a kind. It's unlikely Selma will ever see anyone like him again.

CHAPTER FORTY-TWO:

*-30-

One of the good (or bad) things about "old age" is the ability to remember what once had been. That's what made 2002 such an enjoyable year for me. I took part in two reunions that year. One involved my 2 ½ year initiation into the wonderful world of daily journalism, thanks to *United Press International*. The other was my career stepping stone, thanks to the Marine Corps.

I had been thinking about hosting some of my old *UPI* buddies for a long time. It began to materialize in the spring of 2001 when I won the support of Cam Martindale and Sandi Gouge at Troy State University Montgomery and *Montgomery Advertiser* Publisher Scott Brown. Martindale, TSUM's president, quickly gave her blessings which was an important first step. Sandi handled the logistics while Scott provided the money. It couldn't have happened without the three of them.

When I first proposed a reunion, I wasn't sure where it would be held or what it would entail. We decided on the Rosa Parks Museum in Montgomery. I couldn't think of a better spot. It's located in the area where, in 1955, Parks got on a city bus, refused to give up her seat to a white passenger and, in so doing, blazed a new trail toward equality for all Americans. Her courageous, singular act launched the modern civil rights movement.

UPI **veterans gather for a photo on the
Edmund Pettus Bridge in Selma.**

Slowly, but surely, I got commitments from former *UPI* colleagues
to attend. Tim Robinson flew in from San Francisco. Joe Chapman
came down from Connecticut. Leon Daniel and John Lynch—both
of whom covered "Bloody Sunday" on the Pettus Bridge in Selma in
1965—arrived from Virginia and North Carolina respectively. Tony
Heffernan—my first and only *UPI* boss—drove over from Atlanta. By
the time we held our reunion in late April 2002, we had quite a program
lined up. It was a weekend event filled with memories of the good old
days that weren't always so good for those of us who found ourselves in
the front lines reporting often-violent events linked to the civil rights
movement.

Gov. Don Siegelman welcomed our group. It was something that
former Gov. George Wallace wasn't likely to have done in 1963 after
giving his "segregation forever" inaugural speech. My selling point to
Don, a man I got to know when he was starting out in politics more
than 20 years before the reunion, was a chance to welcome those who
knew Alabama only from the violence and discrimination of years past.
It was a chance to show that it was a different state today. He was in the
middle of what would be an unsuccessful reelection campaign at the

time and one of his young assistants didn't seem particularly interested in bothering him with my invitation. So, as has been my practice through the years, I went through the barricade. I met Siegelman at an industrial announcement ceremony in Selma and personally delivered an invitation. He read it on the way back to Montgomery and notified me immediately that he'd love to come.

He spoke on a Saturday morning when he could have been elsewhere in the state looking for votes. We appreciated his appearance and his words. He told us it wasn't the same Alabama that we knew as young reporters. Don was right and he was one of the reasons for that progressive change. Two years later, he would be indicted by a federal grand jury on fraud charges stemming from his term as governor. The federal government dropped the charges against him on the second day of his trial. On Oct. 26, 2005, Siegelman was indicted again, this time on a federal racketeering charge. Jim Bennett, my old buddy from the *Birmingham Post-Herald*, dropped by to extend his welcome as Alabama's Secretary of State. Montgomery Mayor Bobby Bright also issued greetings to our little group of writers. Events included panel discussions and an interview on public television with Tony, Elvin Stanton and me. Elvin was news director of WSGN-AM in Birmingham when I first got to know him. He also worked for *UPI* for awhile. He's also Cam Martindale's husband and that didn't hurt our reunion plans a bit. Cam got a refresher course from Elvin on what it was like during those days so long ago. She didn't realize how important her husband had been in reporting events of earth-shaking importance. Elvin even brought along tapes of the violence he covered, including the chilling sound of gunshots.

**Tim Robinson, left, Joe Chapman, center,
visit Benn at his Selma office.**

We ended our reunion by hopping aboard a bus provided by the Alabama Bureau of Tourism and Travel and going to Selma to have pictures taken on the Edmund Pettus Bridge where "Bloody Sunday" led to the march to Montgomery in 1965. It had been a one-year project and took place during my busy work schedule. I was the only reporter still actively doing what I had done when we all were young and aggressive decades before in Alabama.

A few months after the *UPI* reunion, Sharon and I flew to Orlando, Fla. to take part in a Marine Corps Combat Correspondents Association conference. I didn't think I was eligible to join because I hadn't been in combat during Vietnam. But I was told I could join because of my experience in the Corps on Okinawa and stateside during the Vietnam era as well as future employment in the "real world" of journalism.

I couldn't wait to go because I hadn't seen Ed Schultze and Marv Deaton in 40 years. They were the two men who gave me the boost I needed to become a journalist. Marv pointed me toward journalism school at the Great Lakes Naval Training Center in 1961 and it wasn't long before I was headed toward *UPI* and Birmingham. Marv and his wife, Annabel, met us at the Orlando airport and took us to the hotel where we'd spend the weekend. We met Ed and his wife, Eleanor. Later that day, I also met Don Gee, a Marine buddy I hadn't seen since journalism school graduation day when we drove through the night from Illinois to begin our new duties. Don became an official with the Marine Corps association and helped put the conference together.

I was on a panel with Joe Galloway, co-author of "*We Were Soldiers Once...And Young.*" It was made into a popular movie starring Mel Gibson. John Laurence, a former network television correspondent who covered the war in Vietnam, also was on the panel. We told the Marines on hand—active and retired—what it was like to cover events during wartime. Galloway had covered some of the bloodiest fighting of the Vietnam War and was as skilled with a camera as the printed word. I told the Marines that Joe may not have been in the Corps, but he came pretty close since he worked for *UPI* during that time. A former *Associated Press* writer in the audience gave me some raspberries over that. I also mentioned that Joe and I had covered two different wars—his was foreign and mine was domestic. By the time we wrapped up and headed home, I had been able to renew some valuable old friendships. Ed is in his 80s and Marv is a bit long in the tooth as well. Both looked great, though. I'll never forget them or what they meant to me personally and professionally.

Since "retiring" in May of 2003, I'm still trying to understand the meaning of the word. It's been a fun arrangement—writing two columns a week, working the Saturday shift to give our young reporters the weekend off and, occasionally helping when needed on breaking news. I've also been asked to speak before civic clubs and area schools, especially to students interested in the civil rights era. I guess I'm somewhat of a fossil to them, but I don't mind. It's disappointing, at times, to see how little so many black kids know about a movement that helped them obtain rights unavailable to their parents and grandparents. I guess we all take things for granted at times. I tell civic club members my age or older that my career has been different from most. "We all hope to climb that ladder of success to the top one day," I tell them. "In my case, I started at the top with *UPI* and it's been a slow, steady downhill slide ever since." It always gets a big laugh.

Several months after my retirement, I covered the Alabama Academy of Honor induction ceremony at the State Capitol in Montgomery and ran into Nelle Harper Lee, Pulitzer Prize-winning author of *"To Kill A Mockingbird."* Whenever Nelle sees me, she usually has a smile, a hug and an admonition not to ask her any questions. Of course, I always try to ask at least one. On this occasion, she looked up at me prior to the ceremony honoring Selma author Kathryn Windham and exclaimed: "You retired, you bastard." It took awhile for me to stop laughing. She had made my day. Famous authors don't usually call me a bastard, so I took it as a compliment. At least, I hoped it was extended that way.

On June 5, 2004, we got word that former President Ronald Reagen had died. It happened on a Saturday and I had already written several stories for our Sunday edition. One was about the 60th anniversary of the D-Day invasion and Montgomery soldiers who took part. I also covered a law school graduation and an air show at Maxwell-Gunter Air Force Base. Word of Reagan's death knocked the D-Day story from its priority position on Page 1 as it should have. As Sharon and I left the newsroom and headed down the steps, I stopped and told her: "There's no way I'm going home when something like this is happening." So, we went back up the steps and I helped put together a reaction story to Reagan's death. It became the top local story on Page 1, just above the D-Day story which slipped into second place at the bottom of the page.

Among those I was able to contact were former U.S. Sen. Howell Heflin, former U.S. Rep. Bill Dickinson and former Alabama Gov. Guy Hunt. Heflin, who served on the Iran-Contra Senate Committee during Reagan's administration, said he had received numerous phone calls, but mine was the only one he was returning. He said he did so because he thought I was a "fair" reporter whenever I covered him. I wish he had said I was a good reporter. But, hey, I'll take it.

One of the newest trends in journalism these days is "blogging" in which reporters file their "thoughts" in column form on a newspaper's Website. I guess the stories, themselves, aren't good enough now. We've got to tell our readers what we really think. Another trend involves "On-Line" versions of daily newspapers. People can strike a key on their computer and read their paper without having to pay for it. Are newspapers competing against themselves by giving their product away? Newspaper circulation figures these days are enough to give owners and editors a big case of bottom line indigestion. Daily circulation at the *Baltimore Sun*, for instance, dropped a staggering 11.5 percent during a one-year period that covered 2004. Other major metropolitan daily newspapers are experiencing similar fates. *USA Today*, which is Gannett's flagship national newspaper, reported a circulation gain of 7,000 which is good. Even better is the total figure—2.2 million copies sold around the country. Only time will tell if newspapers will be able to meet the challenges of today's visual society. It's hard for me to admit, but millions of Americans just aren't reading. That's a shame.

I feel sorry for young reporters today. I've said the same thing about myself, at times. If I had been born in 1900 instead of 1940, I'd have been able to cover events of the Roaring Twenties—a time when Al Capone ruled Chicago and Babe Ruth owned baseball. But, I was able to report on earth-shaking events just the same. Included were the space race, Vietnam and, of course, the civil rights era in which I had a ringside seat. In a way, it's been kind of boring the past decade or so—until I hear a police or fire truck roar by. That's when I hop into my car to find out what's happening.

*"30" is a newspaper term meaning "the end" of a story.

That's what this is. Thanks for reading.

Printed in the United States
47770LVS00005B/1-72

9 781420 861853